W9-DAC-952

ALVIN

To: Garnet & Marie
"progressive conservatives"

ALVIN

A Biography of the Honourable Alvin Hamilton, P.C.

Patrick Kyba

Canadian Plains Research Center
Regina, Saskatchewan
1989

Canadian Plains Research Center
University of Regina
Regina, Saskatchewan S4S 0A2
Canada

Canadian Cataloguing in Publication Data

Kyba, Patrick, 1942–
Alvin: a biography of the Hon. Alvin Hamilton, P.C.

(Canadian plains biographies, ISSN 0823-8936 ; 2)
Includes bibliographical references and index.
ISBN: 0-88977-056-5

1. Hamilton, Alvin, 1912–. 2. Politicians – Canada – Biography. 3. Politicians – Saskatchewan – Biography. 4. Cabinet ministers – Canada – Biography*. I. University of Regina. Canadian Plains Research Center. II. Title. III. Series.
FC616.H365K92 1989 971.064'2'0924 C89-098075-6
F1034.3.H365K92 1989

Cover design: Amanda Maslany
Typeset by Lines & Letters, Regina, Saskatchewan
Printed and bound in Canada by
Hignell Printing Limited, Winnipeg, Manitoba

for
Jennifer, Robin and Alexandra

Contents

Illustrations

Acknowledgements

I wish to express my thanks to the following copyright holders for permission to use passages from their publications.

I am grateful to The Brunswick Press for permission to use material from Robert Coates's *The Night of the Knives.*

The Right Honourable John G. Diefenbaker Centre, University of Saskatchewan, kindly permitted me to use quotations from Mr. Diefenbaker's memoirs, *One Canada*, published by Macmillan of Canada.

Robert M. Campbell, author of "The Diefenbaker Years Revisited: The Demise of Keynesian Strategy in Canada," consented to the use of material from his article, which was published in the *Journal of Canadian Studies* 18, no. 2 (Summer 1983).

Passages from Peter C. Newman's *The Distemper of Our Times: Canadian Politics in Transition, 1963-1968*, and *Renegade in Power: The Diefenbaker Years*, have been used by permission of the Canadian publishers, McClelland and Stewart, Toronto.

McGill-Queen's University Press granted permission for the use of material from G.C. Perlin's *The Tory Syndrome: Leadership Politics in the Progressive Conservative Party.*

Permission was extended for the use of a passage from *Managing Canada's Renewable Resources*, edited by Ralph R. Krueger and Bruce Mitchell, copyright Nelson Canada, 1977, a division of International Thomson Limited, 1120 Birchmount Road, Scarborough, Ontario M1K 5G4, Canada.

I am grateful to the University of Toronto Press for permission to use quotations from three of its publications: *Canada Since 1945: Power, Politics, and Provincialism*, by Robert Bothwell, Ian M. Drummond and John English; *Prairie Liberalism: The Liberal Party in Saskatchewan, 1905-71*, by David E. Smith; and *Diefenbaker: Leadership Lost, 1962-1967*, by Peter Stursberg.

This book is illustrated with photographs which have been obtained from four sources. Unless otherwise noted, the photographs have been drawn from the private collection of Alvin Hamilton himself, and I wish to express my thanks to Mr. Hamilton for his generosity in this respect particularly. In addition, the Saskatchewan Archives Board (SAB), the National Archives Canada (NAC), and the Right Honourable J.G. Diefenbaker Centre are owed my thanks for providing a number of photographs from their collections.

Introduction

Several years ago, impressionist Rich Little recorded a very funny parody of a House of Commons debate on the steps the Diefenbaker government should take to protect visitors to national parks from attacks by bears.[1] The main characters in the sketch were John Diefenbaker, Lester Pearson, and Tommy Douglas, and Little captured to perfection Diefenbaker's sonorous self-righteousness, Pearson's childlike lisp and mock outrage, and Douglas's clipped accent and pious concern. Eldon Wooliams, member of Parliament for Bow River, who brought the matter before the Commons in July of 1960, and Alvin Hamilton, then minister of northern affairs and national resources, whose response sparked both laughter and anger across the country, were not mentioned at all. The truth of the matter was that Wooliams, in light of incidents in Banff and Glacier Parks where bears had mauled tourists, asked the minister if his department would consider changing park regulations so that people could carry firearms to protect themselves. Hamilton's reply pointed out first that, under the National Parks Act, his principal responsibility was to protect the bears, second that park wardens warned tourists of the dangers of feeding the bears, and third that:

> At the present time if any bear becomes too friendly along the highways we trap the animal and remove him to a very distant spot, and paint his rear end red. If this bear with the red posterior reappears in the settled areas where people are visiting the parks, then he is trapped a second time and removed permanently.[2]

Hamilton also informed the Commons that the programme had been in operation for two years.

In the midst of a slow session halfway through a stupefying Ottawa summer, the press pounced on the story with gleeful gratitude. For a few days, the affairs of the "Bears' Backsides" attracted national interest and Alvin Hamilton became the focus of a whirlwind of controversy. Some people thought the minister's behaviour scandalous. The editor of the *Calgary Herald*, for example, charged that:

> Mr. Hamilton's statement would be downright amusing were it not dealing with such a serious subject. There is some merit in his refusal to permit tourists and park visitors to carry firearms, but it is sheer nonsense for him to say it is his responsibility to protect the bears, not the people, regardless of what the National Parks Act says.[3]

Others considered the episode simply hilarious and the editor of the *Lethbridge Herald* was moved to pen this doggerel:

> While good bears learn their twice times ten
> Bad bears (in parks) just count on men
> For food and fun and venting rage —
> A problem in this tourist age.
>
> But problems are for government
> Mere nothings. So in Parliament
> The answer's given, briefly said —
> "We'll paint the bad bears' backsides red."
>
> We hail this ingenuity,
> But still remains a mystery —
> How do you tell a bear's unkind
> When running, if the bear's behind.[4]

The affair became the highlight of that year's Press Club dinner, then Little's record, and finally entered the mythology of the period — all the while becoming further removed from its essential truth. Even twenty-eight years after the event, Hamilton cannot recount what began as a sincere attempt to respond to a serious question without breaking up in gales of laughter.[5]

This anecdote illustrates the tendency in Canada to ignore politicians other than party leaders at the expense of those who may have had as great or even greater impact on the policies of governments. Canadian political biography over the years has focussed on prime ministers and, to a lesser extent, leaders of the opposition. This should not be surprising perhaps, since the tradition of political biography has never been as highly developed in this country as it has in other countries, such as Great Britain. Whatever the reasons, however, the fact remains that there are many men and women whose contributions to the governance of Canada have gone unrecognized at worst, or have been treated as mere adjuncts to their more prominent leaders at best. Alvin Hamilton is one such man. For some who remember, Alvin Hamilton *is* the man who sparked the incident of the "Bears' Backsides," who recommended that a nuclear device be exploded in south-central Saskatchewan to hasten construction of the Gardiner Dam, and whose ill-timed remarks concerning the devaluation of the Canadian dollar may have cost his party its majority in the election of 1962. For others, he is the man who opened the resources of Canada's north to development, the father of the Agricultural Rehabilitation and Development Act (ARDA), and the minister of agriculture who sold Canada's wheat surplus to China. Still others think of him as the ideas man of the Diefenbaker government, a Diefenbaker loyalist, and the man who won the West for the Progressive Conservative party. All these recollections contain kernels of truth and some are vital to an understanding of his contributions to this country. Yet they are only a small part of the story of his political career, which began in Saskatchewan more than fifty years ago and continues in Ottawa and far-flung places all over the world today despite his decision not to run in the 1988 election.

The chapters which follow begin at the beginning as all stories should. Nevertheless, this is not a biography which gives equal weight to Hamilton's private and public lives. Although his early life, and the circumstances which brought him to Saskatchewan as an orphan at the age of fifteen, are treated in some detail, succeeding chapters do not dwell at any length on anything but his public persona. Almost nothing is said about the long and happy marriage which provided a stable foundation for his political career. No mention at all is made of his relationships with his two sons, his brothers, his supporters in Qu'Appelle, his office staff, his friends and acquaintances all over this country and abroad, or anyone else, except when they are or were of direct relevance to his political life. Nor is this a psychobiography. While Hamilton's sense of humour and his personal integrity, compassion, and determination undoubtedly affected his career — again, they are discussed only when of direct relevance to his story. Furthermore, the book does not attempt to give equal weight to all the many events and people of importance to him during his long life in politics. Nor does it treat in depth all the many successes and failures of his career. For example, Alvin Hamilton set in motion much of the planning for the 1967 centennial celebration, yet this is mentioned only fleetingly in the text. As well, he was never able to convince the premiers of the Atlantic provinces to merge their separate identities into a single province to give them a stronger voice in national affairs and to exploit the resources of the sea-bed which separated them, and which he was prepared to give them. This is not mentioned at all. It is simply impossible to cover everything that occurred over a long political career in a book of this length. Many difficult decisions have been made as to what has been included and excluded. Finally, it will be noted that more attention has been devoted to Hamilton's successful contributions to Canadian political life than to his failures. This was not done with any intent to write a hagiography. Quite the contrary. Alvin Hamilton was no saint in politics. Nor does he aspire to the deification which has attended J.S. Woodsworth. Rather, the book took this turn because very few of these failures can be documented. Furthermore, many of these failures, to which Hamilton admits freely, were in the realm of ideas which never found a responsive ear, proposals which never were adopted, or actions of his party or the Diefenbaker cabinet for which responsibility must be shared. It is my hope that judgements such as these have added to, rather than detracted from, the story which follows.

Chapters one and two take Hamilton from his birth in 1912

to his appointment as provincial organizer for the federal Progressive Conservative party in Saskatchewan in 1948. Chapter three assesses his difficulties as organizer, and then leader of a third party, in that competitive two-party province, until his election to the Canadian House of Commons in 1957. Chapters four and five treat his years as a minister in the Diefenbaker cabinets from 1957 to 1963, and outline not only his manifold responsibilities as first minister of northern affairs and national resources and then minister of agriculture, but also his major successes and failure in those portfolios. Chapter six reviews the reasons for the decline and eventual defeat of the Diefenbaker government and Hamilton's rôle in these events. Chapter seven discusses the battle within the Progressive Conservative party over Diefenbaker's leadership between 1963 and 1967, and Hamilton's attempts first to save and then to replace the Chief. Chapters eight, nine and ten recount his activities as a front and back bench member of Parliament under the three leaders he has served under since 1967: Robert Stanfield, Joe Clark and Brian Mulroney. The book ends with a brief review of Hamilton's lifetime of public service, emphasizing those personal qualities which make him and his career worth remembering.

One does not complete an undertaking such as this without incurring debts of gratitude which must be acknowledged. I must thank the Social Sciences and Humanities Council and the Department of Political Studies at the University of Guelph, for generous financial support. I wish also to express my appreciation to Carman Carroll and Geoffrey Ott of the National Archives of Canada; Iain Campbell and Ed Morgan of the Saskatchewan Archives Board in Regina; Douglas Bocking and Lloyd Rodwell, formerly of the Saskatchewan Archives Board in Saskatoon; and Laurie Farrington of the Privy Council Office. All these and their staffs made available to me the necessary documents, often at short notice. I owe a good deal to all those from London, England, to Victoria, British Columbia, who gave me access to their papers, those who submitted to interviews, and those who responded to my written requests for information. I would like to thank the many research assistants who helped at various stages of the project, in particular Linda Cracknell, Gretchen MacMillan, Jim Whitechurch and Peggy Schenk. I am grateful to Fred Vaughan and David Murray of the University of Guelph, Jack Granatstein of York University, John Hilliker in the Department of External Affairs, and James N. McCrorie and Gillian Wadsworth Minifie of the Canadian Plains Research Center for their many useful comments on the manuscript, almost all of which I have incorporated into the final draft. Muriel Hunt and Linda Robar and their staff in Hamilton's office deserve mention for their efforts to ensure that interviews went off as scheduled, and for providing personal glimpses of what it is like to work for Alvin Hamilton. I wish to thank Lorraine Black of Guelph for typing the manuscript. I am grateful to my sisters, Sharon of Saskatoon and Valerie of Calgary, their families, and my parents in Melfort for providing a friendly base from which to undertake the research in the West. I thank my wife Alison, and our children Jennifer, Robin and Alexandra, for their moral support and for never complaining about the length of time I spent away from home. Finally, I owe an enormous debt to Alvin Hamilton himself for his generosity in giving me his time, and access to his public and private papers. Although this biography is neither commissioned nor even authorized, it is fair to say that it would not have been completed without Hamilton's patience and understanding. I hasten to add, however, that any errors of fact or judgement are mine alone.

Patrick Kyba
University of Guelph
1989

Chapter 1
Palma ad Ardua

Five of the passengers on the Canadian Pacific Railway out of Kenora, Ontario, in the summer of 1927 were the sons of Frank and Alice Hamilton. One train eastbound took the oldest boy, Ralph, to Montréal. Another carried the remaining four west to Saskatchewan. Two of them, Ross and Hubert, got off at Summerberry, on the main line seventy miles east of Regina. The other two, Fred and Alvin, changed trains in the capital and continued to Delisle, twenty-five miles southwest of Saskatoon. All five were met by relatives, but they had not left Kenora to spend the summer holidays with their cousins. The boys, aged eight to seventeen, were orphans who had been split up and shipped off to their late father's family to be looked after until they could fend for themselves. The five would not meet together again for ten years.

The boys' parents, Francis Robert (Frank) Hamilton and Alice May Jamieson, were both descended from United Empire Loyalist families who came to Canada near the end of the American Revolution. The Hamiltons crossed the St. Lawrence River from upper state New York to settle near Verona, twenty miles north of Kingston. The family farmed there for more than a hundred years, and Frank might have continued the tradition had the holdings been larger and more productive. By the turn of the century, however, it was clear that the farm would no longer support the family. Someone had to supplement the income from the two hundred acres of rock, bush and lake, and Frank, the eldest son at twenty-two, was the obvious choice. He had worked for the New York Central Railway while completing his education and the Canadian Pacific Railway (CPR) needed experienced men to lay additional track in northwestern Ontario. The company offered him a job in Kenora, and he left Verona for good in 1905. Other members of the family followed suit over the next few years. One sister went to Kenora, two others followed their husbands to Saskatchewan, and his brother moved to Montréal. All of them would repay their debt to Frank by taking care of his orphaned sons after his death.

The Jamiesons had left Québec for the West a generation earlier. The Thurber side of their family had come to Megantic County in the 1780s, and over the next century they had moved east and north to Leeds County where Eliza Thurber married George Jamieson. However, fear of the growing French Canadian Catholic influence in the region caused some of them to pull up stakes once again. In 1882, three Jamieson brothers and their families, including Alice, born earlier that year, took the CPR west to the end of its track, near what was to become the Manitoba-Saskatchewan border. One entered a partnership in the first store at Moosomin. The other two filed homesteads near McAuley, Manitoba, and Welwyn, Saskatchewan. Alice Jamieson went to school at McAuley and worked for a time in Fleming, but this determined young woman soon decided that life as a clerk in a general store was not for her. She chose to become a nurse instead, and an offer of board and lodging from a married cousin brought her to Kenora to begin her training at the local hospital. She never returned to Saskatchewan to nurse. In 1909, Alice Jamieson married Frank Hamilton and they began their family without delay. Their second son, christened Francis Alvin George, was born in Kenora near the end of a long and bitter winter on 30 March 1912.

Kenora, during the eighteen years the Hamiltons lived there, was a frontier lumber, mining, and railroad town. Possessing many of the worst characteristics of each industry,

Kenora was a rough town and more akin to the new settlements on the prairies than the older towns and cities of southern Ontario. Nevertheless, Kenora possessed some redeeming qualities, among them a public school staffed with several competent teachers, many churches with their attendant social and cultural groups, a fine hockey tradition, and a proximity to nature, all of which added to the quality of life of its citizens. Beyond this, Frank and Alice Hamilton were able to provide their sons with a standard of living a cut above most other families in town. Men who worked on the railroad were better paid than either loggers or miners, and Frank Hamilton's pay packet was larger than most of those who worked with him. His experience with the New York Central stood him in good stead with the CPR and he advanced quickly to become the second most senior engineer in the division. The Hamiltons built a large two-storey house on Second Street, situated conveniently near to both the business section and the station, and added to it later to accommodate their growing family.[1] Alice dressed the boys invariably in white shirts and ties for school, a style not always appreciated by her sons. She bought a piano to accompany her fine singing voice and to supplement readings from the Bible and *Pilgrim's Progress* on sedate Presbyterian Sundays. After World War I the Hamiltons could afford a new Chevrolet, which they acquired despite the fact that there were few but logging roads outside the town limits.

Hamilton looks back on his fifteen years in Kenora with mixed emotions. Most of the fond memories, of course, are from the period prior to the tragic deaths of his parents, for both played important rôles in his early development. Frank Hamilton was an outdoorsman, an excellent hunter, and he introduced all his boys to life in the bush as soon as they had the strength to lower the hammer on a loaded shell without setting it off. He taught them to hunt and to fish and, of equal importance, he taught them to love the country around the Lake of the Woods. This training enabled young Alvin to pass through the scouting programme with ease, and to win shooting competitions twenty years later after he joined the Royal Canadian Air Force. He was to build a bush camp on

Dogtooth Lake, just east of Kenora, as soon as he could afford to after World War II, and he has spent as much as possible of every summer there ever since.

Alice Hamilton created a warm and loving home environment and she took a special interest in her boys' education. She taught them to read before they entered Central Public School and she followed their progress closely. Her son Alvin caused her more concern than did his brothers. He completed nine grades in the nine years he went to school in Kenora, but he did not advance through the grades at the usual rate of one per year. He lacked neither intelligence nor application. One year, in fact, his overall average was the second highest in his class. However, he simply did not fit the school curriculum well and the school found it difficult at times to accommodate him. He spent two years in the first grade before his teacher realized that he could read and belonged in a higher grade. As Hamilton remembers his predicament, "They didn't do much reading in the first year — all manual work. I couldn't draw, I couldn't colour, I couldn't fold . . . and I seemed to be getting into fights occasionally." His situation did not improve immediately, for "the next thing I knew I'm yanked out of that class and put into a grade where I was in trouble immediately because I couldn't spell very well and I got pounded over the head and shoulders quite a lot."[2] Hamilton's fate was to move through his early education in fits and starts. He would spend two years in one grade, jump to where he should have been or beyond, remain there for a couple more years and then leapfrog again. This process continued until the school decided to advance him to high school far ahead of his peer group. Now Alice intervened to hold her son back until she was satisfied he could cope with both the academic and social demands of secondary education. This proved to be a wise decision, for although Hamilton had to spend two years in the eighth grade, he turned to history to dispel the boredom of having to repeat the subjects he had mastered the previous year. He became a voracious reader, and devoured the school's entire collection of history texts and the children's books in the public library long before proceeding to high school.

Hamilton's final two years at school in Kenora were not happy ones. His mother's lingering death from tuberculosis, in March of 1924, was a dreadful shock, and schoolwork proved to be of little solace. He was expelled three times in his first year of high school, failed his English class, and had to repeat the ninth grade. Athletic competition seemed to ease his grief and he plunged headlong into every available sport, also to the detriment of his grades. He boxed, did gymnastics, played basketball and Rugby football, and participated fully at the school's track meets. He also played hockey. Kenora was a hotbed of hockey at the time, and the organization of the sport reached down to the lowest age. Hamilton received excellent coaching in the fundamentals of the game and this, combined with his large size and talent, made him a first-rate hockey player either at centre or on defence. Hamilton turned out to be a superb athlete. He won several events at the school track meets, especially in the sprints, and was chosen to be a member of the school's senior basketball and Rugby teams, no mean feat for a junior. In Kenora, athletics helped fill a void in Hamilton's life. Later, his well-developed skills as a hockey player would pave the way for his acceptance by the people of Delisle.

Just three years had gone by since the death of their mother when tragedy struck the Hamilton boys once again. According to the local newspaper at the time:

> Death, under tragic circumstances, came to Frank R. Hamilton last night about six o'clock at his home, 541 Second Street South. He was in his room upstairs preparing to come to the evening meal, and when told that supper was ready, replied that he would be down in a minute. Shortly after an explosion was heard, and on one of his family going upstairs he was found dead from a wound in the head. It is presumed that he had been handling the gun when it exploded from cause not known.[3]

The lamentable irony is that he must have forgotten the very rules of gun safety that he had drilled into his sons. The writer of the obituary went on to add that:

> The late Frank Hamilton had been engaged by the CPR as an engineer for many years and given the most efficient service to the company. He was a splendid type of man and enjoyed the esteem of everyone with whom he came in contact, being of a most likeable disposition, his first thoughts being for his family of boys, who were his every care.[4]

Care of the boys now passed to Frank Hamilton's brother and sisters, and their life together in Kenora came to an end.

It is difficult to find many clues in Alvin Hamilton's early life in Kenora which would explain his later interest and career in politics. The Hamiltons were not a political family. Although Frank participated actively in his union, the Brotherhood of Locomotive Engineers, his concerns tended to be related directly to his job, and broader political issues were rarely discussed at home. None of Hamilton's brothers chose to enter politics at any stage of their careers. He is unique among the Hamilton sons in this respect. Ralph apprenticed in the film industry and eventually formed his own production company. Ross completed a doctorate in education and pioneered techniques in the rehabilitation of the physically and mentally handicapped. Fred became a geologist, and his explorations in the Arctic proved the potential of the far north as a source of oil and natural gas. Hubert took a job with Goodyear Rubber during World War II and rose to the position of foreman before he retired. Furthermore, neither Frank nor Alice pushed their partisan preferences on the boys. Indeed, Hamilton never did learn his parents' politics. He thinks his father may have been a Conservative, but only because Frank came from that staunch Conservative region north of Kingston. Finally, Hamilton's introduction to politics did not happen at home, but rather through the Heenan family who lived nearby. The Hamilton and Heenan children played together constantly and Peter Heenan was the member of Parliament for the Kenora constituency. It is interesting to speculate on what might have happened to the political career of Alvin Hamilton had fate not dealt his family that devastating double blow in such a short span of time. Had either parent survived, it is likely that the family would have remained in Kenora and, had this occurred, it is quite possible that an ambitious Alvin Hamilton might have embraced the major political philosophy of the area and joined the local Liberal-Labour party. However, this did not occur. The political socialization and career of Alvin Hamilton began in Saskatchewan, and his story now shifts to that province.

Alvin Hamilton went to Saskatchewan in the unhappiest of circumstances, and it is not difficult to imagine the emotions which swept over him as he journeyed to Delisle. He mourned the loss of his father and the life he had shared with his brothers in Kenora, and he feared his unknown future in a new and different environment. Furthermore, he was alone except for the younger brother who travelled with him, and within weeks Fred would be sent a hundred miles away to another aunt at Prongua, near North Battleford. Hamilton owes to his aunt, Annie Chambers, and her husband Mark a debt of gratitude for they helped him through this traumatic period, but they did not recreate for him the home he had left behind. They provided food and shelter and ensured that he continued his education, but he was not treated as a fully-fledged member of their family. Mark Chambers regarded Hamilton more as a hired man, one of several he employed to help run his large farm, the Delisle Farming Company, and he treated his ward accordingly. He paid Hamilton a monthly salary, renegotiated each year, and Hamilton was expected to earn it. This meant many long hours feeding pigs, herding cattle, and tending to the horses which were the farm's principal source of power at the time, but the hard work did not bother him. He was big for his age — over six feet tall and filled out already to 170 pounds. Mark Chambers was not an easy man to work for, but Hamilton survived, and once he proved his mettle his major job-related problem turned out to be Chambers's decision to improve his cattle-feeding operation. Alvin Hamilton, by his own admission, does not possess a "mechanical mind" and the repairs he had to make to the complex new machinery lengthened many a long day. With that exception, Hamilton fulfilled his uncle's expectations, and he remained on the farm for three years until he completed his senior matriculation. The experience convinced him, however, that he did not wish to spend the rest of his life working as a hired hand on someone else's farm.

During the 1920s most prairie children old enough to work on the farm did not finish their schooling. Those who did crammed ten month's education into five or six months, coming to school in October or November, after the harvest, and leaving in April or May to prepare for seeding. Hamilton flourished under this regimen. Perhaps because of his new circumstances or greater maturity he resolved to alter the pattern of his last years in Kenora and to take full advantage of his opportunity to learn. He applied himself diligently and used his time at school purposefully. Together with other students in the same situation, he convinced his teachers to curb their natural inclination to lecture so that he could finish his assignments during school hours. According to Hamilton:

> I couldn't afford to have teachers talking to me all the time. I had to get the work done because I had no time to get the homework done at night. I had to do everything in school hours or I wouldn't get it. So we just pleaded with the teachers not to talk. We'd do the work and if we had any problem we'd take it up with them. And the principal approved . . .[5]

He also appointed himself class policeman and dealt severely with any student who disrupted his studies. His industry and determination paid off handsomely. Hamilton rose to the top of his class in Grade XI, held that position in Grade XII, and passed the province-wide Department of Education final examinations with an 80 percent average. He had little trouble with most subjects. His best grades were in history and mathematics, his worst in English literature and composition, and French and Latin grammar.

It would be wrong to leave the impression that Hamilton's three years at the Delisle High School were a time of unremitting hard labour. It is impossible to hobble high spirits and a keen sense of humour forever and Hamilton was thrown out of more than one class, once by a teacher of Scottish heritage who could not understand why anyone would object to the playing of the bagpipes at a distance of less than a mile and a half. Such episodes were rare, however, and never as serious as those which had led to his expulsions from school in Kenora. In addition, there were dances and other social events to attend at the school, especially in the winter when he was not needed as much on the farm. Hamilton speaks highly of his teachers at Delisle and their contributions to his later success. He is particularly grateful to one of his language teachers who spent many hours with him to help overcome the stutter which would have hindered, if not prevented, his career in politics. He encouraged Hamilton to take up public speaking as part of his therapy, and the venture was so successful that within months he had gained sufficient confidence to enter the provincial Bryant Oratory Contest.[6] His topic, "Canada's Need for a Strong Navy and Merchant Marine," must have sounded strange to judges fifteen hundred miles from the nearest coastline, but that did not stop them from awarding Alvin Hamilton the prize for the best speech by a student in Saskatchewan in 1928.

Small towns tend to view strangers with suspicion and Delisle did not accept Alvin Hamilton immediately, despite his family connections. Hamilton's attendance at school helped break down the reserve, as did his skill at hockey, and his participation in the local United Church. There are few hockey fans who grew up in Saskatchewan in the 1930s and 1940s who do not remember the Bentley brothers of Delisle. This large family produced several fine hockey players, three of whom — Max, Doug and Reg — made it to the National Hockey League, and for years every Delisle team had two or three Bentleys on it. As it happened, it was the Bentleys who invited Hamilton to join their team at the beginning of his first winter in Delisle, an invitation which he accepted with alacrity. Alvin Hamilton played a great deal of hockey during his three years in Delisle. He played for the junior team, the church team and, despite his age, for the senior team. Some of these teams did well, winning provincial championships in their divisions. Hamilton played some defence, but more often he centred the senior team's "Scoop" and "Bull" Bentley, both of whom delighted local crowds by converting his crisp passes into pretty goals. Alvin Hamilton became a popular player and there is no doubt that hockey eased him gently into the good graces of the townspeople. As he explains, "If you have two guys who are destined to be superstars and somebody's feeding them the puck all the time they have nothing against you at all."[7] Years later, after he had built a reputation in politics, people from Delisle, the Bentleys especially, would refer to him as "Hamilton the hockey player," rather than "Hamilton the politician."

Hamilton never played hockey for money, but his skills as an athlete enabled him to supplement his wages from the farm during the summer months. In the days before the Depression, most rural towns would sponsor sports days and give cash prizes to the winners of the track-and-field events. His uncle gave Hamilton time off to compete at these and he did very well for himself. In his words, "Ordinarily there weren't too many people at a sports day in a rural town who could pole vault eleven or twelve feet and broad jump twenty feet and high jump over six feet. The result was that two or three of us could pretty well clean up all the first and second prizes."[8] During the winter, the rink was the social centre for the youth of Delisle as well as being the hockey arena, and it was there that Hamilton began to skate with one of the more attractive girls he knew from school. Although he had a great deal of competition for the attention of Beulah Major at the time, eventually she would become the first and only Mrs. Alvin Hamilton.

The church, together with the farm, the school, and the rink rounded out Alvin Hamilton's life at Delisle. His parents had been Presbyterian and the Chamberses counted themselves as such, but the Presbyterians had merged with the Methodists and Congregationalists in the West in 1924 to form the United Church, and this was the one Hamilton attended. He enjoyed his Sundays. They provided an escape from the farm, an additional avenue of acceptance by the community and, as it turned out, an introduction to the world of politics. The church's senior Sunday School class was led by Nathaniel Given, the mayor of Delisle, whose interests went far beyond religion. He enjoyed music, drama, and politics, and involved his students in all three. In time he formed the Excelsior Club, and began to hold additional sessions on Monday evenings devoted solely to the major political and social issues of the day, sessions which Hamilton attended whenever he could. If anyone deserves credit for pointing Alvin Hamilton in the direction of a political career that person must be Nathaniel Given. His classes stimulated Hamilton's interest in politics, made him aware of problems which required political solutions, and gave him a base from which to judge the merits of party philosophies and government actions he would encounter over the next few years. Given led discussions on political philosophy, the fundamentals of democracy, and issues of current importance to Saskatchewan. He hated any practice which he believed corrupted the Canadian system of government, and he attacked the Liberal machine in Saskatchewan as an example of the worst type of abuse that can befall the democratic system, in particular its practice of giving road-building contracts to party supporters. This left the province with no paved roads and a mere sixty-four miles of gravelled highway after twenty-three years in office.[9]

Given happened to be a Conservative and he asked some of his students to help him with his campaign during the 1929 provincial election. Then, as now, the chief task of a candidate was to meet as many voters as possible, so meetings would be scheduled for the same evening in two or three towns and the candidate would rush from one to another as quickly as possible. Since the meetings overlapped, someone had to entertain the crowds until the candidate and his entourage arrived, and Hamilton was one of those used for this purpose. He could neither sing nor dance, so he relied on the speech which had won him the Bryant Oratory Contest the year before. Given's guest speaker on one of those evenings was John Diefenbaker, then a rising star in the Conservative firmament and a candidate for Prince Albert constituency. This was the first time Diefenbaker had seen Hamilton in action and Alvin Hamilton remembers Diefenbaker shaking his head in amazement on hearing a seventeen-year-old boy preaching the virtues of a strong Canadian navy and merchant marine to a group of dryland farmers.[10] Neither this experience nor the Excelsior Club turned Alvin Hamilton into a committed Conservative at the time. Nevertheless, Given did leave his students with a faith in the democratic political process and a dislike of machine politics. As the Conservative candidate for Rosetown, he also provided Hamilton with a powerful personal counter to Mark Chambers's attempts to make his nephew work for the Liberal party during the election of 1929.

The 1929 campaign was among the most bitter ever fought in Saskatchewan. The Conservative party knew that it could not defeat the Gardiner government by pitting its promises against the Liberals' record of economic achievement or the government's close links with the organized farmers' movement. The Conservatives needed issues which transcended traditional economic concerns if they were to break up the long-standing coalition of Catholic, European immigrant, and Protestant Anglo-Canadian farmers which had guaranteed Liberal success so often in the past. The four they chose as the basis of their campaign were: abolition of sectarianism in the public school system; introduction of a scientific and selective scheme of immigration; return of natural resources to provincial control; the scandalous behaviour of the Liberal political machine. The first two fed upon the religious and racial antagonism created by the Ku Klux Klan since its appearance in the province two years previously. The Conservative party maintained a discreet distance from the Klan, but its spokesman had no hesitation in directing the emotions aroused by the Klan into political channels. Conservatives charged that the government had pandered to the province's Catholic and European minorities in order to win votes, that under Liberal immigration policy the Anglo-Protestant population of Saskatchewan would soon lose its majority status, and that the premier had allowed Catholicism to infiltrate the public school system. Hamilton remembers this aspect of the 1929 campaign well, just as he remembers Klan crosses burning on the outskirts of Delisle, but, despite his impressionable age, these were not the issues which drew him to the Conservative party. Rather, he was attracted by Anderson's determination to gain control of Saskatchewan's natural resources and, of greatest importance, he was repelled by his encounters with the Liberal machine in action.[11]

The Liberal machine in the late 1920s consisted of a network of committed partisans spread across the province, whose principal tasks were to identify Liberal sympathizers and to ensure that they voted on election day. Patronage fuelled the machine and alcohol kept it well-oiled, despite Prohibition. Mark Chambers was one of the machine's men in the Delisle area and, when the election was called, he set out immediately to fulfill his responsibilities. He travelled from poll to poll to check on the state of the organization, and he took his young nephew with him. Hamilton's job was to bring out the liquor whenever his uncle thought it would be useful, and to hide it from the police during the trips from farm to farm. Chambers also dispensed contracts for road work to deserving supporters and he used his position for personal benefit. Usual practice dictated that those given contracts put their hired men to work for a day or two to fill a slough or level a grade. They then billed the Department of Highways for a week's labour. His uncle's actions offended Hamilton's sense of propriety. Nathaniel Given's lectures on abstinence and corruption had impressed him deeply and he needed little encouragement from his friends to join them in their mentor's campaign.

Nathaniel Given won the Rosetown constituency easily on 6 June, amassing more votes than both his opponents combined, and the Conservative party took sufficient seats to form a government with the cooperation of the five Progressive and six Independent members elected. This success provincially buoyed local Conservatives and convinced them to make a full-fledged effort to win the Rosetown-Biggar federal seat the following year. They chose William Loucks, an area farmer and superintendent of the Delisle United Church Sunday School, as their candidate. Once again Hamilton campaigned for a man he knew and respected, and once again the Conservatives won the seat and the election. Thus, in less than thirteen months, Alvin Hamilton had been a part of two successful Conservative election campaigns. He may not have been a member of the party when he first became involved, but by the summer of 1930 he had travelled some distance down the road to a permanent commitment to Conservatism. The process would be completed a few years hence.

The election which brought R.B. Bennett and the Conservative party to power federally in 1930 coincided with Hamilton's graduation from high school, and the beginning of the harsh years of the Depression, which settled like a pall over the prairies. Young Hamilton had to plan a future for himself in most inauspicious circumstances and his alternatives were limited. He might have stayed on with the Chamberses, but he did not want to waste his life working as a hired hand and the Depression guaranteed that he could never borrow enough money to buy land for himself. In any case, he knew by this time that farm life would not satisfy him. He considered the prospect of a legal career and had visions of becoming a criminal lawyer as prominent as John Diefenbaker, but he simply could not afford the required number of years at university to obtain a law degree. He had saved enough money to finance just one year of further education and, as did so many of his contemporaries in similar situations, he decided to become a teacher. One year at normal school would earn him a teaching certificate and he hoped that a few years in the classroom would leave sufficient savings to see him through university. Teachers' salaries in 1930 were not high by any standard, but they had not yet been reduced to mid-Depression levels. Having made this decision, Hamilton applied for admission to the teachers' college in Saskatoon, only to be turned down because his application did not include a letter of recommendation from his local Liberal member of the Legislative Assembly, or, in the case of students from Rosetown constituency, the defeated Liberal candidate at the last provincial election. This rejection confirmed Hamilton's low opinion of machine politics and destroyed whatever chance the Liberal party may have had to bring him into its ranks. The Liberals had been out of office in Saskatchewan for some months, but the principal of the school, C.P. Seeley, remained committed to the party, and he would not admit anyone without its stamp of approval. Such blatant partisanship enraged Hamilton and he protested vehemently, but to no avail. Even a letter from the new member for Rosetown, Given, failed to move the man and it appeared for a time that Hamilton's plans would founder. Once again, however, his hockey skills smoothed the way for him. Seeley wanted his school to ice a competitive team that coming season, and when he learned that Hamilton had played for Delisle, he offered to ignore his initial objections if Hamilton would agree to organize the school team, play for it, and write a thesis on Sir Wilfrid Laurier. He also promised to find Hamilton a school in a district which paid its teachers well if Hamilton graduated and if the hockey team proved to be a winner. Alvin Hamilton accepted these conditions reluctantly, but fulfilled his part of the bargain. He put together a successful team, wrote the paper on Laurier, and passed all his courses, albeit with a third-rate average which reflected the time he spent on hockey and as president of the Student Assembly. Seeley's replacement also honoured the deal, and when Hamilton received his teaching certificate, a school was waiting for him in the Rhondda school district near Rosetown.

One-room schools, such as Rhondda, were the backbone of the Saskatchewan public school system in the early 1930s. Consolidation of those rural schools into larger units, which allowed teachers to specialize, would not take place for another fifteen years. Thus, when Hamilton arrived at Rhondda in the autumn of 1931, he was expected to teach all academic subjects to forty students from Grades I–XII, as well as organize all extra-curricular activities, such as music, art, drama and sport. These schools also served as the social centres for their communities at a time when people had little or no money to spend on entertainment, and again, it was assumed that the teacher would participate fully in all the dances, concerts, and whist evenings that took place, despite the attendant hazards. According to Hamilton:

> The teacher had a real place in those things. He had to dance with all the mothers of the children or he was a dead duck. Secondly, his great risk was in the form of mothers trying to get matches for their daughters with the school teacher because they looked on the school teacher, as a male, as a natural target for their oldest daughter.[12]

Hamilton fitted well into life in the Rhondda area. The school board persevered with him while he learned his craft and he contributed much to the community in return. The difference between the first and last reports done on him by the Department of Education inspectors indicates his progress. The first, in September 1931, read: "Mr. Hamilton has the work fairly well organized. He is having some difficulty in keeping the junior grades occupied. He is working hard and am sure the results will be quite satisfactory."[13] The last, in February 1934, stated:

> Mr. Hamilton is doing splendid work. He has a very heavy school. Work is well prepared and well presented. Supervision is well managed in classroom as well as playground. He is doing excellent work in this district, not only in school but in community. Am pleased with his work.[14]

Hamilton taught three years at Rhondda and the school board was good to him. They paid him twelve hundred dollars his first year, which made him one of the highest paid teachers in western Saskatchewan at the time, and tried hard to keep his pay high when other school boards slashed teachers' salaries as the Depression deepened. The board kept his salary at one thousand dollars his second and third years there, while teachers in other parts of the province saw their pay cut to as little as two hundred dollars per annum, and much of that given in kind instead of cash. The generosity of the Rhondda community meant a great deal to Alvin Hamilton. Without it, he could neither have supported his brother Fred through high school, nor saved enough to send himself to university.[15]

Life in the early years of the Depression should have been easier for Alvin Hamilton than for most of his contemporaries. He had a job which brought him a steady income, and he never experienced an unemployment line, the loss of a year's labour due to crop failure, or the vagaries of the international wheat market. Nevertheless, money dominated his thoughts as much as those around him, for he wanted to save as much as possible to go to university, and there was not much left over after he deducted the cost of Fred's schooling and his own room and board from the one hundred dollars he received each month. He forced himself to live frugally and it is perhaps fortunate that his duties at the school occupied most of his time. He played some hockey in the winter, but beyond that went into town only once a month for a haircut. He tried to find work during the summer holidays to supplement his income and, in the summer of 1932, when no one would hire him, he lived in the bush near Kenora for seven weeks to save money. The one luxury he allowed himself was the occasional bus trip to visit Beulah at her parents' farm seventy miles away. They had seen each other once in a while when Hamilton was in Saskatoon, and they had kept in touch during the year Beulah worked in Montréal. By the time she returned to Saskatchewan in late 1932, Hamilton knew he wanted to see her more often and he acted accordingly. He would walk the six miles into Rosetown, catch a bus to Biggar, change to another bus which took him to Kinley, and then hope that Beulah's father would meet him and save him the further seven-mile walk to the farm. Such devotion could not be denied. The romance flowered during these visits and, in other circumstances, they would have married before Hamilton left Rhondda. However, Hamilton had decided on a career in politics by this time, and they postponed their wedding so that he could go to university to acquire the tools he believed essential for the task. He had saved enough money to support himself alone and, not yet convinced that two could live as cheaply as one, they would wait another two years.

Alvin Hamilton came to Rhondda in 1931 with a definite bias against the Liberal party, but not yet a member of the Conservative party. He left three years later a committed partisan determined to sit in Parliament as a Conservative member at a time when thousands of people, in Saskatchewan especially, were fleeing that party for the new Cooperative Commonwealth Federation (CCF) and Social Credit movements.[16] Hamilton may not have been unique in this respect, but his decision was certainly a departure from the norm. The Depression came close to destroying the Conservative party in Saskatchewan. Outrageous fortune placed

Conservative governments in power at both Ottawa and Regina in the early 1930s and both bore the brunt of public anger when neither could cope with its destructive ferocity. The new political movements, which promised relief and a return to prosperity, benefitted greatly at the expense of the Conservatives, attracting large numbers of people whose hopes had been shattered by the failure of the traditional economic and political system. The Rhondda area suffered no less than most and the Rosetown-Biggar constituency soon became a battleground from which the socialist forces emerged victorious. It sent to Ottawa M.J. Coldwell, Woodsworth's eventual successor as leader of the federal CCF, and elected CCF candidates time after time to the provincial legislature, among them Woodrow Lloyd, who later became premier. The CCF should have appealed to an idealistic young man anxious to find a solution to the problems created by the Depression and ambitious for a political career and, indeed, Alvin Hamilton gave much serious consideration to the socialist alternative. He read the party's literature and attended its meetings, but in the end he opted for the Conservative party.

Hamilton's decision to reject the CCF in favour of the Conservatives emerged slowly over the three years he taught at Rhondda, and for a number of different reasons — personal, pragmatic, and philosophic. He spent a good deal of his spare time attending political meetings and reading political history and philosophy. He stayed with the secretary of his school board, Charles McKenzie, a graduate of the University of Edinburgh, who possessed an enormous library, and wiled away many a long winter evening with his landlord, reflecting on what he had heard and on the merits of the various competing political philosophies. He learned to distinguish between and among the parties' views of the nature of man, the proper relationship between individuals and the state, and the rôle of government in society — the cornerstones of all political philosophies. Over time he became convinced that the Conservative approach not only made the most sense philosophically, but also offered the best solution to practical problems of economic and social progress. Hamilton came to distrust both Utopians and fanatics, many of whom he found in the new CCF. He accepted the socialist premise that reform was necessary, but he would accomplish this in a different way. He would not pit class against class to build a new Jerusalem in that then brown and unpromising land. Furthermore, the CCF at that time promised to replace private enterprise with state enterprise as the basis of the country's economic life and this was more that Hamilton could stomach. While he understood that the existing system needed improvement, he was not prepared to accept total state domination of the economy or any other aspect of society. This offended his Presbyterian sense that individuals should turn to the state only as a last resort and, in addition, his experience of the Gardiner government and its legacy of corruption cautioned him against substituting one evil with a potentially greater and more dangerous one.

Hamilton also found a hypocrisy in the CCF at the level of the individual which he did not expect and this drove him further from socialism. In his words:

> What really turned me against them was the fact that when you got digging real deep the individual selfishness still remained. Here they were talking this dogma that as socialists we'd lose all selfishness, we'd do everything for the state, and yet every form of dirty trick seemed to come from these great spouters of humanitarian philosophy.[17]

One such dirty trick occurred when the school board in one of the districts adjoining Rhondda, most of whose members belonged to the CCF, cut the teacher's salary in half to effect an average annual saving of two dollars per taxpayer. Hamilton had a great deal more respect for Conservatives such as McKenzie, who did everything they could to maintain his salary when they were no better off financially. Such incidents convinced him that the CCF had no panacea for the Depression and confirmed the positive impression of individual Conservatives that he had obtained from people such as Given, Loucks and his prospective father-in-law.

The attempts of the Anderson and Bennett governments to bring the country out of the Depression provided the last nudge necessary to push Alvin Hamilton into the Conservative party. Unlike many, Hamilton did not lay the blame for the catastrophe at the feet of the Conservatives. Instead, he regarded their policies as appropriate to the circumstances — designed to restart the stalled economy and to alleviate the plight of those who could no longer fend for themselves. Anderson's plans to develop the province sparked Hamilton's imagination. The premier spoke of the need to tap the vast resources of Saskatchewan, to use these resources to build a strong economy, and to pay for the social programmes he deemed essential to the welfare of his people, and he won a permanent convert to this philosophy in Alvin Hamilton. Hamilton also welcomed the federal government's efforts to save the family farm and to improve the western economy. In fact, he attended some of the early discussions which led to eventual passage of the Farm Loan Act, the Farmers' Creditors Arrangement Act, and the Canadian Wheat Board Act. Bennett appointed William Loucks to a committee established to investigate the problems of western agriculture and, in the summer of 1934, Hamilton drove him to committee meetings held in Saskatchewan. Hamilton was not a member of the committee, but he was allowed to sit in on the discussions and so gained firsthand knowledge of the Conservative party's efforts to cope with this aspect of the Depression. These meetings sealed Alvin Hamilton's fate, for men such as E.E. Perley, the member of Parliament for Qu'Appelle, and M.A. McPherson, attorney-general and provincial treasurer of Saskatchewan, impressed him greatly with the breadth of their knowledge of agricultural problems in general, and the depth of their concern for individual farmers in particular. When these men suggested that Hamilton should join them in their attempts to bring Canada out of the Depression, he needed little persuasion. His experiences the past five years had convinced him that no other party possessed such an appealing combination of principles, policies, and personnel. Thus, by the time he left Rhondda, Alvin Hamilton was a Conservative — a policy-oriented Conservative inspired by the philosophy of resource development for economic and social purposes, and a young man resolved to pursue a political career in the Conservative party when he graduated from university.

Hamilton performed one last service for the Conservative party in the Rosetown constituency before he left for Saskatoon. He worked on Nathaniel Given's campaign for reelection in the provincial contest in June 1934, although without the same success as in 1929. Despite its self-proclaimed record of achievement in difficult circumstances, the Anderson government could not counter opposition attacks which blamed it for the Depression. "Impossible as it may seem, the net agricultural incomes for 1931 through 1939 [in Saskatchewan] . . . were reported in minus figures, a reduction in income quite unmatched in any civilized country."[18] No government could turn statistics such as these into votes, and Given went down to defeat, as did every candidate who supported Dr. Anderson.

When Alvin Hamilton registered at the University of Saskatchewan in the autumn of 1934, political clubs were not allowed on campus. Walter C. Murray, president of the university, believed that politics had no place at such a state-financed institution, but this did not prevent Hamilton from continuing to work for the Conservative party. It meant simply that he had to carry on his activities away from the campus and this did not hinder him unduly. He gave R.B. Bennett his thoughts on the rôle of the Bank of Canada in a depressed economy, and the prime minister used some of them in the party's *Speakers Handbook* prepared for the federal election in 1935. Hamilton also managed William Louck's campaign in that election, again without success, as Loucks lost to M.J. Coldwell. Such defeats, however, did not detach Hamilton from his allegiance to the Conservative party. If anything they convinced him more than ever of the need for a stronger Conservative presence in Regina and Ottawa. In this he had the full support of John Diefenbaker, who Hamilton began to see quite often while at university. Diefenbaker's parents lived close to the campus, and whenever Diefenbaker visited them, he would invite students known to have Conservative sympathies to drop in to discuss political affairs, including the state of the party in Saskatchewan.

The provincial Conservative party was in turmoil in the mid-1930s. The party had split between those who supported Dr. Anderson and his coalition government and those who wanted the party to remain true to its principles, even if this meant the loss of power. Anderson beat back the threat from the "True Blues" but, by 1936, it was clear that he had lost the confidence of a powerful section of the party and he tendered his resignation. The party now had to find a new leader, and the provincial executive called a convention for November to replace Anderson and to write a new platform, both of which it hoped would restore party fortunes. It established a committee, chaired by Nathaniel Given, to draft resolutions for discussion during the convention and Given asked Hamilton to participate in the process. As Given explained to Diefenbaker after the event:

> I named young Hamilton as I have been personally interested in his welfare for years and he has proven his worth. He is at present attending University and paid his own expenses to be at Regina . . . I named him because I know [*sic*] he was interested in education and he did get in his resolution on education.
>
> [He is] a good thinker and good talker and he has one or two of the Professors who think quite a lot of him.[19]

Hamilton had nothing to do with the campaign that brought Diefenbaker the leadership, but he did participate in the work of the Resolutions Committee, and the convention did adopt his suggestions for education which committed the party to an adequate minimum salary schedule for all teachers, payment of all arrears of teachers' salaries, a lower price for school books, revision of primary and secondary curricula, and scholarships for students who otherwise would not be able to go to university.[20] The convention passed a host of resolutions on many subjects, but made no attempt to arrange them into a coherent statement of the party's policy. When Hamilton realized that all this work might go for naught, he suggested to Diefenbaker that the resolutions, if organized properly, could be an important source of publicity for the party. Diefenbaker agreed, and Hamilton spent the winter months of 1937, while still at university, at the task. The result of his efforts, with minor modifications made by the Provincial Council, became the Conservative party's platform in the election of 1938. Beyond this work he did on the resolutions, Hamilton found himself spending more and more time on political matters throughout 1937. He became the representative for the Rosetown constituency on the Provincial Council and attended several meetings in this capacity. He began to research and write speeches for the new leader, and drove Diefenbaker from meeting to meeting across northern Saskatchewan in the summer. He helped to build the party organization in Rosetown and tried to sell memberships there, although raising money for political purposes was not easy at the time. As Senator Aseltine wrote Diefenbaker about Hamilton and his fellow canvassers, "They are very willing and hard workers but the average crop of wheat was less than one bushel to the acre in this constituency and that means that no one has any money."[21] Then, just before the end of the year, he volunteered to become Diefenbaker's organizer for northern Saskatchewan. He used what spare time he had in the winter of 1938 to sell memberships, to build local party organizations, and to locate potential candidates. All these efforts brought him to the attention of his party's federal leader. In April, Bennett sent Hamilton one hundred dollars in recognition of his services and "to promote interest among young people in the Conservative Party." Hamilton asked Diefenbaker's approval to hire another organizer in a "good Conservative seat."[22] Thus, by the time Alvin Hamilton graduated from university, he had begun to build a reputation for himself in the Conservative party. If he needed to prove his commitment further, he would have the opportunity to do so at the forthcoming provincial election.

Alvin Hamilton had left Rhondda in the autumn of 1934 because he believed a university education would further his career in politics, and he was active politically while a student, but politics by no means dominated his life between registration and graduation. The decision to attend university cost Hamilton a great deal. He had to scrimp and save for three years, to postpone his wedding, and to leave a secure job at the height of the Depression, so he was determined that these sacrifices would not be in vain. Furthermore, he was not wealthy, had little prospect of becoming so, and knew that he would have to earn a living to provide the financial base from which to launch his political career. Consequently, while university may have been a stepping stone to a life in politics, politics definitely played second fiddle to his education during his four years in Saskatoon.

Politics, nevertheless, did provide a unifying theme for the programme of study he chose to pursue at university. He registered in Type B Arts, which gave him access to the maximum number of social science courses possible, and he decided to specialize in history and economics, the latter more properly called "political economy" given the state of the discipline then. He took courses in national and imperial history, and Canadian and international economics from professors such as W.S. Morton, W.C. Murray and G.E. Britnell. He wrote essays, led seminars, and exposed his ideas to the criticism of faculty and students alike on topics ranging from constitutional law to Keynesian economics. He also took courses in English and other languages to improve his ability to speak and write well.[23] All these courses carried on where his evenings in Charles McKenzie's library left off. Over those four years at university, his reading, research, and classes broadened and deepened his knowledge and understanding of history, politics, economics and philosophy, and the interrelationships between and among them. They taught him the causes of the Depression and added to his knowledge of the solutions to it offered by various political philosophies and economic theories. They convinced him that the only way to build a strong Canada was to develop its natural resources, and that governments must be active participants in economic affairs when the free market failed and private enterprise proved unequal to the task of national development. They also confirmed his belief that the Conservative party was the best political instrument to help the country realize its potential, and that it promised the most hope of pulling Canada and Saskatchewan out of the Depression.

Hamilton enjoyed his classes. He worked hard at them and they caused him little difficulty. He achieved high second-class standing in each of his first two years, raised his average to the first-class level in his third year, and kept it there his last year. He did so well, in fact, that he won a bursary which enabled him to remain at university for his Honours year, and he received serious consideration for the Rhodes scholarship. Furthermore, he was so encouraged by his success that when he learned he would have financial support for a fourth year, he decided to register in the College of Education as well as Arts and, in effect, take two full years of study in different programmes at the same time. He came through with flying colours, much to the chagrin of the deans of Arts and Education, neither of whom learned of his endeavours until it was too late. At the spring convocation in 1938 Alvin Hamilton graduated with distinction from the College of Arts and returned to the platform to receive his Certificate in Education. It is not surprising that an intelligent young man should be able to combine academic excellence with some work for a political party during his years at university. What is unusual, however, is that Alvin Hamilton did both while engaged in a remarkable number of extracurricular activities on campus at the same time.

Hamilton knew that he would have but one chance to sample all that university life had to offer, and he set out from his earliest days as a freshman not to waste a moment of the opportunity. The only constraints he recognized were those imposed by the demands of his courses, lack of money, and the unfortunate fact that then, as now, a day consisted of a mere twenty-four hours. His many extracurricular activities followed the Greek model — improvement of one's physical and mental abilities, and participation in the governance of one's polity. Hamilton played for the Arts hockey team for four years, the Arts Rugby team for three, the Arts and Education basketball teams for two, and he competed for both the Arts and University track teams in his final year. He also managed the Arts hockey and Rugby teams during his third year. He joined the International Relations Club as a freshman and remained a member throughout his university career. He also joined the Historical Association, served as its secretary-treasurer in his sophomore year and as its president when a senior. In addition, he made the university debating team in his second and third years, won the national debating competition sponsored by the Canadian Broadcasting Commission in 1936 and lost it the following year. Finally, as if he needed the extra work, he accepted a nomination for the presidency of the College of Arts and Science and his fellow students elected him to the position for his last university year.

In the midst of all this, Alvin Hamilton and Beulah Major decided that two could live just about as cheaply as one if his bus fares to see her on weekends were taken into account, and they married on 14 November 1936. They planned a quiet family affair, but Hamilton was well known on campus by this time, and when word spread that he would be married in Saskatoon on a Saturday afternoon after classes ended, his college friends packed the church. These "friends" also staged a chivaree after the wedding, refusing to leave the newlyweds alone until the groom paid them to go home. Unfortunately, Hamilton did not have enough money to satisfy the crowd and the revellers did not depart until the early hours of the next morning. The Hamiltons, in fact, had a very difficult time financially throughout the first two years of their marriage. Hamilton's savings from Rhondda had long gone to support him during his first two years at university, and he could not earn enough in the summers to meet all their expenses for the rest of the year. He had no choice but to work part-time and, at one stage in his Honours year, he held five different jobs. He lectured at the university, marked essays and examinations, translated Latin for other students, managed the campus skating rink, and taught arithmetic a few periods a week at Nutana Collegiate — all this while taking a full programme in Arts and another in Education. Luckily, Hamilton was a healthy well-organized young man, but even he admits that by the time he graduated "I was kind of tired."[24] Hamilton's marriage to Beulah Major also meant that he had to withdraw from the competitions for the Rhodes scholarship because, by the rules in force then, Rhodes scholars had to be single.[25] Nevertheless, Hamilton did not regret his decision for one moment. In his words:

> When this was told me there was no great moaning at the bar. I was sort of relieved I didn't have to go through this silly business of spending three years studying at Oxford. And I couldn't see any real purpose in studying at Oxford being a school teacher . . . In retrospect, I'm glad I didn't get it. It pitches you in the wrong direction. You get a type of muddleheaded thinking — you seem to lose contact with common sense. This is not sour grapes either . . . The prestige would have been there, but . . . I was interested in politics by this time.[26]

The orphan had come a long way in the eleven years since he had to leave Kenora. By the spring of 1938, Alvin Hamilton had the woman he loved, the university education he wanted, an offer of a full-time position at Nutana, and a start on a promising political career, albeit in a party then in decline in Saskatchewan.

Chapter 2

Per Ardua ad Astra

Alvin Hamilton, B.A. (Hon.), had little time to savour his graduation from university. W.J. Patterson, who had succeeded J.G. Gardiner as premier in 1935, asked Lieutenant-Governor McNab to dissolve the legislature in mid-May and to call an election for 8 June. In normal circumstances the Conservative party would have welcomed an election in 1938. The Liberals, in power provincially for four years and federally for three, could be attacked for their failure to cope with the Depression. The Conservatives had a new and dynamic leader, John Diefenbaker, and a new platform designed to appeal to those willing to try all measures, however drastic, to bring the province back to economic prosperity. This programme seemed to some observers at the time to be "more to the left than the CCF's."[1] It committed the party to debt adjustment legislation to prevent mortgage foreclosures and to force creditors to share with their debtors losses occasioned by crop failure and low prices; to re-fund the public debt at lower interest rates; to abolish the education tax; to encourage cooperative buying and selling of agricultural commodities; to various social welfare measures, including state medical and hospital care; to an increased minimum wage; and to several development projects to reduce unemployment.[2] Nevertheless, the election came at an inopportune time for the

Conservative party because its circumstances were anything but normal.

The Conservative party in Saskatchewan in 1938 was divided as never before in its history. All Conservatives were united in their desire to rid the province of the Liberal machine, but they could not agree on the best method to accomplish the objective — whether to try it on their own or by joining either Social Credit or the CCF. Splits in the party over this issue began shortly after the 1934 election which saw the Conservative share of the popular vote drop below 30 percent and every supporter of the Anderson government go down to defeat. After this debacle many Conservatives came to the conclusion that their party would never win office again on its own, and they began to look to the new parties as the better hope of defeating the Liberals. Some constituency associations, inspired by Aberhart's success in Alberta, went over to Social Credit, as Hamilton was to find out to his chagrin. Other Conservatives looked to the CCF and in 1937, a group led by Dr. Anderson proposed an alliance with the socialists at the provincial level. Diefenbaker, backed by Alvin Hamilton and others, was able to stall the attempt, but he did agree to investigate the possibility of an agreement with the CCF not to oppose each other's candidates at the next election. The overtures were made late in 1937 and the negotiations were carried out in the strictest secrecy at the highest levels of both parties in Regina and Ottawa. The path to agreement was by no means smooth. In early April, F.W. Turnbull, one of the principal Conservative negotiators, informed Diefenbaker that:

> George [Williams, CCF provincial leader] claims the CCF are the dominant party in the Province, and that we should recognize that we are distinctly inferior. He expresses the belief that the CCF will have a clear majority in the next house and I presume, for that reason, does not intend to give us a clear field in very many seats . . . It is hard to negotiate with a man without any balance.[3]

Later the same month, he advised H.E. Keown, president of the Saskatchewan Conservative Association, that:

> Conversations with the CCF Leaders have not been one hundred per cent successful. They appear to have difficulty that does not affect us, with their constituents. They cannot restrain activities of their followers in the constituencies. On the other hand, we cannot arose [*sic*] enthusiasm among our followers.[4]

Just the same, Turnbull thought it would be inadvisable "to impair what success we are having just because we do not succeed in full,"[5] and there is no doubt that the Conservatives believed they had more to gain from the arrangement than the CCF. As early as January, E.E. Perley, the lone Conservative from Saskatchewan in the House of Commons, told Diefenbaker that he was "more convinced than ever, we must go through with the arrangement and nothing must be left undone in carrying it out."[6] At the same time, the advantages of an agreement with the Conservatives were not lost on the entire CCF leadership. At one stage in the process Tommy Douglas warned Williams that:

> If we make it too tough on fellows like Perley and Diefenbaker . . . we may well have a Conservative in almost every constituency, with strong financial backing from the Group [R.B. Bennett and the federal Conservative party] . . . who are endeavouring to get the Conservative party on its feet again.[7]

Despite Williams's intransigence and the refusal of some local CCF organizations to stay out of the campaign, by the time the election was called, an informal agreement had been reached on a majority of the province's fifty-two constituencies. After nominations ceased, Conservative and CCF candidates opposed each other in only seventeen seats. The saw-off of seats with the CCF proved to be of little help to the Conservatives as it turned out. As Williams informed Woodsworth after the election, "We stayed out of a number of seats and gave them a clear field and also gave them considerable voting support. They failed to show any strength."[8] The election returns showed just how low the once proud Conservative party had sunk. In Diefenbaker's words:

> I could not get sufficient candidates in the field to be in a position to form a Government, and that militated against

> the Party, the reason being that there were no local finances, nor could candidates be found to finance themselves.[9]

The Conservative leader could find only twenty-nine candidates in total, his party's share of the popular vote fell to 12 percent, and again no Conservative candidate won a seat. In contrast, both new parties ran more candidates, elected more members and received a larger proportion of the total vote on election day.

The election of 1938 taught Alvin Hamilton a great deal about the real world of politics, and the lessons he learned during that campaign have stayed with him to this day. He learned first hand never to take one's supporters for granted, the importance of loyalty to one's party, and that the threat to an independent Conservative party in Saskatchewan was equally as ominous from the right as from the left of the political spectrum. Hamilton entered the campaign with great expectations, for he had been chosen the Conservative candidate for Biggar at a convention held before he graduated, and he had been promised the support of the riding's prominent Conservatives. Diefenbaker had suggested that Hamilton run in Tisdale, perhaps because he knew that Biggar headed the list of seats to be left to the CCF under the agreement then being negotiated, but Hamilton decided to run in a constituency closer to his home territory. There is no evidence that Diefenbaker or any other Conservative put pressure on Hamilton to withdraw in favour of the CCF candidate but, nonetheless, the ballot in Biggar on 8 June did not include his name. The plans he had laid so carefully went awry at the last moment because his "friends" deserted him for another party. Hamilton spent the first part of the campaign carrying out his duties as Diefenbaker's northern organizer, finding candidates, and building local election committees, but he returned to Biggar in time to submit his nomination papers. To his shock and surprise the very people who had chosen him their candidate a few months previously, including Given and Loucks, would not sign the papers. They told him they had decided that Social Credit offered the best chance of defeating the sitting Liberal member, and Loucks, in fact, stood as the

Social Credit candidate in the neighbouring constituency of Rosetown. The news stunned Hamilton. He might have found sufficient loyal Conservatives in the riding to sign his papers, but he decided that without the support of the party executive it would not be worth the effort. Diefenbaker again suggested that he run in Tisdale, but Hamilton declined on the grounds that, as he was not well known there, his task would be hopeless. He gave his leader the one hundred dollar deposit he had scraped together so painfully and left Biggar to help Conservative candidates elsewhere for the remainder of the campaign. He left embittered by his betrayal and, decades later, he still has no use for the Conservative who will sacrifice his party simply to defeat a rival.[10]

The election over, Hamilton returned to Saskatoon for a much needed rest and to prepare for his new position at Nutana Collegiate. He would spend the next three and a half years there, although his duties at first were not those one would expect of a graduate in history. G.A. Bonney, the principal at Nutana, hired Hamilton initially to run the school's athletics programme and during his first two years there Hamilton spent most of his time at the track, on the football field, or in the gymnasium, rather than in the classroom. Despite his love of athletics, those two years were not an unmitigated joy. In his words:

> The first couple of years I was there were just murder on me. I only spent, the first year I taught, about one hour and a half or maybe two hours at the most a week in the classroom and all the rest was out in the sweaty gymnasium . . . I didn't mind teaching boys because you could kick them around and they didn't seem to mind but the girls used to cry and weep and so on and their parents would come to see you when you had to reduce your number on the team. I suppose I enjoyed it, but I knew it wasn't for me.[11]

The retirement of one of the school's history teachers gave Hamilton a chance to get out of his track suit, and he grasped it gratefully. He continued to coach Nutana's track teams but, as of the beginning of the school year in 1940, his principal responsibility was to teach history and he continued to do so as long as he remained at Nutana. He became, by all accounts, an excellent teacher. He loved his subject and transmitted his enthusiasm to his students.[12] He altered the curriculum to suit his priorities and those of his students, and his classes became so popular that the College of Education at the university began to send its trainees to Nutana to observe his teaching techniques. Hamilton also served as the staff representative on the collegiate yearbook committee every year he taught at Nutana, and he earned the gratitude of the students for the "untiring efforts and hard work" he contributed to making the publication a success.[13]

Alvin Hamilton continued to work for the Conservative party while at Nutana, although the demands of his job curtailed his activities somewhat. The school did not object to his partisan activities. He simply did not have the time to do everything he wanted to do for the party. He did what he could to help Diefenbaker. He attended meetings of the Provincial Council and spoke at party functions and, in fact, saved half his first year's salary of fourteen hundred dollars to buy a new car, which would make it easier for him to carry out his tasks as northern organizer.

After the 1938 election, most of Hamilton's political activities were directed at the federal level. War was on the horizon, all parties expected a federal election shortly, Diefenbaker received the nomination for the federal riding of Lake Centre in the summer of 1939, and he accepted Hamilton's offer to campaign there on his behalf.[14] Hamilton also helped the party find candidates to run federally and convinced former Premier Anderson to take on M.J. Coldwell in Rosetown-Biggar, the seat he might have had for himself. Hamilton did not contest any seat at the election held in March of 1940. Instead, he worked for both Diefenbaker and Anderson during the campaign, speaking and fund raising, and had the pleasure of seeing Diefenbaker elected, if by a narrow margin. Diefenbaker's victory that year proved to be important to Hamilton's later career, because the defeat in 1938 had come close to driving Diefenbaker out of political life in Saskatchewan. Shortly after his nomination in Lake Centre, he informed Hamilton that "if things go bad politically this year, I intend to go East and establish myself where I can associate with kindred political souls, instead of forever battling against what sometimes appears like insurmountable odds."[15] The victory in Lake Centre kept Diefenbaker in politics and in contact with the man who would eventually become a minister in his cabinet.

After the 1940 election, the nation turned its attention increasingly to the war effort and so did Alvin Hamilton. He continued his involvement with the affairs of the Conservative party, but there wasn't much incentive to work federally after the election, and H.E. Keown, the lawyer from Melfort who had replaced Diefenbaker as provincial leader after the Chief's victory in the 1940 election, believed that partisan politics should cease for the duration of the war. In addition, Hamilton began to feel that he could no longer remain teaching when so many of his students were joining the army, navy and air force.

The first three and a half years Hamilton spent at Nutana were happy ones for the most part, with the exception of the time he spent in the gymnasium. He enjoyed teaching, the position provided both the time and the money to pursue his political career, he bought a small house in Saskatoon, and in June of 1940 he and his wife had their first child, a son they named Robert Alexander. The one dark shadow which hung over his life throughout this period was the threat and eventual onset of war. The outbreak of hostilities caught the Hamiltons holidaying in Ontario, and they drove back to Saskatchewan as quickly as possible. Hamilton was a member of the Saskatoon Light Infantry reserve and he thought he might be called up at any moment. However, the army at that time could not supply its militia units with the requisite weapons and materiel, and the call did not come. Hamilton then tried to join the Royal Canadian Air Force (RCAF) as a pilot, but it rejected him on the grounds of age and poor eyesight. He next enrolled in the Canadian Officers Training Corps at the University of Saskatchewan in the hope that this would catapult him into the fray, but to no avail. Two years passed by with Hamilton in the militia while every month his students left Nutana to join the forces. By the autumn of 1941 he could wait no longer. He could have remained at Nutana for the duration of the war because teaching was a protected occupation, but he could not justify his security in light of the casualty figures among his former students. In his words, "You can't see your students get all fired up with the propaganda that goes on in early wartime and go off and join up and pay the price. You can't face those students. You go yourself and join them."[16] Finally he resorted to the subterfuge which had cleared the way into the RCAF for so many young men with less than perfect eyesight — he memorized the eye chart — and this time the air force accepted his application. He took a leave of absence from Nutana as soon as he received his orders to report for duty and just after Christmas 1941 he left Saskatoon for the manning depot in Toronto. His departure did not go unnoticed by the students at Nutana. Their yearbook for 1942 was dedicated

> To Pilot Officer Hamilton in particular whose four years' service on the Hermes staff saw a vast improvement in our publication, and in general to all those former students and teachers of Nutana who have cheerfully given up their security to fight for ours.[17]

Life was such during the war that Hamilton did not learn of this tribute until he returned to Nutana after almost four years with the Royal Canadian Air Force.

Hamilton spent most of his wartime service in Canada. He did not plan it that way. He would have been quite happy to serve as a combatant in any theatre of the war, but the air force decided that his greatest contribution would be as an instructor in air navigation. The Commonwealth Air Training Plan based in Canada needed teachers and Hamilton's experience made him an obvious choice. When he completed basic training the air force posted him to the No. 1 Air Navigation School at Rivers, Manitoba, to learn the tools of his new trade. The course lasted two months and, after he graduated in April of 1942, he spent the next two years teaching others how to plot courses by instruments and the stars, and how to arrive at their destinations safely in all forms of weather. His postings were first to No. 4 Senior Flying School at Saskatoon, where he spent fifteen months, and then to Portage la Prairie for the next nine, which meant that he could be with his wife Beulah for the birth of their second son, William Alvin, in October 1943. Hamilton knew the importance of his rôle and he proved to be a competent instructor. Nevertheless, after two years at the same task and despite promotions to flying officer and then flight lieutenant, he began to look for a way overseas. A married man of thirty-two with two young children, he was no thrill-seeker. He simply wanted to experience in action what he had been teaching for so long and, by the spring of 1944, it was clear that the war would not last that much longer. His opportunity came in May when the air force sent him to Patricia Bay, British Columbia, to teach long-range navigation techniques to an operational unit preparing to go abroad. By chance, Hamilton had to scrub the navigator for one of the crews from the course before it ended and, rather than see the rest of the crew miss the course as well, he posted himself to them for the remainder of their training. After that, his departure from Canada was quick and remarkably uncomplicated. The commanding officer at Patricia Bay could see only that all his crews were fully manned, and Hamilton's superiors at Portage could not dispute the orders which transferred the crews from Patricia Bay to Britain, even if one of their instructors had been posted with them. After short stops in Saskatoon to say good-bye to his wife and the boys, and in Portage to pack his gear, Hamilton hitched a ride to Halifax for the Atlantic crossing to join Pilot Officer Jim Flett and Sergeant Bill Ulrich in Britain. His ship sailed from Halifax for Scotland on 11 July.

The men knew before they arrived in Britain that with their skills they could be posted to Ferry Command and spend the rest of the war jockeying aircraft back and forth across the Atlantic. This prospect did not appeal to them in the least, and they applied immediately on arrival for courses which would train them in the low-level transport of troops and supplies. This meant extra practice in low-level flying for Flett and Ulrich, whereas Hamilton's talents would not be required, so he enrolled at the Pathfinder Navigation School at Cranwell. To his dismay, the course offered nothing he did not know already and, as soon as Flett and Ulrich completed their training, all three volunteered for active service. In early August, they drew tropical kit and left for Cairo via Rabat, French West Africa, and Castel Benito, Tripoli. Their stay in Cairo was brief, just over a week, but while there they had their first taste of action. They flew twice to Taranto on the heel of Italy, loaded their Dakota with weapons and delivered them at night to partisan groups in Yugoslavia. These were exciting missions and they might have spent much longer at them, but Mountbatten's "Forgotten Army," which had stopped the Japanese advance into India and had begun to push them back into Burma, needed all the transport it could get. So the crew moved again, this time to an Royal Air Force (RAF) squadron based at Mauripur in northeastern India, travelling via Iraq, Bahrein and Karachi. They went into action immediately, carrying supplies to the troops at the front but, once again, their experience of combat was brief, for their arrival coincided with the Canadian government's decision to pull all Canadian aircrew out of the RAF and unite them in Canadian units. This, of course, took time and Alvin Hamilton and his mates spent most of the autumn months of 1944 with a Gurkha regiment stationed near Rawalpindi, then in India but now capital of Pakistan, honing their skills. As Hamilton summarized the experience years afterward:

> They learned how to drop mass formations of parachutists at precise places within seconds of the target hour. They went through the gruelling business of lugging a heavily loaded glider off the ground and pulling it to a prescribed spot. They practised dropping supplies by parachute on small clearings. In short, they were low-level combat supply squadrons.[18]

Finally, in December, they were posted back to the fighting as part of RCAF squadron No. 436 based at Imphal. By this time the Fourteenth Army had reached the Chindwin and Irrawaddy rivers, and had begun to stockpile equipment in preparation for the crossings which would take it to Mandalay. Transport Command played a vital rôle in the build-up and Hamilton and his crew flew mission after mission, carrying troops and materiel and dropping agents behind enemy lines. On 14 January, the Nineteenth Indian Division crossed the

Chindwin north of Mandalay, and for the next month Hamilton flew up to six missions every day, ferrying food, gasoline and ammunition to the front and the wounded back to the hospital. In mid-February the crew was transferred to Akyab on the Burmese coast to support the Twentieth Division in its attack across the Irrawaddy towards the vital rail and road junction at Meiktila, south of Mandalay. The battle for Meiktila was one of the most decisive of the Asian theatre and the Allies spared no effort to capture the town.[19] Once it was in their hands, they would encircle the main Japanese army in Burma, and the Japanese were equally determined to force their way south through the town to Rangoon. The British dropped a parachute brigade ahead of their main force to take the airfield at Meiktila, and Transport Command flew its planes right into the heart of the battle to keep the troops fed and supplied with ammunition. On one of these missions, a Japanese attack caught Hamilton's Dakota on the ground packed with wounded men and they had to leave in a hurry through a hail of rifle, machine gun and mortar fire and into the sights of a 40-mm cannon. As Hamilton tells the story:

> The plane acted like a wild horse as we shuddered our way down the strip and I thought we were going to get it because here were these guys aiming right at us and sooner or later they would get a round in that thing and sooner or later they would fire it. But some British soldiers saw the trouble we were in and jumped in a jeep and went swinging around past our aircraft and they raced full-tilt at that gun going about thirty miles an hour . . . and they must have sprayed enough lead around there that kept those fellows nervous and they never did get their round fired off . . . So that plane took off I would think in about nine hundred or a thousand feet. We got up to fifty feet and then turned over, banked back down to the ground again and went skimming off across the country at ten feet above the ground. Our plane had a whole bunch of holes in it from all those guys firing their rifles and machine guns, but we didn't get that big 40-mm cannon going off at us.[20]

A few days later, Hamilton wasn't so lucky. On another mission to the front, Japanese gunners once again caught

Hamilton's crew unloading cargo and, as they sprinted back to their aircraft, a piece of shrapnel smashed into his foot breaking five bones. The foot should have been placed in a cast, but Hamilton wanted to finish his tour and pursuaded the doctor to give him painkillers instead. Ten days later he was back in the air, just as the fighting at Meiktila reached its climax. As he remembers the battle:

> The Japanese recaptured the airfields . . . When the planes could no longer land with supplies and reinforcements, the airmen reverted to parachutes. When the area between the lakes got too small for all the parachuted supplies to hit, they flew at 20 feet above the ground to roll the ammunition right up to the guns. After six weeks of terrible effort and dying the battles of Mandalay and Meiktila were over. The Imperial armies of Japan had been defeated for the first time.[21]

Meiktila fell first, then Mandalay, and the army wheeled south towards Rangoon. Transport Command stayed with the troops every step of the way and Hamilton continued to fly missions until he left for home.

On 22 April Hamilton received word that Prime Minister Mackenzie King had called a federal election. As a candidate, he had the right to return home immediately to campaign, but he could not leave without orders and these did not come. Finally, he contacted Diefenbaker, who took up his case with the Defence Department, and eventually he left Burma on 4 May, the day the Fourteenth Army marched into Rangoon. His crew gave him the traditional liquid send-off and his commanding officer added the following commendation: "F/L Hamilton is an above average navigator — His job in this squadron has been outstanding."[22] Hamilton's trip home was neither easy nor quick. Victory in Europe celebrations delayed him in Malta. The end of the war in Europe also meant that all special leaves were cancelled in expectation of repatriation, and he had to find his own flight from Scotland to Canada. This caused him to miss the Trans-Canada Airlines flight from Montréal to the West, which he had booked in advance, so he had to take the train to Saskatoon. As a consequence, he did not arrive home until 19 May, less than three weeks before election day.

The war did not leave Alvin Hamilton much time for politics. In fact, he did not play any part at all in the provincial election of 1944, which brought the CCF to power in Saskatchewan. Nevertheless, his desire to sit in Parliament burned as strongly as ever, and his postings to Saskatoon and Portage la Prairie allowed him to keep in touch with key people in the province and in the constituency of Rosetown-Biggar. He corresponded regularly with J.F. Anderson, the provincial organizer, mostly about his chances of winning the nomination in Rosetown-Biggar and, in the spring of 1944, the riding association chose him to carry the Progressive Conservative banner in the next federal election. This time he planned to leave nothing to chance to avoid a recurrence of the embarrassment in 1938. As he informed Diefenbaker just before he went overseas:

> I have just finished spending two days out in the constituency . . . I found that all our fellows are still full of fight, and made some thirty calls, so the feeling is reasonably widespread. Secondly, the Liberals, including their organizers, are talking up some form of coalition with the Conservatives. This I did not commit myself on because I am opposed to any type of medicine mixing . . . If this sample of feeling is any indication as to what the rest of the constituency feels like, it is absolutely imperative that a campaign to popularize my name be started immediately *so as to ensure our people that we are in the fight right from the word go.*[23]

Hamilton did what he could from India and Burma to stay abreast of developments in the constituency, and to keep his name before the electorate. He exchanged many letters with E.J. Ewing, the president of the riding association, as well as other prominent Conservatives, urging them to build an election organization and to ensure that he received coverage by the local media. Ewing did both and, when the election was called, he also began to advertise as follows on Hamilton's behalf:

> Word has been received by his committee that Flight Lieutenant Alvin Hamilton, Mr. Bracken's candidate in the forthcoming election, is on his way home from his R.C.A.F. duties in India, on leave. He will vigourously contest the election in this constituency on behalf of the Progressive Conservative Party which stands for a Square Deal for all, security for the aged, the right of every man to a job at a fair wage, a guarantee to agriculture of a fair share of the National Income by floor prices and arbitrary price adjustments of farm products.[24]

Thus, by the time Hamilton arrived home, his campaign was already underway and he did not have to waste any of the time remaining before election day on details of organization. He could begin immediately to meet the electorate and to convince voters that he deserved their support. He held several meetings across the riding and bought radio time for five major broadcasts. In these he outlined what a Progressive Conservative government, led by John Bracken, would do for western agriculture, and he drew upon his experiences during the war to describe the type of world he wanted to see emerge when hostilities ceased. The ideal world he envisaged would be capitalist, not socialist as promised by his major opponent, M.J. Coldwell, and the economy would be based on resource development. In his words:

> Let us free Canadian enterprise. Tell the little man that he is safe to invest his savings in small business without the danger of confiscation or ruthless state-bonused business competition. Tell the big man that his millions are welcome to develop the country, to provide wealth, and with jobs rapid circulation of money which is true prosperity. The key thing is an aggressive, intelligent development of our natural resources to provide us with the wealth that is ours. Only so can we increase our well-being and at the same time afford the social services our conscience dictates.[25]

Hamilton campaigned in uniform, which proved to be a mixed blessing. While his air force "blues" attracted crowds, the uniform also led to more questions about his service in the Far East than his qualifications as a candidate, or the platform of his party. All in all, Hamilton waged a creditable campaign in the short time available, but it was not enough to unseat the CCF leader. He received 20 percent of the popular vote, less than half Coldwell's total, and not sufficient even to place him above the Liberal candidate in second place.

At the end of the campaign, F/L Hamilton reported back to the air force and was told to draw tropical kit once again. The war with Japan continued unabated and Transport Command in that theatre needed navigators experienced in long distance and monsoon flying. This time Hamilton asked not to be sent to Asia. He pointed out that he had completed one tour of duty there already, and that there were many equally qualified navigators in Canada and Britain who had never seen action, and who would welcome the chance to take his place. To his great relief the air force accepted his arguments and posted him instead to Portage la Prairie as station navigation officer. There he spent the rest of the summer training other crews and reacquainting himself with his young family. It was a happy three months for the Hamiltons, but by this time Alvin Hamilton had had his fill of life in the services. He had been in the air force for almost four years and had spent ten months overseas. He had flown 113 missions and had served with fifteen different units. He wanted out and on 12 September, the day the Japanese surrendered to Mountbatten, he applied to be discharged. His discharge came through immediately and within days the Hamilton family was back in Saskatoon and Hamilton had resumed his teaching career at Nutana. He left the air force with a thousand dollars in war service gratuities and several decorations, including the Burma Star. Of greater importance, he left convinced by his experiences that other wars were a distinct possibility in the future; that these might be prevented if nations traded together to raise living standards everywhere in the world; that Canada, and the prairie provinces in particular, could contribute a great deal to lessen global tension and to feed the world's hungry; and that he wanted more than ever to play a prominent rôle in national and international politics in the years to come.

Politics played a large part in Alvin Hamilton's life after he left the air force although they did not dominate it altogether, at least not for a few years. In fact, between demobilization and his election as leader of the Progressive Conservative party in Saskatchewan, he spent more time at home with his wife and their two sons than at any time before or after. Hamilton slipped back easily into his career at Nutana. He returned to his history classes, to coaching the senior boys basketball team, and to advising the school's yearbook committee. Outside the collegiate he continued his association with the Air Cadets, brought into being a second Kiwanis Club in Saskatoon, and helped organize its track and field programme. Nevertheless, the sirens of politics continued to call and Alvin Hamilton never could resist them.

The political facts of life in Saskatchewan had changed considerably in the four years between the time Hamilton enlisted and the end of the war. In the first place, the CCF, led by Tommy Douglas, now governed the province having taken the reins from the Liberals, and many Conservatives had come to regard socialism, not liberalism, as their principal enemy. Secondly, the Conservative party was now the Progressive Conservative party and had chosen new leaders — John Bracken federally in 1942 and Rupert Ramsay provincially in 1944.[26] Hamilton welcomed the choice of both men for he shared many of their interests and political principles. The changes in leadership, however, did little to solve the basic problem of the party in Saskatchewan. It had entered a period of severe decline and had reached the stage of a third party in a two-party province. Not one of the forty Progressive Conservative candidates ran better than third in the provincial election of 1944 and only John Diefenbaker would win a seat at the federal election a year later. Ramsay, who held the dual positions of provincial leader and director of organization for the federal party in Saskatchewan, was correct when he reported in 1946 that prospects for the party were not bright.

> So often I feel that our followers are followers in name only . . . During the past year I have written to the Provincial Executive asking for specific information six times. Less than 10% troubled to answer. Last winter I offered to provide free study material of an interesting type to 160 of our own Associations. One took advantage

> of it. We send P.C.P. News to 2,200 people fortnightly. Less than 100 have sent in the postage for it. Last year from all Saskatchewan, the money collected for our party totalled $1,200. I have attended and addressed 66 party meetings during the year . . . the average attendance has been about 20 . . . Many times during the past year, I have felt like a chap in the front line without ammunition. I use the time that should be put on policy and organization worrying about paying month end bills.[27]

A year later, facing the prospect of an election, his refrain was much the same:

> Today a weakness dominates the thinking of many of our supporters. They will not fight . . . Personally, I feel convinced the C.C.F. will be returned to power. Even if the Liberals had a straight two-way fight in this Province against the C.C.F. they could not win half the seats. The Liberals are still not trusted by the rank and file of the voters. For this reason I do not see that it would make any difference to the possibilities of defeating the C.C.F. government if we nominated as well as the Liberals. But it is hard to persuade some people to see this. And this makes it difficult to get candidates in the field.[28]

Ramsay's problems were compounded by the fact that the new Liberal leader, Walter Tucker, believed that the CCF could be defeated only by the combined efforts of the non-socialist parties, and he worked assiduously to convince local Conservative associations not to run against Liberal candidates who stood a good chance of defeating their CCF opponents.[29] Ramsay himself wanted nothing to do with the Liberal party, but felt that he could not force his views on the riding associations, and so he left the final decision on the matter to them.

The difficulties his party faced did not daunt Alvin Hamilton in the least. Within a month of his return to Saskatoon from the air force the *P.C.P. News* (the official publication of the Saskatchewan Progressive Conservative party) reported that the "Saskatoon Progressive Conservative Association is holding its annual meeting October 15th for the election of officers. The guest speaker will be Alvin Hamilton."[30] Two weeks later it noted that "An excellent reorganization meeting was held at Rosetown on October 13th. F/L Alvin Hamilton is building up a strong working organization."[31] Hamilton had wasted no time in picking up the threads of his political life and, over the next few years, he served his party in several varied capacities. He continued to build his constituency organization in Rosetown-Biggar, he accepted almost all speaking engagements offered to him, and he assumed the presidency of the Saskatoon Progressive Conservative Association as well as a position on the party's provincial finance committee. In addition, he developed a close working relationship with Rupert Ramsay, who also lived in Saskatoon. Both men had a keen interest in party policy, and it was not long before Ramsay began to call on Hamilton to make radio broadcasts on behalf of the party, putting forward the issues of concern to them. The major task was to differentiate the Progressive Conservative party from its rivals and this Hamilton attempted to do, first by a statement of party philosophy, and second by attacks on the Liberals and CCF. From two of his speeches:

> We believe that progressive capitalism is synonymous with liberty. We believe that the great natural resource of the Canadian people is their independence and that in the tradition of their fathers Canadians will show by private enterprise that they can do more to solve their problems than by any other system. We believe that progressive capitalism will provide equal opportunity for all and must not be for the enrichment of the few.[32]
>
> The people of this Province do not wish to go back to a government of the Gardiner-Tucker character. It took the better part of forty years to get rid of the Liberal machine and many people had to vote C.C.F. to do it. Now with the actions of the C.C.F. Party leaders estranging democratic-minded people, the progressive people of Saskatchewan have no intention of jumping back and forth from the Gardiner frying pan to the C.C.F. fire. Democracy can be lost by machine politics as well as by state compulsion. Liberal-minded, progressive people in Saskatchewan look to this democratic leadership of Rupert Ramsay and the Progressive Conservative Party

> for the alternative to the present government and its controls and as an alternative to going back to the machine politics of earlier years.[33]

In other broadcasts, Hamilton outlined some of the policies his party would legislate if elected to power: stabilization of grain prices; construction of the South Saskatchewan River Dam; and development of the prairies' natural resources.

Hamilton performed one last task for Ramsay prior to the 1948 provincial election: he arranged the nomination of a Conservative candidate in Rosetown. The successful nominee turned out to be Alvin Hamilton, although Hamilton had no intention of running provincially when he set out to find a candidate. His interest lay in federal politics and he wanted a seat at Ottawa, not Regina. However, he was willing to work for the provincial party because he believed that success at one level could lead to success at the other, and Ramsay had asked him to locate a suitable person for Rosetown. This he did. In Hamilton's words:

> We called a meeting for Rosetown and I had two delegates in from every poll. I had three good candidates lined up — a Presbyterian Minister, a Secretary-Treasurer of a Municipality, and a leading businessman — but when the delegates heard these three fellows speak, the only one that they knew was me. I was the only one who had been at all their homes. I was the one that got them there. So, they got up and said: "Look, we like these fellows, but we'd like Alvin to run" . . . So, I was overwhelmed in effect by the convention and I found myself running provincially in 1948.[34]

He did not have long to wait as Premier Douglas called the election for 24 June. It turned out to be a bitter campaign. Politics in Saskatchewan have never been gentlemanly and the Marquis of Queensberry would have been appalled at the fight in 1948. That campaign reflected not only the deep divisions within Saskatchewan society but also the temper of international politics at the time. The Soviet Union faced the Western allies at the beginning of the Cold War and the forces later known as McCarthyism began their witch hunt to purge the United States of alleged Communist influence. Douglas led the only socialist government anywhere on the North American continent, and Tucker was determined to bring the province back to the path of capitalist righteousness. He campaigned on a slogan of "Tucker or Tyranny"[35] and did not make much of the distinction between democratic socialism and totalitarian communism. Neither did some Conservative candidates. Alan Embury, for example, asked the voters of Regina to consider the following:

> Do you wish to join with those who prefer the Russian form of Government to that of Canada and the United States?
>
> Do you wish a completely communistic or socialistic form of government to be substituted for [our] democratic form of government?
>
> Do you wish to have your business taken away from you and operated by the state?
>
> Do you realize that with the completion of socialism in Saskatchewan, we shall all be cogs in a government machine and that individual ambitions and ability will count for nothing?
>
> We have fought through generations to be free of feudalism and serfdom. WOULD YOU RETURN TO SUCH A DICTATORSHIP ???
>
> DO YOU WANT SUBTLE TYRANNY ? ? ?[36]

The enemy was socialism. It did not seem to matter much what weapon was used to defeat it.

Conservative strategy in general did not rely on this tactic. Ramsay believed his party should wage a positive rather than a negative campaign, and he preferred to rely on the appeal of the comprehensive and detailed programme he had prepared over the past four years. The platform, called The P.C. Plan for Saskatchewan, dealt with many issues in nine major areas of concern: agriculture, health care, education, highways, taxation, labour, industry, pensions, and natural resources. In it the Conservatives promised to establish a wheat stabilization fund; to cooperate in a national health plan; to reduce local school taxes; to construct one north-south and two east-west paved highways; to abolish the education tax; to guarantee all workers two weeks paid vacation per year; to sell all public utilities not suited to government ownership; to raise old age pensions to forty dollars per month; and to speed power development from all sources within the province.[37] It was a programme which dealt with the major issues then confronting the province and it was designed to meet both the long and short-term needs of Saskatchewan. Unfortunately for Ramsay, he could find but eight candidates besides himself to take it to the electorate.

Walter Tucker had undercut Ramsay, although not in the way he had planned. Tucker had wanted a coalition between his party and the Conservatives, but Ramsay would not accept his terms and many powerful Liberals, including former Premier Gardiner, disapproved of the idea. "Gardiner's opposition, which was not surprising if one remembered his antipathy to coalition, prevailed so that only four coalition candidates were nominated"[38] — three who ran as Liberal-Conservatives and A.H. McDonald in Moosomin as a Conservative-Liberal. Nevertheless, many local Conservative associations accepted Tucker's plea not to split the anti-socialist vote and, despite Ramsay's wishes, refused to nominate a candidate of their own. Liberal candidates faced Conservative opponents in only six seats on election day. For his part, Tucker was able to convince only one Liberal constituency executive not to run against the Conservative candidate — Alvin Hamilton in Rosetown.[39]

Hamilton staged a campaign which belied his initial reluctance to enter the lists. In fact, he looks back on 1948 as "the best organized campaign I have ever been in."[40] He asked William Elliot, a former bomber pilot, to act as his campaign manager and Elliot organized the campaign with military precision. They sold over twelve hundred memberships to finance the campaign and fitted an aeroplane with loudspeakers to publicize Hamilton's meetings, probably the first time this had been done in Saskatchewan. Hamilton spoke to packed houses all over the riding. He advised his audiences that there was an undemocratic strain in socialism. He attacked the government's policy of state corporatism, which he claimed drove private enterprise out of the province, with a consequent loss of jobs and opportunities for the young people of Saskatchewan. He pointed to the Conservative platform and promised that a Ramsay government would pay half the costs of local education, would develop the energy resources of the province in order to bring industry to Saskatchewan, and would construct an all-weather highway system. Hamilton's obvious success, and the fact that no Liberal candidate stood to split the anti-government vote, combined to cause the CCF organization a great deal of concern. The CCF candidate, J.T. Douglas, was the minister of highways and, to bolster his fortunes, he resorted to a tried and tested expedient perfected by the old Liberal machine. In Hamilton's words:

> Well, when the campaign got going, and the minister of highways realized he was in serious trouble, all of a sudden every highway crew in Saskatchewan moved into Rosetown and we ended up that election campaign with over half the paved roads in Saskatchewan in one little seat.[41]

Whatever the reason, Douglas retained his seat, though barely. While he raised his popular vote by almost 500, Hamilton increased the Conservative tally by more than 2,000 and came within 450 votes of victory. Hamilton, of course, saved his deposit as did Ramsay, the only bright spots in an otherwise dismal Conservative showing. With only nine candidates, the Conservatives share of the popular vote dropped to 8 percent, far behind the CCF, Liberals and Social Credit, and only McDonald won as a coalition candidate in Moosomin.

No one likes to lose, especially after coming so close to victory, but Hamilton was by no means crushed by his defeat. He always believed his future lay in federal politics and Richard Bell, the national director of the party, impressed by Hamilton's success, offered him another opportunity to prove himself at that level. John Bracken resigned as leader of the party on 17 July and a joint leadership and policy convention was scheduled for Ottawa in early October. Bell asked Hamilton to take responsibility for the Saskatchewan contingent — to find delegates and to prepare its policy positions — both of which he accepted with relish.

Hamilton delivered a full delegation and a comprehensive set of resolutions to the convention. Bell's request coincided with the beginning of a year's sabbatical leave from Nutana, so he was able to give his undivided attention to the tasks at hand. As it happened, it did not prove difficult to find delegates willing to go to Ottawa. Hamilton simply pointed out that if anybody wanted a new car they could buy one in Oshawa or Windsor and the money they would save on freight charges would pay their fares to the convention. While there, they could also support Saskatchewan's own John Diefenbaker for the leadership against Bay Street's George Drew, which ninety-two of the ninety-three delegates from Saskatchewan did do.[42] On arrival at the convention, Alvin Hamilton and Donald Johnston, a young law student at the University of Saskatchewan who had helped Hamilton prepare the Saskatchewan delegation's policy recommendations, headed immediately to meetings of the Resolutions Committee where the preparatory work they had done gave them a position of some status. According to Hamilton, "We proposed at least half of the resolutions before that policy committee"[43] and they succeeded in pushing most of them through. Their obvious concern and expertise convinced the chairman of the committee, J.R. MacNichol, member of Parliament for Toronto Davenport, to let them prepare the committee's report to the convention. Hamilton's stamp is evident in the Declaration of Policy which the delegates finally approved. They committed the Progressive Conservative party to many of those principles and positions on which Hamilton had fought the previous provincial election in Saskatchewan: free enterprise; opposition to socialization of major industries and financial institutions; permanent floor-price legislation for grain producers; health insurance; immediate completion of a hard-surface trans-Canada highway; and conservation and development of natural resources and maximum industrial production.[44] Diefenbaker did not win the leadership at that convention, but, after the report of the Resolutions Committee, one Drew supporter was overheard to complain to another that "John sure got everything he wanted in that committee."[45] To Drew's credit, he did not hold

Hamilton's open support for Diefenbaker against him. In fact, he had been much impressed by the young man from Saskatchewan, who had not only contributed so much to the party's policy discussions but who had also brought a full delegation to Ottawa from one of the weakest Conservative areas in the country. Thus, when Rupert Ramsay resigned a short time later, he had no objection to the recommendation that Alvin Hamilton be appointed director of organization for the Progressive Conservative party in Saskatchewan.

The results of the 1948 election had devastated Ramsay. Despite his work since becoming leader, he could not find enough candidates to provide a credible alternative to the CCF and Liberals and could not win a seat himself. Within days of the voting he wrote Bell:

> I am forced to believe that Progressive Conservatives are through provincially in Saskatchewan. There will always be conservatives here, but not enough and too widely scattered to be effective politically. The man on the street admits we had the best candidates and the most reasonable policy, but he still associates "conservative" with the hungry thirties, the Grain Exchange, Bay and St. James Street and Ontario. He is afraid that we are against the laboring man and the primary producer.[46]

He informed Bell of his intention to resign both the provincial leadership and his position with the federal party as soon as possible, and he recommended that Alvin Hamilton replace him, at least as provincial organizer. In this he received the support of H.O. Wright, treasurer of the provincial party, who also wrote Bell at the time:

> I cannot help agreeing with Rupert that it might be better for him to eventually resign the leadership. Rupert never was a politician at heart . . . If his resignation takes effect I would suggest that a Provincial Organizer should be secured to immediately start organization for the Federal campaign . . . It is just possible that we might be able to obtain the services of Alvin Hamilton as organizer. He is going on his sabbatical year, and he is a staunch, capable fighter who loves a political contest. He is young and full of vitality.[47]

Bell approached Hamilton with the suggestion and they corresponded sporadically during August and September, neither man forcing the issue. The job attracted Hamilton, but he did not want to give up his sabbatical year or the money the school board had advanced him to carry out his research. Matters finally came to a head shortly after the federal convention in October when Ramsay's wife, Eva, who was ill, had to leave Saskatchewan immediately. Ramsay resigned formally later that month and Bell and Wright increased their pressure on Hamilton. Eventually he gave in when Bell accepted all his conditions for taking the post. The federal party agreed to pay Hamilton six thousand dollars per annum for the next five years, to compensate him for the loss of his sabbatical year, to establish a trust fund to ensure that his salary would be paid regardless of the state of the party's finances, and to contribute a further two thousand dollars towards renovation of the provincial office.[48] It was an uncommon arrangement for the Conservative party, but one dictated by Hamilton's circumstances and the dependent position of the provincial party.[49] His financial security guaranteed for the next five years, Hamilton resigned from Nutana "in order to avoid any suggestion of impropriety"[50] and took up his new position as director of organization on 1 November 1948.

Hamilton began the job with one objective in mind — to turn Saskatchewan into a Progressive Conservative stronghold, although he did not delude himself that this would be done easily or overnight. As he explained to one supporter:

> My own point of view is that we have to look on constituencies not only as just winning them but of starting an educational campaign and organizational drive on a permanent basis over the next five to fifteen years that will put our party in a position different from what it is today. This may sound foolish when it comes to worrying what happens in each particular constituency but in the long run I think it is sound.[51]

Of necessity, virtually all of Hamilton's attention during his first few months as director focussed on federal politics. Although he was expected to keep an eye on the provincial party Bell expected a national election sometime in 1949, and he instructed Hamilton to devote himself primarily to preparations for that campaign. Hamilton's duties, as he understood them, were:

> First, to prepare for successful public meetings for the official visit of our National leader. Secondly, to get as many Federal candidates in the field over the winter and next spring as possible. Thirdly, to build up organizational staff that will be ready to move into action if an election is called. Fourth, to give full publicity to the P.C. program by radio, public addresses and by other means.[52]

Hamilton wasted no time in setting about his responsibilities. By happy coincidence he was able to deliver a nomination the day after his appointment began — his own in Rosetown-Biggar. Within a week, he bought time on the radio to pay a tribute to Ramsay and, thereafter, spoke as often as party coffers could afford the cost. In these addresses he extolled Drew's virtues as leader of the Progressive Conservative party, attacked the failings of both liberalism and socialism, and gave his party's stand on national issues of concern to the Saskatchewan electorate, in particular the marketing of grain, taxation, and the need for a nation-wide development policy. He handled all the arrangements for Drew's tour of Saskatchewan in January 1949. He ran the "Joiner Campaign" which was intended to increase the party membership and help finance the forthcoming election. Finally, he visited as many constituencies as possible across the province to find candidates and to establish local election committees. In his words:

> I went out and got candidates in every riding, tried to get the basis of organization, tried to get the basis of finance set up for them. It was probably the best organized effort that Saskatchewan had made in a quarter of a century at least. We went at every seat like a military operation to get the maximum number of votes.[53]

Unhappily for Hamilton, his efforts did not reap the hoped for dividends. Although Progressive Conservative candidates contested every one of Saskatchewan's twenty constituencies, the party's popular vote dropped sharply and once again only John Diefenbaker won a seat.

Progressive Conservative candidates all over Canada ran headlong into a swing to the Liberal party in the 1949 election, and Saskatchewan had no more immunity to the appeal of the Liberals led by Louis St. Laurent than any other province. The Liberals increased their number of seats in the province from two to fourteen at the expense of the CCF and the Conservatives' share of the vote fell from 19 to less than 15 percent. Alvin Hamilton did not fare much better in Rosetown-Biggar. There he faced not only a strong Liberal candidate but also M.J. Coldwell, leader of the CCF, and he attacked both with equal enthusiasm. In one broadcast he charged that:

> The Liberal party does not seem to have the strength or the energy to tackle problems vigorously. The CCF has got lost in its big plans of socializing our economy and going back to prehistoric barter principles of trade. The only Party that can provide the vigour is the Progressive Conservative Party.[54]

According to Hamilton, the Liberals and CCF were indistinguishable for all intents and purposes. Even before the election he claimed that:

> The Gardiners, the Abbots, the Howes have accepted the C.C.F. idea of state planning to such a degree that liberalism is a mockery in their hands . . . that personal freedom which is the essence of liberalism has been sacrificed under St. Laurent . . . that private enterprise has been limited at every turn under socialist policies at Ottawa . . . that free trade which is the life blood of an exporting nation has been forgotten at Ottawa which accepts the C.C.F. idea of state marketing, which has meant the loss of hundreds of millions of dollars to western farmers [the Wheat Agreement with Britain].[55]

One fact, however, made the Liberal party the greater enemy in Saskatchewan for Alvin Hamilton, and that was the omnipresent presence of the minister of agriculture, J.G. Gardiner.

> Again and again let me repeat to you. A vote for any Liberal candidate in this province is a vote for the continued boss-rule by James G. Gardiner over both the Provincial and Federal political fields. If you want to get rid of Gardiner vote against Gardiner candidates for no

> candidate is selected by the Liberal Party unless he is palatable to Mr. Gardiner's taste.[56]

Gardiner also provided Hamilton with his best line of the election. As he remarked midway through the campaign:

> Mr. Gardiner describes himself as the spark plug of the Liberal Party. Those of us who have worked with engines know that sparks need cleaning and occasionally replacement. I would like to suggest that the time for replacement of one spark plug has now arrived.[57]

Hamilton promised that a Progressive Conservative government, led by George Drew, would rid the country of the evils of both liberalism and socialism, and would start Canada on the road to a new and prosperous era. He insisted that development of the nation's resources should be the central issue of the election, and he focussed most of his campaign on this theme. In his major election advertisement, he assured the voters of Rosetown-Biggar that his party would reduce income and sales taxes to free money for investment; introduce floor price legislation to provide security for the farming community; restore the Canadian Wheat Board to its original position as the sole market agency for wheat producers and embark on an aggressive attempt to increase grain sales; develop new lands for farm production; develop the water and mineral resources of the north; pave the Trans-Canada highway and extend its feeder lines into the north; and begin the South Saskatchewan River Dam without delay.[58] This was not enough. On 27 June he received less than twenty-seven hundred votes, nearly five hundred fewer than in 1945, and he ran a poor third to both Coldwell and Noble, the Liberal candidate. He could overcome neither the widespread support for Coldwell in the riding nor the general western antipathy towards George Drew. Even Coldwell referred to the latter in a message of condolence to Hamilton the day after the election. "Yesterday's results which affected my Party as well as your own were, I am certain, due to a determination on the part of the electorate to keep Col. Drew from power. This was cleverly played up by the Liberals to their great advantage."[59] Hamilton accepted this explanation of the

Conservatives' poor showing in Saskatchewan to some degree. Certainly, his report to Bell after the campaign listed "the successful Liberal and C.C.F. attack on Progressive Conservative wheat policy," "the Party's too close links to big interests and big business," and "Drew's unpopular stand on Dominion-Provincial relations and Family Allowances," as the three most important reasons for the party's defeat.[60] He also stressed the need to "sell Drew in small towns and villages" in the future.[61] Nevertheless, he realized that all the blame could not be laid at Drew's feet. As he wrote in a post-mortem to Ramsay:

> The most public reason given and of course the one that is being used to alibi us, was that Drew was entirely to blame. However, we all know who are on the inside that our organization and the ability of our workers is almost non-existent in Saskatchewan . . . But organization is not the only thing required. We need people to understand what we stand for and also to believe in us. For the present time, we lack both these things.[62]

He talked in terms of a four-year programme of education before the next federal election and so set out the course of his work for the party for that time. Alvin Hamilton would try to convince the Saskatchewan electorate that the Progressive Conservative party had both the policies and the people to provide Canada with the farsighted government it needed. The task at the federal level would have been formidable in itself. The problems of the provincial party made it even more difficult, but he could not ignore its fate.

Chapter 3
Provincial Leader: Per Ardua

Provincial politics in Saskatchewan since 1905 have been characterized by one-party dominance in a competitive two-party system. "Third" parties have not found it easy to win large-scale electoral support, and those which have been successful have made their gains at the expense of one or other of the dominant parties. Likewise, any party which has slipped to "third" party status has found it extremely difficult to regain its former position. For the first three decades of Saskatchewan history, and again recently, the Conservative party has been one of the two major contenders for power. In the interregnum, however, the very survival of the party was at stake.

Between 1934 and 1948 popular support for the Conservative party dropped from 27 to 8 percent and changes in leadership had done nothing to stem the tide.[1] By the late 1940s, the Progressive Conservative party in Saskatchewan was in desperate straits — its share of the popular vote low; its representation in the legislature limited to a single "Conservative-Liberal";[2] and its remaining supporters divided among those who wished to unite with the Liberals to defeat the socialists, those who wanted an alliance with Social Credit, and those who believed the party must rejuvenate itself on its own initiative, free from marriages of convenience. In these daunting circumstances the party chose Alvin Hamilton to replace Rupert Ramsay and to restore Conservative fortunes in the province.

The convention which chose Hamilton was not called until October 1949, nearly a year after Ramsay resigned. This was done deliberately because the party's Executive Advisory Board wanted Ramsay to stay on and, in effect, gave him a leave of absence in the hope that "the circumstances which made this resignation necessary will have changed and that Mr. Ramsay will be in a position to reconsider."[3] Rupert Ramsay, however, had no wish to return to political life and, after the federal election in 1949, the party ordered its director of organization to find a replacement for him. Hamilton called a convention for the Hotel Saskatchewan in Regina for 11 and 12 October 1949, and approached several of the party's leading personalities to let their names stand in nomination. At first, Hamilton did not think of himself as a successor to Ramsay. He knew his own failings: "In a frank analysis of my own position, I do not think that I have the behaviour characteristics of a good leader . . . Therefore, my own personal reaction would be to have someone else take on the leadership."[4] He understood the enormous difficulties facing the next leader of the party, he feared the sacrifices he and his family would be expected to make, and he wanted a career in federal, not provincial, politics.[5] Furthermore, he was young by prevailing political standards — thirty-seven, he did not have a seat in the legislature, and he could not command the respect in the party that others could.

Nevertheless, he realized that the party might have no choice but to turn to him, and he was prepared to accept the consequences in that event. As he reported to national headquarters:

> However, I see the practical considerations, that in spite of my handicaps of personality, I may be the only one who is available to do the job on a full time basis and even though I will not go out of my way to push myself

> forward, I will, if voted in by the Convention accept the position.[6]

This remained his position until the convention, despite the pressures on him to declare his candidacy — he would be a candidate if necessary, but he would prefer to see someone else in the job. Some of the pressure came from people such as H.O. Wright and R.A. Bell, for financial considerations made Hamilton a very attractive candidate. The party could raise very little money within the province and Hamilton already received a salary from the federal party. For Wright, in fact, lack of funds left the provincial party no choice in the matter.

> From present indications the party will not be in a position to pay a salary such as was paid to Rupert Ramsay, and under the circumstances it seems to me that the only course to follow is to recommend to the Convention the appointment of Alvin Hamilton as leader. Speaking purely from a financial standpoint, that would eliminate the duplication of salaries for officers for this province at the present time.[7]

He could have added that since the Hamiltons lived in Saskatoon where the party's headquarters were located, a Hamilton victory would avoid the cost of moving the office to Regina or elsewhere. An additional selling point for others was Alvin Hamilton's unswerving commitment to the Conservative party. Although he was not yet prominent in provincial affairs, he had recorded an enviable record of service to the party in several capacities over the past two decades. Furthermore, throughout the entire period, he had remained loyal to the Conservative party and free of the suspicion that he was prepared to sacrifice his party's interests just to keep some other party out of power.

The pressure on Hamilton grew greater as the date of the convention grew nearer. Ramsay urged him to run, as did Keown, who also promised that "if elected I will give you all the support I can."[8] Furthermore, some of those Hamilton asked to run, such as M.A. McPherson, refused to accept a nomination.[9] Others, such as Allan Embury and Hammy

McDonald, agreed to take the leadership, but only on condition that the party form an alliance with the Liberals to defeat the CCF. The prospect of either "coalitionist" as leader removed Hamilton's remaining doubts as to whether or not he should let his name go forward. He could not accept an alliance with the Liberals because "I hadn't left my teaching job to preside over the demise of the Conservative party."[10] Therefore, "I had to fight, and the only way I could fight as Organizer was to say — 'All right, if that is going to be your policy I won't stand for it. I'm going in as a Conservative and I am going to run and beat you'."[11] Which he did. He accepted a nomination and, when both Embury and McDonald withdrew before the voting, easily defeated the only other candidate in the race — Ed Hudson of Moose Jaw. With his victory, Alvin Hamilton now held simultaneously the two most important posts in the hierarchy of the Progressive Conservative party in Saskatchewan — provincial leader and federal director of organization. His attempt to meet the onerous responsibilities of both positions would come close to driving him out of political life altogether. At that time, however, and despite Ramsay's prophetic caveat that "Many times it will seem to you a thankless job — uphill and in second gear,"[12] he accepted the accolades of his party and for one brief moment could not imagine any place he would rather be.

Two provincial by-elections fought within four months of the convention provided the new leader with a taste of what lay ahead for him. Hamilton found candidates for both constituencies, Gull Lake and the Battlefords, but despite active campaigns waged on their behalf they received less than 10 and 6 percent of the vote respectively.[13] Nevertheless, this was still early days. Alvin Hamilton had just begun to fight and his enthusiasm remained high. He identified three causes of these disasters: "the idea we cannot win," "the view that we must beat socialism even if we ruin our own party in so doing," and "hatred of Liberals which causes PCs to vote CCF."[14] He began at once to try to overcome them.

The first objective, as he saw it, was to convince party supporters, and the electorate generally, that the Progressive Conservative party in Saskatchewan was not a spent force.

The party needed publicity and he acted quickly to obtain it. He resumed publication of the *P.C.P. News*, a fortnightly bulletin of Conservative party philosophy and activities, and sent it to the party membership and anyone else who would subscribe to it.[15] He bought time on the radio for a number of broadcasts, and he wrote a series of forty-seven articles for the press in which he set out the party position on a host of issues of federal and provincial importance. He attended the sessions of the legislature in Regina and did what he could while there to draw media attention to himself and his party.[16] He participated in all-party debates and spoke at public meetings whenever he was invited. He attended Conservative party functions all over the province and carried out preliminary organization in nearly half of Saskatchewan's fifty-two constituencies during 1950. He also devoted a good deal of attention to the party's programme, partly because of his interest in policy, but also because he recognized the need to distinguish the party from the CCF and the Liberals. In sum, Hamilton attempted to advance the Conservative cause in every possible way during his first year as leader and at the end of it he reported that:

> The year opened with very dubious prospects as far as party organization and educational work was concerned. The by-elections of Gull Lake and the Battlefords had strained our financial resources. It was questionable whether much activity could be carried out in the summer months.
>
> However, with hardly anything else but faith we went ahead and 1950 marks the end of a critical period in the life of the party in Saskatchewan. During the year we put our P.C.P. News on a financially sound basis. We sold enough memberships in the party to carry out organization work in 25 of the Provincial Constituencies. We inaugurated a 20-week radio program over five stations in Saskatchewan. Therefore 1950 was a year that I personally will look back upon as one that demonstrated that we can accomplish objectives if we set our minds to them.[17]

Such activities would be part and parcel of Hamilton's life throughout his entire term as provincial leader and, if activity had translated into votes, then Alvin Hamilton might have had a better fate in Saskatchewan politics. However, although he did not know it at the time, neither 1950 nor any other year during his leadership marked the end of a critical period in the life of the party in Saskatchewan.

Hamilton might be forgiven his mood of cautious optimism as he began the second year of his leadership. After all, in just over a year he had laid the groundwork for his party's revival. He did not underestimate the remaining obstacles to making the Progressive Conservative party of Saskatchewan a force capable of fighting the CCF and the Liberals on equal terms, but he did believe that he was now in a position to overcome them. The following year and a half — months that ended with the election of 11 June 1952 — brought him face to face with the appalling enormity of the task and the awful prospect that perhaps he would fail. In those eighteen months Hamilton did everything a leader of a third party has to do to wage a successful campaign. He toured the province seeking memberships, candidates, and publicity. He attacked the CCF and the Liberals equally — the CCF for its failures in office, and the Liberals because of the lingering influence of Jimmy Gardiner.[18] He took up issues such as the financing of education and the need for a provincial oil policy which he thought put as much distance as possible between his party and its competitors. For example:

> The Progressive Conservative Party puts Education first. The P.C. Party is the only party in Saskatchewan definitely pledged to 50% support of local Education.[19]
>
> Saskatchewan needs an Oil Policy today which will take advantage of the mistakes made in the United States and in Alberta. This Oil Policy should have a conservation program and a development program based on fairness to producers and at the same time protect the long term interest of the people in our very valuable resources.[20]

He addressed issues of current concern to the farm population, such as the outbreak of foot and mouth disease, and the need for advances on farm stored grain, and put forward his solutions. He also assured farmers that his party was pledged to "stability of income for farmers."[21] He organized a convention in Saskatoon in October 1951 which gave him a Ten Point Program of Development on which to fight an election and to which he referred at every opportunity. Development was the keystone of his plan for the province. As he put it:

> We have emphasized repeatedly that the job is to *build Saskatchewan*. This can be done only by development projects that make it possible for individuals to produce more and make more wealth to pay for the services we all want . . . Every one of those proposals that make up the Conservative program of development of resources . . . *will* make the province money.[22]

In addition, he left the Rosetown area, which he had cultivated for so long, for Lumsden, part of Diefenbaker's Lake Centre constituency, in the hope of winning a seat in the legislature.

Hamilton continued his efforts right through the election campaign. He spent the early weeks canvassing in Lumsden, then left to help his candidates in other areas when convinced he had sufficient support to win. He had Diefenbaker prepare a personal message to the electors of Lumsden and all of Saskatchewan which extolled his virtues. According to Diefenbaker:

> I honestly believe that Alvin Hamilton would, if elected, make Lumsden the best represented constituency in the Legislative Assembly . . . of all the young men I know in public life in this Province, I do not know of anyone with a finer mind, or anyone who is a greater student of public affairs . . . Earnest and conscientious, able and farseen as he is, the election of Alvin Hamilton will assure that the voice of the Progressive Conservative Party will be heard in the Legislature, and above all that a voice of a man whose life is dedicated to public service will be given the opportunity to serve the people of his province and Canada as a whole in these days of twilight peace as he did during the night of war.[23]

Hamilton accused both the CCF and the Liberals of partisanship of such extremism that it lowered the tone of all politics in Saskatchewan. In his words:

> I have sat in the Legislature for two years and listened to grown men fighting and quarreling for six hours a day and not only for 90 minutes on the radio. What Saskatchewan needs is a voice in the Legislature to speak out above the quarreling, bickering and name-calling, to ask questions and advocate policies of a constructive nature.[24]

He pointed to the fact that William Manning, brother of Alberta Premier Ernest Manning, had come out in support of the Progressive Conservatives, and he appealed to all "independent-minded" voters to do the same. Most important of all, he publicized his party's Program to Develop Saskatchewan. According to the programme, a Progressive Conservative government would:

1. Set up a Saskatchewan Valley Authority to start immediate work on the South Saskatchewan River Dam by the Province
2. Open up the 3 million acres of valuable agricultural land in the Carrot River Valley
3. Start a Soil Conservation and Utilization program to put Agriculture on a more secure economic basis
4. Inaugurate a five-year program to build 2,000 miles of hard-surfaced through highways
5. Build up a $50 million Tourist Industry in 10 years by the use of such devices as the Recreation Homestead
6. Provide cheap electrical power for industries by using natural gas
7. Guarantee economic transmission of natural gas by allowing no gas pipeline monopolies
8. Provide an oil policy and atmosphere that will bring large-scale scientific development of our oil resources in less than 24 months
9. Give surface right holders a percentage royalty on all oil and minerals found on their lands
10. The Provincial Government to assume 50% of the costs of local education[25]

According to Hamilton:

> A vote for Progressive Conservative candidates on June 11th will indicate that you want this province developed, that you want the Saskatchewan River Dam built, that

> you want the Carrot River Valley opened up, that you want roads into the tourist and mining areas of the north, that you want the natural gas and oil made available for industries in this province so that we can have a diversified economy and not always be dependent on federal subsidies and handouts.[26]

This programme of development was also an attempt to stem the flow of young people from the province, which had reached "crisis proportions." A valiant effort, but one which would be in vain, and Hamilton knew it long before voting day.

Hamilton could find only eight candidates to stand with him in 1952, and one of these ran as an Independent Progressive Conservative.[27] He tried to place his predicament in the best light possible by pointing to the "high ability and integrity" of all eight, and by predicting that this small band would hold the balance of power in the legislature after election day,[28] but this did not fool any astute observer of provincial politics. As the editor of the *Star-Phoenix* summarized his predicament:

> The decision to concentrate the party strength behind a few strong individuals is realistic enough in practical politics. But it removes the Progressive Conservative party from any claim to consideration as a political force in Saskatchewan . . . The decision is the fullest recognition by party strategists that the Tory party is a spent force in provincial politics.[29]

The election results bore out this assessment. On 11 June the Progressive Conservative party in Saskatchewan did appear to be a spent force. No Conservative candidate won a seat and the party's share of the popular vote dropped from 8 to 2 percent. Hamilton came third in Lumsden despite his early hopes and no Conservative came closer to victory than he. The result hurt, especially the vote in Lumsden, and Hamilton gave some thought to resigning as provincial leader.[30] However, as his disappointment faded he advised party supporters that:

> There is a real need in Saskatchewan for a party that believes in private enterprise and is willing to educate the

> people of the province to what is possible if certain simple things are done. If we continue to make our views known, there will be increasing support for these views. It is disheartening to meet defeat continually, but if a real purpose is being fulfilled, it is our duty to carry on.[31]

Despite the loss, there was still reason to carry on, and Alvin Hamilton was not ready to quit just yet. He would take some time to reflect on the causes of the debacle and then return to lead the fight again.

There were several reasons why the Progressive Conservative party did so poorly in 1952 despite Hamilton's indomitable efforts. First and foremost among them was the propensity of traditional Conservative supporters to look to parties other than their own in order to defeat the government in power. This tendency, at times encouraged by leading figures in the party, began in the mid-1930s and was directed first at the Liberal "machine" and later at the "socialists." Thus, by the 1950s the Conservative party had been weakened severely. It had lost to the CCF those Conservatives who were determined to prevent the return of the Liberals to power and it had lost to the Liberals those who saw that party as the best hope of defeating the CCF government. Hamilton had to return both groups of Conservatives to their former allegiance in order to be successful, and this he was not able to do because both the CCF and the Liberals did everything in their power to keep their new Conservative supporters in their camps, and the Liberal party went after the remainder of the old Conservative vote.

As indicated previously, Walter Tucker, the Liberal leader, had returned to Saskatchewan from federal politics in 1946 convinced that there was no way to defeat the CCF without the support of all non-socialists within the province, and he tried hard to build an anti-socialist coalition.[32] He came close to success in the election of 1948. A few hundred votes distributed appropriately in a half dozen seats would have brought him to power and, encouraged by this result, he redoubled his efforts in anticipation of the next election. His first priority was to bring as many prominent Conservatives into the Liberal fold as possible and an obvious target was the lone Conservative elected in 1948 — Hammy McDonald. Over the objections of Gardiner, although with the approval of Mackenzie King, Tucker invited McDonald to attend meetings of the Liberal caucus on the grounds that he owed his seat, in part at least, to Liberal votes. Hamilton was well aware of the attempt to detach McDonald from the Progressive Conservative party. Within months of the 1948 election he warned Bell:

> We will have to watch Hammy very carefully because the Liberals are after him hot foot. He makes no bones about it that he is a PC but feels that because he was elected by our joint effort, he has to play ball with the Liberals. The Liberals are noted for their technique in making a man change completely to their party.[33]

Nevertheless, Hamilton could not keep McDonald with him. McDonald ran as a Liberal in 1952 and, to add insult to injury, became Liberal leader a year later when Tucker returned to federal politics. Nor could Hamilton prevent other party supporters and potential Conservative candidates from going over to the Liberals. Tucker's second objective was to prevent three-cornered contests in as many constituencies as possible, and this too caused Hamilton difficulty. He wanted to run a full slate in 1952 but could not because Conservatives in the constituencies had been convinced that they had no hope of winning and that, therefore, they should support the Liberals, or perhaps Social Credit, if they wanted to defeat the socialists.

Although Tucker and the Liberals posed the greatest threat to the Conservative party during this period, Hamilton also had to keep an anxious eye on Social Credit. He had long feared that "a third party which [was] private enterprise and had good candidates and wasn't an old party could cut a terrific swath in a provincial election in this province,"[34] and there is evidence that he tried to prevent a contest with them in 1952. As he explained to a supporter at the time:

> I had a long talk with the Social Credit organizer in Regina and I do not think there will be any clashes between the Conservative and Social Credit parties in the next provincial election . . . I have done other things as well to get Social Crediters to help us out.[35]

Internal schisms within Social Credit staved off the menace for the moment. Although Social Credit ran twenty-three candidates in the 1952 election, they were not well financed and posed little threat to anyone, including Progressive Conservatives. Hamilton could look forward to this four years later.

The tendency of Conservative voters to abandon their party in order to defeat the CCF brought the party to the lowest point in its history and made Hamilton's task doubly difficult, for it deprived him of the candidates, workers, funds, and publicity he needed if he was to be successful. Leaving aside the problems of finance and publicity for the moment, with Conservatives leaving for other parties Hamilton had trouble keeping constituency associations alive; without organization at the local level he had difficulty attracting candidates at election time; without sufficient candidates to form a government, if elected, the Conservative voter looked elsewhere for a credible alternative to the CCF. The following is typical of the response Hamilton received from party stalwarts throughout the period. "I am writing to say there is nothing I can do to help . . . There were only 2 votes in our poll for the P.C. I think it is useless to spend any time in our district."[36] Hamilton had no illusions about the problem. His letters to W.H. Kidd, by then national director of the party, make this quite clear. For example:

> The truth is that the boys who hold office in our constituency organizations have lost the will and ability to fight . . . The most frustrating part of all is that every place I go I get such encouraging reactions from the ordinary voter, but no life from the leading Conservatives. It tries the patience of Job.[37]

Hamilton began his term as leader with the hope that he would run candidates in all fifty-two of Saskatchewan's seats. By mid-1950 he started to talk in terms of "thirty to thirty-five" candidates and by the autumn of 1951 he informed Kidd that "I am trying desperately to get about 10 or 12 nominations . . ."[38] "Desperation" is an appropriate word to describe Hamilton's growing concern over the problem. As he wrote to a friend in Regina:

> Things have got to the stage now that we have either got to produce candidates or no one is going to listen to my press statements or speeches. So any practical thing that you can do to get me a candidate in any constituency will save me from making a complete fool of myself.
>
> All over the province rank and file people tell me that they are willing to leave the CCF and Liberals and ask who our candidate is. I feel so silly when I have to tell them that there is no candidate because the older generation have lost the will and ability to move. So get me a candidate and I will be forever in your debt.[39]

The problem bedevilled Hamilton right up to the election. Again he had to inform Kidd that "several of the candidates . . . are quite concerned over the scarcity of candidates. They say that is hurting their chances not to have a sizeable number in the field."[40] Lack of candidates also hurt Hamilton's chances of obtaining all the money he needed to wage a campaign equal to those of his competitors. Kidd rejected his request for additional funds on the grounds that "a big show without seats isn't worth a damn."[41] Unfortunately for Hamilton, reminders of the problem did not contribute to its solution. Despite his best efforts he could not convince more than the eight to carry the party's colours in 1952.

Lack of money plagued Hamilton throughout the period. Although his salary was paid by the federal party, and national headquarters contributed a large proportion of the funds required to keep the provincial office in operation, Hamilton could never raise enough money within Saskatchewan to undertake all the activities he knew were needed to resurrect the party. This complaint from the party's official agent in Swift Current that "our friends here are so desperately short that we are having a difficult time getting through the winter"[42] typifies the financial crisis in the party. Hamilton did not have the money to hire enough organizers to canvass all parts of the province, and those he did send out most often did not sell sufficient memberships to cover their expenses. Lack of money meant that he could not pursue issues that might bring favourable publicity to the party. For example, when he wanted to attack the Liberals and CCF over their support for the wheat agreement with Britain, which brought prairie farmers less than the prevailing market price, he had to write Kidd that "it is going to be nip and tuck with us to survive for the next two or three months till we get our bills for the radio paid off. Therefore I cannot take advantage of the opportunity."[43] Lack of money also meant that he could not pay candidates' expenses or wage a comprehensive election campaign. Two months prior to the 1952 election, he advised Kidd that "there is no possible way of financing an election in this province on the basis of the contribution of the little individuals that we are depending on."[44] The problem of money dogged Hamilton from the moment he took on the leadership but, as with the other major problems which beset him, while he recognized it, and tried to overcome it, he could not succeed.

The last link in the chain of interrelated problems which led to the party's defeat in 1952 was lack of publicity. Hamilton knew he had to attract people's attention before they would consider the party seriously, but he could neither buy nor obtain sufficient free publicity to do so. He simply could not compete with the CCF, for example, which put out a weekly newspaper and had a regular radio programme, although he tried to counter with the *P.C.P. News* and radio broadcasts whenever he could afford to purchase the air time. He wanted a weekly radio programme of his own because "in the face of a hostile press which ignores us, it is the only way that we can get our ideas across."[45] He did broadcast sporadically in his first years as leader but could not raise enough money within the province, or from national headquarters, to continue on a regular basis. Compounding the problem was the fact that even during the election campaign most of the press did not consider either Hamilton or his party newsworthy. For example, the *Star-Phoenix* eve-of-poll editorial did not mention the Progressive Conservative campaign at all.

A seat in the legislature would have helped Hamilton enormously, for it would have given him access to the fount of free publicity which party leaders in Parliament attract. In addition, because the debates were broadcast, it would have provided him with a free platform from which to reach voters in every corner of the province. Hamilton did what he could to get into the legislature and he received help from unexpected quarters early in the process. Premier Douglas offered to help clear the path for him shortly after the leadership convention. As Hamilton informed Diefenbaker:

> Mr. Douglas invited me over for a long talk in Regina and said that he would do anything he could to get me in the House next January. He suggested that if I could get McDonald to resign in Moosomin and if I could get the Liberals to agree to stay out that he would call a by-election immediately and ask publicly that an acclamation be given me.[46]

Hamilton did consider asking McDonald to stand aside for him but decided not to for fear that the Moosomin Liberal association would contest the by-election and deprive the Conservative party of its only voice in the legislature.[47] Thus, Hamilton was forced to lead his party as best he could from outside the legislature. He did attend debates and committee meetings, thanks to an arrangement with Douglas and Tucker, but without speaking privileges his contributions did not reach the same audience as those of his opponents. A seat meant a great deal to Alvin Hamilton. To repeat, it would have given him and his party publicity that he could not purchase or generate elsewhere. Had he been successful in 1948 or 1952, it might have convinced potential Conservative candidates that they stood a chance and party workers that their cause was not hopeless. Most important of all, in Hamilton's own words — "I would have been credible"[48] — and credibility was imperative if the electorate was to be convinced that the Progressive Conservative party offered a realistic alternative to the CCF and Liberals.

The four years between the elections of 1952 and 1956 must have seemed a cruel practical joke to Hamilton because all of the problems he had encountered in his first years as leader continued to haunt him. Hammy McDonald carried on Tucker's attempts to build an antisocialist coalition and again this met with some success.[49] He talked Alex Jupp, the lone Conservative candidate in Regina in 1952, into running as a

Liberal in 1956, and he convinced several Conservative riding associations not to nominate candidates in order to keep the anti-CCF vote united. Throughout the period Hamilton had to remind potential candidates not to seek alliances with the Liberals. In addition, inactivity at the constituency level remained the norm, not the exception. As one supporter wrote, "Whether I can get enough interested to form a Local Organization is a 64 dollar question. No one seems very interested any more and the old stand byes of the party have either moved away or passed on."[50] In fact, the state of the party in the constituencies was so bad that Hamilton had to report to a provincial convention in the autumn of 1954 that: "Organization in the usual sense of the word is non-existent in several areas of the province . . . In those constituencies local executives are inactive and supporters make no effort to form local associations in their towns."[51] Prospective candidates refused to run because:

> Frankly, having covered the Yorkton constituency intensely for the past thirty years I see no hope for electing a Conservative in it. We have been so long without any organization of any kind that two generations have grown up with little or no knowledge of Conservative principles and policy except in a critical manner from our opponents.[52]

Party finances were in no better condition. "Our financial drive was a complete failure."[53] "The Provincial Office is [in a] dire financial state at the moment."[54] The repercussions were obvious. It became even more difficult to find people willing to run as Conservatives. As Hamilton complained, "It appears that we can't collect money unless we have candidates sufficient to form a government and we can't get candidates unless we have money. So it is a vicious circle which is difficult to break."[55] There was no money to buy radio time. As early as the autumn of 1952 Kidd had to inform Hamilton that: "With reference to the question of your radio program, I must tell you that I cannot see any possibility of any further funds . . . over and above the regular monthly commitment."[56] Even worse financial embarrassment forced Hamilton to suspend publication of his *P.C.P. News* in 1955, and to beg the postmaster in Saskatoon for "any indulgence that you may grant us in this period of difficulty."[57] Hamilton did try to break the "vicious circle." He even contributed a portion of his own salary, as he informed one candidate seeking help a few months before the election:

> You will remember the high hopes that we had last January and the big plans that were made last June to collect funds. Those funds have not materialized and the result has been that I felt obligated, personally, to pay a good deal of this [candidate support] out of my own pocket. I can not afford any more personal financial support and so far the Party has not come up with a Provincial Finance Committee to collect any money.[58]

As if that weren't sufficient, in the lead up to the 1956 election Hamilton also had to deal with several other problems which were either new, or had existed previously, but had not caused him much concern. The most important of these began in 1955 when Social Credit supporters, led and financed by the governments of Alberta and British Columbia, attempted to take Saskatchewan by storm. Their strategy was similar to the Liberals — to build an antisocialist coalition and to attract prominent Conservatives to their banner. Social Credit, however, was willing to be led by one of these Conservatives and was also prepared to pay for the privilege. Late in 1954, Social Credit representatives from British Columbia and Alberta met with Robert Kohaly, the sole Progressive Conservative in the Saskatchewan Legislature,[59] and offered him "close to half a million" to lead their forces in the province.[60] The offer caused quite a stir in the Conservative party. As Hamilton informed national headquarters:

> Our organization work in selected areas became a secondary interest when Social Credit Leaders in British Columbia and Alberta made a definite offer to take over our Party. The technique was to offer to our single member substantial sums to carry out an election drive for the Social Credit. They were quite willing to let us make policy, pick candidates, etc., as long as we called ourselves Social Credit.[61]

Kohaly considered the offer carefully but, in the end, he refused to go over to Social Credit unless Hamilton did so as well and as Hamilton would not sacrifice his party, the temptation was rejected. Nevertheless, this did not deter Social Credit from its determination to capture the Conservative vote and to bring Conservative supporters over to its cause. In the following months, members of Conservative constituency executives resigned because Hamilton would not accept any form of alliance with Social Credit. Some local associations refused to nominate candidates for the 1956 election because they believed their members had defected to Social Credit. Just prior to the election, one long-term party worker in Tisdale advised Hamilton that:

> For us to put in a candidate would only be political suicide for the candidate and would do the party no good . . . I have talked to the Executive and they all agree that it is hopeless. At least 80% of the Conservative vote has decided to vote Social Credit and possibly as much as that of the Liberal vote.[62]

Moreover, men who had run as Progressive Conservatives in previous elections ran as Social Credit candidates in 1956. Social Credit contested all fifty-three seats in the 1956 election and did enormous damage to the Conservative party and its leader.

In addition to all these difficulties, Hamilton had to contend with several other problems concerning the organization of the Progressive Conservative party in Saskatchewan which, while not of major importance in themselves, nonetheless together added substantially to his plight. The first of these stemmed from the fact that even after several years as leader he still had very little assistance in running the party. In essence, he was the Progressive Conservative party organization in the province. He was its chief organizer, fund raiser, publicist, theorist and campaigner. Although the party possessed a president and an executive, and these individuals helped him on occasion, by and large the formal organization contributed little to ease his burdens. At times he soldiered on without a treasurer and could count on the services of more people than his permanent secretary only during election campaigns. By 1956 he was beginning to feel the strain. As he complained to one supporter: "As you know one trouble is traceable to a very simple fact that one person cannot do all the work."[63] Too often he had to confess to members who wanted his help in their areas that: "I am the only one in our Provincial Headquarters and I am only able to cover a certain part of the province."[64] Furthermore, he had to carry on his work during winters not conducive to travel and over roads that only recently had been gravelled, not paved.

Another problem concerned the nature of party organizations in the constituencies as they existed when Hamilton took on the leadership. Local associations had languished since the thirties and, where they existed, had taken on the characteristics of feudal fiefdoms controlled by powerful barons jealous of their positions. Many of these local overlords resented the attempt to shake them out of their lethargy and to impose direction from the centre, especially by a leader so much younger and less experienced than they. Regina proved to be the most ticklish problem area for Hamilton, especially after he decided to keep the party's headquarters in Saskatoon. Perhaps the sole point on which all Regina Conservatives agreed was that the party's central office should be in the capital. Furthermore, the party in Regina had split into several factions and, try as he might, Hamilton could not bring them together. His difficulties are illustrated in the following letter he sent to the president of the Regina Progressive Conservative Association late in 1955:

> I noticed the story on page eleven of the Leader Post the other day of your re-election of officers, congratulations.
>
> I wonder if you could send me the addresses of each of those people named to the executive so that we would have a proper list for our files.[65]

Not only did this party activity not receive the publicity it warranted, but this type of information should have been sent to the leader of the party as a matter of routine. Hamilton never did resolve his problem with Regina. If anything, the situation there deteriorated over time. Just prior to the 1956 election the new president of the Regina association informed Diefenbaker that:

> Early last month the Association held a meeting in Regina, ostensibly to decide whether or not to run candidates in the city at the forthcoming provincial elections. I attended this meeting and found, to my amazement and disgust, they seriously suggested folding up the whole association in Regina, giving up their committee rooms and, in short, fading out of the picture.[66]

Although the man took on the presidency "to stop the rot," he could not do so in time — no Conservative candidates ran in Regina in 1956. Relations with Regina may have caused Hamilton the most trouble during his years as leader, but similar difficulties with other local associations also existed, if to a lesser degree.

The last of the problems of lesser importance arose out of Hamilton's dual position as provincial leader and federal director of organization. Hamilton never viewed the two rôles as being in conflict. To his mind the Progressive Conservative party in Saskatchewan was in trouble at both levels and the task was to rebuild it as a credible alternative to the Liberals and CCF. Thus, actions directed at one level were deemed to produce desirable results at the other as well. Not all people in the provincial party agreed, however, as evidenced in this complaint:

> As stated my opinion is that the political strategy of the Leader Hamilton is not practical and is leading us further into the wilderness from day to day . . . Hamilton is dealing with Federal policies that have no bearing upon the Provincial election and the average elector is not interested . . . The unfortunate part of it all is that he doesn't know what its all about.[67]

The link with federal politics also caused Hamilton difficulty in other ways. In the first place, it prevented him from finding a candidate for the Prince Albert constituency in the 1956 election. Diefenbaker had won the federal riding by playing down the partisan nature of his candidacy, and he wished to maintain a discreet distance from the provincial party. As the president of the Prince Albert association informed Hamilton:

> I have spoken to some of the leading Conservatives here and they are of the opinion that as Mr. Diefenbaker

> represents this seat Federally and as his Diefenbaker Club movement is at variance with straight Conservative organization of the constituency both Federally and Provincially, they can see no point in doing anything from a straight Conservative basis.[68]

Secondly, it diverted Hamilton's attention to matters of federal concern. Diefenbaker, among others, would often invite him to "write me a resume of things and your suggestions on matters that I should bring before Parliament"[69] and Hamilton, deeply interested in federal politics, was only too happy to oblige. This is not meant to suggest that provincial politics stood second in Hamilton's priorities when he was leader of the party in Saskatchewan. Nevertheless, he had many duties to perform as federal director of organization. He carried them out conscientiously; he hoped some day to win election to the House of Commons; he began to believe that success in Saskatchewan would only follow a Conservative victory federally; and all of this took time — time he might have devoted to the provincial party alone.

In the face of these manifold and seemingly insurmountable difficulties, it is not surprising that Hamilton considered quitting as provincial leader on more than one occasion prior to the 1956 election. After Robert Kohaly's by-election victory in 1953, the prospect looked even more inviting, because Kohaly seemed a logical successor. In fact, Hamilton did submit his resignation to the party president, Robert Svoboda, in 1955 in the hope of forcing the issue, but Kohaly would not agree to take on the leadership, so Svoboda would not accept the resignation. Thus, as Hamilton explained to a friend early in 1956:

> For your confidential information I can tell you that I expect to be running in the next provincial election in Saskatoon. I had hoped to develop our young member Bob Kohaly as a replacement for Provincial Leader which would leave me free to concentrate on the Federal field. However I cannot leave the Party leaderless with so much at stake. Kohaly does not want the leadership so this means that I will have to make my contribution . . . in the provincial arena.[70]

He would plug away as leader to the best of his abilities, even though he no longer wanted the job with "every fibre of my being"[71] as he had once advised national headquarters.

Hamilton's public persona belied his innermost feelings in those years. He put on a brave face and took his party's case to every corner of the province. His strategy was simple — to keep Conservative supporters loyal and to attract as many new voters as possible. To these ends he attacked Social Credit over its lack of principle for:

> The offering of the Social Credit leadership in Saskatchewan to any responsible person regardless of his politics is the best evidence in the world that they do not care what the principles or qualities of the leaders are as long as he is called Social Credit.[72]

He reminded voters of McDonald's treachery and his links to Jimmy Gardiner. McDonald "stabbed the mass of Liberals in the province by joining with the Gardiner machine even as he stabbed his Conservative supporters in the back some years ago."[73] He charged the CCF government with responsibility for most of the ills then facing the province: the loss of young people; rent controls; the act which permitted the adoption of Protestant and Catholic children only; unemployment; spending less than the monies the legislature voted for old age assistance; the high cost of natural gas; overcentralized government; and degradation of the legislature.[74] Most often, he criticized the government for its failure to develop the province. In his words:

> This government went to the people in 1952 with a promise of development of our natural resources. This promise has not and is not being carried out. We need highways to open up our North — to make available our pulp, lumber, our fish, our minerals and our tourist attractions . . . It is on this issue that the C.C.F. party will be defeated — it is on this issue that the Conservative party can speak with pride — it was our party that fought to get natural resources as a provincial responsibility in 1905 — it was our party that won those natural resources back in 1930 — it is our party that will develop those resources.[75]

Frank Hamilton (right) and unidentified friend holidaying on the West Coast, c. 1908.

Alice Jamieson Hamilton, c. 1911.

Francis Alvin George Hamilton and older brother Ralph, 1912.

Frank and Alice Hamilton, c. 1914.

At Normal School, 1930.

Alvin Hamilton and Beulah Major on their wedding day, 14 November 1936.

Alvin Hamilton, B.A. (Hon.), 1937.

The five Hamilton brothers at their first reunion since their separation — from left to right Ross, Fred, Ralph, Hubert and Alvin, 1937.

Alvin and Beulah and their first automobile, 1939.

The "coach" and the Nutana Girls' Basketball team, c. 1940.

F/O Alvin Hamilton, c. 1943.

Beulah Hamilton, c. 1943.

F/L Hamilton and his crew in Burma — left to right F/S Bill Uhrich, F/O Jim Flett, F/S Ray Toth and F/O Jack Webb, 1945.

Leader of the Progressive Conservative party of Saskatchewan, c. 1949.

With national party leader George Drew, 1949.

Alvin and Beulah with their sons Bill (far left) and Bob, c. 1953.

Alvin and brothers Ralph (left) and Fred at Dogtooth Lake, c. 1955.

SAB R-B 2990

Alvin Hamilton with left to right T.C. Douglas, J.G. Gardiner, Mr. Ismond, A.P. Gleave and A.J. Loveridge at the Indian Head Farm Movement Day, 19 August 1955.

SAB S-B 2656

Leader of the Saskatchewan delegation to
the Progressive Conservative national leadership convention,
December 1956.

In his opinion, Saskatchewan could not depend on Ottawa for its economic salvation. The province itself had to promote its resources and industry because:

> If Saskatchewan people had the courage and the vision they could find the money for expansion that would provide cheaper power, highways, tourist and mining industries, farm credit, municipal credit, and a host of new enterprises arising from natural gas and minerals.[76]

The government's attitude towards natural gas and its potential were extremely important to Hamilton at that time because "gas represents our first real opportunity in the southern settled areas of Saskatchewan to build a more diversified economy."[77] Natural gas had come to the province in 1953, but its high price had restricted its use and Hamilton wondered why when his calculations showed that gas could be delivered in Regina at one-third less than the cost then being charged.[78] He knew that the price charged for natural gas could be lowered and he demanded that the government act immediately to do so.

In a similarly positive vein Hamilton made suggestions to improve the work of the legislature by making the public accounts available at an earlier date, providing opposition parties with qualified research assistance, and giving members adequate office space and stenographic service.[79] He advocated creation of a royal commission to study the province's liquor laws.[80] He suggested rehabilitation programmes based on the principle of "self-help."[81] He urged the province to proceed with the South Saskatchewan River Dam on its own if the federal government would not agree to help.[82] Most important of all, he added a development fund to the Ten Point Program he had taken to the electorate in 1952. At its convention in June of 1954 the party passed the following resolution:

> The province is in need of funds for development and assisting our communities. The Crown monies derived from oil, gas and minerals should be used for such development . . . Be it resolved to request a provincial development fund. This fund to receive all revenues from non-renewable resources. The principle shall be used for

> self-liquidating projects, permanent public buildings and retirement of provincial debt.[83]

This put the finishing touches to the Program of Development Hamilton campaigned on in 1956.

Publicly, Hamilton exuded confidence in the eventual success of the Conservative cause. On the radio he claimed that "the tide can turn here with devastating suddenness. It has happened before. It will happen again."[84] He predicted that "once the Conservative Party begins to rise in Saskatchewan, the C.C.F. will disappear because large numbers of C.C.F. votes are not socialist votes, but anti-Liberal votes."[85] To the party faithful he announced that:

> With the failure of the Liberal Party to provide a constructive opposition and failure of the Social Credit Party to find men of weight in the community to support them, the path of success and eventual victory is becoming increasingly clear.[86]

Furthermore, "Saskatchewan desperately needs a stronger opposition and an alternative to the present government."[87] Hamilton did not predict victory at the very next election. However, if the electorate could be convinced of the worth of a stronger opposition and the need for more Conservatives in the legislature, then the party would be on the road to ultimate success. This tactic was one used by most third parties — first win a few seats to establish a presence, then enough to become the official opposition, and finally a majority to form a government. At all times the leader of the party must appear certain of the final victory.

Hamilton had some grounds for optimism as the 1956 election approached, despite the impression created earlier. His work seemed to have paid off in some ridings. The campus Progressive Conservatives at the University of Saskatchewan won a majority at the Mock Parliament elections in 1955 — the first time this had happened in twenty-five years. By far the greatest encouragement, however, was Kohaly's by-election victory. Not only was Kohaly living proof that a Conservative could win a seat in Saskatchewan, albeit with Liberal support, but his presence in the legislature also gave

Hamilton the mouthpiece he had wanted for so long, and he worked very closely with the new member to ensure that the Progressive Conservative stand on issues was put forward. Thus, Kohaly reminded the legislature in his maiden speech that:

> Many of the members of this House have noticed that the leader of the Progressive Conservative party in Saskatchewan, Mr. Alvin Hamilton, has through the press and radio, asked for a statement of policy for the use of wealth received from the sale of our expendable resources such as petroleum and minerals.[88]

Later that session, he moved unsuccessfully to abolish the Saskatchewan Government Insurance office. Next year he proposed a development fund for public buildings, municipal waterworks, and highways to open the north, and he pressed the government successfully to adopt a new and better system of public accounting, especially with respect to highway construction and maintenance.[89] In the last session before the election, he returned to many of the same themes. He also attacked the government for its failure to provide an adequate system of care for the aged, and for driving oil exploration companies out of the province with its high taxes and royalties — issues of importance to his leader.[90] Kohaly was by no means Hamilton's puppet. The two men did not always see eye to eye on issues and tactics and their relationship became strained at times. On balance, however, Hamilton was delighted to have Kohaly in the legislature because it gave him the opportunity to publicize the Progressive Conservative platform, and brought the party some of the media attention it needed so desperately prior to the 1956 election.

In many ways, the 1956 campaign turned out to be a repeat of the one fought in 1952, as far as Alvin Hamilton and the Progressive Conservative party were concerned. In terms of policy, Hamilton once again entered the fray with a development program to place before the electorate. Party literature claimed, in general, that "we have the best program for the future development of this Province" and, in particular, that:

> We are the only Party that challenges the Province to start work on the Saskatchewan River Dam as the first step in providing cheaper power which will attract industries and lower rural power costs.
>
> We are the only Party that calls for a program of building hard-surfaced through highways as the only method to get extra revenue to pay for municipal roads.
>
> We are the only Party that continually presses for the building of access roads into the North to open up lakes, mining areas, timber and pulp to private enterprise development.
>
> We are the only Party that has worked out a comprehensive land development policy to open up over a million acres in the North-East for economic farm units under private ownership.
>
> We are the only Party that officially advocates 50% support for the costs of local education.
>
> We are the only Party that has pushed for a policy of loans to young farmers of sufficient size to enable them to make a success of modern operations.
>
> We are the only Party that has a policy to make available low cost loans to municipalities for development of services such as sewer, water, roads, public buildings, etc.
>
> We are the only Party that has a far-sighted and practical program on natural gas distribution based on a zone system.
>
> Finally we are the only Party that proposes a Development Fund.[91]

Hamilton's tactics were then to travel the province to make the programme better known and to attack the government for its shortcomings in office. The Liberals, too, he criticized for their ties to the federal government, which refused to build the South Saskatchewan River Dam and whose attitude towards agriculture had left the province's farmers in a perilous condition. "The P.C. party has put its faith again in a program of development."[92] "The P.C.s believe that . . . revenues from non-recurring resources should be put into a development fund available for self-liquidating projects . . ."[93] "The Government has had twelve years in office and seems to have run out of ideas . . . half of our young people have to leave the province each year in search of work and opportunity."[94] "It [the Dam] is a Provincial issue because we must have the Dam if this City [Saskatoon] and Province are going to have a firm base for industry . . . Since the Federal Government will not build it, the Province must."[95] Western agriculture needs "the Federal Government to accept full responsibility for an active policy of selling our products by every legitimate means."[96]

Some things had changed in four years however. In the first place, Hamilton left Lumsden to run for one of the two seats in Saskatoon. He did so because:

> In Saskatoon we have a government minister pledged to socialism . . . [and] I would like to give the people in this city an opportunity to choose between the two ideas . . . Saskatoon is the best place to discuss this issue because it is here that the difference between the two approaches to government action are felt by the pocketbooks of all our citizens.[97]

He might have added that as Saskatoon was one of the two largest media centres in Saskatchewan he could expect better coverage of his campaign. Secondly, he was able to make one of his concerns — the high cost of natural gas — one of the major issues of the campaign. He compared the user-price in Saskatchewan [85.8 cents per million cubic feet] with the price in Calgary and Edmonton [26 cents], and advised voters that "we can't expect to meet the Alberta prices, but we should eventually get gas for 40 cents . . . This is not a dream but based on the orthodox economics of natural gas."[98] He hammered the government constantly over this and eventually the press took up the cause. For example, on 9 June the editor of the *Star-Phoenix* pointed out to his readers that:

> Mr. Alvin Hamilton maintains . . . that a 25 per cent reduction in the price of gas might easily result in a doubling of consumption. He argued that present customers would use more gas and new customers would be more inclined to lay out capital for conversion to gas in order to enjoy its benefits. His figures have never been challenged by a government official that we

> know of. Why, then, does the SPC not move at once in that direction.[99]

Three days later, David Cass-Beggs, president of the Saskatchewan Power Corporation, announced that the cost of natural gas would be reduced by 9 percent and 7 percent for domestic and industrial users respectively. Hamilton was quick to claim credit for the change although he complained that it was not enough to increase consumption substantially. Thirdly, the Progressive Conservative campaign, thanks in part to the issue just discussed, began to obtain the publicity it did not get in 1952. It did not receive as much as either the CCF or the Liberals or even Social Credit, but this time at least it was not ignored. The party's platform in particular caught the attention of the media. An editorial in the *Star-Phoenix* just two days before the vote advised readers that:

> The Progressive Conservative party has one of the best thought-out programs, one which puts the emphasis where it belongs — on development, not welfarism. The P.C.'s advocacy of a revolving development fund financed by the province's non- renewable resource revenues, is an example of the party's generally sound approach to Saskatchewan's needs.[100]

The editor also noted, however, that "the party . . . is running only nine candidates and this weakens the pertinency of its program to a degree."[101] That much had not changed. Finally, Social Credit mounted a full-scale effort to add Saskatchewan to its bag of western conquests. The movement ran a full slate of candidates and both Premiers Bennett of British Columbia and Manning of Alberta visited the province to help their forces. This Social Credit onslaught did Hamilton and his party no good whatsoever as the results proved on election day.

On the evening of 20 June Hamilton must have felt as if he were watching a rerun of election night 1952. The same number of Conservative candidates won exactly the same percentage of the popular vote — just under 2 percent. No Conservative won a seat and Hamilton lost badly in Saskatoon — coming seventh behind both CCF, both Liberal and both Social Credit candidates. He obtained over thirty-five hundred votes, but this did not bring him anywhere close to the more than fifteen thousand received by each of the winning CCF candidates — J.H. Sturdy and A.T. Stone. The results were a personal embarrassment and a public humiliation for Alvin Hamilton and placed his leadership of the provincial party in question, at least as far as he was concerned. He had predicted prior to the campaign that the Progressive Conservatives would form the official opposition after election day, but with only nine candidates in the field they could not have displaced the Liberals even if all had been elected. Furthermore, with no seats at all compared to Social Credit's three, he could no longer claim to be the *only* alternative to the CCF and Liberals. Social Credit's success was especially galling because Hamilton believed that most of the people who voted for Socred candidates were those who would have been attracted to the Conservative platform had he been able to find enough candidates to make his appeal credible. As he explained to the president of the Lumsden association:

> The election is now over and once again it is clear that all that happened was that the Conservatives got fooled once again and voted Social Credit over two-thirds of the Province. If our fellows could only learn to stand fast and vote for what they believe, rather than in the hope of beating someone, we wouldn't be in the position we are.[102]

Furthermore, "they did succeed in destroying me as a Provincial Leader and my position must now be considered in the light of my failure to attract candidates to the Party."[103] The writing was on the wall and Hamilton knew it. No one would have to push him. He would step aside as leader and let someone else try to succeed where he had failed.

Hamilton's nickname at University was "Happy." This had been bestowed on him by his Rugby teammates who admired his enthusiasm for the fight and his determination to win. These characteristics were tested severely during Hamilton's years as leader of the party in Saskatchewan. The terms he uses most often to describe that period in his life are "cruel," "awful," and "frustrating,"[104] and he had an overabundance of reasons to be discouraged, especially by the 1956 results. Publicly, he maintained the pretense of cautious optimism tempered by the reality of electoral defeat. As he wrote one of the eight who stood with him at that election:

> I know how you feel because I have been through the mill so many times before. It takes tremendous courage to maintain your faith, but you know and I know that there was nothing personal in this for any of us and that the measure of respect that we will hold in the community is in how we bear this defeat. They will admire us if we hold up our heads and continue to fight because in their own hearts they know that we are right and eventually that feeling will bear dividends.[105]

Privately, however, he was very discouraged. He had been leader for seven years and yet support for the party had dropped to its lowest level ever. He could not find people willing to run for the party, he could not win a seat himself, and even Kohaly had gone down to defeat in Estevan. He reported to another new national director, W.L. Rowe, in his election post-mortem that "the loss of Kohaly was a tragic blow . . . The PCs are in a desperate position . . . our backbone is broken."[106] Furthermore, he informed Diefenbaker that "I've been defeated several times before but this is the first time that I was left so completely numb. Never did I expect to win the City, but never did I expect such a loss."[107] With respect to his leadership, he advised another longtime friend that "our first reaction is to call it quits."[108] He continued as leader for another year when Svoboda again refused his resignation, but it is clear that his enthusiasm for the struggle at the provincial level had been extinguished.

Hamilton did not make the decision to leave provincial politics quickly or irresponsibly. The process went on for some time, and it is certain that he stayed on as leader much longer than he would have liked, because he did not want to desert the party at that blackest of periods in its history. After the 1956 election, however, although still titular head of the party, he transferred as many of his provincial responsibilities as possible to Svoboda and concentrated his efforts on federal politics — the leadership convention, policy development based on the resolutions passed by that convention, speechwriting for Diefenbaker, the nomination of candidates, and the organization of his own constituency prior to the 1957 federal election. He did this for both personal and political reasons. He had always regarded his work at the provincial level as a stepping stone to the federal House, and he had concluded by 1956 that if he did not win election to Parliament at his next attempt, he would have no alternative but to give up his political career altogether. In his words, "I have one more chance in Qu'Appelle Federal. If that fails, I will be looking for a job."[109] In addition, he had become convinced that the party would never succeed in provincial politics without victory first at the federal level. Again, as he put it, "My own personal opinion now is that we will have to come back federally before we can restore our fortunes here provincially."[110] It would take twenty-five years, but eventually his assessment would prove to be correct. In sum, the national party offered him a chance of compensation for the years of frustration in Saskatchewan politics and he was determined it would not pass him by.

Hamilton looks back on his years as leader of the Progressive Conservative party in Saskatchewan from several different perspectives. In terms of electoral politics, he tends to regard that period as "eight lost years" and with some justification. He failed to raise the party's percentage of the popular vote, he failed to win personal election to the legislature, he failed to attract sufficient candidates to the Progressive Conservative standard, and he failed to build a winning election organization. Above all, he failed to break the stranglehold the CCF and Liberal parties had on the province. There are considerations, however, which, when taken into account, make the failure less overwhelming and certainly less personal. No one could have devoted more time and effort to the attempt to improve the Conservative party's position in Saskatchewan than did Alvin Hamilton. At the same time, it is unlikely that anyone could have done better given the obstacles that had to be overcome.

In the first place, one must remember the sorry state of the party when Hamilton became leader. As the party treasurer concluded at that time:

> I believe quite sincerely that Alvin is making progress, but please remember that he pretty well started from zero. All Rupert Ramsay was able to do was arouse sufficient interest after we had lain dormant for many years, to make it possible for Alvin to get away to a reasonable start.[111]

Hamilton had to rebuild the party from scratch and lack of funds forced him to do it almost alone.

Furthermore, he had to restore public confidence in a party whose reputation had been damaged severely, almost fatally, by its years in power both federally and provincially during the great Depression. The problem was not new to Hamilton. Ramsay had encountered it and had recognized its rôle in his lack of success. When Hamilton succeeded Ramsay, a vast majority of the Saskatchewan electorate did not believe that the Progressive Conservative party had their interests at heart. The choice of George Drew as federal leader in 1948, with his image of Bay Street corporate plutocracy, had done nothing to shake that belief.

These were two strikes against Hamilton. The third was that he had the misfortune to lead a third party in a competitive two-party province. The decline of the Conservative party in the 1930s had paved the way for the CCF to become the major opposition to the Liberals. Likewise, its continued weakness had left the Liberal party free to pose as the only realistic alternative to the CCF after Douglas came to power. By 1949, Saskatchewan had divided into two camps, those who supported and those who opposed the CCF, but it was the Liberals who benefitted from the polarization. The Conservative party was squeezed between its opponents and, try as he might, Hamilton could not establish a middle ground between them. He could not convince CCF supporters that his party would provide better government than the Douglas regime. He could not persuade members of the Liberal party that the Conservatives stood a better chance of defeating the CCF. Then, to compound his difficulties, his remaining base of hard-core Conservative support came under attack from another direction altogether — Social Credit. For the first few years of his leadership, hopeless though his position may have been, Hamilton could claim that the Progressive Conservative party offered the only realistic alternative to those voters who favoured neither the Liberals nor the CCF. By 1956 this was no longer the case. The appeal of the Liberals and CCF made Hamilton's electoral prospects dim from the very beginning. The threat from Social Credit made his success even less likely. Together with all the other problems he had to surmount, difficulties which reinforced each other at every juncture, Hamilton was caught in a conundrum he could never solve. He tried, but the Progressive Conservatives' third-party status tipped the scales against him. Whatever he did it seemed he was doomed to fail. In these circumstances, and Hamilton understood them well, it is little wonder that he turned to federal politics for salvation both for himself and the party he led.

When Hamilton left the province for Ottawa, the editor of the *Saskatoon Star-Phoenix* portrayed his political career to that point in the following way.

> Mr. Alvin Hamilton departs the Saskatchewan political scene after having made a considerable contribution to the development of the province without ever having gained a voice in the Legislative Assembly . . . His course was to insist that there was a place for the Conservative voice in provincial affairs. He tried to make that voice both reasonable and insistent . . . By so doing, Mr. Hamilton won respect even at a time when respect could not be translated into votes.[112]

Likewise, Hamilton does not view his contributions to his party and to Saskatchewan politics in electoral terms alone. He points to the issues he raised over the years, his concern for propriety in government, and his attempts to moderate the tone of political debate in the province as evidence of the value of his participation as leader of the Progressive Conservative party. He claims credit for, among other accomplishments, forcing the government to lower the price of natural gas to consumers, to change the accounting procedures of the Department of Highways, and to consider the relationship between resource development and the province's ability to pay for social services.[113]

Beyond these, Alvin Hamilton left behind him at least three other achievements of which he can be proud. First and foremost, he kept the provincial party alive in the face of overwhelming odds, and passed on to his successor an organization better in most respects than Ramsay had bequeathed him. He left an extensive collection of party records and a widespread network of informal contacts on which his successor, Martin Pederson, could build. Pederson admits, "My job was enormous, but Alvin gave me a good start."[114] Hamilton also attracted to the party a number of young people, of whom Pederson was one, who eventually became leading figures in the party at both federal and provincial levels. Secondly, he convinced members of Saskatchewan's ethnic communities that they would be welcome in the Progressive Conservative party. Prior to his term, and especially after the 1929 election, the party gave the impression that it catered solely to the interests of the dominant Anglo-Protestant group in the province. Hamilton did not turn his party into a well-balanced ethnic collage overnight, but he took steps in that direction by bringing people such as Svoboda into the higher echelons of the organization, and this helped make the party more acceptable to Saskatchewan's non-Anglo-Saxon non-Protestant population. The election of Grant Devine, a Roman Catholic, as leader in 1979, completed the process begun by Hamilton and laid to rest the ghost of 1929, which had haunted the Conservative party in Saskatchewan for two generations. Finally, Hamilton left his party a policy direction on which to base its future appeals to the electorate. The central theme of his philosophy was the vigorous state-led economic development of the province. In his view, economic development, through private enterprise preferably but with state participation when necessary, and it would be necessary in Saskatchewan, would solve most of the problems then facing Saskatchewan. Economic development would open up virgin areas to agriculture, logging, mining, and tourism. It would create the jobs required to halt the outflow of young people from the province. It would generate the revenues necessary to pay for all those services desired by the people of the province such as roads, health care, and education. The Ten

Point Program of 1952, and its later refinements, provided both a motivating and unifying political platform and a ready means by which the Progressive Conservative party in Saskatchewan could distinguish itself from both the Liberals and the CCF/NDP and may have been Hamilton's most important legacy to the party he led for eight years. It is more than coincidence that Devine's victorious appeal to the Saskatchewan electorate in 1982 had its roots in the philosophy of development expounded by Alvin Hamilton thirty years earlier. It is also no coincidence that the philosophy of development could be applied equally well at the federal level, which helps explain why Hamilton insists that his time in Saskatchewan politics was "excellent training for my years as Minister" and not just a waste of his time and energy.[115]

Hamilton's experience in Saskatchewan politics confirms the importance of the federal system to third parties in competitive two-party provinces. Much has been written about the relationship between party success and failure at the provincial and federal levels, most of it to show that powerful provincial parties can contribute substantially to the federal party's chances of election. It is often forgotten, however, that a strong federal party can have significant repercussions on its provincial counterparts at and between elections, sometimes deleterious but more often beneficial. In the case of the Saskatchewan Progressive Conservative party when led by Alvin Hamilton, its relationship with the federal party was almost entirely to its advantage. National headquarters paid Hamilton the salary which permitted him to carry out his responsibilities, both federal and provincial, across the province. It contributed funds for provincial election campaigns and provided most of the provincial party's operating budget between elections. In fact, it is no exaggeration to conclude that, during Hamilton's eight years as leader, the provincial party owed its very existence to the federal party. National headquarters did not make these sacrifices out of simple altruism. All three national directors to whom Hamilton reported understood the importance of a viable provincial organization to the federal party's chances in Saskatchewan and events proved them correct. The provincial party they kept alive, weak as it may have been, provided both the candidates and the workers who led the federal breakthrough in 1957 and the sweep in 1958.

It must be remembered that Hamilton served as the party's federal director of organization for Saskatchewan throughout his entire term as provincial leader. Between elections his tasks were to strengthen the party organization and obtain favourable publicity for the party and its leader. At election time he was to find candidates for every riding and do everything possible to elect them. Between the elections of 1949 and 1953, therefore, Hamilton held seminars for prospective candidates and workers, set up Young Progressive Conservative Clubs, undertook membership and other fund-raising drives, travelled the province to encourage local associations, arranged for delegates to attend the party's annual meetings, organized tours for Drew and other party prominents, advised caucus by letter and in person on matters pertaining to Saskatchewan, and spoke often on issues of current concern. The most important issues of a federal nature to him during the period were the South Saskatchewan River Dam and the plight of western agriculture. He regarded the dam as vital to the development of the province, as we have seen, and he made certain the public knew that he held all Liberals responsible for the failure to begin its construction. In his words, "My complaint is that Saskatchewan Liberals make statements out here that they favour the dam, then when they go to Ottawa they haven't the courage to vote against the Cabinet."[116] He also blamed the St. Laurent government for the crisis of prairie agriculture. Grain sales had slumped, farmers' bins were full, and farm families were cash poor. He urged the federal government to do more to promote sales abroad, to pay storage costs to farmers, and to advance initial payments on farm-stored grain. He believed the existing system made it impossible for farmers to prosper, and he said so time and again. In the autumn of 1951, for example, he told farmers that "the only solution that seems practical at the moment is that the government should do what we asked some weeks ago, that is arrange for advances on wheat that has to be kept at home."[117] The following summer his views had not changed:

> In my opinion, the long range answer to this problem of annual crisis in grain storage should be the building up of a flexible farm storage plan. The farmers would do this themselves if there was no discrimination against them as there is under the present system where elevator companies are paid storage out of the farmers' pockets, and the farmer who stores at home receives nothing for the same service. It is only fair that the farmer who stores grain at home receive comparable returns to the farmer who is lucky enough to get his grain in a commercial elevator.[118]

Unlike the Liberal government, in other words, a Progressive Conservative government at Ottawa would help western agriculture because it understood the problems facing the farm population. In this way, Hamilton attempted to persuade rural voters that his party was a legitimate heir to the Liberals in the agrarian communities of the province.

Hamilton fulfilled his pledge to Drew to find candidates for all seventeen Saskatchewan constituencies in the 1953 election. One of these, of course, was Alvin Hamilton, although this time he chose to run in Qu'Appelle. He accepted the advice of Diefenbaker and others to give up his futile attempt to unseat M.J. Coldwell in Rosetown-Biggar and left for the greener Conservative pastures where E.E. Perley had once grazed. It was a decision he would never regret. He continued to emphasize agricultural issues during the five weeks he campaigned in the riding. The seat was predominantly agrarian and its farm population had suffered as much as any from declining sales and increasing costs. Again Hamilton blamed the Liberals for causing the problem and promised action from a Progressive Conservative government to solve it. The government's refusal to acknowledge that a crisis existed angered him especially. As he told the audience at one of his meetings:

> If the Prime Minister or Mr. Howe were to take time to listen to our farmers in Western Canada, they would not

> complain of no interest in the election or make fatuous statements about how prosperous they (farmers) were and how content they were with the present government.[119]

In comparison, his party would act immediately in the following areas:

1. 100% Wheat Board
2. Stronger producer representation on the Wheat Board at policy levels
3. Initial grain prices based on costs of production
4. Advances on grain stored on the farm
5. Immediate steps to restore and expand world markets for farm products
6. Floor prices related to farm production costs and announced well in advance of each crop season [120]

He also promised that a Progressive Conservative government would "ease the tax load," provide "contributory health insurance," and "develop our resources," in particular "build the Saskatchewan Dam," "provincial-federal co-operation in building . . . highways into the North," and "full use of our oil, gas and power resources to build industries in Saskatchewan."[121] This fit well with the national party platform which referred to natural resources as "a heritage which Canadians of our generation hold in trust," and which committed the party to "promote and develop our natural resources for the benefit of the people of every part of Canada."[122]

This campaign had some impact on the voters of Qu'Appelle. Hamilton did not win. In fact, he ran third behind the Liberal incumbent and the CCF candidate. However, he doubled the Conservative vote to almost five thousand and won several of the polls in the riding, an achievement not common among Progressive Conservative candidates in Saskatchewan when the national party was going down to its second massive defeat under the leadership of George Drew. Diefenbaker, the only Progressive Conservative to win in Saskatchewan, was delighted with the result in Qu'Appelle. After all, he had pressured Hamilton to run there in the first place, and he urged him to stay there and prepare for the next campaign. In offering his congratulations, he wrote:

> You received a wonderful vote in Qu'Appelle and that is a constituency you can win. I hope that you do not give up trying even though the result in this election was disappointing. Qu'Appelle is a different proposition than Rosetown-Biggar. It can and will be won by you. The former constituency had neither of these alternatives. Nothing disappointed me more on election night than your defeat for if ever a person merited a victory both for yourself and for the benefit of the country as a whole you did.[123]

It was a good result in the circumstances and Hamilton needed no reminders of its future promise. He would cultivate the electors of Qu'Appelle at every opportunity over the next four years, knowing that he stood a good chance of eventual victory.

National headquarters renewed Hamilton's contract as director of organization for Saskatchewan late in 1953 and he continued his efforts to strengthen the federal party in the province. It was not an easy task because many of the same problems he faced as provincial leader also afflicted the federal party. In 1954, for example, when the party president George Hees visited the province, he gave the media an advance copy of the speech he was to deliver that evening in Star City. Unfortunately, nobody in the small northeastern town came to the meeting and, rather than make the press unknowing dupes in an event which never occurred, Hees read the speech to Hamilton while they sat parked on Star City's main street.[124] In addition, he had to contend with the unpopular George Drew as leader, as did his counterparts in the other western provinces. In fact, at a meeting of three of the four in 1955, "There was general acceptance of the fact that under the present leadership the Party could not make gains in the three Western provinces."[125] Nevertheless, Hamilton persisted, knowing that the federal party had the better chance of success in the province. He maintained his organization work and continued his attempts to convince the public that the Liberals must bear the blame for the deteriorating condition of prairie agriculture.

The issues which attracted most of Hamilton's attention in the mid-1950s, however, were natural resources in general, and oil and gas in particular. He had learned something of the prospects and problems of the industry from his brother Fred, a geologist with Imperial Oil and then Texaco, and other friends active in exploration, production and transportation of the resource, such as George Cloakey and Jack Gallagher. These men convinced him of the need for a pipeline from the west to markets in the central provinces and of the benefits which would accrue to Western Canada if the pipeline were built, and if a pricing system could be found which satisfied both producers and consumers. By early 1954, Hamilton and the other western Progressive Conservative leaders agreed to urge the construction of an all-Canadian pipeline subsidized but not owned by the federal government.[126] They wanted the resource developed and distributed by private enterprise but argued that the losses incurred in building the line north of Lake Superior should be borne by all Canadians because security of supply was in the interests of all Canadians. The benefits, especially to the producing provinces, were obvious. As Hamilton explained in a radio broadcast:

> In simple terms, we have in Western Canada a great natural resource, petroleum and its by-products. If fully developed and properly arranged this resource can double and triple our provincial revenues: it can cause a continuation of the present 200-400 million dollars a year spending program which is bringing prosperity to our province; it can provide jobs to keep our young people in the province; and it can provide the wealth to open up our great resources in the North. It can give us roads, schools and services which our taxpayers are now struggling to provide.[127]

He made much the same claims in a letter to the editor of the *Calgary Herald* a few months later:

> Alberta, Saskatchewan and Manitoba stand to benefit tremendously from the completion of the Trans-Canada Pipeline. I hope it is a start to many other pipelines to the south and to the west. Once we start exporting our gas then exploration will really begin to move in Western

> Canada and supplies will grow as we have a right to hope that they will. By-product industries will be our biggest gain from the whole proposition and the prairies have a fine future if this thing goes through.[128]

Hamilton wanted the pipeline built with as little delay as possible, and he used his contacts in the oil companies and all governments involved to try to hasten the date of its construction. He wrote or visited people such as Cloakey in Calgary, Leslie Frost in Toronto, and Diefenbaker in Ottawa in 1955 and early 1956 in an attempt to smooth the negotiations and to ensure that the volumes carried would be sufficient to provide a reasonable profit for the producers when delivered at as low a cost as possible to the consumers. He followed closely the debates in the House of Commons which finally approved construction of the line and benefitted politically from them as did the Conservative party in general. The pipeline debates, and the government's unprecedented use of closure to force its bill through Parliament, allowed Conservatives such as Hamilton to have their cake and eat it too. The line would be built but Conservatives could attack the Liberals for their arrogance and disdain for the rights of the Commons.

The pipeline debate proved to be George Drew's last hurrah as leader of the Progressive Conservative party. He was in poor health and had to resign later that summer, forcing a convention in December to choose his successor. Hamilton attended the convention but played little rôle in the struggle for the leadership. It was not that he lacked interest in the contest. Rather, he knew that the Saskatchewan delegation, which he had brought together, was solid in its support of John Diefenbaker, and he had good reason to believe that Saskatchewan's "favourite son" would win handily. Instead of canvassing for delegate votes, therefore, he spent his time on the Resolutions and Policy Committee with Donald Johnston, Erik Nielsen and others, updating the platform adopted by the party in 1948. Hamilton had brought to Ottawa a number of resolutions on behalf of the Saskatchewan party which he submitted to the committee for its consideration. They included for farmers "a fair share of the national income," "price stabilization," "national marketing boards," "grain storage assistance," and "retention of the Crows Nest Pass [*sic*] rate structure."[129] For all of Canada he proposed a National Development Policy:

> At home we must embark on a national development policy that will strengthen Canada by strengthening all areas, that will see that all classes and groups get a fair share of the national income, that will give us a reasonable chance to share in our own prosperity and that our human resources will be developed to the full by making use of every aid to education.[130]

The idea of national development policy was not unique to Alvin Hamilton or the party in Saskatchewan. In fact, its roots could be traced back to the National Policy of Sir John A. Macdonald and it had been tailored to fit virtually every Conservative leader since. In this century, men as different as R.B. Bennett and John Bracken had pledged their party to "a policy of protection for Canadians in the development of our national resources"[131] and to "the principle of managing, developing and conserving our natural resources so as to achieve the greatest possible annual return from them consistent with their preservation as a continuing source of wealth for future generations."[132] Thus, when Hamilton asked the Resolutions and Policy Committee to adopt his national development proposal, he invited it to continue a tradition "as old as the party itself."[133]

The convention gave Hamilton everything he wanted. The committee accepted his recommendations in substance and the convention, with delegate attention fixed firmly on the leadership vote about to take place, accepted the report of the committee almost without debate. A short while later, the delegates chose John Diefenbaker over Donald Fleming and Davie Fulton to lead them in the next election. Hamilton would await that contest with eager anticipation. He had a constituency he could win, a leader he could sell in Saskatchewan, and a policy direction he could use to guide the party during and after the election. He returned home convinced that the Progressive Conservative party stood the best chance in a generation of winning power and determined that he would share in its exercise. If he could win a seat in the House of Commons he would have the opportunity to put forward the many ideas he had for the betterment of the country. If he won a seat and were asked to join the cabinet, then he could see those ideas in effect as legislation. In either case, a seat in Parliament would help compensate for the years of frustration as provincial leader. Perhaps it would also prove that the eight years he spent in Saskatchewan politics were not "lost years" but indeed "excellent training" for his years as minister.

Chapter 4

Minister of the Vision of National Development

The "Vision" which John Diefenbaker offered the Canadian people is often treated as little more than a successful campaign slogan. It is true that the picture of opportunities in the north, which the prime minister painted during the 1958 campaign, helped the Progressive Conservative party to one of the greatest victories in Canadian electoral history, but it must not be forgotten that the "Vision" was much more than just a political gimmick. It was backed by a platform which contained several specific policies designed to develop the north and, further, it was part of a broader programme of national development — a programme which provided both the unifying theme and the motivating force for much of the Diefenbaker government's innovative legislation during its term of office. It is often forgotten as well that just as the Conservative party won its huge majority over two elections so the policy enunciated in the 1958 campaign evolved in two distinct stages. The first began at the leadership convention in December 1956 and ended with the 1957 election. It laid the philosophic foundation of a New National Policy and spelled out in general terms the programme a Diefenbaker government would implement if elected to office.

The convention which chose John Diefenbaker to replace George Drew also passed a host of resolutions on various matters of concern, including national development. After the convention ended, Alvin Hamilton took on the task of placing these resolutions in a systematic statement of party objectives and, two months later, he produced the Declaration of Principles by the Progressive Conservative National Convention. Most of the specifics in the document were taken from the resolutions adopted by the convention but, in addition, he sought and accepted suggestions as to content from Conservative premiers and others in the party. As well, he borrowed freely and heavily from both British and Canadian Tory thinkers in shaping the philosophic framework into which he placed the convention's resolutions. The result was a national development policy based on three fundamental principles: resource development, social justice, and government intervention. Development of the nation's resources would be the engine which propelled the country to social justice for all, and the government would be an active participant in the attainment of both goals. Individual Canadians would be expected to take the lead in both the development of their resources and the improvement of their circumstances, but a Progressive Conservative government would not be an idle bystander in either case.

> We must embark on a national development policy that will strengthen Canada by strengthening all areas and groups and regions [which] must have equal opportunities to share in the National prosperity . . . [It will] develop natural resources for the maximum benefit of all parts of Canada; encourage more processing of these resources in Canada; foster the widest financial and other participation by Canadians in the development of our resources; [and] promote greater opportunity and employment for a steadily increasing population.[1]
>
> In order that a National Development Policy and a strong political state may bring equitable and increased advantage to all there must be a program of human betterment. This program will be a comprehensive contributory system that covers the aged, the unemployed, the sick, and the injured. It must be such a system that

> preserves the individual, the home, the volunteer group, the Provincial and Municipal powers. There must be incentive to encourage the individual to be a proud, participating member in a self-reliant society. When contributions cannot be made and where need exists our principles will guarantee assistance of the state.[2]

Diefenbaker refused to let Hamilton publish the Declaration of Principles for fear that it would provide the Liberals and CCF with an easy target for attacks on the Conservative party.[3] Nevertheless, it stands as an important step in the evolution of the New National Policy, for it placed the party's commitment to national development on the record, and Hamilton was able to use it with telling effect to overcome opposition to his proposals in cabinet when he became minister of northern affairs and national resources.

Another significant step in the process occurred when Dr. Glen Green, a close friend of Diefenbaker's from Prince Albert, introduced the new leader to the ideas of his brother-in-law, Dr. Merril Menzies, a young agricultural economist from Saskatchewan. Prior to the leadership convention, Green had asked Menzies for his thoughts on the direction Progressive Conservative economic policy should take in the future and, on 1 December 1956, Menzies replied at length. His principal theme was that if Canada were to maintain her national identity, the federal government had to abandon the doctrine of laissez faire, which to his thinking characterized the economic policy of the St. Laurent government, and intervene actively in economic affairs in order to foster development. In his words:

> What is lacking is a national policy and the realization that without one we must invariably drift into economic continentalism in which we can have little economic independence or effective sovereignty. The regional north-south pull of the American industrial colossus is such that only by the most determined and ceaseless efforts can we hope to maintain our integrated national economy. Only by great thought and effort can we prevent the unconscious betrayal of the national heritage bequeathed to us by Sir John A. Macdonald.[4]

Specifically, the government should aim to build an industrialized nation by expanding energy sources, utilizing non-renewable resources in the most efficient and profitable way possible, processing more of our resources within Canada, encouraging projects that would open up remote areas, and by providing Canadians with the opportunity to invest in their own country.[5] Furthermore, this could be accomplished without repudiating the party's commitment to free enterprise or its belief in social justice. According to Menzies:

> If the role of government is to provide the framework for development, the field of resource development is the essential preserve of private enterprise. The government's task is to encourage, not discourage the risk-taker. Surely it is here that the Conservative party can make a major appeal . . . In view of the Liberal's concern with stability and security and the concern of the C.C.F. with welfare, it should be possible for the Conservatives to become in the public mind the party of enterprise and national expansion. This need not imply hostility to welfare.[6]

Green showed the letter to Diefenbaker who, at first, "was not deeply impressed with it."[7] On second reading, however, Diefenbaker began to realize the political potential of Menzies's proposals when combined with Hamilton's work and, early in 1957, brought Menzies to Ottawa to help him prepare for the forthcoming election. Over the next few months, Menzies elaborated his thesis and, either singly or in conjunction with the party's research department, provided Diefenbaker with a development programme even broader in scope and detail than that contained in Hamilton's Declaration of Principles.

The result of these labours was a fourteen-page document called The Progressive Conservative National Development Policy. The paper began with a general statement of the reasons why a new national policy was essential and why the government must assist economic growth.

> A new national development policy is needed, one which will contain a clearer vision of the essential role Canadians in every region and occupation should play in

> making this nation grow . . . Our Federal government has responsibility to guarantee all our people a share both in the building of our prosperity and in the benefits flowing from it. The government should assist every region of this broad land to participate in national growth, and should assist the business of this country to be as productive and efficient as possible. In addition, the Federal government should preserve our nation's integrity, and ensure that growth benefits Canadians in every part of Canada.[8]

It continued with a list of the areas in which a new Conservative government should act to promote economic development, and to distribute the benefits of growth fairly across the country, including: a national energy policy; a national resources inventory; a national farm development policy; increased markets for both farm and industrial products; greater processing of Canadian resources in Canada; greater investment by Canadians in Canadian ventures; a policy to protect and promote small business; an immigration policy to enlarge the domestic market; and northern development. In elaboration of the section on northern development, "the Federal government should become aware of the vast potential of our northland frontier, and should take steps to broaden this country from north to south, as the Conservative government of Sir John A. Macdonald broadened it from east to west."[9]

National development continued to fill Hamilton's mind in the months prior to the 1957 election. Not only did he prepare the Declaration of Principles, he also wrote Diefenbaker several times to impress upon the new leader his belief that a new national policy should highlight the party's appeal at the forthcoming election. In his words:

> A National Development Policy is the keystone of the Conservative Platform. It is the heart and life blood of our program to build Canada. It is what most clearly distinguishes our Party from others. It is the means by which we can increase revenues so that we can reduce taxes and pay for a program of human betterment in Canada.[10]

This focus on national development formed a major part of the advice he gave Diefenbaker on the issues to emphasize once the campaign began. The Chief had asked him "to prepare a full outline in detail of all the matters you think I should deal with when I am in Saskatchewan"[11] and Hamilton replied that Diefenbaker should stress the following points:

> In Ottawa [at the convention] I pledged myself to a policy of One Canada with equality to all parts. To bring equality to areas that are lagging in the economic boom there must be a National Development Policy. This is the heart and soul of the Conservative Program . . .
>
> By this policy we hope, not only to increase the tempo of activity in the Prairies, the Maritimes, and the North West Territories, but to help increase revenues for the Federal Government in order to lower taxes, provide a larger share of the tax dollar to the provinces, municipalities, and school boards.[12]

At the same time he also suggested that Diefenbaker speak on development "as it relates to agriculture" when in Saskatchewan.[13] Resource development in itself would not be sufficient to attract rural voters. To win Saskatchewan and the farm population generally the Progressive Conservative party would have to pledge itself to "a fair share of the national income for farmers" and detail its plans for "cash advances," "grain storage," and "the need for greater exports."[14]

Diefenbaker accepted many of the suggestions made by Hamilton, Menzies, and Donald Eldon, the director of research at party headquarters, and they became part of the platform he set forth during the ensuing election campaign. In it he pledged the Progressive Conservative party to a policy of national development for the benefit of all, and promised Canadians that:

> To assure economic development in all parts of the country the Conservative Party will offer a new National Policy founded on a renewed sense of national purpose. Whereas Sir John MacDonald was concerned with opening the West, we shall be concerned with developments in the Northern frontier . . .
>
> We believe that the welfare of Canada demands the adoption of such a policy as will develop our National Resources for the maximum benefit of all parts of Canada . . . [and] will foster wide financial participation by Canadians . . .

> That being my philosophy and since I wish to bring about the concept of one Canada with special rights and privileges to no area, I would advocate a new national policy of resources embracing every part of this country to assure prosperity in Canada and a maximum capacity to discharge her international responsibilities.[15]

The platform also outlined the five major areas in which a Diefenbaker government would first concentrate its efforts to attain these objectives, as well as the principal methods it would use:

> **Natural Resources Policy**
>
> 1. Every encouragement must be given to the processing of domestic raw materials in Canada to a much greater degree than exists today . . .
> 2. Foreign investment must not be discouraged, but it must be directed to the maximum benefit of Canada.
> 3. Canadian subsidiaries of foreign concerns . . . should be required to provide a substantial interest in their equity stock to Canadian investors.
> 4. Wherever possible foreign companies should employ Canadians in senior management and technical posts.
>
> **National Energy Board**
>
> To meet the industrial demands of Canada's future . . . there is need now for the setting up of a Canadian Energy Board . . . to the end that the most effective use of the energy resources of Canada in the interests of the public welfare may be assured.
>
> **Roads to Resources**
>
> A National Highway policy should be launched to provide highways for peace and development wherein the Federal Government will make contributions to or share in cooperation with the provinces.
>
> **Tax Structure to be Revised**
>
> The entire tax structure in Canada needs to be overhauled with a view to providing encouragement to the promotion of primary and secondary industries in our country.
>
> **A Fair Share for Farmers**
>
> We will assure the farmer of his fair share of the national income by maintaining a flexible price-support program

> to ensure an adequate parity for agricultural producers based on a fair price-cost relationship . . . Agriculture and its welfare is a basic cornerstone of [our] policy.[16]

Although Diefenbaker stressed many other issues in his campaign, it is also true that during the 1957 election he laid the foundation for the national development programme to come. Its major goals would be resource development and human betterment, presided over by a government determined to play an active rôle in achieving both objectives.

Hamilton took his own advice to heart with respect to his fight for Qu'Appelle. He had spent one week of every month in the riding after the provincial election, and once the federal election was called, he informed national headquarters that he would be in Qu'Appelle for the duration of the campaign.[17] He had fulfilled his responsibility to the party as director of organization for Saskatchewan — he and Svoboda had found candidates for all seventeen seats in the province. Now he would try to win a seat for himself. Despite his concern for national development, he knew that this alone would not win over the farm vote in his predominantly agrarian constituency. He had to address their concerns, not his, and so he emphasized the party's agricultural policies and downplayed its plans for the other regions of Canada. The press release he put out near the beginning of the campaign is evidence of his tactics. It reminded the electors of Qu'Appelle that "the Conservative Party is pledged to a fair share of the national income for agriculture," and outlined a comprehensive programme for agriculture in both the short and long-terms. In the short-run a Progressive Conservative government would implement: (1) advance payments in the autumn; (2) a grain storage policy; (3) a stepped-up selling programme; (4) a domestic wheat price (in effect a two-price system which would give farmers a higher return on wheat sold in Canada than abroad). In the long-term the party was committed to: (1) building up markets abroad; (2) increasing producers' democratic control over their own affairs; (3) credit policies to build up smaller farmers; (4) taxation policies that encourage efficiency. In addition, floor prices would be "the keystone to stability of agriculture in Canada."[18] Hamilton ignored neither resource development nor other issues he thought would advance his cause, but to his mind agriculture was the key to victory, as the following advertisements indicate:

> Alvin Hamilton P.C. Candidate for Qu'Appelle Constituency says to Build a United Canada with equality between groups and regions, we need a national development program which has Agriculture as its cornerstone.[19]
>
> In Saskatchewan, people are disgusted with the outright disregard by the Liberals of our most urgent needs — a fair share of the national income for farmers, cash advances on farm-stored grain, credit for farm expansion, construction of the Saskatchewan River Dam project, higher tax exemptions and higher Old Age Pensions.[20]

Hamilton campaigned for no one but himself during this election. He travelled the main line of the Canadian Pacific Railway east of Regina to the Manitoba border, speaking at every town enroute, and he visited as many of the other parts of the riding as possible to attend all-candidates' meetings, to encourage his workers, and to add the personal touch to his campaign. All the hard work finally paid off. On election day, 10 June 1957, Saskatchewan elected three Progressive Conservatives — John Diefenbaker in Prince Albert, Harry Jones in Saskatoon, and Alvin Hamilton in Qu'Appelle. In a close race Hamilton won 34 percent of the vote and defeated the previous member, Liberal Henry Mang, by 705 votes — 6,217 to 5,512.CCF and Social Credit candidates also went down to defeat. Nation-wide, the Conservatives won 112 seats, the Liberals 105, the CCF 25 and Social Credit 19 — a minority of seats, but enough to return the party to power after twenty-two years.

The day after the election the *Star-Phoenix* headed one of its articles "Hamilton Jubilant," and jubilation, together with relief, seem appropriate terms to describe his feelings after the result. After defeats at three federal (not to mention defeats at three provincial) elections, finally his dream of a seat in the House of Commons had come true. The *Indian Head News*, the local newspaper in the town where Hamilton had his campaign headquarters, also commented after the election that:

> Alvin Hamilton, newly-elected Conservative representative in this constituency, was jubilant after the win though feeling . . . a great sense of responsibility . . . In downtown Indian Head, there were glowing smiles on staunch Conservative faces that hadn't been able to do quite that in nearly three decades.[21]

A week later, the same editor pointed out that "it will strike many in Saskatchewan that Mr. Hamilton is of cabinet calibre and should rate serious consideration in one or another capacities."[22] In fact, it was not long before Hamilton supporters in Qu'Appelle and elsewhere began to flood the Prime Minister's Office with requests and/or demands that Diefenbaker appoint him to the cabinet. Some asked that he be made minister of agriculture. Others suggested that he be made a junior minister in the Department of Trade and Commerce, with special responsibility for the Wheat Board. Still others believed he was best suited to be minister of northern affairs and national resources. For the editor of the *Star-Phoenix*:

> Mr. Hamilton is one of the most dedicated and hardest-working members of the Conservative party in western Canada. We believe he had a good deal to do with thinking out the imaginative national development program which Mr. Diefenbaker advocated during the campaign. We think Mr. Hamilton would be a good choice for minister of northern affairs and national resources.[23]

For his part, Hamilton made no attempt to obtain a cabinet post. When Diefenbaker held out the prospect shortly after the election he informed the prime minister-elect that he would be quite content to remain free from the responsibilities of a portfolio so that he could work on the policies he believed the new government should legislate.[24] Diefenbaker replied that he thought "a Colonel House would not work in the Canadian system . . . that the only way to put forward your views and defend yourself in Ottawa is to have a portfolio and get yourself to a position of political clout,"[25] but he did not appoint Hamilton to his first cabinet, and Hamilton took his family to their bush camp near Kenora for their traditional summer vacation.

The prime minister called him back to Ottawa in late July and took him on a trip through the prairies where he broached the subject of a portfolio once again. Once again, Hamilton pushed the claims of others rather than his own, although after this visit he did force Svoboda to accept his resignation as provincial leader, causing further speculation in the media of an impending appointment to cabinet.[26] The conjectures proved correct. On 20 August, Diefenbaker announced that Alvin Hamilton would be the next minister of northern affairs and national resources, replacing Douglas Harkness, who had carried the double burden of this department and agriculture since June. The prime minister declared that:

> Mr. Alvin Hamilton is well-known throughout Western Canada for his devotion to public affairs over many years and particularly for his interest in and appreciation of the need for the development of Canada's remaining frontier lands. His keen, analytical mind, together with his energetic approach to responsibility, assures that the direction of the affairs of his department will be in keeping with our national development policy.[27]

The media in Saskatchewan welcomed the appointment. The *Star-Phoenix* stated that:

> The two latest appointments [Waldo Monteith was made minister of national health and welfare the same day] brought news particularly pleasing to Saskatchewan, where there were many who were convinced that Mr. Alvin Hamilton not only deserved the honours of appointment but also had the ability to make valuable contributions to cabinet deliberations and to the country's affairs . . . The northern affairs and resources post is a natural for the new Saskatchewan member.[28]

The press in Qu'Appelle took especial pride in the announcement. According to the *Grenfell Sun*:

> Electors in Qu'Appelle federal constituency are both pleased and proud at the recent appointment of Mr. Alvin

> Hamilton as the new Minister of Northern Affairs and Natural [*sic*] Resources . . . Prime Minister Diefenbaker's choice of portfolio for the newly elected Qu'Appelle member could hardly have been a wiser one.[29]

Everyone seemed to know of the appointment before Hamilton himself because he had gone back to Dogtooth Lake to finish his holiday after his trip with Diefenbaker, the camp had no telephone, and he left for Saskatoon before he could be reached by any other means. He learned he had received some position when he caught the tail end of a news broadcast on the car radio as he neared home, but did not find out it was a cabinet post until he arrived in Saskatoon, and telephoned the Prime Minister's Office. Derek Bedson, Diefenbaker's private secretary, informed him that he would be sworn in as minister of northern affairs and national resources if he could make it to Ottawa by ten o'clock the next morning. Hamilton took time to meet the press and express his "surprise" and "gratitude" to the prime minister for the appointment and then he fled for Ottawa as fast as he could. Car, plane, train and army escort delivered him at the ceremony unshaven but on time.[30] He attended his first cabinet meeting later that day — 22 August 1957 — and also met with his senior officials in his new department. Thus began a very hectic period in his life, months of feverish activity in advance of the election of 1958.

Alvin Hamilton brought to his portfolio a novel mix of philosophical principles, and his philosophy of government is important in this context because it explains, in large part, the vantage point from which he judged the merits of issues and the realm in which he sought solutions to the problems which confronted him. Hamilton was a "Conservative," and so shared some of the attitudes and beliefs which bound Conservatives together in all parts of the country. He accepted that mankind was imperfect and probably imperfectible and, therefore, that government was necessary to provide the order required for any civilized society. He had a highly developed sense of nation, and was convinced that the nation had both the right and the duty to ensure that the interests of the whole took precedence over those of any part of society.

He believed that individuals and groups in society had both rights and responsibilities, and that the privileged must show concern for those less fortunate than themselves. He accepted politics as the paramount activity in the state, and believed that without ultimate government control over economic forces political sovereignty would be eroded. He was a "Progressive" Conservative. He had faith in both the individual and the political process, and shared the populist belief that citizens should cooperate to better their lot whenever and wherever they could not do it on their own. He was also a "prairie" conservative akin, although not identical, to John Diefenbaker — a type which has become increasingly rare in recent years, even in that region of the country which gave birth to it. He had an understanding of the importance of history, a love of his country, a concern for the underprivileged, an understanding of the farm population and its problems, and a conviction that the powers of government should be used to develop the nation.[31]

Nevertheless, Alvin Hamilton did not fit precisely into any of these strains of Canadian conservatism at that time any more than he does today. He neither feared nor was suspicious of change, nor did he have any nostalgia for the past. He agreed that change for the better was likely to be incremental, but was willing to accept sweeping change whenever he was convinced that it was warranted by the circumstances. He viewed Canadian society in organic terms, but not in hierarchical ones, and had a healthy dislike of privilege in any form. He believed wholeheartedly in the party system, but not that party took precedence over nation. He was pro-Canadian, but no fanatical nationalist. He was a firm believer in the merits of independent individual enterprise, but had no fear of big business so long as it acted in the national interest. In sum, Alvin Hamilton's political philosophy was an amalgam of many of the strands found in the Conservative party in the late 1950s, some complementary, some contradictory, and the emphasis he gave to the particular strains within his thought at any given time depended on the practical question at hand. He was not a typical "Tory," "Red Tory," or "Tory populist" — all labels which have applied to him at one time or other. He combined elements of all three within his philosophy, and any one could dominate his thinking in any particular set of circumstances.

To these philosophical underpinnings Hamilton added several practical principles he thought would push his causes forward from the realm of theory to action. Some of these concepts he brought with him to his ministries, others developed as he gained experience in office. They may be summarized in the following words and phrases — activism, common sense, self-help, interventionist government, belief in technology, faith in the ability of reasonable men to cooperate, and the necessity of planning. Hamilton was, above all else, an activist in government. In his words, "the question of policy-making has been one of my main interests, if not *the* main interest throughout my political career."[32] Furthermore, although he can lay claim to the title — "the Ideas Man" of the Diefenbaker cabinet — he was never satisfied until he saw his proposals enacted as legislation. Again, as he puts it, "there were people who just talked about policy, who just talked about what was wrong, but I had a compulsion to do something about it."[33] Furthermore, he soon discovered how to propel his proposals through the system, often at some personal cost, and took the lessons to heart. He quickly became "a politician who learned how to get things done."[34] His approach to most issues which arose during his term of office was based on what he calls "common sense." He did not subscribe to any particular theory of problem-solving, and preferred in most instances to seek the advice of those "in the field," rather than those high-ranking civil servants who had spend most of their careers in Ottawa. In his words, "never forget that your main source of information is not your elitist, it is not your scientist. The bulk of useful knowledge comes from John T. Rabble who has to face the realities of doing things."[35] Although this annoyed his civil servants a great deal, when it came time to choose between and among alternative courses of action, he would "ask the people affected before making up his mind on policy."[36] Whenever possible, "I would always listen to the guys who actually did the job."[37]

As far as Hamilton was concerned, as many problems as possible should be solved by the people themselves. He viewed government as a court of last resort for those in difficulty, and believed that countries everywhere would be better off if their citizens were self-reliant and self-sufficient. Nevertheless, he was never afraid to use the power and resources of government whenever people could not cope, or when he became convinced that a little encouragement from government would hasten the move to self-sufficiency. He did not agree with "hand outs," or that all problems could be solved by "throwing money at them," but he did accept that, occasionally, one had "to spend money to make money," and that sometimes governments had to make the initial investment. In addition, he had no doubt that government had a legitimate rôle to play in preserving and fostering private enterprise. As he once wrote to Diefenbaker:

> It is the role of government to create the conditions where free enterprise may prosper, and to ensure that the social justice measures obtain which are an increasingly necessary part of the conditions which are essential to the survival of the free enterprise system.[38]

Closely related to the above was his faith that modern technology, used by private enterprise and applied to Canada's natural resources, would not only provide the foundations of this country's future prosperity, but also produce the wealth which would enable governments to finance the welfare measures necessary to ensure minimum standards of living for all Canadians. For Alvin Hamilton, nothing was beyond the highest aspirations of any people if they would cooperate to achieve their goals, and he proceeded on the assumption that reasonable men and women would recognize their own best interests and act accordingly. Finally, the longer Hamilton served in cabinet, the more he became convinced that the government should not sit idly waiting for urgent problems to arise before taking action. The more he came to understand the interconnections between and among the multifarious concerns and activities of modern government, the more he came to realize the necessity of planning — planning to avoid problems in the future and to achieve complex objectives.

This unconventional combination of philosophical principles and practical statecraft gave direction to Hamilton's desire to serve his country, and he worked very hard at his job. In particular, once installed in office, Hamilton "devoted himself to the 'Vision' with vigour"[39] and, indeed, the second stage in the evolution of the policy which helped the Progressive Conservative party to its enormous majority in 1958 dates from his appointment to the northern affairs and national resources portfolio. Hamilton interpreted his ministry's title literally, and concluded that he bore responsibility not only for the resources of the north, but all national resources wherever they existed and of whatever type they might be. Thus, he decided that nothing concerning national development fell outside his purview, and he involved himself quickly in all fields of government activity related to it. In this, Diefenbaker proved to be of considerable assistance, for the prospect of an early election and the need to present the electorate with a comprehensive development programme appears to have been on the prime minister's mind from the moment he took office. This was one of the matters the two men discussed during the summer and Hamilton believes that the prime minister appointed him to the cabinet with that end in mind. In his words: "He made it very clear that I was to get a programme ready of precise development proposals because in a short time he said we'll be facing the possibilities of a minority government election and he said . . . work it out and get through step by step the things you want preparatory to getting them accepted by cabinet."[40] Diefenbaker also appointed Hamilton to several cabinet committees established to prepare legislation to fulfill the promises made during the previous election campaign, and chose him to chair two others which were to formulate the government's position on two longstanding problems related to development — the Columbia River and the upcoming Law of the Sea Conference.

With this mandate in hand, Hamilton set out immediately to make national development, as he defined it, an important part of the new government's legislative programme, and he met with some success. In the field of energy production and distribution, within a week of taking office Hamilton asked cabinet to pass an order-in-council setting aside those regulations governing oil and gas exploration on Crown lands in the north. Regulations as they had stood gave almost all oil found to the prospecting companies. He also began a series of discussions with the companies to obtain for the Crown more benefit from new reserves discovered. Shortly thereafter he helped draft the terms of reference of the Royal Commission on Energy (the Borden Commission) announced on 15 October. They directed the commissioners to make recommendations in regard to:

> the export of energy and sources of energy from Canada; the regulation of the transmission of oil and natural gas between provinces or from Canada to another country; the regulation of prices or rates to be charged or paid, the financial structure and control of pipeline corporations in relation to the setting of proper prices or charges, and all other matters as it is necessary to inquire into and report upon, in order to ensure the efficient and economical operation of pipelines in the national interest; the extent of authority that might best be conferred on a national energy board to administer, subject to the control and authority of parliament, such aspects of energy policy coming within the jurisdiction of parliament, and, such other related matters as the Commissioners consider it necessary to include in reporting . . .[41]

At the end of the month, as part of the Atlantic Provinces Power Development scheme, cabinet agreed to loan New Brunswick the funds to build the Beechwood hydroelectric plant; to construct thermal power plants and transmission lines in the Maritimes, and to sell them to provincial power commissions; and to subsidize coal used for power production in the Maritimes to bring rates down to those charged consumers in Ontario.[42] Hamilton introduced a bill for these purposes in the House of Commons the following January. As well, during these months Hamilton helped Gordon Churchill, then minister of trade and commerce, fight through cabinet the Atomic Energy Research and Development programme which produced eventually the CANDU nuclear reactor.

In the field of human resources, the Department of Northern Affairs devised a trial works programme designed to alleviate the high seasonal unemployment which occurred annually in the winter months and, in late December, cabinet authorized Hamilton "to contribute assistance towards provincial expenditures on forest road and trail construction for fire protection purposes," "to assist provinces develop camp ground and picnic areas," and "to start clearing rights-of-way for interconnection lines forming part of the Atlantic Provinces Power Development program."[43] In short time, the roads construction part of the programme would become the Roads to Resources, an important feature of the "Vision" which John Diefenbaker brought to the electorate in the 1958 campaign.

Within northern affairs and national resources, Hamilton's first objective was to make resource development in the north a higher priority among his department's concerns. Under the St. Laurent government, the department's principal interest was in the human population under its control, and development of the region's natural resources proceeded slowly. With Hamilton's appointment, the emphasis within the department shifted. While concern for the human side remained and native education and welfare programmes continued, Hamilton "brought a tremendous new emphasis on the resource side."[44] In particular, he quickened the pace of work already underway by the department to determine the extent of the north's resources and how they could best be exploited. His second major concern was to meet Diefenbaker's request for a list of specific development proposals on which to fight the next election. To this end, Hamilton sought advice from both inside and outside his department, and brought to his personal staff people who shared his interests in resource development. The result of their endeavours, according to Hamilton, was as follows:

> It was a very active time, and even though the media and I'm sure my colleagues thought I was very enthusiastic, but very naive, the fact is I was laying the groundwork for a conviction across the country that this was action at long last after the government had done nothing for twenty-two years. And when the election was called in 1958, I had ready that whole development program that Diefenbaker announced in February in Winnipeg to

> open up his campaign — ten points. And nine of those ten points came out of my Department.[45]

Not surprisingly, half of these proposals concerned the development of Canada's northland.

Despite all the above, one cannot conclude that a comprehensive national development programme was in place by 1 February 1958, when Diefenbaker called on the governor-general to ask for an election. It was not, and it was probably too much to expect from a new minority government in one session. Indeed, the Speech from the Throne in mid-October had committed the government only generally to "a national development policy carried on in cooperation with the provinces, and in the territories . . . to enable all regions of Canada to share in the benefits to be realized in developing the resources of this great nation."[46] The only specifics mentioned in the speech were power development in the Atlantic provinces, construction of the South Saskatchewan River Dam, and settlement of international problems in connection with the Columbia River in order that its power potential might be realized. The government could not launch a full-fledged national development programme at that time. In the first place, it did not have a comprehensive and detailed programme ready to be legislated. Secondly, it had to keep the other promises made during the 1957 campaign in the social sphere — promises dear to Diefenbaker's heart. Thus, the few pieces of legislation concerned with resource development, including those such as the Prairie Grain Advance Payments Act and the Agricultural Stabilization Act aimed at alleviating the plight of the farm population, pale in comparison with loans for low cost housing; increases in old-age security pensions; raised levels of assistance to the blind, the disabled, and war veterans; amendment of the Unemployment Insurance Act to increase the period of supplementary benefits; income tax cuts; the doubling of grants for hospital construction; and action to prevent increases in telephone rates. Nevertheless, some important steps on the road to the New National Policy had been taken in this period. The government's commitment to the principle of development had been made clear in the Speech from the Throne, some practical measures to that end had been introduced, and Hamilton and his staff had been given the time needed to prepare the development portion of the platform on which the Progressive Conservative party and its leader would fight the next election.

Within days of the announcement of the election Hamilton wrote Diefenbaker to outline his proposals. He stressed both national development in general and northern development in particular, and these recommendations became the essential elements of the "Vision." There is reason to believe that Menzies also urged a campaign based on a development strategy, and pointed out to Diefenbaker that:

> The first Prime Minister of Canada, John A. Macdonald, united this nation from east to west both politically and economically. His national policy laid the foundation of industrial prosperity and growth of Canada. All governments since have followed his lead, but now we are long overdue on the task of developing Canada to its full. This means that instead of an east and west outlook, we must turn all our attention northwards. In future years it may well be said that Canada, under its present Prime Minister, Mr. Diefenbaker, set this nation on a path as significant to our future wealth and national sovereignty as the course followed by John A. Macdonald ninety years ago.[47]

Diefenbaker, long an admirer of Macdonald, found the concept attractive. Furthermore, it confirmed his belief that a new national policy might swing the nation to the Conservative party — a belief he had held at least since his instructions to Hamilton the previous summer. Thus, northern development, within the context of national development, became the central theme of his campaign, and he greeted his first audience in Winnipeg with the promise that:

> This national development policy will create a new sense of national purpose and national identity. . . The only party that can give to youth an Elizabethan sense of grand design — that's my challenge.
>
> The faith to venture with enthusiasm to the frontiers of a nation, that faith, that assurance will be provided with a

> government strong enough to implement plans for development.[48]

Specifically, he pledged his government to the following ten objectives:

1. A $100 million roads programme in the Yukon and Northwest Territories to open exploration of new oil and mineral areas
2. A joint federal-provincial plan to build access roads to the north, tying in with the Territories roads at a cost of $75 million, and perhaps double that amount if all provinces join the programme
3. Federal aid to "economically sound" rail lines to resources, including the proposed Pine Point railway from northern Alberta to Great Slave Lake
4. Exploration of the Arctic archipelago aimed at developing Arctic sea routes with the prospect of developing atomic icebreakers in the future
5. A ten year, $105-million scheme for thermal power plants in the Atlantic provinces, provided for in legislation last session
6. A $75-million development at Frobisher Bay on Baffin Island in the Arctic
7. A possible second route via Saskatoon and Edmonton for the trans-Canada highway [sic] in western Canada
8. Federal sharing in Saskatchewan's power irrigation development of the South Saskatchewan River
9. Hydro power development of British Columbia's Columbia River and signing of an agreement with the United States to share downstream power benefits
10. A national conference to be called later this year [1958] to map a national conservation policy[49]

These were the substance of the Vision of the North and the New National Policy as they had evolved to date and they were sufficient to capture the electorate's interest and imagination. "The Conservatives won an overwhelming victory in the 1958 election, successfully pursuing the theme of a policy of 'vision' in economic development,"[50] and, just as his party won easily nation-wide, so Hamilton won readily in Qu'Appelle. Now the government had to meet the expectations it had created at a time of increasing economic difficulty for Canada.

The difficulties of minority government left behind, Hamilton and his coterie of advisers began at once to put together a comprehensive set of specific policy proposals intended to make national development the centrepiece of the government's domestic legislation over the next four years. In fact, and in anticipation of a Progressive Conservative majority, some had started to plan before the campaign ended. As Roy Faibish, the minister's private secretary, wrote to Hamilton:

> He [Menzies] proposes to make a recommendation to the Prime Minister as soon as the election is over, that he and I, Bill Morrow and Don Eldon be asked as a group to develop and formulate, in book form, the Conservative National Development Policy along the following lines:
> 1. Resource development principles
> 2. National employment principles
> 3. Trade principles
> 4. Public investment principles
> 5. Economic and fiscal planning principles[51]

Faibish also added that "I am convinced that we now have one of the best pipelines into the Prime Minister's Office and it is now becoming clearer all the time we are going to be called upon for more and more ideas."[52] Faibish's conclusion turned out to be prophetic. The cabinet decided in April that "early consideration would have to be given to legislation to lay the foundations for the National Development Policy."[53] The proposals which came out of the Department of Northern Affairs and National Resources "meshed beautifully"[54] with Menzies's thinking, and Menzies brought them to the attention of the prime minister, most often in convincing fashion.

Hamilton took pains to attract gifted individuals to his personal staff and, by his own admission, owes a great deal to them. In his words, "Those men made my ideas possible."[55] Eventually, his ministerial "think tank" came to include people such as Baldur Kristjanson, Morris Miller and, in time, Menzies, as well as Roy Faibish and Donald Johnston in the private sector. All these intelligent, hard-working and dedicated men from the prairies were not afraid to challenge conventional wisdom or to circumvent traditional channels to achieve their goals. In their approach they were at one with the minister and this, more than any other reason perhaps, explains the mutual attraction which kept them with Hamilton for such a long time. With the exception of Johnston, Hamilton met with this group every day,

> to set objectives and to discuss what we had done the previous day to move these objectives forward. Every morning we had a glorious hour and a half tearing each other apart. A minister has to have people to check his ideas, to say "No" to him. For example, if I could get an idea by Kristjanson then my idea would stand up economically.[56]

A minister also needs people to provide him with ideas for new policies and programmes and as Hamilton gave the group its head the members delivered in abundance. Inspired by a common belief in national development and led by a minister who not only "met them on their own level" but also "wanted to get things done," together they made a formidable team.

These men and others spent much of 1958 working out the details of a coherent programme of national development, and by November Hamilton was able to bring a plan to cabinet for its information and approval. The document, titled Action for a National Development Program, outlined the major areas in which the government would have to act if it were to achieve its objectives: research to determine the location and extent of Canada's renewable and nonrenewable resources; the opening of the north to development; a national energy policy; conservation and multiple use of resources; monetary and fiscal policies; trade and commerce; and public education to inform Canadians in general and businesses in particular of the government's intentions.[57] It closed with a suggestion to establish a Cabinet Committee on Development, assisted by a Development Planning Staff in the Privy Council Office, to undertake the long-range and coordinated planning of the programme.[58] The cabinet committee was set up and proved to be the channel through which Hamilton brought his specific proposals to the attention of his colleagues, although his office remained the source of most of the planning he intended should be carried out by the Privy Council Office.

The activist philosophy espoused in the action program provided the impetus for the New National Policy and its elaboration in public and private over the next few years provided the rationale for much of the government's significant domestic legislation. The long-range objective of the programme was:

> an industrial nation of 50 to 100 million people, living in the northern half of the North American continent, processing its resources cheaper and better than its competitors. Such a nation maintaining a high level of living would need the support of an intensively developed industrial and agricultural base. We have arable farm lands sufficient to support more than double our present population, but the challenge is to facilitate and accelerate the building of industrial complexes so that large numbers of people could be attracted to Canada.[59]

The agricultural base would be taken care of by the National Agricultural Program begun in 1957 and added to throughout the Conservatives' term of office. The industrial base would require a national programme of resource development founded on three essential propositions — economic nationalism, interventionist government, and partnership between public and private enterprise. According to Hamilton:

> The resources are the property of the people of the country as a whole, and, therefore, the government must ensure that they earn for all Canadians a fair share in the benefits. The role of government is not passive but dynamic. It should stimulate resource development and create the conditions that will make it possible. Private enterprise has an essential role in the actual development of the resources available.[60]

This was the philosophy Hamilton and other government spokesmen expounded to all who would listen on countless occasions over the next few years. First and foremost, Canadian resources would be used to benefit Canadians and to lessen foreign domination of the Canadian economy.

Development capital from foreign sources would not be refused. However, to be welcome it had to make provision for the participation of Canadians in development projects. Second, and of equal importance, the government had a responsibility to intervene in the economy to provide the basic services essential to development, especially in northern Canada. Third, and of no less importance, private enterprise would play a major rôle in future development. The government did not see itself in competition with the private sector.

> This is the expression of a belief in the role of public or government enterprise as a necessary catalyst for the fullest functioning of our system of private enterprise. It envisages a policy of practical partnership of public and private enterprise in which the government will find the necessary funds to overcome the initial problems of expanded communications, and other essential public services.[61]

The government would proceed with its plans for national development in three stages: first, to delineate the resources of the country; second, to encourage the creation of regional power grids which would have the eventual capability of forming an integrated national energy grid; and third, to advance keeping in mind the need for conservation of resources defined as multiple use of resources, as "intelligent utilization rather than passive preservation and irrational exploitation."[62] The action programme would also help the government fulfill one of its other election promises — to reduce taxes. Part of this would be done by economy, but much of it would be done by "development of our country and producing a growth economy that would provide the additional revenues to enable us to reduce the tax rate."[63] The extra revenue would also pay for the expanded social services implemented and envisioned by the government.

The opening of the north was, of course, an important first step for the minister of northern affairs and national resources. To Hamilton:

> The North represents a new world to conquer — but it is much more than that. It is like a great vault, holding in its recesses treasures to maintain and increase the material

> living standards which our countries take for granted, and which other countries must soon attain. As populations grow, and as the more readily available resources come increasingly into use, we can no longer afford to ignore our northern hinterland.[64]

The federal government of necessity would have to be involved in northern development because the task was far too large for the private sector alone.

> The development of this vast area requires the cooperative effort of government and individual enterprise. The essential task of government is two-fold — to provide first the basic services that are necessary to enable development to occur, and second the general economic climate in which individual enterprise can feel confident that its efforts will be rewarded if it puts money and effort into northern development.[65]

The first stage would be research to find out the extent of the region's resources. Then, a plan would be formulated as to how these resources could best be utilized. Finally, the actual construction of the infrastructure would begin.

To these ends Hamilton reorganized and expanded the Northern Administration Branch of his department. The Arctic Division was replaced by two new divisions — Industrial and Welfare — and these were added to the old Resources, Lands and Timber, Education, Engineering, and Territorial Divisions to reflect better the department's new direction. As well, the department's budget nearly doubled between 1958 and 1960 in recognition of the government's interest in the north and its increased activity there. The new emphasis of the department would be on the physical side, although it would not be allowed to overshadow the department's traditional responsibility for the human resources of the region. As Hamilton warned Diefenbaker: "It is essential that in Development, care be exercised to ensure that resources, both material and human, are not exploited. By human resources, I am referring, of course, to native peoples of the north for whom we have a particular responsibility."[66] The depth of the department's concern for its charges is shown in the many programmes it instituted in these years to improve their standard of living:

expanded school construction to make schooling available to more Eskimo and Indian children; improved adult education and vocational training schemes; better housing for Eskimos; encouragement of local industries to reduce the numbers of people on relief, including native handcrafts and tourist camps; and, expansion of broadcasting facilities across the Arctic.

Nevertheless, the minister's main interest was in physical resource development and between the election of 1958 and October 1960, when Hamilton left the department, a host of old programmes were expanded and new ones begun to meet the government's objectives. By April 1960, Hamilton was able to report progress on three fronts. The first, research and exploration, saw a hastening of the Geological and Hydrographic Surveys due to an "aggressive program" of air photography and ship construction and "an integrated program of research into the characteristics of northern waters, the ice on them, and the seabed under them" by the Polar Continental Shelf Expedition. The second, investment in facilities for development, was divided into two distinct parts. Transportation, the first of these, included the construction of four thousand miles of development roads under the Roads to Resources programme, and three additional routes as part of the Territorial Roads programme; airport and harbour construction at strategic points in the Arctic; construction of the Pine Point Railway to the lead and zinc deposits on Great Slave Lake; construction of additional icebreakers; and purchase of the Canol pipeline. The other part, which modernized the North West Communications Service, also saw the construction of a microwave system from Alberta to the Alaska boundary; improved radio facilities for air navigation; assignment of radio frequencies to oil companies engaged in exploration; and installation of a telephone service to Frobisher Bay. Lastly, policies to encourage private investment included new oil and gas regulations; ninety-eight million acres of exploration permits given out in the Yukon and Northwest Territories; and a further 142 million acres assigned in the Arctic Islands.[67]

The convention adopted at the Law of the Sea Conference in 1958, the oil and gas regulations promulgated in 1959 and 1960, and the Roads to Resources programme of 1958 require comment because all were linked intimately with the government's plans for northern development. The first Law of the Sea Conference, which met in Geneva from late February to late April 1958, was an attempt on the part of the nations of the world to establish a legal framework to govern the exploitation of the resources of the sea and the sea bed. The conference failed to reach agreement on the contentious questions of territorial waters and fishing rights, but it did adopt a Convention on the Continental Shelf which was of great importance to Canada. Hamilton became involved directly with the conference in his capacity as chairman of the Cabinet Committee on Territorial Waters, and he was assisted ably by his deputy minister, Gordon Robertson, who had worked for years on Law of the Sea matters while in the Privy Council Office and at northern affairs and national resources. Hamilton's major interest was in the resource potential of the continental shelf for he had been convinced by his brother Fred, and others, that it contained an enormous amount of wealth just waiting to be tapped. Originally, he thought solely in terms of mineral wealth, but he soon became entranced by the prospect of oil and gas reserves in the shelf as well. Hamilton had to fight the 1958 election, so he was unable to lead the Canadian delegation himself. Cabinet, therefore, delegated that task to George Drew, then high commissioner in London, but Drew went to Geneva with definite instructions to ensure that the Canadian position on the continental shelf prevailed. According to Hamilton:

> We went in, not only with proposals on fishing which was one of the main controversial issues, but also with a very strong proposal, purely Canadian, that the lands at the bottom of the sea, without interfering with the water or the resources in the water, were the sovereign property of the littoral state, and we put a limit out as far as two hundred metres because that was their [the experts] guess as to the capacity to explore for minerals and oil.[68]

Hamilton left for Geneva as soon as the election was over and he arrived in time to see the Canadian proposal accepted. The Convention on the Continental Shelf gave the littoral states control over the natural resources in land covered by water to a depth of two hundred metres and another agreement declared that territorial waters could be measured by drawing a straight line from headland to headland and made bays with mouths of twenty-four miles or less into territorial waters, thus adding greatly to the area governed by Canada. In fact, Canada obtained more than Hamilton had hoped. The conference also accepted a Russian amendment to the Canadian proposal which gave nations the right to resources covered by deeper water if they could develop them. Other matters, such as Canadian sovereignty over the entire Arctic archipelago, would have to be resolved at a later date but, with the adoption of the Continental Shelf Convention, the government could proceed with development of the resources off all three of its coasts, including the Arctic.

One of these resources, both off-shore and on-shore, was the oil and gas potential of the north. Exploration on Crown lands in the region had been underway for some time but, under the existing regulations, the Crown received virtually no benefit from any discoveries made by the oil companies. This appalled Hamilton and as soon as he joined the government, he moved to protect the public interest in these resources. As he explained to Diefenbaker:

> When one realizes that we have from 300 million to 1500 million potential oil and gas acreage you realize the enormity of what the previous government, by lack of interest, was giving away of the resources of future generations of this country.[69]

The order-in-council passed in late August 1957 declared the offensive section of the regulations null and void and, over the next three years, cabinet amended them three times to bring them into line with Hamilton's philosophy. His objectives were straightforward: "To encourage exploration, discovery and development of northern oil and gas areas; to maximize economic returns and prevent waste; and, to ensure protection of the public interest and also ensure an acceptable measure of public control."[70] Another goal was to guarantee Canadian participation in exploration and development. The changes to the regulations accomplished all four objectives. The August 1958 amendments reserved one-half of any discoveries of oil and gas for the Crown to dispose of as it saw fit. The June 1959 amendments gave companies exploring north of 70 degrees north latitude twelve years instead of nine to complete their work. The April 1960 amendments required that oil and gas leases in the north *not* be granted to "a person unless the Minister is satisfied that he is a Canadian citizen . . . a corporation incorporated outside of Canada; or, a corporation, unless the Minister is satisfied that at least 50% of the issued shares of the corporation is beneficially owned by persons who are Canadian citizens; or that the shares of the corporation are listed on a recognized Canadian exchange and that Canadians will have an opportunity of participating in the financing and ownership of the corporation."[71] Further amendments in 1961 permitted the government to issue exploration permits on the continental shelf after the Law of the Sea convention had been ratified. Taken together, these new Territorial Oil and Gas Regulations set the ground rules for the future development of Canada's northern energy resources.

Once exploration to determine the extent and location of the north's resources was in progress, and a plan formulated as to how these resources could be best utilized, construction of the development infrastructure could begin. Transportation would have to be an essential feature of the programme and the government, again of necessity, would play an important rôle in the provision of these facilities. A first and obvious step was to build highways in that part of the north under the direct control of the federal government. Thus, a Territorial Roads Program was begun in 1958 to connect the southern parts of the Yukon and Northwest Territories with their valuable mineral, oil, and natural gas areas to the north. At the same time, however, it made little sense to open these regions to development but leave them unconnected to the settled parts of the country where the resources would be processed and distributed. Therefore, roads would have to be built through the northern areas of the western provinces to link up with the highways of the Yukon and Northwest Territories. These roads would also open up new regions for development within the provinces. The access roads programme might have been limited to the above had Diefenbaker not decided during the election campaign, on the advice of Menzies and Faibish, that the offer be extended to all the provinces. He argued that every province should have the opportunity to develop whatever resources it possessed and, as a consequence, the concept of the Roads to Resources programme was expanded to include even the opening of new areas to tourism.[72] Cabinet accepted both the basic Roads to Resources policy and the expanded version,[73] and over the next twelve months Hamilton travelled from St. John's to Victoria to sign agreements on behalf of the federal government. The government contracted to pay the provinces a maximum of $7.5 million apiece for Roads to Resources projects, and all provinces except Québec welcomed the scheme. Under the auspices of Roads to Resources close to four thousand miles of new roads were constructed and, whether or not the government was aware of "the wonderful opportunities for regional patronage that the Vision could present,"[74] these roads did open new areas to tourism, connected fishing villages, and linked mining towns with the more populated south, as well as providing easier access to much of the north for geological surveys.

The second stage of the development plan laid down in the action programme dealt with energy. If Canada's resources were to be used to industrialize to an extent capable of supporting a population of fifty million to a hundred million people, then the nation's energy sources had to be developed to the fullest and no source could be ignored — not coal, uranium, oil, natural gas, or hydroelectricity. The government decided to proceed at first with schemes intended to increase the energy output in low growth areas of the country in order to supply the power for industrialization. It began with the Atlantic provinces and passed in 1957 and 1958 several bills designed to expand the power producing capacity of the region culminating in the umbrella Atlantic Provinces Power Development Act.

Another of the nation's low growth areas at the time was the prairie region and there projects dear to the hearts of both the prime minister and the minister of national resources could be undertaken as part of the government's energy policy, in particular the South Saskatchewan River Dam. Power generation may have taken second place to other objectives such as irrigation in the the minds of the planners, but it was definitely a factor of considerable importance. The agreement signed with Saskatchewan in July 1958 committed the federal government to pay 75 percent of the cost of the dams and 25 percent of the penstocks and connecting lines to deliver water to power generating installations.[75] In addition, Hamilton promised the House of Commons a year later that, as far as the government was concerned, "The whole Nelson-Saskatchewan-Churchill system [which drained all three prairie provincies] will have to be examined to plan for the eventual full utilization of the hydro power in this area"[76] and, in August 1961, it agreed to pay half the development costs of an integrated plan for the water resources of the Nelson basin.

In that same speech Hamilton also drew attention to a third major project in the government's national energy programme — the Columbia. Development of the power potential of the Columbia had been discussed for years, with negotiations between Canada and the United States going back as far as 1944. The government decided very early in its term to bring the matter to a successful conclusion as soon as possible. In October 1957, it issued a statement on the Columbia which promised development in accordance with the following principles:

1. The great potential heritage of the Upper Columbia in power and resources be not permanently alienated
2. The United States to pay for flood control, irrigation, land reclamation, navigation and similar benefits occurring in the United States as a result of dams to be credited against cost of dam construction in Canada
3. Downstream power benefits resulting from dams to be paid for by the United States in terms of power, not cash

4. Responsibility for financing to be allocated in accordance with benefits derived.[77]

The third principle is especially important because it confirmed the government's determination to use Canada's power-producing resources for the benefit of Canadians. In the context of the Columbia, this meant that the United States would have to pay for the energy it generated from the dams built in Canada by the export of power to British Columbia, rather than by money payments. The Columbia River negotiations involved two national governments — Canada and the United States, two American state governments — Washington and Montana, the government of British Columbia, several departments of these governments, the International Joint Commission, liaison committees between governments, innumerable smaller committees to investigate all important aspects of the matter, and several private consulting firms on both sides of the border. Discussions with the United States went on for almost two years and with British Columbia for five. On the Canadian side, it is a story of diplomatic intrigue, bluff, and perhaps betrayal, and it ended in frustration and humiliation for the federal government and Alvin Hamilton.[78]

Hamilton has said that "If they do an autopsy on me after my death they will find the word 'Columbia' carved on my heart."[79] He was involved with the Columbia from the moment he entered the cabinet until he left office in 1963. He was chairman of the Cabinet Committee on Columbia River Problems throughout the period and inspired, and later cochaired, the Canada-British Columbia Policy Advisory (later Liaison) Committee when it was established in the spring of 1959. His goals in this context were straightforward. As he informed the cabinet committee shortly after he became its chairman, he wanted "first the development of public power, second optimum power from the Columbia River basin for Canada, and third Canadians must build any dams constructed."[80] Unhappily for him, the path to these objectives was not as direct, and the negotiations with the United States proved easier to conclude successfully than those with British Columbia. Cabinet accepted his recommendation that Davie Fulton lead the Canadian team in the discussions with

Washington, and Fulton brought back a treaty under whose terms Canada would provide 15.5 million acre-feet of storage in the Columbia basin to improve the flow of the river which would require the erection of three dams. The United States would pay Canada for the better flood control which would ensue because of the dams, and would also return to British Columbia half the power generated downstream by the project. The treaty was signed on 17 January 1961, and the prime minister waxed eloquent at the ceremony calling the agreement "a splendid example of cooperation between neighbours," "without precedent in the relations between nations," and predicted that "through the great investment involved and by reason of the low-cost power it provides [it will] serve as a most important stimulus to the Canadian economy."[81]

Unfortunately for the federal government, Premier W.A.C. Bennett would not ratify the treaty and without British Columbia's adherence none of the expected construction could begin. Bennett wanted to develop the power potential of the Peace River as well as the Columbia, and to sell the American west coast states the power from the Columbia to be returned to British Columbia under the terms of the treaty in order to pay for his Peace River project. The federal government would not agree to this, and this is what caused Bennett to retreat from his earlier assurances that British Columbia would ratify the treaty, despite his misgivings, so that construction would not be delayed. As late as 4 January, Ray Williston, Victoria's principal representative on the Canada-British Columbia Policy Liaison Committee, agreed that "the British Columbia Government is prepared to proceed with the Columbia River Development in accordance with the Treaty now being negotiated between the U.S. and Canadian negotiators and that the studies scheduled [by the British Columbia Energy Board to determine the costs and benefits associated with the Peace and Columbia Rivers] are for the purpose of speeding up the preliminaries to ratification."[82] Bennett's delaying tactics therefore "came as a complete surprise to the federal representatives."[83] Lengthy and often heated negotiations between the two governments continued throughout the year, until the federal government reversed its position on the main issue at contention and agreed to let British Columbia enter into long-term contracts with American states to sell for cash the province's share of the power generated by the Columbia. By this time, however, it was too late. Bennett now wanted more than this and an agreement between Ottawa and Victoria could not be worked out until after Lester B. Pearson replaced Diefenbaker as prime minister.

The failure to come to an accord with British Columbia on the Columbia River dealt the Diefenbaker government a severe blow in many ways, not least its plans for a national power policy. As early as 1958, it was clear that a policy directed at the Atlantic provinces and based on the Saskatchewan and Columbia rivers would not meet the needs of the national development plan envisioned in the action programme. Hamilton saw that some areas of the country would never be able to produce sufficient power to satisfy the dual demands of resource exploitation and industrialization, while others would have more than they required. He realized that the problem of low generating capacity in some regions could be overcome by the development of nuclear power, but the solution which caught his imagination was the idea of a national grid linking all regional power sources. Power would be moved from areas of surplus to those in deficit as needed, even on a daily basis to take advantage of time zone differentials across the country. This would reduce the need for greatly increased generating capacity in most regions of the country and, in addition, any power not required by Canada could be exported to the United States via linkages with American power grids. Hamilton had no doubts as to the importance of a national energy grid. In his words:

> One of the most important elements in the National Development Policy is the creation and rapid expansion of a flexible energy grid on a national basis. Perhaps this more than any other single factor will determine our future national growth . . . without ample sources of energy, it is impossible to build an industrialized nation . . . Fortunately, although energy sources have their special uses, they are becoming increasingly inter-

> changeable. . . Thus, the concept of a flexible National Energy Grid suggests a network throughout the country by which energy can be quickly and economically transported by means of the interconnection of electrical system and pipelines etc. This network, or grid, will help build a more unified Canada, allow a better utilization of our other resources, and make for a more even distribution of our prosperity. Furthermore, ample amounts of low cost energy, not only for present use but future expansion, will give us a pronounced comparative advantage in processing our own resources — a matter of great significance for our future development.[84]

The scope and potential of the project appealed to the prime minister's sense of grandeur. Using a speech written by Faibish for Hamilton, he opened the huge aluminium smelter at Kitimat in 1959 with the prediction that at some time in the near future there would be "a national energy grid anchored at one end on the Hamilton River [in Labrador] and at the other end on the Columbia and the Taku [in northwestern British Columbia]."[85] Hamilton did everything he could to put the national grid in place. He lobbied his cabinet collegues, he established a committee headed by the director of Radio and Electrical Engineering at the National Research Council to investigate the problems involved and, as he informed the House of Commons in July 1959, "We have called in provincial power commissions, private power companies, [and] electrical equipment companies to join with our research agencies in a coordinated attack on the problem of long-range transmission of electric power."[86] Unfortunately for Hamilton, however, his enthusiasm for the project was not shared by all, the technical problems encountered could not be solved quickly, and the government was defeated before the grid could be established.

Oil and natural gas would have been major sources of energy for the national power grid, but they were also important to the government in their own right. Given the fact that together they provided over half of Canada's total domestic energy requirements at the time, they were resources that could not be left out of the government's plans for national development. The new Territorial Oil and Gas Regulations solved some of its problems with respect to exploration and ownership in the north. However, several others remained concerning the distribution of oil and gas produced anywhere in Canada, especially the proportion which should be reserved for domestic consumption and that which could be exported to the United States. Hence, the government established the Borden Commission to advise it on these and related matters, and the commission submitted two reports. The first, in October 1958, recommended that the export of oil and natural gas be allowed only under license — an annual license for oil, a twenty-five year one for natural gas. It further suggested that the Board of Transport Commissioners should regulate both oil and gas pipeline companies and proposed the creation of a National Energy Board.[87] The government established the board in May 1959 with powers to deal with "the whole problem of the utilization of the abundant sources of electrical and petroleum energy in our country in the national interest."[88] Specifically, it gave the board the authority to collect statistics related to oil, gas and power; to grant or withhold approval of new pipeline construction; to give or deny authorization to export electric power or natural gas; to set tolls charged by all pipeline companies; and to determine the prices at which gas and power could be exported.

The commission's second report, in July 1959, dealt more particularly with the need for a national oil policy. It recommended that it be national policy:

1. To ensure the continual use . . . of Canadian crude in refinery areas of Canada accessible to it by existing pipe line facilities, thereby increasing the market outlets for such crude oil
2. To implement such national policy the oil companies concerned take steps as soon as possible to displace, with products refined from Canadian crude, a volume of petroleum products now moving into the Ontario market from the Montreal refinery area equivalent to approximately 50,000 barrels daily of crude oil
3. No Government action should at this time be taken to ensure the constructon of pipe line facilities to trans-

port Canadian crude oil to the Montreal refinery area . . .

4. The Canadian oil industry take vigorous and imaginative action very substantially to enlarge its markets in the United States on a basis that will ensure the continuing participation of Canadian crude in these markets and in their expansion.[89]

The commission also proposed, in a switch from the previous year, that it be national policy "to encourage and permit the export of Canadian crude oil without license."[90] The government at this time was under great pressure from the oil companies, the Alberta government, and Alberta Conservatives to open the Montréal market to Alberta crude, which would require an extension of existing pipelines. This was especially important to those concerned because, in March, the American government had imposed limits on oil imports to the United States, thus leaving the companies with a large surplus on their hands and the Alberta government with declining revenues. This placed the government in a quandary. It wanted to ensure that Canada's resources were used in the best interests of all Canadians but, at the same time, it also wished to see the oil and gas industry increase its exploration and production. It convinced the Eisenhower administration to remove the import quotas on Canadian oil by the end of April, but it could not dispose of the other part of the problem so easily. The government wanted Canadian oil used in the nation's houses and factories, the oil companies continued to press for a pipeline to the Montréal market, and yet the cabinet knew that Québec and eastern Canada could be served more cheaply with oil imported from outside the country, especially from Venezuela. The government took a long time before it finally accepted the Borden Commission's recommendations. It was not until 1 February 1961 that it announced its National Oil Policy to be to close the market east of the Ottawa River to Alberta oil, to reserve the Ontario market for Alberta crude, and to further compensate western oil producers for the loss of the Montréal-serviced market by permitting increased exports to the United States. Caught in a conflict of principles, and subject to severe pressures, this is one occasion in which the government could not square its determination to develop Canada's resources with its desire to see the nation's resources used for the benefit of all Canadians first and foremost.

The third stage of the national development programme dealt with conservation, and for the minister of national resources it was no less important than the other two. To his mind, "because resource development is for the general national advantage in the long as well as the short term, it is also important to ensure that our development proceeds with a due regard for the future — with a genuine use and genuine conservation of the resources that are exploited."[91] It must be pointed out that conservation to Hamilton was a positive, not a negative, principle. In his words:

> This, I should emphasize, doesn't mean simply sitting on resources like a hen on a china egg! It means using our resources as rationally as we can, and resisting the temptation to dissipate them for a momentary advantage or a quick one-shot profit. It means, whenever possible, a multiple use of our resources.[92]

It also meant cooperation with the provinces and the private sector to achieve this end because the federal government did not have the constitutional authority to enforce a comprehensive policy of conservation itself.

The practical result of this outlook, in the context of the government's national development programme, was the Resources for Tomorrow Conference held in Montréal from 23-28 October 1961. Hamilton gives credit for the conference to Diefenbaker but, in truth, it was Hamilton, on the advice of Faibish, who raised the idea with the prime minister early in the 1958 election campaign.[93] After the Conservative victory, Hamilton continued to pursue the matter and called a meeting of provincial resource ministers in November of the same year to sound them out on the potential of such a conference and to decide its nature and scope if they agreed the conference should be held. The ministers concluded that a National Conference on Conservation could be of benefit, that the federal government should establish a secretariat to organize the conference, and that it should be limited to renewable resources only.

Work on the conference was delayed a year while appropriate people were found to staff the secretariat but, by the end of 1959, they were in place and the planning began to proceed quickly and smoothly. In June 1960 the secretariat announced that the conference would have these general objectives:

1. To appraise the use of renewable resources in Canada
2. To identify the needs, gaps or weaknesses in resource management
3. To develop principles and general guides for the improved use of our renewable resources in the developing Canadian economy.[94]

The conference would focus on six specific sectors: agriculture and land use, water, fisheries, forestry, wildlife, recreation, and regional development. To provide a basis for the discussions, experts would be commissioned to prepare eighty background papers on various aspects of resource utilization, and the conference would proceed by means of workshops in order to involve the expected five hundred participants as fully as possible. Hamilton was no longer minister of northern affairs and national resources nor chairman of the Conference Steering Committee in October 1961, but he attended the conference and had to be pleased with its results, for it confirmed much of his thinking on resource development.[95]

The conference recommended specifically that, in order to realize the possibilities opened up by the meetings, "The National Steering Committee be reconstituted, with a rotating chairmanship and with a secretariat responsible to all governments jointly."[96] The Canadian Council of Resource Ministers was in fact established on 5 February 1962, later changing its name to the Candian Council of Resource and Environment Ministers "in response to a growing public concern about the deteriorating quality of our environment, and the establishment of a federal and several provincial government Departments of Environment."[97] The council's charter gave it the right to advise governments on the most efficient policy for the development of natural renewable resources; to give counsel to governments on proposals relating to programmes to be adopted, agreements to be reached and coordination of their policy with respect to these resources; to stimulate the sound development of these resources; to promote the inventory of production capabilities; and, to study the economic trends with a view to establishing priorities.[98] In sum, the Resources of Tomorrow Conference provided the impetus for increased federal-provincial cooperation in the field of renewable resources and it also marked the beginning of a new concern for the environment in Canada. As well, the co-equal status of the federal and provincial governments on the council provided a model of effective cooperative federalism important then and now.

Just as agriculture headed the agenda of the Resources for Tomorrow Conference, so it was high on the government's list of priority problems and the government regarded agricultural policy as an integral and important part of the national development programme. Grain sales to China, and increased exports to other countries, had solved the immediate cash flow problems of many Canadian farmers, especially in the west, but in the early 1960s one group continued to live a perilous existence — those farmers whose land was marginal or whose holdings were too small ever to achieve prosperity. According to the 1956 census 21 percent of Canadian farms produced less than $1,200 of income annually, from a low of 4 percent in Saskatchewan to a high of 78 percent in Newfoundland. The Agricultural Rehabilitation and Development Act (ARDA) was designed to remedy this situation.

Although the legislation followed a recommendation of a Senate special committee, Alvin Hamilton is regarded generally as the father of ARDA and deservedly so. He made rural development an integral part of the National Agricultural Program, he defended the proposal in cabinet, and against skeptical civil servants, and he headed the cabinet committee which drafted the legislation. In addition, he sought the opinions of farm leaders on the scheme and created such a groundswell of support for it among the farm organizations that the act passed through the House of Commons without a single adverse vote. In fact, when it became apparent that no member would oppose the legislation on third reading, he felt compelled to draw attention to some of its faults himself — an instance rare in Parliamentary history when a minister criticized a bill he had introduced. Finally, Hamilton conducted with the provinces the negotiations necessary to put the plan in operation, an exercise which he considers a classic example of cooperative federalism."[99]

The bill, introduced on 25 January 1961, authorized the minister of agriculture to enter into agreements with the provinces to fund projects "for the alternative uses of lands that are marginal or of low productivity;" "for the development of income and employment opportunities in rural agricultural areas;" and "for the development and conservation of the soil and water resources of Canada."[100] In detail, as he explained to his counterparts in the provinces:

> The General Agreement implies two basic development stages in areas designated as rural development areas under ARDA. The first is a research and planning stage carried out in close liaison with the local rural development committee. At this time, full information would be collected relating to existing conditions and potential development possibilities. Based on an analysis of the technical and economic information, and with suitably qualified consultative assistance, the committee would work out a comprehensive plan for the development of the individual rural area.
>
> The second stage contemplates joint action on the implementation of this plan, involving the carrying out of projects which might cover the whole range of economic development of physical resources and of social and cultural development.[101]

Government action would be important to the success of the programme, but self-help would also be emphasized in assisting marginal farmers to improve their lot. In fact, for Hamilton the concept of self-help was key to the success of the legislation. In his words: "We believe that . . . parity of income should not be achieved by charity, but by providing opportunities for the farmers to help themselves."[102] As with most aspects of the National Development Program, the rôle of government would be that of creating the conditions whereby development could occur. The government's intention was not to move people off the land, although this was recognized as a possible outcome of the programme. Rather, its objective was "to help by various means to improve the income and standard of living of the small and more marginal family farms, and in that way improve the over-all position of agriculture."[103]

Cabinet finally approved a Draft General Agreement with the provinces in the spring of 1962, and on 1 May Hamilton announced that $50 million would be available for ARDA projects over the next three years. The money could be used for:

1. The alternative use of marginal agricultural lands — such as pasture, tree farming, and recreation and wildlife projects
2. Soil and water conservation — such as reservoir, irrigation and wind-break construction
3. Rural development projects — such as the establishment of local industries
4. Research projects designed to help determine the most productive use of rural resources[104]

Two years later, in its annual report, the Department of Agriculture listed the following as some of ARDA's accomplishments:

> Projects underway include a wide range of physical, economic and social research; improvement of stream channels for drainage; purchase of poorer lands for reforestation or recreation; establishment of community pastures; and other projects related to diverse activities, such as blueberry culture and production of maple sugar.[105]

The first ARDA agreements with the provinces expired in March 1965, and the new Liberal government signed others to cover the next five-year period. In 1970, ARDA came under the jurisdiction of the Department of Regional Economic Expansion and over the next decade the ARDA agreements were replaced by General Development Agreements, although as late as 1980 special ARDA agreements remained "to improve job opportunities for people of Indian ancestry living in slow growth areas of the country."[106]

Assessments vary as to the difference ARDA made to rural life in Canada. No one denies the utility of the many projects begun under its auspices but, likewise, no one claims that it solved all the manifold problems of rural underdevelopment in Canada. Even Hamilton laments the fact that he was out of office before the entire programme was in place and that the Liberals altered its direction when they came to power.[107] Nevertheless, ARDA proved to be important to both Hamilton and the philosophy of rural planning in Canada and abroad. It provided concrete evidence to the farm population of central and eastern Canada that the minister of agriculture had an interest in their problems as well as those of the prairie region. Indeed, as Hamilton explained to a cousin whose family had remained on a farm much like the one his father had left fifty-five years earlier, "The type of farm land near Kingston was very much in my mind when I drafted the ARDA bill."[108] As well, ARDA represented a radical departure from traditional approaches to the problems of rural underdevelopment. In fact, it was "an example of the development of a social philosophy almost diametrically opposed to the ruling philosophy of North American governments forty to fifty years ago."[109] ARDA attempted to break down the historical economic subordination of the hinterland to the metropolis through a strategy which integrated indigenous regional development and balanced regional growth, and which also involved the rural population itself in the planning process. The concept of "self-help" was new to rural planning and, as Hamilton envisaged the process, suggestions for ARDA projects would come not from governments but from the farmers themselves. Eventually both the Vatican and the United Nations adopted the doctrine of self-help as the basis of their plans for rural development in other parts of the world. Thus, despite "all its false-starts, shortcomings and limitations, ARDA . . . made a constructive and promising beginning in a public attempt to come to grips with rural poverty and regional disparities."[110]

Re-election is never far from the mind of a practicing politician and Hamilton never doubted the electoral potential of the New National Policy. He believed the "Vision" had swept the country in 1958. Perhaps a revised and expanded version could do so again. As early as the summer of 1959 he advised Diefenbaker that:

> The Canadian people . . . ask for 'Vision' in their leaders; a sense of national purpose and national destiny. . . As I see it, the great task before the Party in the next election is to evolve the second step in our National Policy and construct a program of action capable of recapturing the imagination of the Canadian people.[111]

Thus, over the next two years Hamilton and his closest advisers, Faibish, Menzies, Johnston, Miller and Kristjanson, with the knowledge and approval of Diefenbaker, sketched the major features of what they called the Second Stage of the National Development Program. By this time they possessed much more expertise than they had had prior to the 1958 election. They had a few years experience of government behind them, they had access to all the information the civil service could provide, they had a greater knowledge of the gaps in the first programme, and they had a much more sophisicated understanding of the possible solutions to both the short and long-term problems facing Canada. They came to be known as the Manotick Group because they met at Hamilton's home in that small town on the Rideau River, just south of Ottawa, and the result of their deliberations in the summer of 1961 was a comprehensive set of policies on which the Progressive Conservative party could fight the next election. The underlying philosophy of activist government remained as it had been.

> The day of passive government is gone. Today we need a partnership of government and private enterprise. . . Government is not just an organization to collect taxes and pay for social welfare services. It is a partnership in which the government on behalf of all the people sets planned objectives and does its part with its resources to direct private enterprise towards those targets.[112]

The Second Stage of their National Development Policy, however, integrated what the government had done already with what it would have to do in the future. If implemented fully, it would include:

1. A National Power Policy — development of a national grid beginning with regional grids
2. A National Oil Policy — tax changes to stimulate exploration, especially by Canadian companies. A second pipeline to Eastern Canada may be necessary before 1970
3. A National Transportation Policy — an integrated policy respecting all competing forms of transport
4. A National Resources Policy — an integrated national program to achieve the most efficient multiple use of our renewable resources
5. A National Agricultural Policy — including ARDA
6. A National Policy for Vocational and Technical Training — such a program can provide the skilled labour Canada will need in the future under a Government dedicated to economic growth and full employment
7. A National Housing Policy — provision of all the social capital required for housing, sewage systems, urban development, and recreation facilities
8. A National Productivity and Trade Policy — the Government must relate increased productivity to increased markets
9. A National Policy for Social Justice — fully portable pensions, unemployment insurance improvements, perhaps a national food allotment program to ensure all Canadians have a reasonable supply of food
10. A National Policy for Full Employment — to ensure that all Canadians have an opportunity for gainful employment
11. A National Development Corporation — to enable the small investor to acquire shares in Canadian companies
12. National Development through Canadian Participation — a Development Corporation would be part of this. In addition, the Government must be prepared

> to help develop Canadian industries and to develop export markets[113]

Hamilton and the Manotick Group wanted to fight an election on this programme in the autumn of 1961 and they appear to have convinced Diefenbaker to do so. However, when the prime minister brought the idea to cabinet it met with great opposition from the Ontario ministers. The government of Leslie Frost had just levied a 3 percent sales tax and they feared that this would hurt the federal party's chances at the polls.[114] Diefenbaker succumbed to this resistance and postponed the election until 18 June 1962. Nevertheless, he turned to the Manotick Group for assistance in drafting the keynote speech with which he would open his campaign in London on 5 May.

As might be expected, Hamilton, Faibish and Menzies prepared a draft based on the work they had done the previous September. National development was its central theme, and it listed both the accomplishments of the first stage and the promises of the second. Diefenbaker did not use the speech as intended that night in London. Instead, he stupefied his audience with an agglomeration of statistics in defence of his government's past record and ignored almost entirely the new policy areas of the second stage. According to Hamilton, the prime minister made the mistake of showing the speech to Donald Fleming and George Hees, the ministers of finance and trade and commerce, as they travelled to London by train that afternoon, and they convinced him that he could not use the second part because it had not yet received the approval of cabinet.[115] As far as Hamilton is concerned, that speech ruined the Conservative party's chance of being returned with a majority, for it not only started the prime minister's campaign in dreadful fashion, it also left the impression that the government had no comprehensive or coherent programme for the future. Furthermore, although the platform published by party's central office listed many of the specific policies of the second stage, it too lacked the allure of the Manotick Group's plan for Canada.

There are many reasons which together explain the government's loss of its majority in 1962, not least being the poor performance of certain sectors of the economy and the run on the dollar during the campaign. Nevertheless, Diefenbaker's refusal to utilize fully the Second Stage of the National Development Program must be included among them and the election results sounded the death knell of the programme. Hamilton and his advisers continued to exchange memoranda on various aspects of development, especially those that might be used profitably for electoral purposes; Hamilton urged the prime minister to create a National Development Fund as "an excellent election ploy";[116] Johnston joined the Diefenbaker campaign in 1963 as a speech writer; and the prime minister did use some of the policies from the second stage in his speeches during that election. However, by this time the tide had turned even further from John Diefenbaker and the Progressive Conservative party and their defeat in 1963 ended the Manotick Group's chances to legislate an integrated programme of national development.

The New National Policy was an attempt on the part of a small group of men to set the country on a new course after what they considered to be twenty-two years of drift under the King and St. Laurent governments. They were motivated by Canadian nationalism, a commitment to social justice, and a conviction that government must create the conditions whereby private enterprise could develop the nation. They believed Canada possessed a treasure house of wealth waiting to be tapped, and they were determined to see these resources used to achieve both economic and social goals. They did not come to power in 1957 with a comprehensive programme of specific policies to be legislated, but one evolved over time as they came to understand better the linkages between and among the multifarious activities of the federal government. They concentrated at first on natural resource development to spur the economy, create employment, and provide additional revenues for the government's social programmes. Later, in the second stage of the programme, they attempted to tie together all aspects of governmental endeavour related to development, added an emphasis on human resources, and focussed on the relationship between productivity, investment, and foreign trade.

Alvin Hamilton, Roy Faibish and Merril Menzies were the principal architects of the New National Policy. Hamilton, of course, was its chief proponent in cabinet.

Hamilton, with the occasional assistance of the prime minister, had some success in winning cabinet approval of his plans for national development, especially in the early years. Most of the promises made in the 1957 and 1958 campaigns which contained the essence of the "Vision" were kept. Roads to Resources were built, construction proceeded on the South Saskatchewan River Dam and a regional power grid in the Atlantic provinces, completion of the geological and hydrographic surveys of the north was hastened, and much was done to tackle the immediate problems of the farm community. Other accomplishments include the Continental Shelf Convention, the Territorial Oil and Gas Regulations, creation of the Department of Forestry in 1960, the Resources for Tomorrow Conference, and the Agricultural Rehabilitation and Development Act. Nevertheless, the record is not untarnished by failure. Neither Hamilton nor anyone in cabinet could convince British Columbia to accept the federal position on development of the Columbia River, and Hamilton could not win his colleagues' approval to create a national energy grid or to establish a national development fund. In fact, cabinet often found it easier to accept the concept of national development in principle than in practice. Likewise, both cabinet and officials in the Department of Finance found it easier to approve development proposals designed to assist specific sections of the population or regions of the country than those which would have given the government a powerful and permanent rôle in directing the economy. It must also be remembered that the comprehensive and integrated Second Stage of the National Development Program did not come before cabinet until late in the government's term when the economy was in difficulty, and many ministers were fearful of the political repercussions of any dramatic departure from traditional economic theory and policy.[117] On balance, however, it can be said that much of short and long-term benefit occurred under the auspices of the New National Policy, although it must also be noted that much of its potential remained unrealized. Economic exigency and political defeat intervened to prevent its legislation in toto, and for the latter half of the government's term of office Alvin Hamilton was no longer minister of northern affairs and national resources but minister of agriculture.

Chapter 5

Minister of Agriculture: The Doctrine of Hope

Hamilton's move to the Department of Agriculture did not evoke the surprise which attended his initial appointment to the cabinet. In many ways agriculture seemed better suited to his background and experience. He had been a member of the Wheat Committee of cabinet since its creation in late August 1957, and he had helped prepare much of the agricultural legislation introduced by the government during its first three years in office. In fact, Hamilton believes that his expertise in agriculture may have convinced Diefenbaker to bring him into the cabinet in the first place. Over and above the prime minister's expectations in the field of resource development,

> Diefenbaker knew when he appointed me that I had been working on this subject [agriculture] for a good many years . . . and he knew that I had worked on agriculture policy at the 1948 convention and again at the 1956 convention. So I knew what I was there for — he wanted me to take over the Wheat Committee of cabinet.[1]

The prime minister had long been a recipient of Hamilton's views on all sorts of issues, including agriculture, he wanted to fulfill his pledges to the farming community as soon as possible, and he had plenty of reasons to believe that the new member for Qu'Appelle could contribute to that end.

In his first *Report from Ottawa* after his initial appointment to the cabinet Hamilton assured his constituents that "this is the most friendly government to agriculture in over twenty years,"[2] and the government's actions over the next few months bear out the truth of his claim. Among the spate of activity in the autumn and winter of 1957-58 four measures were designed specifically to treat the immediate concerns of the agricultural community — the Prairie Grain Advance Payments Act, the Royal Commission on Price Spreads in Food Products, the Royal Commission on the Distribution of Railway Boxcars for Prairie Grain Movement, and the Agricultural Stabilization Act. The first of these provided payments to farmers for harvested grain stored on their farms, and it was meant to give farmers sufficient funds to tide them over until the Wheat Board could reduce the huge surpluses of grain that had built up during the 1950s. Advance payment had been high on the list of the new government's promises, and it was determined to see the concept enshrined in legislation as soon as possible, despite the opposition of some civil servants, including Mitchell Sharp, the deputy minister of trade and commerce. Sharp opposed the idea on the grounds that no way could be devised to ensure that the monies disbursed under the scheme would be returned to the treasury. Hamilton found a way. Existing legislation required all farmers to sell their grain through the Wheat Board and this could not be done unless the farmer had a permit book. The permit book would provide the required collateral and the act, which came into effect on 25 November 1957, made it so. Any payments made under the act would be deducted from the farmers' initial payments for grain sold and, during the government's entire term of office, it did not have to prosecute a single farmer for repayment of a loan.

The battle over the cash advances was important to Hamilton's career as a cabinet minister. He knew it and, in fact, gave his maiden speech in the House of Commons in support of this legislation, rather than on matters related to northern affairs and national resources. It was his baptism of fire and he emerged from the fray with his reputation enhanced. He had proved to his cabinet colleagues that he could get things done, he had demonstrated to his department that its minister was no lightweight, and he had shown the mandarins, that tight-knit group of top-rank bureaucrats who had risen to prominence during the King and St. Laurent years, that its members would not be permitted to obstruct the government in its pursuit of the public interest. Hamilton and the Wheat Committee, which more appropriately could have been called the Cabinet Committee on Agriculture, had much less difficulty in obtaining civil service acquiescence to the Royal Commissions on Price Spreads and the Distribution of Boxcars and the Agricultural Stabilization Act.

The first commission, chaired by Dr. Andrew Stewart, was directed "to enquire into the extent and the causes of the spread between the prices received by the producers of food products of agricultural and fisheries origin and the prices paid by consumers and to determine whether or not such price spreads . . . were fair and reasonable or were excessive."[3] The second, a one-man commission headed by John Bracken, was to investigate the fairness of the system by which the railways allocated their rolling stock to grain collection points. The Agricultural Stabilization Act superseded the old Agricultural Prices Support Act and provided mandatory price support for several agricultural commodities: cattle, hogs, sheep, cheese, butter, eggs, and grains produced outside the jurisdiction of the Wheat Board. It allowed also for other commodities to be added from time to time, and established a revolving fund of $250 million to pay the intended subsidies. The formula on which the subsidies would be based would be established by the government in consultation with the representative farm organizations, and would be announced each year well in advance of production periods so that farmers could plan ahead with some assurance of receiving an adequate return on their investments. According to Hamilton in the House of Commons, "this stabilization bill is necessary to give some peace of mind to a group of people who have always been considered to be the backbone of the country, and who have not had that security over the past few years."[4] With the two royal commissions in motion, the cash advances and the stabilization legislation on the books, and the government's promise to provide crop insurance, easier farm credit, and to consider deficiency payments on wheat, oats and barley, the Conservative party looked forward to a favourable response from the farm community at the 1958 election. Their confidence was justified. Progressive Conservative candidates swept to victory in rural seat after rural seat, not only on the prairies but all across the country.

The election successfully behind them, Hamilton and the Wheat Committee turned their attention to the legislation that would fulfill the remainder of the prime minister's oft-repeated promises to the farm population. The result of their deliberations was a six-point proposal they presented to cabinet in the summer of 1958. It consisted of accelerated sales abroad, a forage bank programme to protect livestock producers, a comprehensive crop insurance scheme in co-operation with the provinces, amendments to various acts to make increased credit available more easily to farmers, a rural development programme to improve the standard of living of small farmers, and a national conservation conference. The programme did not have an easy passage through cabinet. Some ministers opposed specific parts of the package, others objected to the degree of government intervention the proposal entailed, and Diefenbaker, as was his wont, waited on his colleagues to reach a consensus. It did not come and, eventually, Hamilton, exhausted and exasperated after weeks of argument, decided he could do no more. He left Ottawa, took his family on holiday, and waited for Diefenbaker to act. Finally the prime minister intervened, and when he did, he came down on the side of the Wheat Committee in no uncertain terms. According to Hamilton:

> He came through. I wasn't at the cabinet meeting but several of my colleagues told me afterward that it was bloody murder . . . He just took each of those cabinet ministers, pointed his finger at them, went through their records and every mistake they had made, all their wrong conclusions and judgements, and said "Hamilton has

> fought steadily for this programme, got it through the policy meetings in 1948 and 1956, and here they were revising the policy of the party, adding one more great mistake to their record of mistakes." It was an awful business. He took their hides off without anaesthetic, stuck their hides on the wall and threw darts at them. Well, there was no vote — there was complete unanimity.[5]

On 30 August, Diefenbaker rose in the House of Commons to announce his government's National Agricultural Program — a programme based on the Wheat Committee's six proposals and "the belief that the national welfare demands positive action to meet the basic causes of distress and maladjustment in particular industries and regions."[6] The National Agricultural Program provided the rationale for the government's agricultural legislation over the next two years.

In July of 1959, the government introduced the Crop Insurance Act and the Farm Credit Act. The former authorized the federal government to pay 20 percent of the premiums and 50 percent of the administrative costs of crop insurance schemes established by the provinces. The latter extended the existing Farm Loan Act and created the Farm Credit Corporation with responsibility to administer a new system of long-term mortgage credit, which made it easier for young people to begin farming, and for established farmers to expand their operations. In January 1960, Parliament passed the Prairie Grain Loans Act, which provided short-term credit to grain producers who could not harvest their crops, and the Prairie Grain Provisional Payments Act, which authorized the Wheat Board to make payments for the 1959-60 crop year in respect of future deliveries of unthreshed grain.

In addition, from time to time during this period, the government provided other assistance as emergencies arose which threatened the livelihood of the farm community. When drought struck parts of the prairies three years in succession beginning in 1958, cabinet agreed to pay provincial governments half the cost of haying equipment, fodder, and livestock brought in to ease its effects. When the Board of Transport Commissioners granted the railways a 17 percent rise in freight rates in November 1958, the cabinet immediately raised its subsidy on feed grains shipped by rail to absorb most of the increase. In addition, at Hamilton's request and in response to pressure from the farm organizations and Conservative backbenchers, cabinet agreed shortly thereafter to pay the railways a $20 million subvention to reduce their rates on other commodities; in May 1959, cabinet established a royal commission to investigate all aspects of rail transportation in Canada.[7] Finally, cabinet approved acreage payments as part of its short-term strategy to alleviate the plight of farmers whose income had "declined markedly" in recent years.[8]

The farm community welcomed most of these initiatives, but the decision to make acreage payments proved costly to the government in the short run, for the monies distributed came nowhere near to meeting the expectations of the farmers. The farm organizations calculated that farmers' costs had risen by over 50 percent in the ten years since 1947, while the average price for wheat, barley and oats had fallen by 21, 27, and 37 percent respectively during the same period.[9] The agricultural sector of the Canadian economy was just about the only one which had not benefitted from the postwar boom and the western farm organizations wanted government action to set matters right. Their solution was to have the federal government make deficiency payments to the grain growers to bridge the gap which occurred from year to year between the price the farmer received for his produce, and a floor price based on an average of prices received in previous years. Many farmers, caught in an impossible situation, came to regard deficiency payments as the only way out of their difficulties, and they urged the government to introduce them as soon as possible. The following is typical of the letters Hamilton received on the subject during the summer of 1958, when the Wheat Committee was meeting to put together the National Agricultural Program: "Being a small farmer of half a section, I find myself in a cost price squeeze which is gradually worsening. Trying to pay for my land, taxes, machinery, groceries, repairs, etc. is impossible with prices as they stand today."[10] A year and a half later, the refrain was exactly the same:

> As a farmer in your constituency, I would like to draw your attention to my problems which I think are similar to many western farmers. After having worked five years and farmed twenty-five years on the same land since 1929, I find myself in a position worse than I was during the "dirty thirties." I have accumulated 640 acres of land worth $20,000, machinery worth $10,000, buildings another $10,000. I have 10,000 bushels of wheat stored on hand and after taking the advance on my 1959-60 crop and paying my expenses, I find myself left with $88 to live on for a very indefinite period.[11]

Both farmers insisted that deficiency payments were their only salvation, as did hundreds of local farm organizations and municipal councils across the prairies, and they warned that they would not be content until they received them.

The government was caught on the horns of a dilemma with respect to this issue. For years, the Conservative party had promised to institute a price-support system for western grains if elected, and the party platform in the 1958 election had committed the government to "sympathetic consideration to federal deficiency payments on wheat, oats and barley."[12] Furthermore, the government had continued the system of deficiency payments for several other agricultural products instituted by its predecessor. Nevertheless, by the time the Wheat Committee came to consider the place of deficiency payments in the National Agricultural Program, its members had come to the conclusion that they would not be in the best interests of either the western grain producer or the nation as a whole. In their opinion, deficiency payments would help only the larger farmers and would do next to nothing for the smaller farmers, many of whom grew grain solely to feed to their livestock. As the prime minister explained to the House of Commons in defence of this position:

> The government has come to the conclusion that deficiency payments, however attractive they appear to be at first glance, would not provide a solution to the problems facing prairie agriculture but would indeed create new

> problems. Deficiency payments applied to deliveries of grain would fail to help those producers most in need and, if adopted, would require very large subsidies from the treasury, would inevitably lead to increased surpluses and would add further burdens in financing the disposal of those surpluses. Such payments would tend to impede essential adjustments to changing conditions of technology and demand which are essential both to the welfare of the producers and the health of the Canadian economy as a whole.
>
> It is obvious, furthermore, that the greatest benefit from such payments would accrue to the large producer rather than to the small farmer upon whom the situation which has prevailed during the past years presses most heavily.[13]

The long-term problems of western agriculture would be solved by the several actions contemplated in the National Agricultural Program. In the interim, and in recognition of the short-term needs of the farm community, the government would pay each grain grower one dollar per acre up to a maximum of two hundred dollars. This temporary measure was intended to help farmers over the current crisis until the longterm programme took effect.

These acreage payments did not in the least satisfy the vast majority of prairie producers. As one of his constituents summed up prevailing sentiment: "Now, Mr. Hamilton, no sane person can stretch their imagination enough to say that $200 is adequate, or if the PM was sincere that we should be satisfied with it."[14] Farmers wanted more and their leaders were determined that they would get it. In the autumn of 1958 Jack Wesson, president of the Saskatchewan Wheat Pool, began a campaign to convince the government that the people of western Canada would accept nothing less than sizeable deficiency payments. He wanted to present cabinet with a petition signed by every farmer on the prairies and, in a short span of time, obtained the support of all ten of the major western farm organizations for his scheme. Beyond this he also sought the backing of other groups who believed that deficiency payments would be the saviour of the western economy, and he succeeded in organizing a massive demonstration of prairie protest. Over three hundred thousand people signed the petition, almost twice as many individuals as there were farmers with permit books in western Canada, and support came forth from church, women's, labour and business groups all across the prairies. Hamilton admits that he could find only one farmer in his constituency who did not sign.[15] The next step was to present the petition to the government and, for this purpose, Wesson chose a strategy employed by western farmers in 1942 at the urging of a young member of Parliament from Saskatchewan, J.G. Diefenbaker, who had advised them to march on Ottawa to protest low wartime grain prices. Furthermore, Conservative candidates in the 1958 election had exhorted voters to "Follow John" and so in March 1959 they did — a delegation a thousand strong trekked to the capital to argue the merits of deficiency payments with the prime minister and the Wheat Committee, backed by the threat of thousands of disenchanted voters who had signed the petition and had contributed the money to finance the Farmers March on Ottawa.

The Wheat Committee, those members of the cabinet most concerned with agriculture, reacted negatively to the march. Even before the delegation left the prairies, Harkness all but rejected the idea of deficiency payments out of hand, and Hamilton, on the advice of friends in the west, claimed that the march was not a genuine grassroots movement at all, but rather a plot concocted by the CCF and Liberal parties to embarrass the government.[16] Needless to say, this was not the response the delegation and its supporters either wanted or expected to hear, and they were quick to express their disappointment. According to Edward Nelson, president of the Alberta Farmers Union and one of the delegation aboard the train:

> I was a little bit surprised and shocked that Mr. Harkness would turn us down before we even had a chance to present our case to the government. It comes close to being bad manners.[17]

Tommy Douglas, premier of Saskatchewan, condemned Hamilton's remarks as "a gratuitous insult to the farmers of western Canada"[18] and others followed in like vein. The editor of the *St. Walburg* (Saskatchewan) *Enterprise* advised that:

> Mr. Hamilton would do well on this occasion to listen to the grassroots rumble among western farmers. They should be heard. The government owes them that right.
>
> We will be greatly disappointed in the Progressive Conservative Government at Ottawa if they fail to give the coming delegation the hearing they deserve. Mr. Hamilton's recent remarks did neither his party nor the people he represents justice.[19]

The official position of the Saskatchewan Wheat Pool was that:

> Mr. Hamilton should be under no illusion on this point. Up to January 30 more than 151,000 residents of Saskatchewan had signed petitions being circulated in the province and had contributed an average of slightly more than 70 cents apiece to make it possible for a mass delegation to go to Ottawa in support of a new deal for western agriculture.[20]

Even Hamilton's supporters were moved to point out his mistake. As one wrote to him:

> You are quoted as saying this is not a genuine grassroots march. You are quoted as saying the CCF and Liberals are behind this march to Ottawa. I should tell you Alvin that a great many Conservatives are also behind this drive, and I think, Alvin, you should remember it was the agricultural people of this constituency that put you in office, hoping that you would at least give agriculture a fair and reasonable break.[21]

In the face of this outcry the government backed off. The march continued and the meetings between the delegation's leaders and the cabinet took place as scheduled. The government, however, did not retreat from its previous position on deficiency payments. Diefenbaker repeated his belief that such a course would not be in the best interests of either the farmers or the nation, and he asked the delegation to bear with the government until the National Agricultural Program proved its worth. This did not satisfy the marchers, of course, but at least the prime minister did not close the door completely on deficiency payments. He promised that the cabinet would review its position on the matter and, in fact, it grappled with the issue for the next seventeen months, caught between its principles and its instinct for political survival.

Most ministers did not want to introduce deficiency payments, and yet they were fully aware of the possible political consequences if they did not. Individual farmers made this crystal clear:

> The tories were elected on their election promises and they are going to be put out of office for not fulfilling these promises. The next election will see to that. I can sweat it out for another three years. I went through the dirty thirties, this is no better, and your party is doing nothing to alleviate the cost-price squeeze.[22]

In addition, the farm groups maintained their united front in favour of deficiency payments, and they had the support of many of those on whom the Conservative party had built its large majority in the west.

By the spring of 1960, there could be no doubt that support for the government on the prairies had fallen dramatically. Opinion polls showed this and so did reports from party organizers who indicated that many Conservative members were in danger of losing their seats unless cabinet did something soon to retrieve the situation. According to Nick Roth, one of Hamilton's key workers in Qu'Appelle:

> My own opinion is that if the Government can come through with legislation which will make it possible for farmers to make a living off their farms, we won't have any trouble electing Alvin. If conditions remain as they are, however, I'm afraid the party that can make the most appealing promises could be the successful candidate.[23]

Cabinet ministers who visited the region that summer came back to Ottawa convinced that their members in rural areas were in grave jeopardy. After a visit to Saskatchewan in June, Hamilton warned his colleagues that "the hostility against the Diefenbaker administration was such that not one of us would be re-elected."[24] Clearly the government had to take some action or it might lose the west and the next election. The prime minister knew this and had known so for some time. In his opinion, "it would be politically disastrous if nothing were done,"[25] and he concurred completely with the view that "support in rural areas would wane unless some steps were taken to improve the position of agricultural producers."[26] His problem was that neither he, the Wheat Committee, nor anyone else in the party had any solution to propose at the time which was acceptable to both the government and the farmers.

The government had created expectations during the 1958 campaign which it could not fulfill. The farmers simply would not wait for the long-term policies of the National Agricultural Program to take effect. On the other hand, the cabinet would not accept deficiency payments on the grounds that they would not help those farmers most in need of assistance. Furthermore, the minister of finance would not countenance deficiency payments estimated to cost over $300 million at a time when the economy had begun to turn down and every demand on the treasury played havoc with his hopes for a balanced budget. Cabinet considered several other options that summer such as a two-price system for wheat but, in the end, it fell back on the policy it had adopted in 1958. On 2 August 1960, cabinet approved a recommendation from the Wheat Committee that acreage payments worth $41 million be made to Canada's grain producers, and Diefenbaker sent Hamilton out west immediately to sell the decision.

Hamilton made three trips to the prairies late that summer at the prime minister's instruction, speaking day after day to as many audiences as could be arranged, presenting the government's reasons for choosing acreage payments over deficiency payments, and defending the decision. He had some success, particularly among smaller farmers who stood to gain more from acreage payments. Overall, however, the approval he obtained was a grudging acquiescence from people who concluded that half a loaf was better than none at all, a reluctant acceptance of a handout they believed would treat merely the symptoms of their troubles and not the major problems themselves. In short, neither the payments nor Hamilton's defence of them retrieved the government's political fortunes in the west. As one observer at the time summarized the situation, "A general disillusionment with the Diefenbaker government is evident throughout the Western provinces."[27] In these circumstances, the prime minister decided that more drastic steps were needed to bolster the government's position on the prairies, and he sought the advice of the man who had just spent so much time among the farmers of the region. Hamilton advised him to shift Harkness out of agriculture. Despite his high regard for his colleague:

> I said get rid of the minister of agriculture. He was the only person who could make both farmers and city folk mad in the same speech. He was always reading the Riot Act to them. He was against all forms of subsidies to farmers and you don't say that sort of thing to farmers. Then he'd go out and blast city people for trying to get low prices for agricultural goods when they already had the lowest priced food in the world.[28]

Furthermore, "eastern agriculture was in a mess."[29] Hamilton suggested several candidates for the position other than himself, but Diefenbaker accepted only part of his advice. He moved Harkness to national defence, but rejected Hamilton's proposed replacements, and instead chose as his next minister of agriculture his present minister of northern affairs and national resources.

Hamilton did not want the portfolio at first. He was happy where he was and several of his pet projects, such as the Resources for Tomorrow Conference, had not yet reached completion. In his words:

> When I went to the cabinet meeting (the morning of October 11th) and Diefenbaker said he had a few changes to announce and the first change was to name me minister of agriculture, well, I died and went back to my department in a state of shock.[30]

Nevertheless, Hamilton soon realized that he had no real choice in the matter. As he explained to friends and political associates alike once he had come to terms with the move:

> I think you will realize with what mixed feelings I assume my new duties. Not only because Northern Affairs and

> National Resources was my first portfolio am I reluctant to leave it, but also because I have always been vitally interested in the development of Canada. However, the development of any country depends to a great extent on the agricultural industry and I know that I will find my new job a real challenge.[31]
>
> You can say you knew me when I was a busy, happy man opening up a new continent. Now you see a politician fighting for his own and his party's political life. Approximately 100 out of the 265 members of Parliament depend on Agriculture. The odds are heavily loaded against the Minister. However, try I will. If I can persuade the farmers that the facts of life must be faced maybe they will believe and not all follow the demagogues who promise instant relief.[32]

The prime minister made it clear that it was up to him to restore the government's failing popularity in rural Canada, especially in the west, and Hamilton, after some hesitation, took on the challenge with his customary enthusiasm and vigour. The one condition he insisted on before he would accept the new portfolio was that responsibility for the Wheat Board be transferred to agriculture from trade and commerce. If his principal task was to solve the farmers' cash flow problems, then he wanted control over the agency responsible for selling Canada's grain abroad.

Diefenbaker had no objections to this, and within hours of the transfer Hamilton asked the board for a list of countries to which Canada did and did not sell grain. Shortly thereafter, he instructed Canadian diplomats and trade representatives to start alphabetically at the top of both lists and make a sales pitch. Initially, he did not single out China for special attention. In fact, his early hopes were for increased sales to countries bordering the Mediterranean.[33] However, he knew that Beijing had bought wheat from Canada in 1958 and that officials in trade and commerce had asked his predecessor for permission to approach the Chinese again. Therefore, China was a potential customer and, in his words, "I asked the Trade Department to give me their man out of Hong Kong to go in. External Affairs insisted that their man go along so we got those two fellows to go to Peking [Beijing] and raise with the

Chinese if they would consider mixing our wheat with their wheat, which was the argument we used all over the world."[34] The two salesmen reported on their return that:

> There is no question that in the next six months the food situation in China will become acute as a result of the poor harvests experienced in 1959 and 1960. Nor is there any doubt that China could use substantial wheat imports to good advantage.[35]

Nonetheless, although the Chinese had been receptive, they had placed no orders. This state of affairs changed dramatically almost overnight. According to Hamilton:

> Almost before I finished reading the report . . . in late November, I got this telephone call from the clerk at the Queen Elizabeth Hotel in Montréal saying there were two Chinese gentlemen at the desk asking for me. Apparently they had flown on Canadian Pacific Airlines . . . which took them to Montréal. They got to this hotel and asked for me and he had enough sense, bless his heart, to call me directly . . . I said, well, if they are from China it must be in response to the wheat sales pitch. So, I told this chap on the phone to give them the best suite, put it on my account, look after them, and I had those fellows on a plane as fast as I could to Winnipeg where the Wheat Board was because only the Wheat Board could negotiate the deal.[36]

The Chinese had come to buy as much wheat and barley as they could for the amount of money they had available, approximately $60 million. Since the Wheat Board's charter permitted cash sales only, this bought 28 million bushels of wheat and 12 million bushels of barley. The agreement was signed in mid-December, although Hamilton did not announce it to the House of Commons until six weeks later, on 2 February 1961.

The circumstances of this sale intrigued Hamilton, for the Chinese negotiators apparently had shown more interest in the quantity of grain they were buying than its quality. This, together with the reports coming out of Hong Kong, convinced Hamilton that China might be interested in further purchases, and just after Christmas he sent the chief commissioner of the Wheat Board, W.C. McNamara, to Beijing to investigate the possibility. Early in January he received word that China indeed faced an acute food shortage, that she would soon enter the international grain market as a buyer in volume, and that she had begun negotiations with Australia already.[37] The Department of Trade and Commerce recommended that in order to compete with the Australians "the Canadian Wheat Board should be authorized to continue their negotiations on the basis of a gift of a limited quantity of high grade wheat and the sale of a much larger quantity of wheat to China."[38] Hamilton took this proposal to cabinet but was turned down. The Departments of External Affairs and Finance opposed the idea for fear that the Chinese would misconstrue Canada's charity as an insult, that it would disturb existing agreements with the United States and Australia with respect to the disposal of surpluses of grain, and that the government could not justify an outlay of almost $7 million which would benefit only the farm community at a time of high levels of urban and industrial unemployment.[39] Green and Fleming won the day. Cabinet decided that "no gift of wheat be made to Red China, notwithstanding the fact that a gift might make possible a large sale of wheat to China."[40] At the same time, however, cabinet also agreed that "the Minister of Agriculture should discuss further with the Canadian Wheat Board the availability of lower grades of wheat and the possibilities of mixing grades in order to make possible a large sale to China at prices consistent with the prices normally quoted for the various grades."[41]

Although he lost the battle over the gift of grain, cabinet's approval of continued negotiations was all the encouragement Hamilton needed to proceed, for by this time he had no doubts whatsoever of the benefits to be derived from the sale of grain to China. He instructed McNamara to persist in his discussions with the Chinese, and by early March, was able to report to cabinet that the China Resources Company would buy approximately 190 million bushels of wheat and 47 million bushels of barley from Canada over a two-and-a-half-year period "if flexibility in payment arrangements could be negotiated."[42]

These "payment arrangements" proved to be an obstacle on which the deal nearly foundered. The Chinese wanted a large quantity of grain, but had very little cash to pay for it. They needed credit and, if the deal were to be struck, then the Canadian government would not only have to guarantee any bank loans made to the Wheat Board in order to finance the sales, but also agree to let the Chinese make their payments over time. Hamilton had no difficulty with these arrangements, but others in cabinet, especially the minister of finance, did not like them at all. The opposition in cabinet was not ideological. There is no evidence that any minister objected to trade in nonstrategic goods with Communist China. Rather, the major reservations were financial and political. Some ministers doubted that the Chinese could meet their obligations and believed they would default, others disliked the specific terms of the proposed agreement, and still others feared the effect the sale might have on Canada's relations with the United States.[43]

> But the big obstacle turned out to be the city members of cabinet who realized there were ethnic groups in these areas that were pretty worked up all the time about Russia's domination of their home countries and they didn't distinguish between communism in Russia and communism in any other country and they were terrified they would run into very strong opposition.[44]

Hamilton, and those in cabinet who agreed with him, tackled each argument in turn, although not with much success at first. Initially, cabinet instructed the Wheat Board to attempt "to effect sales on a cash basis."[45] The issue came to a head a month later when Hamilton reported to cabinet that "the Mission fully explored the possibility of a sale of grain to China on a cash basis and is fully satisfied that the Chinese are not in a position to conclude an agreement on that basis."[46] He also pointed out that a potential sale of over 230 million bushels of grain might be lost unless cabinet approved the credit arrangement requested by the Chinese.

By this time, opposition in the cabinet had abated somewhat. Reports from the cities indicated that most of the ethnic communities, with the exception of the Chinese Canadians, would not be antagonized by grain sales to China and even Fleming agreed that a large sale of grain would save the treasury the money now being paid as a subsidy to farmers to store their surpluses. Nevertheless, sufficient opposition remained to force Hamilton to play his trump card. He wrote to Diefenbaker threatening to resign from the cabinet and to publicize his reasons for leaving unless his colleagues accepted his recommendations. This spurred the prime minister to intervene in the debate and he did so decisively. In Hamilton's words:

> That ended the discussion very quickly. The prime minister said, "This man is willing to lay his portfolio on the line because he believes this is a sound proposal for Canada. Are you fellows equally prepared to lay your portfolios on the line?" Well, there was no more discussion. I got what I wanted.[47]

Cabinet authorized the minister of agriculture to instruct the chief commissioner of the Wheat Board to conclude an agreement with the China Resources Company on the basis of 25 percent cash and the balance payable in a maximum of nine months. Cabinet also authorized the minister of finance to guarantee bank loans made to the Wheat Board to permit credit sales to China to a maximum of $50 million.[48] This upper limit was raised two months later to $100 million despite Fleming's protests.[49]

Hamilton paid a short visit to Hong Kong at the end of April, and when he returned he informed cabinet that China would purchase $362 million worth of Canadian wheat and barley over the next two and a half years.[50] The Liberals claimed later that this visit was no more than a political ploy to gain publicity for the government since the Chinese had approved the contract several days before he arrived, and it is true that the larger issues had been settled before the trip took place — N.A. Robertson (undersecretary of state for external affairs) informed Green that McNamara had signed a long-term agreement with Chinese authorities in Beijing on 22 April.[51] It is also a fact that not all the Canadian officials involved in the negotiations appreciated the minister's last minute appearance. They feared that Hamilton's presence in

Hong Kong would emphasize the importance the Canadian government placed on the deal and would make future negotiations more difficult. It should not be forgotten, perhaps, that as late as 28 April McNamara cautioned Hamilton that "details have yet to be worked out,"[52] but Hamilton did not go to Hong Kong for the purpose of participating in the negotiations. Rather, because he had put his political career on the line for this agreement and believed he would have to resign if the Chinese did not meet their obligations under its terms, he wanted to find out for himself how China planned to pay for her credit purchases.[53] The Chinese told him that they would be able to pay only if they could sell more of their own products abroad and, on hearing this, Hamilton stuck out his neck even further and promised to help China expand her export markets. That commitment forged a bond between Alvin Hamilton and China which has lasted to this very day.

On 2 May 1961, Hamilton rose in the House of Commons to proclaim the sale to China of approximately 187 million bushels of wheat and 47 million bushels of barley to be delivered by the end of December 1963. This would be over and above the original contract announced in February. The benefits of the sale, as he saw them, were as follows:

> Not only will it provide a welcome increase in western farm incomes, but this in turn will release new purchasing power for the goods and services required by farmers from the business community at large. Additionally, the sale will generate increased employment for country and terminal elevator operators, railway and dock workers, and others engaged in the domestic handling and export movement of grain and flour. It is apparent that new grain sales of this magnitude will add significantly to Canada's total earnings from exports. Business activity in general will therefore be stimulated to a marked extent by the conclusion of this new sales contract with China.[54]

The opposition parties welcomed the sale at the time, although not without the expected reservations, which included fear of an adverse reaction from the United States.

Concern over America's attitude surfaced in cabinet as soon as it became apparent that the Chinese were serious about a large-scale long-term purchase of grain. Diefenbaker and Eisenhower had agreed back in 1957 that their countries would not undercut each other in the fiercely competitive international wheat market, and they had established a Joint Committee on Trade and Economic Matters which met quarterly to exchange information. The arrangement worked to the advantage of both countries. The United States undertook not to interfere with Canadian markets by gifts of grain or sales at cut-rate prices and Canada agreed not to protest American largesse if convinced it would strengthen the NATO alliance and the "Free World." No one in the government of Canada wanted to upset this quid pro quo. As early as January 1961, officials in external affairs warned Green of the possible adverse reaction of the United States and advised that Washington be informed of the impending sale. One argument used to support the proposed sale to China was that it "would not displace an existing U.S. Market,"[55] but at the same time it was recognized that:

> The strongest argument against the proposal was the fact that a communist country was involved . . . Some Ministers said that the extension of credit to Communist China might cause serious concern in the U.S., and might lead to retaliation, e.g. in defence sharing or in the form of a reduction of U.S. investment in Canada.[56]

In these circumstances, the ministers involved took pains to keep their American counterparts informed of the progress of the negotiations. According to Hamilton, "I phoned down to Kennedy's agriculture minister, Orville Freeman, every detail of the negotiations with the Chinese."[57] In addition, in early March cabinet authorized the minister of agriculture:

> to communicate privately to the Secretary of Agriculture of the United States, at the forthcoming meeting of the Joint Committee on Trade and Economic Matters, the fact that consideration was being given by the government of Canada to further sales of grain to China on a cash basis, but that, if cash sales proved impossible, the Canadian

> government was prepared to consider facilitating short-term credit.[58]

The meetings of the joint committee took place on 13 and 14 March 1961, during which time the Canadians also met President Kennedy. Hamilton reminded Kennedy of the deal struck between Diefenbaker and Eisenhower and the new president agreed to honour it. As well, Hamilton tried to convince the Americans that the first step towards a lasting peace with the Chinese was to begin trading with them. In his words, "in that '61 series of meetings . . . I offered the president half the sales of our grain to the Chinese . . . because I could visualize even then there would be lots of markets for both our farmers."[59] The idea attracted Kennedy and, although he did not accept Hamilton's offer, the Americans did not object at that time to Canada's grain sales to China. As Fleming reported on his return to Ottawa, "the Minister of Agriculture and the U.S. Secretary of Agriculture discussed, informally, the proposed sale of grain by Canada to Communist China. No objection or adverse comment had been made by the U.S. Minister."[60] Furthermore, when Kennedy visited Ottawa two months later, the Americans did not even raise the matter.[61]

The first indication that the United States might have changed its opinion with respect to the sales occurred in June when the Treasury Department halted the export of grain unloading pumps (vacuators) to Canada on the grounds that this violated American legislation forbidding trade with enemy nations. The crisis broke on 5 June when the general manager of the Shipping Federation of Canada warned Hamilton that the ships contracted to deliver the grain to China would not sail without the vacuators. External officials immediately lodged a protest with the State Department and the Americans responded favourably to the Canadian appeal. Within forty-eight hours Howard Green, the minister of external affairs, was able to inform Diefenbaker that:

> Mr. White (Deputy Assistant Secretary for European Affairs) is in the process of clearing a policy statement along the lines that the United States Treasury Department is prepared to license exports of these items of

> equipment to ships in Quebec engaged in carrying wheat to mainland China, in those cases where orders have already been received by the supplier company in the United States.[62]

Despite the fact that the statement would "emphasize that this action is being taken as an accommodation to the Government of Canada and is not to be regarded as a precedent," the decision did enable Canada to meet its commitments and also gave the government time to make alternative arrangements to avoid similar difficulties with the Treasury Department in the future. The United States also cautioned in early 1962 that Canadian grain would be used by the Chinese to assist North Vietnamese aggression in South Vietnam, but it never raised the issue to the level of a formal protest.[63] Shipments of grain to China proceeded apace, much to the relief of those who regarded them as the salvation of prairie agriculture.

The sales to China transformed farm opinion in the West. Shortly after their announcement Hamilton and other ministers began to receive letters in the following vein:

> Grain sales to China and other countries behind the iron curtain will be a life saver to Western Canada. You have done a good job selling wheat. Canada will end the year with good exports. Qu'Appelle you will win . . . and you will have helped all Government members in Western Canada to win their seats.[64]
>
> Selling wheat to the Chinese was a step in the right direction, disposing of quite a bit of surplus and at the same time creating a better understanding among the people of Asia.[65]

Even the farm organizations, which had led the protest march on Ottawa in 1959, approved the sales. The National Farmers Union was the first to congratulate the government. In its annual submission to cabinet in February, just after the first sale became public knowledge, it declared:

> We have watched with interest the efforts of the Minister of Agriculture to increase foreign sales of western grains, and have expressed to him our appreciation on the occasion of the recent transaction with China covering 40,000,000 bushels of western grain.[66]

Then, after the announcement of the long-term agreement, the president of the union wrote to inform Hamilton that:

> The farm unions were very pleased with the successful negotiations for the sale of grain to China. The officials of the Canadian Wheat Board and yourself have shown initiative in negotiating this sale. I want to express to you my personal appreciation as a grain farmer and, as well, that of the farm union membership.[67]

And, after Hamilton's stand during the debate in cabinet came to be known, various Wheat Pool associations passed resolutions such as the following:

> Resolved that the delegates . . . wish to express to the Federal Minister of Agriculture, Hon. Alvin Hamilton, our appreciation of his efforts in having the necessary credits made available in order to make it possible to negotiate grain sales with China.[68]

In sum, the grain sales to China brought a much needed influx of money to the economy of western Canada and did much to restore the government's popularity with the prairie electorate.

Just the same, the impression must not be left that everybody welcomed the deal with China. The Cold War had not yet thawed, memories of the Korean conflict remained, and some people would not countenance any trade with a Communist country. Within days of the announcement of the first contract, Hamilton and his cabinet colleagues began to receive letters of protest, such as the following:

> Regarding the forthcoming transaction pertaining to the deal with China for 40,000,000 bushels of grain from Canada. It should be pointed out to you that such a trade transgresses the treaty amongst Christian democratic nations; this treaty was formulated for the specific purpose of countering Communist aggression.[69]

Months later the criticism was just as pointed:

> In the name of reason, responsibility, and the 25 million urban Canadians [*sic*] who must ultimately face the awesome legacy of 800 million Chinese communist imperialists that we are leaving for them, let us have no

> more of such jingoistic junk as "Breaking the Embargo" or "feeding our enemies."[70]

Merril Menzies dismissed such dissent as "rather childish and need scarcely be dignified by serious rebuttal,"[71] but Hamilton did not treat it so lightly. He took pains to reply to each critic and invariably used the counterargument which formed the basis of his belief in seeking peace through international trade:

> We hold to the belief that world peace is only possible when you are talking and trading with potential enemy countries. Naturally, we do not trade in strategic or military goods. We feel that peace will be helped by building up trade and contact between nations.[72]

Nonetheless, he must have taken some comfort from the fact that a mere 5 percent of letters to him opposed the sale, that most of these were from urban Canada east of Manitoba, and that his political contacts in the west were reporting a favourable reception for the sales and his part in them. In fact, he was so impressed with the response he received that he advised Diefenbaker to call an election in the autumn of 1961 to "take advantage of the China sales."[73]

Fleming's fears that the Chinese would renege on their commitments and that the government would be forced to make good the $100 million guarantee of bank loans that financed the long-term agreement, proved unfounded.[74] The Chinese met their obligations and the untarnished success of the arrangement moved Hamilton to promise farmers that he would sell as much grain as they could grow. Such optimism had not been heard on the prairies for a generation, it restored farmers' faith in their future, and Hamilton's audiences were delighted, even though they proved reluctant to follow him everywhere he wanted to go. They welcomed the sales, but were not prepared to share the risks if the Chinese should default.

Fleming continued to fret over the government's guarantee of credit despite China's payments on the dates they were due, and this finally led Hamilton to conclude that the farmers should place a small amount of their profits in a reserve fund to ensure credit sales. After all, farmers were accustomed to setting aside funds for various contingencies, and Canadian businessmen took 15 percent of the risk of any credit extended to foreign purchasers by the Export Credit Insurance Corporation. It seemed a good idea at the time and Hamilton, on his own initiative, suggested the idea to the farm organizations in the autumn of 1962. The farmers, however, wanted nothing whatever to do with the proposal and expressed their feelings directly and pointedly. The National Farmers Union, in its brief to a federal-provincial agricultural conference held in November, stated that "we do not think that farmers or groups of farmers should be expected to set up special funds to help carry possible losses arising out of such credit sales,"[75] and individual farmers were just as blunt in their opposition. According to one of them:

> I'm opposed to the pools financing your political ambitions. You took credit for the sales, you told us to grow all the grain we can and you would sell it. Now you want us to underwrite your sales and sink the earnings of our organization into promotional sales that other companies in the business do not want to take the risk. As far as I'm concerned, Mr. Hamilton, no deal.[76]

The cabinet documents summarize the prime minister's response to his minister's trial balloon as follows:

> (a) that the Minister of Agriculture would prepare a statement for delivery in the House along the lines of the discussion in Cabinet, explaining the Minister's purpose in promoting public discussion of a grain farmers' fund to guarantee sales on credit to foreign purchasers;
>
> (b) that proposed public statements regarding possible future policy matters be first shown to the Prime Minister.[77]

A more colourful, and probably more accurate, description of Diefenbaker's reaction is contained in this account from the *Montreal Star's* Ottawa correspondent:

> It is known that Mr. Diefenbaker summoned the minister of agriculture in a hot fury and berated him violently. Then he informed Mr. Hamilton that he had already

> arranged to have his estimates brought before the House of Commons on Wednesday so that the statements could be debated — in effect so that the Opposition parties could add their chastisement to the one Mr. Diefenbaker had just delivered.[78]

In this instance, perhaps, the road to hell was paved with good intentions.

Hamilton's unbridled enthusiasm also led to warnings from his closest advisers. Faibish, in particular, cautioned his boss against raising expectations he could not meet:

> I want to urge you again not to emphasize to farmers that you will sell all the wheat they can grow in the next two years ... You could be seriously and permanently harmed politically in the future if the breaks on sales don't come your way and grain piles up again.[79]

The caveat proved prophetic when in the autumn of 1962 China marched its troops into territory India regarded as its own and the cabinet, in response to public outcry and pressure from the Indian government, considered stopping the shipments of grain to China from Canadian ports. Most of the correspondence Hamilton received on the subject expressed the following sentiments:

> I suggest you are an opportunistic hypocrite. You are selling wheat for dollars regardless of the ethics involved. You and your government must soon choose whether you are on the side of freedom or of Communism.[80]
>
> Should you continue the wheat shipments in the face of Chinese aggression against India, I will be ashamed to call myself a Canadian, and will do my part to remove you and the whole government from office at the earliest opportunity.[81]

At the same time Canada's high commissioner to India, Chester Ronning, informed Green that "Nehru asked me informally on November 23rd about Canada's wheat sales to China adding that in his opinion, food being such an important factor in China's economy, Canadian wheat was giving strength to China during an aggressive invasion which threatened the very existence of India,"[82] and Green advised his colleagues that India's high commissioner had asked him whether Canada would cancel future grain sales to China in the circumstances.[83]

The debate in Cabinet was protracted and there is some reason to believe that the government came close to bowing to this pressure. As Hamilton wrote to Diefenbaker:

> I am still numbed by our conversation . . . I gather that, because of the India-China situation, the national interest may best be served by slowing down efforts to sell in Communist countries . . . My personal judgment is that, unless open war breaks out, we would lose far more support by weakening our efforts to sell abroad.[84]

Negotiations were then underway for a further sale of grain to the Chinese, and Hamilton feared that not only would Canada lose the contract but also that the government would anger the farm population, the one solid base of Conservative support still intact. Eventually cabinet adopted a compromise position. Canada would meet her obligations under existing contracts and continue the discussions on further sales, but cabinet would not grant permits for the export to China of products other than grains because they might be used to support her "continued aggression against India."[85] In addition, Canada would assist her fellow member of the Commonwealth in other ways. Cabinet agreed in November to give India six Dakota aircraft, and in December reversed its decision to cut Canada's contributions to the Columbo Plan on the grounds that "the suggested assistance to India would be an effective reply to the criticism that the government of Canada was selling wheat to Communist China and reducing its aid to India."[86] By the new year, Hamilton was sufficiently confident to draft the following defence of the government's position:

> We have never refused to sell non-strategic materials such as grain to any country because of its political persuasions. This has also been the case with other Commonwealth countries, including Great Britain, Australia and India itself, all of whom have been trading with China in foodstuffs or other products. It might be noted in this connection that the more of its foreign exchange resources that China is required to use for imported food-

> stuffs, the less is available for manufactured goods which may have a more direct bearing on its military strength.[87]

In the final analysis, and despite their sympathy for India, members of the cabinet did not regard the conflict as sufficient reason to sacrifice either the long-term agreement with China or the prospect of additional sales.

There were some costs, however, that cabinet was not prepared to pay to ensure further sales to China, and this led Hamilton into another lengthy battle with some of his colleagues and their advisers. During 1961, Canadian exports to China totalled $122.8 million — $120.2 million of which were cereal grains, while Canada imported a mere $3.2 million worth of goods from China.[88] The Chinese wanted to reduce this deficit as much as possible and throughout 1962 they pressed the government to grant their products easier access to the Canadian market. The future of the grain sales soon became a bargaining lever and the Chinese used it as best they could. Canada's new trade commissioner in Hong Kong reported in July that:

> From the Chinese side . . . the inference was clear that if the Chinese continue to be thwarted in marketing their textiles in Canada by what they regard as discriminatory and unfair tactics then they would be forced to reconsider the extent of their future wheat purchases in Canada.[89]

Beijing recalled its trade mission to Canada earlier than scheduled because of Ottawa's "intransigence," and in December one of the commissioners of the Wheat Board, in Hong Kong to sign another contract under the long-term agreement, warned Hamilton that:

> It was made abundantly clear, and in fact Mr. Ting, General Manager of the China Resources Company, at the social function held following the signing of the contract, reiterated in unmistakable terms their need for more favourable access to the Canadian market. He bluntly asserted that if we hoped, and it was their wish, to see a long-term development of trade between our two countries, it was essential that China be able to earn part

> of the funds for this by sales of Chinese products to Canada.[90]

The contract signed in December covered the first six months of 1963 only. The Chinese refused to negotiate deliveries for the latter half of the year without some sign that Canada would accommodate them.

Beijing wanted to sell more of her textiles in Canada to reduce the huge disparity in trade between the two countries and asked Ottawa repeatedly to help her do so. She understood that increased sales of textiles alone would not correct the imbalance and, further, that Ottawa could not grant free and open access to the Canadian market, but wanted a change in the tariff which would enable her to compete on more favourable terms with domestic and other foreign suppliers as a gesture of good will. An increase in sales from $1 million to $4 million would have been considered satisfactory.[91] The Chinese position met with some sympathy in Ottawa and Hamilton, as might be expected, led the fight to oblige Beijing. As he explained to Diefenbaker:

> In view of the tremendous importance of the Chinese market for grain in 1963 — and possible continued sales of substantial amounts after 1963 — there is no question in my mind that we have no choice but to allow three or four million dollars' worth of Chinese textiles in each year.
>
> As Westerners, we both understand that to be able to sell 50 million bushels of wheat to these new markets of China and Eastern Europe means that we can probably hold the west politically for years to come.[92]

No argument however, political or economic, could convince the prime minister and cabinet to provide the accommodation the Chinese sought. Canadian textiles companies, fearful then, as now, of increased competition, urged the government to refuse Beijing's request, and officials in trade and commerce and external affairs warned that any favour granted to China might be resented by Canada's other trading partners, Japan and Taiwan, on commercial grounds, and the United States and possibly India on political grounds. They also predicted that China could not afford to go without Canadian grain in light of her shortage of food and advised the government in effect to call Beijing's bluff.[93] Cabinet referred the issue to the Interdepartmental Committee on Low-Cost Imports which recommended nothing more than an extension of the list of goods China could export to Canada, but the government was defeated before even this small concession could be granted.

Thus, the history of the early grain sales to China is not just a series of easy triumphs for Alvin Hamilton and those who regarded them as an enormous benefit to Canada. On balance, however, while he may have lost a few battles along the way, he won the war and the sales did more to enhance his reputation than any other accomplishment of his years in office. Canada's exports of wheat during the 1961-62 crop year were the third highest in her history, and for the same year the Wheat Board made the highest average final payment to farmers in its history. Because of this, Hamilton came to be called the best ever minister of agriculture, cartoonists portrayed him as a modern day Marco Polo, and he acquired a status as high as Diefenbaker in the eyes of the farm community — an elevation which did his relations with the prime minister no good at all.[94] Furthermore, the sales left a political legacy to the Progessive Conservative party on the prairies which is still apparent today. For those who remember, Alvin Hamilton is the man who sold their wheat and revitalized their economy and this to some degree explains the success of the party in the region since that time.

Another accomplishment of his years as minister of agriculture for which Hamilton takes "considerable credit"[95] was the establishment of the World Food Bank. The idea did not originate with Alvin Hamilton. It had been mooted in various international circles since the 1920s, Diefenbaker had proposed it unsuccessfully to the NATO heads of government in 1957, and Harkness had tried with more success to sell it to the United Nations Food and Agriculture Organization (FAO) as early as 1959. Nevertheless, Hamilton played an important rôle in its realization. He had just taken over the agriculture portfolio when the United Nations adopted a joint Canadian-American resolution directing FAO to investigate the possibility of creating a global reserve of money and foodstuffs to be used in emergencies, and to report to the organization's biennial conference scheduled for Rome the following year. Hamilton approved the concept wholeheartedly. He saw it as another means to reduce Canada's huge grain surplus. Furthermore, and of greater importance, he believed that the bank would ensure that gifts of food to nations *in extremis* would be delivered to the people who needed them most. The existing method of bilateral aid was prone to corruption, and he believed the problem could be solved better if the United Nations took charge of the collection and distribution of food and funds as required.

Cabinet appointed Hamilton to lead the Canadian delegation, and he staffed it with care, bringing together a combination of anglophone and francophone politicians and civil servants to ensure that Canada's position was known and understood by all at the conference. His tactics in Rome were simple. "I went over there determined to ram it through and I did it the old fashioned way . . . I treated the exercise as a political campaign — you sell each group in turn."[96] He soon realized that the Vatican held the key to success. If he could obtain the approval of the Papacy he would win support among scores of countries in both Europe and South America. He sought out the Papal delegate immediately and, as luck would have it, found a receptive audience. The Vatican's representative had just completed work on the encyclical which John XXIII issued as Mater et Magistra and shared Hamilton's philosophy of self-help. Once Hamilton explained that the proposed programme consisted of more than mere handouts, that nations would be helped to become self-sufficient, and that the bank would be drawn upon only in emergencies, "he joined the battle immediately. He personally sat down with the heads of the delegations we were having trouble with and warned them of the consequences of going against the Pope's wishes."[97] This intervention, together with the lobbying of the Canadian and American delegations, proved sufficient. The conference approved the World Food Program unanimously. In appreciation of his efforts, Hamilton was given the honour of signing the agreement first and the United Nations accepted his advice on the appointment of the programme's first director, Dr. Boerma of the Netherlands. Today, the programme is one of the United Nation's most successful institutions and Canadians have been chosen to head it the last three times the position has fallen vacant.

The Agricultural Economic Research Council of Canada also warrants mention at this time, not only because of its intrinsic merits but also because the circumstances of its creation shed further light on Hamilton's philosophy of government and his approach to problem-solving in a federal state. Alvin Hamilton came to office convinced that government should act in areas where the private sector faced problems it could not solve by itself. Furthermore, he believed in the utility of cooperation and practiced cooperative federalism even before the term became fashionable in political circles. This was evident throughout the ARDA negotiations, the formation of the Canadian Council of Resource Ministers, and again in this context. George Hutton, Manitoba's minister of agriculture, raised the idea of an agricultural economic research council at the annual meeting of ministers of agriculture in the autumn of 1960. He proposed that a committee composed of representatives of the federal and provincial governments, the farm organizations, and the food industry investigate the idea and report to a special meeting of the four groups the following spring. The committee recommended that a council be established "to strengthen the agricultural industry in Canada by the development of a long-range independent research program in the sciences of agricultural economics and rural sociology."[98] It further recommended that each of the four participants at the conference provide sufficient funds to enable the council to evaluate existing and proposed government agricultural policies, study the effects on agriculture of government policies in other areas, and develop criteria for future agriculture policy.[99] Hamilton accepted the recommendations enthusiastically for they fit perfectly with his views. A problem had been identified and a solution proposed. There was a gap in the research on the difficulties facing Canadian agriculture, one which could not be filled by any of the groups affected. Therefore, the federal and provincial governments should cooperate together and with the interested parties to solve the problem. He obtained cabinet approval to contribute fifty thousand dollars a year for five years, the provinces agreed to contribute a like amount, as did the farm organizations and the food industry, and the council came into being in October of 1962.

The grain sales to China and the Agricultural Rehabilitation and Development Act are the two major initiatives for which Alvin Hamilton, minister of agriculture, is best remembered. The World Food Program and the Agricultural Economic Research Council are two other important accomplishments of his years in that portfolio. Nevertheless, his time in agriculture was by no means spent on those pursuits alone. The Department of Agriculture is one of the oldest ministries in Canada, created at Confederation, and, by the time Hamilton took it over, it had come to be involved with all types of agriculture in the country and all stages of food production, from research into new products to health safety standards at the consuming end. Thus, Hamilton had to oversee a large bureaucracy and administer an enormous array of programmes designed to assist Canadian farmers as well as sell this country's products abroad, develop legislation, and establish new institutions.

The structure of the Department of Agriculture reflected its multifarious activities. As minister, Hamilton bore responsibility for a Research Service, a Production Service, a Marketing Service and an Information Service; the Farm Credit Corporation; the Agricultural Stabilization Board; the Prairie Farm Rehabilitation Administration (PFRA); the Prairie Farm Assistance Administration; and the Maritime Marshland Reclamation Administration; as well as the Canadian Wheat Board and the Board of Grain Commissioners. Responsibility for ARDA, of course, was added during his term of office. Most of the department's programmes had been in existence for some time and Hamilton's task was simply to ensure that they were carried through efficiently and effectively. Much of this he left to his deputy minister. Hamilton's rare involvement in this context consisted primarily of bringing to cabinet for its approval requests for stabilization payments for new products and revised figures for support prices authorized in past years.

As well, he would sometimes be consulted in cases of out of the ordinary projects submitted to ARDA or the PFRA.

Hamilton's greatest involvement in the ongoing affairs of his department occurred when disaster struck some sector or other of the agricultural community. In these crisis situations he would have to seek cabinet acceptance of his plans for relief because almost always they involved the expenditure of funds not included in his budget estimates. As the cabinet record indicates, hardly a season went by without a cry for help. In June 1961, because of drought in the west cabinet approved Hamilton's recommendation that the federal government pay half the cost of transportation of fodder, cattle to feed, and transport of haying equipment to the three prairie provinces. At the same time, it also authorized aid to potato growers in Prince Edward Island because of an outbreak of fusarium rot.[100] In March 1962, cabinet agreed to pay half the transportation costs of seed oats to Saskatchewan and Manitoba because of crop failures in those provinces.[101] In April of the same year, cabinet authorized "as an emergency measure" freight rate assistance on shipments of corn to the Atlantic provinces.[102] In February 1963, cabinet accepted Hamilton's recommendation that the government of Nova Scotia be reimbursed for hay brought in to tide over its livestock producers during a harsh winter,[103] and later that month the government of Prince Edward Island for half the amount paid to its farmers for the loss of their crops the previous season.[104] In addition, in early 1962, cabinet agreed to make another acreage payment, and for the same reasons it had done so on the previous two occasions. As Hamilton explained to Neil Crawford, Diefenbaker's executive assistant:

> The reason why decisions on acreage payments are made annually is because the government believes it has no right to ask the Canadian taxpayer to give transfer payments to any section of the country if that particular section has good returns . . .
>
> Insofar as the fairness of the acreage payments is concerned, the government of Canada does not argue that it is a perfect system. It does give greater benefit to the smaller farmers who are most desperately in need. It

> is much superior to the deficiency payment system since deficiency payments would be paid on the bushel basis and the money would go to those with the most bushels.[105]

The breadth of his department's interests also involved Hamilton in various and sundry other matters domestic and international during his two and half years as minister of agriculture. On the domestic side, the numerous problems of grain transportation were perhaps his most prominent concern. In order to handle the increased volume of exports the railway system had to function efficiently, and Hamilton had to intervene on several occasions to end strikes, keep rates down, prevent rail line abandonment, and to ensure a fair allocation of boxcars. As well, he took up the challenge presented by Reynold Rapp's private member's bill and obtained the approval of cabinet to classify rapeseed as a grain entitled to the benefit of the Crownest Pass rates.[106] And, in the autumn of 1962, at the height of the public's concern over the effects of above-ground nuclear testing, he moved to reassure Canadians that "the nation's milk supply is quite safe . . . despite a certain impression that danger exists from fall-out material, the levels of strontium 90 and iodine 131 are still substantially below those for which remedial action would be considered necessary."[107] In the international sphere, Hamilton had to deal with the impact on Canadian agriculture of Britain's proposed entry into the European Common Market, the General Agreement on Tariffs and Trade (GATT) negotiations which affected Canadian products, the nature and extent of Canada's food aid to the West Indies and the Colombo Plan, and innumerable requests for tariff increases or import controls on agricultural commodities ranging from lamb to filbert nuts. Finally, he spent a good deal of time on the negotiations which led to a new International Wheat Agreement to cover the period 1962 through 1965. The agreement, which Hamilton recommended to cabinet on 10 April 1962, raised the minimum and maximum prices per bushel for the lowest and highest grades from $1.50 to $1.625 and $1.90 to $2.025 American respectively.

In addition, Hamilton devoted a good deal of time and attention to his rôle as a partisan politician. First and foremost, he wanted to create a good impression as minister of agriculture, and he kept a close eye on how the public viewed his performance. To this end, he sought opinions from all over as to improvements which could be made to his department's programmes, and accepted a surprising number of requests for meetings from representatives of the farm organizations and others interested in various aspects of Canadian agriculture. In addition, he established an elaborate feedback system to provide him with information on the public's perception of himself and the department. As Faibish informed the director of Agriculture's Information Division, "The Minister places the highest priority on clippings dealing with policy, criticisms and comments by the public, farm organizations and various political organizations."[108] Secondly, he took pains to ensure that the public knew what was happening in his department. He fed releases to the press continually through the Information Division and prepared briefing paper after briefing paper for use by the prime minister and Conservative members. Finally, he sought to keep in close touch with the farm organizations, provincial and local. He served as honorary president of several agricultural societies. He welcomed their submissions to the government and promised to give careful consideration to their resolutions, even though he may not have agreed with their content. He spoke at their annual conventions to advance his own ideas on how the lot of Canadian farmers could be improved, even though his thoughts were not always well received. On occasion, when they did agree with him, he even used the farm organizations to silence his critics in the House of Commons. Over time, and despite their differences, Hamilton and the farm organizations developed a symbiotic relationship. The farmers came to see him as someone sympathetic to their situation and their concerns and he came to count on them as a forum for his proposals and a source of political support.

All of these activities as minister of agriculture, plus his other responsibilities as a member of cabinet, took time and

Hamilton could not have carried them out alone. In agriculture, as in northern affairs and national resources, he could turn to the department's permanent civil servants for assistance and advice or to his personal staff. Hamilton used both, albeit for different purposes as circumstances and his own experience dictated. Although he distrusted the mandarins as a group, he got on reasonably well with individual civil servants and pays tribute to both Gordon Robertson and C.S. Barry, his deputy ministers in northern affairs and agriculture, for their help in administering the departments. After his years in northern affairs, he came to agriculture determined to separate the policy-making from the administrative aspects of his duties, and to devote himself to the former as far as possible. He informed Barry at their first meeting that the deputy minister would bear responsibility for the effective implementation of all the legislation on the books, and Barry confirms that Hamilton "left the running of the department to him."[109] This does not mean that the twain never met. Hamilton did meet regularly with his deputy minister and at least one permanent civil servant attended all the "brain-storming" sessions Hamilton held with his personal staff. The arrangement did mean, however, that with Barry taking care of the day-to-day administration of the department, Hamilton was free to concentrate on the grain sales to China, the ARDA agreements, the Second Stage of the National Development Program and the government's political difficulties after the 1962 election.

For policy-making, Hamilton came to rely more heavily on the personal staff he had recruited, especially Roy Faibish, to supplement the advice he received from his permanent civil servants. Faibish not only provided useful advice, he also ran his minister's office, and acted as Hamilton's eyes and ears within the federal bureaucracy. He built up an enormous circle of contacts across the civil service, and was able to warn his minister of potential pitfalls in the path of his legislative proposals and possible treachery within his department. On one occasion, for example, he alerted Hamilton to opposition in both finance and the Privy Council Office to his forthcoming recommendation that cabinet establish a National

Development Corporation.[110] On another, he advised Hamilton that a high ranking civil servant in agriculture had held back a much needed piece of legislation the minister had fought through cabinet because of pressure from officials in the Treasury Board.[111] As one might expect, the permanent civil servants, especially those near the top, were not enamoured of Hamilton's reliance on the group of personal advisers he had gathered about him. Barry confesses that he did not like Faibish because he was "pushy, built up his own network, and did not follow channels,"[112] and even Robertson, ever the diplomat, admits that his relations with Faibish were "always a little strained because of Faibish's suspicions of the civil service."[113] Nevertheless, this uneasy alliance served Hamilton well and helped make him one of the most influential ministers in Ottawa.

The manifold burdens of office and a succession of sixteen-hour days finally took their toll on Hamilton's health. In mid-January 1962, while attending the funeral of a former minister of agriculture, J.G. Gardiner, he fell victim to a Saskatchewan chill which so weakened him that within days he had to be hospitalized for shingles, erysipelas and Bell's palsy. He spent six weeks in hospital, at home, and in Jamaica recovering and did not return to the House of Commons until the end of March. Thus, he was in no condition to play his usual rôle in the 1962 election campaign. He had to limit his activities and confine himself to one speech a day to avoid exhaustion and to reduce the pain caused by the metal plate he had to wear in his mouth to keep his face taut and his words intelligible. He had to delay his own nomination meeting by two weeks, and spent a good part of the campaign in Ottawa as acting prime minister while Diefenbaker and the rest of his cabinet colleagues toured the country canvassing for votes.

Despite the illness, however, Hamilton entered the campaign with high hopes. He believed the Second Stage of the National Development Program offered Canadians an attractive blueprint for the future and he knew that his work as minister of agriculture had won the approval of the farm population, at least on the prairies. He had impressed the agricultural community with his sympathy for their condition and his actions on their behalf, and at no time was this more evident than when he took sick. He received hundreds of letters wishing him well from friends, constituents and political opponents; even the press, not known for its affection for the Diefenbaker government at the time, joined in the tribute.

Hamilton, when he did enter the fray, did so with his usual enthusiasm and occasional hyperbole. In a press release at the end of April:

> He called on prairie farmers to grow every bushel of grain they can, consistent with sound agricultural practices . . . Employ every proven technique to conserve moisture and increase your production with complete confidence that there will be hungry markets, good prices and more space available for your grain in country elevators than at any time in the past ten years.[114]

He also provided Diefenbaker the ammunition with which to carry the fight in the rural constituencies. In a memorandum to the prime minister in mid-April he reminded his leader that: the average final payment to wheat growers for the 1960-61 crop was the largest in the history of the Wheat Board; for the first time in a decade grain delivery quotas were lifted; the latest contract with China boosted sales of grain to that country to over 130 million bushels; the government made acreage payments in 1958, 1960 and 1962; federal assistance had been forthcoming to overcome the drought in 1961; expenditures under the PFRA and Prairie Farm Administration Act had risen sharply in recent years; a World Food Program was imminent; rapeseed shipments were now eligible to move at the same rates as other grains; the government spent substantial sums of money to stabilize the prices to producers of several farm commodities and provided assistance to the provinces in the operation of crop insurance programmes; the Agricultural Stabilization Board had been authorized to purchase butter at sixty-four cents and re-sell it at fifty-two cents a pound; and the government had passed the Prairie Grain Advance Payments Act and the Agricultural Rehabilitation and Development Act.[115] These achievements provided the basis of Hamilton's campaign in Qu'Appelle and most Conservative candidates on the prairies. Furthermore, Hamilton did speak in selected constituencies during the campaign, assisted by a recent addition to his staff, Brian Mulroney; he chaired the campaign committee in Saskatchewan; and directed the fight to unseat Hazen Argue, former House Leader of the New Democratic Party (NDP), who had left the new party to join the Liberals and who had been a persistent thorn in the government's side for several years.

The results of the election did not bear out Hamilton's optimism. The failure to defeat Argue in Assiniboia was galling, but not nearly as devastating as the results nationwide. Although the Conservatives lost only five seats on the prairies and the party's vote remained respectable in rural areas all across the country except Québec, the government lost ninety-two constituencies, enough to reduce it to 116 seats and minority status in the House of Commons. Urban Canada swung dramatically to the Liberals and the NDP, and much of rural Québec abandoned both the Conservatives and the Liberals for Réal Caouette and les Créditistes.

The results meant that the government could stay in office, but only as long as it obtained the support of either the nineteen New Democrats or the thirty Social Credit members in the House of Commons. Philosophical and policy differences made the NDP less than reliable collaborators, so the government turned its attention to Social Credit, twenty-six of whom came from Québec. The prime minister and his colleagues were not unaware of the transformation which had begun to sweep Québec under Lesage, Lévesque and the Quiet Revolution. As early as November 1960, Diefenbaker had impressed upon his ministers the need for more French Canadian deputy ministers in the public service,[116] and a year later, at a cabinet meeting held appropriately in Québec City, he noted that:

> It seemed strange to him that in Canada, a bilingual country in which bilingualism was officially recognized in Parliament, in the Province of Quebec and in the High Courts, it had never been practised in the Cabinet. He suggested that Ministers should consider whether bilin-

> gualism should be made applicable within the Cabinet, so that any Minister might speak or present memoranda in his own tongue.[117]

Diefenbaker promised that such matters would be discussed further at a later date, but Québec's aspirations did not rank high on his list of priorities and the issue did not appear again on the cabinet agenda until after the 1962 election. All of a sudden, with the fate of the government in the hands of the Créditistes, steps had to be taken to raise the profile of French Canadians in Ottawa. In agriculture, Hamilton appointed L-J. Pigeon to be his parliamentary secretary, the first Québecker to hold the position, and Pigeon began a weekly column in Québec newspapers in the autumn of 1962; he promoted French Canadians to senior positions in ARDA; he created a new position of associate deputy minister and elevated S.C. Chagnon, one of his assistant deputy ministers, to fill it; and he informed Barry that from that time forward "I shall be indicating to officers of this Department that they are to feel free to correspond with me, or my staff, in French if they so desire. I wish to make quite clear that the use of French in the Department is to be encouraged."[118]

Social Credit support could solve the government's political problems in the short-term, but any long-term solution had to aim at winning back the rural and urban voters of central and eastern Canada before the next election, which would likely come sooner rather than later. Don Johnston believed this beyond any shadow of a doubt. In his words, in a letter to Hamilton just after the 1962 election, "From our own point of view . . . the way back is a continued concentration on the farm program initially, and a new urban program."[119] The government's major problem in the rural areas east of Manitoba was that none of its programmes had improved the situation of these farmers in as dramatic a fashion as the grain sales had for prairie farmers. Despite stabilization payments, many farmers in Ontario, Québec and the Atlantic region continued to eke out a subsistence living and several sectors of their economy, such as the dairy industry, suffered from overproduction and lack of markets. In fact, in the case of butter and milk production for example, the government's subsidies probably aggravated the problem by keeping marginal farmers in the business.

Warnings of the discontent among this part of the farm community began to be heard even before the 1962 election. The editor of the *Family Herald*, for example, advised Hamilton, "I've become concerned about traces I've hit among eastern farmers that western ones are getting the best of the deal from the government and that westerners are shaking the easterners down."[120] In response, and at the prime minister's order, Hamilton began to "speak at once on the subject of what has been done for agriculture and in particular eastern agriculture, to show that no less attention has been given them than in the West."[121] After the election results confirmed the disenchantment with the government in the east, Hamilton took additional steps to try to retrieve the situation. He spoke as often as possible in Ontario, Québec and the Maritimes pointing out that "I am Minister of Agriculture for Canada. I am not Minister for any one Province. I must look at the needs of farmers all across Canada."[122] He reminded his audiences of all the programmes in place to aid eastern farmers and he drew their attention to the new initiatives underway to solve their problems. ARDA was one of these. So were his attempts to help farmers develop new products and find markets for them. In one speech he pointed with pride to the fact that with government help the tobacco industry in Québec had now produced a "good" five-cent cigar,[123] which must also have come as a relief to those who had to endure the "rope" that he smoked incessantly. In addition, he began to compile a list of new programmes for eastern agriculture which he submitted to Diefenbaker early in 1963. Its seventeen pages were devoted to "trying to give the same opportunities to Eastern farmers as the Government has been able to give to the Prairie farmers," and the programme was based on four principles: stability in supply; equalization of price at a larger number of distribution points; opportunity for eastern producers of feed grains to expand with the growing demand in eastern Canada; and price stabilization for a year at a time.[124] He established a Feed Grain Committee to keep the Wheat Board informed as to grain requirements in eastern

Canada. In addition, he obtained cabinet approval for an Eastern Livestock Feed Board and a programme of Feed Assistance for Eastern Livestock, but he could not see these measures through the House of Commons before the government fell and had to face the electorate for the second time in less than a year.

Hamilton entered the 1963 campaign in better health than he had in 1962, and the rôle he played in this election reflected his rejuvenation. First, he helped prepare the party's platform. Shortly after the governor-general dissolved Parliament, Hamilton promised Diefenbaker that he would prepare a set of position papers on varied topics such as devaluation, national development, the problems of suburbia, agriculture and fisheries and that he would deliver them to Dalton Camp, the new national director of the party, within a week.[125] It may seem strange that the minister of agriculture would develop policy for urban Canada, but Hamilton had become well acquainted with the subject while working on the Second Stage of the National Development Program, and had prepared at the prime minister's request a fifteen-page memorandum on the housing, education, economic, transportation, waste disposal and recreation problems of Canada's cities and towns just three weeks before the government's defeat.[126] This memorandum was among the material Hamilton sent Camp and its recommendations proved to be a major part of the Conservative party's appeal for re-election. Second, Hamilton helped staff the prime minister's campaign team. Merril Menzies could not accompany Diefenbaker as he had at previous elections, and Roy Faibish had just undergone an operation and needed time to recover. Hamilton, therefore, turned to Don Johnston and arranged a leave of absence from TransCanada PipeLines for his trusted friend and adviser. He urged Diefenbaker to take advantage of Johnston's availability because "Don is the best writer we have and knows how your mind works better than any of us. He is a good idea man and comes closest to you in your distinctive ability for tactics and strategy."[127] The prime minister did take up the offer and Johnston provided invaluable assistance in Diefenbaker's fight to stave off defeat. Third, Hamilton undertook a national tour on behalf of the party, one of only four cabinet ministers chosen for the task. He concentrated on rural constituencies, as requested, and repeated time and again one central theme — Canadian agriculture needed a Conservative government in office. "The fundamental purpose of the National Agricultural Program is to try to give to farmers a fairer share of the national income"; "A Progressive Conservative government will do for Eastern farmers what it has done for the West"; "In 1956 while Canada was prospering, farm income was declining in relation to other segments of the economy. The Government of John Diefenbaker has not only checked that decline, but has started it moving up again."[128] Finally, Hamilton directed the party's campaign in the province of Saskatchewan. He aimed at holding the sixteen seats already in Conservative hands and winning Assiniboia, the one which had eluded his grasp in 1962. He reminded Saskatchewan farmers that they had been well served by the Diefenbaker government and also warned them of the possible consequences if the government were to be defeated. If the government lost the election, then prairie farmers would lose a good friend in Ottawa and eastern business interests would once again dominate national politics.

Hamilton's rôle in the campaign did not go unrewarded. His popular vote in Qu'Appelle went over 60 percent for the first time, Hazen Argue went down to defeat in Assiniboia, and the party suffered a net loss of only one seat on the prairies. This was not enough to save the government however. Despite the party's new urban policy, the cities went overwhelmingly to the Liberals and the NDP and this, together with the loss of a few rural seats in eastern Canada, spelled the defeat of the government. The Conservatives held on to only 95 seats while the Liberal total rose to 129, not enough to form a majority government, but more than sufficient to convince Diefenbaker that he had no choice but to resign. Governor-General Vanier called upon Lester Pearson to replace John Diefenbaker and the reins of power changed hands on 22 April 1963. Thus, for the first time in almost six years, Alvin

Hamilton found himself out of office and unable to put his ideas into action. While his career in national politics was by no means over, he would never hold office again.

In retrospect, it can be said that Alvin Hamilton did not want to leave northern affairs and national resources for agriculture and many people did not want him to go. He had impressed them with his knowledge of and concern for the north and they wanted him to remain their spokesman in the cabinet. The commissioner of the Yukon territory was one of these, and he wrote to Hamilton just after the shuffle:

> It is with mixed feelings that I tender congratulations on your appointment to a senior Ministry for I feel that the North has lost one of its most sincere and devoted supporters and so many of us in Northern Affairs a true and tried friend.[129]

Even months later others continued to express the same sentiments:

> I think I can understand why the PM wished to have you at the Department of Agriculture, but I don't mind admitting that it was a disappointment to me. For forty years I have been writing and talking about the North, its possibilities and the necessity for recognition by the Canadian people of the importance of northern development. Then, suddenly, you come on the scene and it begins to look as though the North might at long last get a break, but what happens? Almost as suddenly, you get shifted to agriculture.[130]

Nevertheless, Hamilton had no real choice but to move and once in agriculture he set about his tasks without remorse. He did not lose his interest in either the north or in resource development, but had to focus his attention on the manifold problems of Canadian agriculture.

Diefenbaker chose Alvin Hamilton to bring relief to the farm population, especially on the prairies, and to restore the Conservative party's fortunes among the rural electorate, and Hamilton succeeded for the most part in accomplishing both objectives. The massive grain sales to China, which followed quickly on his appointment to agriculture, and increased exports to other countries made his task on the prairies relatively easy. The sales brought a much needed influx of cash to the area and Hamilton received credit for the new prosperity. And, as his personal popularity rose in the west, so did that of the Progressive Conservative party.

He could not duplicate his success on the prairies everywhere across Canada, however. The problems of agriculture in British Columbia, Ontario, Québec and the Atlantic provinces differed substantially from those which faced the grain farmers of the west and could not be solved so readily. For example, he could not get rid of the stockpiles of butter and dairy products as simply as he reduced the surpluses of wheat and barley. Nor could he come up with a quick and easy solution to the plight of the marginal farmers in these areas. These problems required long-term solutions and, while he took steps in that direction, he had to leave office before plans such as ARDA came to fruition. Nevertheless, he received good marks for his attempts from coast to coast. After a speech to the Prince Edward Island Federation of Agriculture, one of the Conservatives in the audience wrote Grosart to inform him that:

> He did an outstanding job, not only in the press conference, but in his remarks to the assembled farmers and in his off the cuff replies to questions from the floor. He showed a firm grasp of the problem facing the industry and what is more important from a PR standpoint he displayed a sympathetic interest in farmers and farm problems without in any sense being condescending, and at the same time he did not give the impression that present policy is a "cure all and end all" program . . . I want you to bear in mind the Farm Federation here is largely Grit controlled and there was no ready made welcome mat out for . . . a Tory minister. But he did a first class job and made friends for the party.[131]

And, after a similar performance before the British Columbia Fruit Growers Association, the editor of the *Penticton Herald* commented that:

> Of the many highlights at the BCFGA convention the most impressive was the speech by the Minister of

> Agriculture the Hon. Alvin Hamilton. Lesser politicians would do well to follow his example.
>
> It was not just that Mr. Hamilton was a fine speaker. Indeed, to critical men like fruit growers, eloquence can be singularly unimpressive. Rather was it the tremendous background knowledge Mr. Hamilton possessed of the problem confronting the Okanagan grower . . .
>
> Fruit growers are not easily moved or swayed. . . It is significant, therefore, that when Mr. Hamilton concluded his speech and rose to leave the platform, every grower, as though pulled by invisible strings, rose from his seat in silent but standing tribute.[132]

Unfortunately for the Conservative party, tributes such as these did not translate into votes and seats as easily as on the prairies.

Alvin Hamilton could not and did not solve all the many problems of Canadian agriculture at the time and his relations with the farm population were occasionally very rocky. Yet, during his two and a half years as minister of agriculture, he acquired a glowing reputation in the farm community. Part of this stems from his successes in the portfolio — the grain sales, ARDA and the like. Another reason lies in his obvious sympathy for the farmers' condition. According to one of his cabinet colleagues, George Hees, "Alvin became popular with the farmers because he would lie down and cry with them."[133] Hamilton believes his popularity at the time to be a by-product of his "preaching the doctrine of hope" and notes with some insight that the exports to China, the ARDA projects and many of his other initiatives as minister of agriculture brought a renewed sense of confidence to the farm population.[134] All this makes sense, but neither singly nor together does it provide a satisfactory answer to the question: why did Alvin Hamilton come to be called "the best minister of agriculture in Canadian history?" Perhaps the answer lies in the following. Another colleague and friend, Gordon Churchill, states simply that "He understood farmers."[135] And, as Richard Hatfield reported to Faibish after a speech in New Brunswick, "Talking with some of the farmers after the meeting, I would judge that their reaction was one of superlative enthusiasm. As one farmer said to me in amazement, 'You know he really does know something about farming'."[136] Alvin Hamilton most certainly did understand farmers. He spent his formative years on a farm in Saskatchewan and he built on this firsthand experience while leader of the Progressive Conservative party in the province. He learned their problems, their hopes and expectations, their frustrations and anxieties, and he learned that farmers are much alike no matter where they live or what they produce. Alvin Hamilton understood that farmers prefer to solve their problems themselves but require government help in some circumstances. Thus, as minister of agriculture he tried to help farmers to help themselves and when they met obstacles beyond their capacity to overcome he had no qualms about bringing the resources of the government to their aid. This was his philosophy and this, together with the other reasons, explains his popularity as minister of agriculture.

Alvin Hamilton as minister of agriculture left legacies to both his party and his country. In the case of the Progressive Conservative party he left a pool of support on the prairies which has remained often tapped but never drained to this very day. He once confided to his former leader, George Drew, that:

> I have always had a personal dream that some day the Prairies would be the rock-ribbed Conservative area of Canada. I felt that by the very nature of their operations, the farmers eventually would move into a traditional conservative position. This is not quite true, yet, but as more and more of the farmers get their feet under them in a permanent type of economic operation, I think this day is coming more rapidly than one could have hoped for ten years ago.[137]

The unbroken skein of Progressive Conservative majorities in the three prairie provinces at every election since 1962 attests to the fact that his dream has become a reality. In the case of Canada, he opened a window to China at a time when most of China's windows were not only closed but shuttered as well. Furthermore, that window has remained open. Today,

Canada continues to sell grain to China and Canadian businessmen travel there in a steady stream searching for markets for new products. There are many reasons why Alvin Hamilton can consider his political career a success, but by any standard these two must rank high among them.

Chapter 6
Leadership Lost

The loss of power in April 1963 angered many Conservatives. They had enjoyed the spoils of victory for less than six years after twenty-two years of frustration and they did not relish the prospect of another lengthy spell in opposition. They sought a scapegoat for their misfortune and found an obvious target in their leader, John Diefenbaker. Diefenbaker personified the Progressive Conservative party for most Canadians, especially those in his own party. Diefenbaker had saved the party from seeming eternal opposition in 1957. Diefenbaker had led the party to the largest electoral victory in Canadian history in 1958. Diefenbaker had come to dominate the public's perception of his government as no prime minister since Laurier. In the elections of 1962 and 1963, however, Diefenbaker had not lived up to the expectations he had created in many Conservatives. Diefenbaker had lost the confidence of the Canadian people and had frittered away his huge majority through apparent inaction and indecision. Diefenbaker had taken credit for all the achievements of his government. Now he had to bear responsibility for its defeat. By accident or design John Diefenbaker had focussed his party's attention on himself. Now he would reap the whirlwind. Covert attacks on his leadership began immediately after the near defeat in 1962. They intensified after the loss of power in 1963, and grew openly and in strength over the next four years, until eventually they brought him down. Diefenbaker fought his adversaries every inch of the way and the struggle involved everyone who had an interest in the future of the Progressive Conservative party. The party split into two camps — pro-Diefenbaker and anti-Diefenbaker — and it is in the character and personality of the man and his style of political leadership that one finds the causes of both the loyalty and the hatred that he evoked.

The myth his admirers would like to perpetuate is that of a man of destiny, a colossus who bestrode his party, the House of Commons and his cabinets, a man with a mission who would let nothing stand in the way of its completion. They point to the Bill of Rights, his stand on South Africa, the legislation to assist farmers and the nation's underprivileged, and his determination to develop Canada's north, among other accomplishments of his years as prime minister, as evidence of his vision and decisive leadership.[1] Those not enamoured of the man paint quite a different picture. They point to the nuclear arms issue, the failure to reduce unemployment during his term of office, and his penchant for royal commissions, among other shortcomings, as evidence of his lack of purpose.

As is almost always the case, the truth lies somewhere between the two extremes. The Diefenbaker government did pass much necessary and valuable legislation, especially during its first years in office, and the prime minister often played a decisive rôle in determining what the policies of his government would be. Examples of this include the debates in cabinet over the National Agriculture Program and the grain sales to China. In the instance of the former, when it looked as if the programme would be lost and Diefenbaker's pledge to the farmers that they would receive their "fair share" of the national income would not be honoured, the prime minister intervened decisively. In the case of the latter, when it seemed as if the cabinet might refuse to guarantee the credit sales of grain to China, Diefenbaker again forced the issue his way. In addition, the record of cabinet conclusions contains statements such as the following: "The Prime Minister said he was not prepared to sign an order for the extension of General McNaughton as Chairman (of the International Joint Commission) beyond his 75th birthday."[2] Diefenbaker gave no reason for his decision and the record reports no discussion of the matter. From these and other available examples there appears to be little reason to doubt that as prime minister John Diefenbaker could provide leadership when he believed it was required.

On the other hand, there is a great deal of evidence to indicate that Diefenbaker did not have firm opinions on everything he wanted his government to do, and that he was prepared to accept the guidance of his colleagues on many matters. The documents for the period show items of all sorts recurring on the cabinet agenda month after month, referrals of most important issues to standing or special committees of cabinet, and deferrals of many decisions until after further deliberation. The record also indicates that the prime minister seldom tried to impose his views on cabinet and that decisions on most matters of import were made by the entire cabinet, almost always after study by and recommendation from a committee or subcommittee of cabinet. The process should have worked better than it did. The use of small committees to investigate issues and report back to cabinet should have provided the information and direction required to make decisions quickly and efficiently. However, as witnessed by the long delays over the AVRO Arrow, the Bomarc, acreage payments to farmers and many other important questions, this simply did not occur.

The reasons why the system did not work well seem to rest in Diefenbaker's philosophy of cabinet decision-making and his rôle in the process. He simply did not believe that the prime minister's views on each and every matter should prevail. Rather, he saw himself as the chairman of cabinet, as "first amongst equals," as the person who should preside over the cabinet's attempts to reach consensus on contentious issues. Thus, in his welcome to the new ministers appointed in the shuffle of 1960, Diefenbaker "urged them to express their opinions freely and vigorously on any subjects raised for consideration."[3] He also went on to emphasize that cabinet decisions were not taken by majority vote and that "it was essential to reach decisions finally by arguments based on mutual confidence and respect."[4] The problem with consensus decision-making, of course, is that it will not function effectively unless ministers who find themselves in the minority are willing to acquiesce in the judgements of the majority and give up their fight. Furthermore, the chairman of the meeting must set time limits on the debates. Neither of these happened with sufficient frequency during Diefenbaker's time in office. He persisted in his attempts to reach consensus in cabinet on most important matters, with the result that decisions were often put off or not taken at all.

The prime minister's preference for complete agreement on disputatious issues sometimes drove his more impatient ministers to extremes of action. Alvin Hamilton, for example, on at least two occasions — over the Agriculture Program in 1958 and the China grain sales in 1961 — resorted to threats of resignation before Diefenbaker would end debate. In the case of the plans for the CANDU nuclear reactor, Hamilton says that "finally, I had to jump in and throw a tantrum and yell and scream that this was the heart of our development programme before Diefenbaker would come down on one side or the other."[5] Nevertheless, the prime minister seldom deviated from the consensus approach while in office and the upshot for him, and his government, was a growing and often deserved reputation for procrastination and inability to cope with the major problems which confronted it. It is not that Diefenbaker could not be decisive. Rather, it appears that the prime minister preferred not to force his views on his colleagues if he could avoid it, not to set time limits on debates on contentious items if possible, and to wait on the discussions in cabinet to effect the desired compromises. Unfortunately, agreements often did not emerge and decisions were postponed until Diefenbaker had no choice but to act in less than propitious circumstances.

Diefenbaker's leadership style had several important ramifications for his ministers in the performance of their duties. In the first place, they had to spend more time in cabinet meetings than their predecessors in the St. Laurent régime because agreements on many issues were not reached readily and were deferred for future consideration.[6] As a result, they had less time to devote to their other administrative and political duties. Secondly, the agenda for cabinet meetings became cluttered as new items competed for time with issues carried over from previous meetings. Furthermore, this state of affairs worsened over time, as the prime minister decided that more and more matters were worthy of discussion by the entire cabinet. By 1959, for example, an agenda selected at random reveals that cabinet considered the following items: a gift for the Queen; price support for sunflower seeds; authorization for twelve-month treasury bills; parking for tourists on Parliament Hill; civil defence; supplementary estimates; the Royal Commission on Energy; a draft bill to amend the Criminal Code; an exchange of land between the National Capital Commission and a private company; expropriation of property in the green belt around Ottawa; the export of oil; and the escort for the Royal yacht during the opening of the St. Lawrence Seaway.[7] Even in the winter of 1963, when the government was fighting for its life, one of the matters cabinet had to decide was whether "an export permit should be granted for the proposed export to Mainland China of crude nephrite jade having a total value of $300.00."[8] In such circumstances a place on the cabinet agenda became harder to obtain, as did time to present one's proposals and, since the prime minister had the final word as to what would come before cabinet, ministers had to convince him beforehand of the merit and/or urgency of their requests. According to Hamilton:

> The technique was to present a paper to Diefenbaker, rewritten sometimes by Merril Menzies who showed it to Diefenbaker in advance so that he wouldn't oppose it when it came up . . . The man who made up the agenda was Bob Bryce, but before it got to Bryce I wanted to make sure that the prime minister knew what was coming and the urgency of getting it on the agenda, so this is where Merril and I worked together.[9]

Diefenbaker's style also had an impact on the relations between and among his ministers as well as on the decision-making process. In the knowledge that the prime minister preferred to let debates in cabinet continue until all views were aired and reconciled, ministers began either to seek the approval of their colleagues before they brought their proposals to cabinet or, at the first sign of opposition, to recommend the creation of a committee to study the matter further and report back. Hamilton used both strategies with some success. In his words:

> As I went on I got smarter. I used to get all the ministers who had an interest in my legislation together with their officials and brief them fully. Then they could say in cabinet "We have examined this in our departments and we are for it." And then shut up. Now that made the other fellows a bit more reluctant to oppose it. So, I was able to get some stuff through pretty fast without much opposition.[10]
>
> Instead of getting into these great big fights . . . I would say "Here is my proposal . . . It is too involved to decide in half an hour of cabinet time so I recommend that the ministers who are affected by this policy sit with me in a sub-committee, go over it thoroughly as to the details and then come back and make a report to cabinet." More often than not the minister of finance would be on that sub-committee. So, by use of that technique, I do admit that I got stuff through pretty easily the last couple of years.[11]

The tactic of referral to committee did not always work as some issues could not be resolved by the smaller group, but it did provide a useful addition to the formal cabinet committee structure and did quicken the decision-making process on occasion. One unintended consequence of these manoeuvrings, however, was that they led to the log-rolling and private accommodations Diefenbaker hoped to prevent by use of his consensus approach where agreements were to be reached after full and open, if lengthy, discussions by the entire cabinet.

Diefenbaker, as a rule, did not interfere with his ministers in the day-to-day administration of their departments. He did reserve certain patronage appointments for himself and would, from time to time, pass on requests for jobs with the note attached that "anything you could do would be greatly appreciated."[12] He also involved himself in any issue he believed warranted his attention, especially in the fields of external affairs and agriculture. Beyond this, however, ministers could run their departments in their own way, free from the prime minister's interference, provided that nothing they did embarrassed the government politically.

Diefenbaker was ever attuned to the political consequences of his government's activities. In fact, in some instances he left the impression of being more concerned with the electoral repercussions of proposed legislation than with its content. Diefenbaker believed that governments defeat themselves by their own mistakes and he wanted to keep these self-inflicted wounds to a minimum. He insisted that he be kept informed of the principal activities of all departments and established an elaborate system whereby he could obtain information quickly. As his executive assistant advised all other executive assistants:

> Where the PM stipulates a reply "at once", it should be made the same day as received . . . "by return", it should be made the next day . . . Where a draft letter is asked for, the draft should be returned in three days. Where no time is mentioned, the reply should be made in not more than one week . . . Weekends cannot be taken into account where a reply is required "at once."[13]

Most requests were as follows: "Re: Maritime Feed Situation. What is the situation? Please reply at once."[14] The prime minister also required that he be consulted in advance of the announcement of any major policy initiative and woe betide the minister who acted without Diefenbaker's prior approval, as Hamilton found out when he proposed that the farm organizations establish a fund to ensure credit sales of grain to China and other "poor risk" countries. The prime minister did not fire Hamilton for this "indiscretion" and, in fact, most ministers, once appointed, had little reason to fear for their positions. Despite the large pool of talent on the back benches Diefenbaker did not play musical chairs with his cabinet and caucus. If anything, he erred in the opposite direction leaving some people in their portfolios for too long and keeping too many of the caucus on the shelf with too few opportunities to advance. This did not mean, however, that relations between the prime minister and his cabinet colleagues were ever close or easy, especially in the latter years. In truth, it would be ludicrous to refer to those governments as the Diefenbaker "team," for he never created that spirit within cabinet and what is more probably never tried to do so.

There appear to be several reasons for this. In the first place, the prime minister did not have a comfortable relationship with several of his ministers including Davie Fulton, Léon Balcer and George Nowlan. Some had opposed his bid for the leadership in 1956 and he never overcame his suspicion of their motives. It would seem that he appointed them to the cabinet in the belief that he could keep a tighter rein on their activities there than if they were on the back benches. Second, there were other ministers whose judgement Diefenbaker did not trust completely. Alvin Hamilton was one of these. Despite the fact that his loyalty was unquestioned and that the prime minister relied on him for advice on many policy and political issues, Diefenbaker also was known to have said that "if you let Alvin loose in a forty-acre field with just three cow pies in it, Alvin would step in all three."[15] Third, the prime minister was extremely jealous of his position and would brook no rivals to what he believed should be his preeminent place in the hearts of the electorate. Davie Fulton says that he "felt the lash more than once" after the press portrayed him as the second Progessive Conservative in Canada.[16] Even Hamilton admits that Diefenbaker no longer treated him with "friendly amusement" after the China grain sales moved reporters to claim that "if Prime Minister Diefenbaker has a rival in the popularity sweepstakes in Western Canada . . . that contender is the Hon. Alvin Hamilton, Minister of Agriculture."[17] Fourth, and closely related to the above, is the fact that the prime minister could be a harsh taskmaster on occasion. There is no lack of evidence to support this conclusion. George Hees described him as "a bully who would bully everyone he could."[18] William Hamilton maintained that Diefenbaker was "not kind to anyone in cabinet, with the exception of the sycophants."[19] Walter Dinsdale talked of the "spanking room" in the prime minister's parliamentary office where he would bring anyone who displeased him and vent his spleen.[20]

Alvin Hamilton was by no means a stranger to Diefenbaker's strategems, but in retrospect he tends to regard them as part of a well-controlled performance by a consummate actor who always had a definite purpose in mind. There is no doubt that he received rough treatment from the prime minister during his first years in cabinet, but he maintains that "Diefenbaker helped me out by savaging my proposals because he made the rest of the cabinet feel sorry for me and so they didn't oppose my ideas as strongly as they might have."[21] Furthermore, as he recounts one of the times he was summoned to the "spanking room":

> I remember an instance when I knew I had run pretty fast and far with the ball and so I said to some of my staff people — "You know, I'm going to be called to the Prime Minister's office one of these days because he doesn't like you to go too far on your own." So one day I got the call and I arrived there and he walked around the office, looked out the window, and delivered this great tantrum — "You're ruining yourself, you're ruining the Government, you're ruining the country." And he carried on saying exactly the same things as I'd said two or three days before that he would say. He caught me smiling and then he really hit the roof. Then he turned around and saw that I wasn't paying much attention and said — "What did I call you here for?" "Well," I said, "you called me in to give me a hard time about such and such a matter." And he said — "Yes, as your leader." And he never said another thing about it. He'd done his duty, he'd pulled off his tantrum, tried to scare the minister who had run too far ahead of the leash. Once he realized that the tantrum technique wasn't working with me, he quit. But, it scared the hell out of most of the guys.[22]

Diefenbaker could browbeat some of his ministers, but even those that he could not felt compelled to pay him homage in other ways. Hamilton, for example, gave the prime minister credit for legislative proposals which originated in his department, and worked at least one reference to Diefenbaker into every speech he delivered. Indeed, many have commented on the practice of ministers hastening to the airport to greet the prime minister on his triumphant return from day trips to places as far away as Montréal and Toronto. Thwarted ambitions and personal animosities could be sublimated for a while in the thrill of victory and the rewards of office, but in an unlikely short span of time the ties that bound some ministers to John Diefenbaker began to loosen. Midway through its term the cabinet was no longer a happy band of warriors united by common purposes and an unswerving love for its leader, if it ever was that, and the unhappiness grew as problems with the economy increased, as issues of defence policy remained unsettled, and as the government's popularity declined in the polls.

The government's honeymoon with the electorate did not last long. The bloom began to fade as early as 1959 and two years to the day after the Progressive Conservative party won its massive majority the *Winnipeg Free Press* summarized prevailing sentiment as follows:

> Government expenditures that were to be reduced have massively increased, with unprecedented deficits. Taxes that were to have gone down have gone up. Trade that was to have been diverted from the United States has been concentrated more than ever in that single market. Money that was to be loosened remains tight. Interest rates that were to be low remain high. Unemployment that was to be cured at a time of recession is still a grave problem at a time of high prosperity and takes on an increasingly permanent look. National defence that was to be re-organized has become only a national botch.[23]

A damning indictment, factual, though somewhat unfair, at least with respect to the economy, because some of the problems were beyond the government's capacity to control. Unfortunately for the Conservatives, they took office just as the western world entered a period of economic recession. Thus, the annual rate of growth in Canada began to decline, unemployment reached levels unsurpassed since the Depression of the 1930s, and the Canadian dollar came under pressure as economic performance could not match its high value compared to the currencies of our major trading partners, especially the United States. Diefenbaker attempted to retrieve the situation by shuffling his cabinet in October 1960, and his appointment of Alvin Hamilton as minister of agriculture and the fortuitous sale of grain to China did revive the government's fortunes on the prairies. However, it remained in electoral trouble almost everywhere else in the country.

Diefenbaker left Fleming in the finance portfolio in 1960 and this exacerbated the division within cabinet as to the best method to pull the country out of the recession.

> On the one hand, fiscal conservatives like Fleming were essentially of the balance-the-budget, classical school. On the other hand, populists like Diefenbaker and Hamilton were less concerned about the logic of aggregated demand reasoning and the merits of market-led economic development than they were about establishing a certain kind of economic development which would be in the Canadian interest.[24]

It would be too facile to characterize the split in cabinet as simply between the "spenders" and the "savers," although this was an aspect of the struggle. One camp, led originally by Alvin Hamilton and Gordon Churchill with the occasional support of the prime minister, believed the government had to intervene actively in the economy to bring the growth rate back to the desired level, even if this meant an increase in the deficit. The other group, led by Donald Fleming with the support of his department, placed its faith in fiscal restraint and a balanced budget, and in this they had the full support of James Coyne, the governor of the Bank of Canada, who had a large say in determining the interest rate and who, therefore, had a powerful impact on whether the economy would expand or contract.

The debate in cabinet was protracted. Fleming won the first round when he convinced Diefenbaker that his "tight money" budget of September 1959 was necessary to combat inflation. This budget angered Hamilton and those others in cabinet who shared his views because they believed that it would curtail the recovery which had begun early in the year and send the country back into recession.[25] The "spenders" persuaded the prime minister to create a committee, which deliberately excluded the minister of finance, to investigate the causes of Canada's economic problems and, after months of discussion, they concluded that Fleming's approach had to be reversed and that the governor had to be dismissed from his position. In Hamilton's words:

> What we had was a . . . clash between the fiscal policies that the Government wanted, that is the elected representatives, and the monetary and fiscal policy that the financial advisors wanted . . . He [Coyne] was dismissed because he was going one way on monetary and fiscal policy and we, the Government, wanted to go the other way.[26]

The Coyne affair is symbolic of the struggle in cabinet over the direction of the government's economic policy from 1959 to 1961. At first, the "savers" had their way. Later, when it became clear that the measures introduced in Fleming's 1959 budget had not produced the desired effect, the "spenders" came increasingly to the fore. According to Hamilton, Coyne was dismissed for his refusal to accept the new direction and, with the decks cleared:

> the Government initiated a series of long-term measures — both budgetary and non-budgetary — whose aim was to reshape the Canadian economic terrain, by increasing the pace of industrialization, strengthening the manufacturing and high technology sectors of the economy, encouraging a more even distribution of economic activity, improving the supply of labour, decreasing dependence on the United States, and making the Canadian economy less open to shocks from the international economy.[27]

None of this happened overnight, of course, and the firing of Coyne should be seen as but one stage in a lengthy process. Nevertheless, as the balance shifted, Hamilton found it easier to obtain cabinet approval of some of the projects he had proposed in the National Development Program of November 1958, and he and his advisers were encouraged sufficiently to prepare the Second Stage of the Program in the autumn of 1961.[28] In fact, many of the government's actions in the economic sphere during its last two years in office had their genesis in these two documents. The Pine Point Railway, the Columbia River Treaty, ARDA, the Technical and Vocational Assistance Act, the National Productivity Council, the Economic Council of Canada, the Royal Commission on Taxation, the Red River Diversion, the Atlantic Development Board and increased subsidies to various industries were all part of this new and renewed determination to use the resources of the government to drag the country out of the recession and, to some extent, it succeeded. Unemployment declined everywhere in Canada in 1962, and other important economic indicators began an upward trend which continued for several years. However, these actions proved to be too little and too late to save the government.

Confidence in the government's ability to manage the economy effectively had been shaken severely and this was reflected by the continued pressure on the dollar after 1960 as investors and currency speculators waited on the cabinet to decide with some finality the direction of its economic, monetary and fiscal policies. The pressure increased dramatically after Fleming announced in his June 1961 budget that the government intended to devalue the dollar without setting a limit beyond which it would not be allowed to fall. This caused a run on the dollar for a time, but one with which the government could live. Eventually the dollar settled at approximately ninety-five cents American and remained there for several months. By March 1962, however, pressure on the dollar increased again and on 10 April Fleming tried to assure the market and the public that the government would use its reserves of foreign exchange to keep the dollar stable. Once again, however, neither he nor anyone else stated unequivocally what the government's "bottom line" would be. In fact, the assurances satisfied no one. By the end of the month, the Bank of Canada had to spend almost as much of its reserves every day to protect the dollar as it had spent in the entire month of March.[29]

On 1 May Fleming recommended and Diefenbaker agreed that the dollar should be devalued further and fixed the rate at ninety-two and a half cents American.[30] Cabinet approved the proposal the next day, although not the whole cabinet as the prime minister, Fleming, and most ministers were out of Ottawa campaigning in the early days of the 1962 election. Thus, it happened that Alvin Hamilton as acting prime minister, David Walker, the minister of public works, Noël Dorion, the secretary of state, Walter Dinsdale, the minister of northern affairs and national resources, and Ernest Halpenny, a minister without portfolio, made the final decision. Nevertheless, there is no doubt that the figure was Fleming's choice. A few weeks later, at the height of the crisis, R.B. Bryce, secretary to the cabinet, noted that:

> WP [probably A.W.F. Plumptre, senior assistant deputy minister of finance] reminds me that par at 92 1/2 was a compromise proposal put forward by the Minister after hearing from his officials all the arguments for and against various alternative proposals (5 in all) that were outlined.
>
> Parity at 92 1/2 was not proposed by any official. Mr. F.'s proposal of it was not objected to by his officials after they realized it was his choice, having heard the case.[31]

Nor can there be any argument that the figure chosen was a compromise between those ministers who wished to defend the dollar at ninety-five cents and those who wanted to lower it to ninety cents, both alternatives that Fleming, Diefenbaker and the cabinet considered.

Alvin Hamilton was one of those who fought hardest for the lower value. He believed Canada's economic condition warranted it, that it would benefit all in the country except the wealthy by lowering the cost of our exports and increasing the cost of imports, and he said so at a press conference in Vancouver on 8 June. In answer to a reporter's question, Hamilton explained that the cabinet had looked at several possible solutions to the problem and that devaluation to ninety cents American had been one of them. The financial community interpreted this immediately as a sign that the government might permit the dollar to fall even further, and it began selling Canadian dollars as fast as it could. The Liberal party attacked Hamilton for weakening confidence in the dollar and the *Globe and Mail* cautioned that "Mr. Hamilton should be made to understand that for a member of the Government to express public doubts about the current value of the dollar is to invite speculative pressure in world money markets."[32] Two days later Fleming moved to repair the damage. In a press release he announced that:

> After consultation with the Prime Minister, I wish to make it clear beyond question that the rate of 92 1/2 cents in U.S. funds is definite and final. We chose this rate after careful consideration of our balance of payments outlook. It has been legally established by the Government with the concurrence of the International Monetary Fund. No other rate and no other exchange system is being considered or will be considered by the Government.
>
> We are determined to maintain the 92 1/2 cent rate against pressures of any sort. The very extensive financial resources available to the Government will be used to defend it. The Government is fully aware that its financial and economic policies basically determine the value of the Canadian dollar and the Canadian people can be assured that these policies will be of a character which involves no further reduction in the exchange value of the Canadian currency.[33]

The damage, however, had been done. The drain on the reserves quickly reached crisis proportions and the government had to resort to extraordinary measures to cope with the emergency. Once the election campaign ended on 18 June and cabinet ministers could return to Ottawa, they met eight times between noon on 20 June and noon 24 June without the secretariat in attendance. The upshot of these meetings was that the cabinet agreed to impose a surcharge on certain classes of imports, to reduce the value of goods Canadian travellers could bring back free of duty, to reduce government expenditure by $250 million in the next fiscal year, to increase Canada's foreign exchange reserves, and to borrow from the International Monetary Fund and other sources sufficient foreign exchange to halt the run on the dollar.[34]

In the economic context, the "financial crisis" of 1962 proved to be of short duration and of no lasting detriment to the Canadian economy. By mid-November, the situation had improved to such an extent that the surcharge on imports could be reduced for certain commodities and removed from others, and the upswing in the economy stimulated by the devaluation and continued exports of grain convinced the government and its Liberal successors to keep the dollar pegged at ninety-two and a half cents until 1970.[35] In political terms, however, it may have dealt the government a telling blow. The crisis occurred in the midst of the 1962 election and reached its peak as the campaign reached its conclusion. As mentioned earlier, the Progressive Conservative party lost ninety-two seats and was reduced to minority status in the House of Commons. It is impossible to determine precisely the impact of any single issue on an election result in a country as large and diverse as Canada. However, it is likely that the government's original decision to let the dollar float, without setting a bottom limit, created a climate of uncertainty in money markets, and that Hamilton's candour in describing the split in cabinet over the decision to devalue to ninety-two and a half cents compounded the market's anxiety. Together, these tended to confirm the suspicion held by many that the government could not manage the economy competently and most probably hurt the party electorally, especially in southern Ontario and urban Canada at large. Certainly, the prime minister blamed his government's near defeat on this issue. In his memoirs, Diefenbaker stated categorically that "I can see no possibility of our having lost the 1962 election but for that so-called financial crisis."[36] Furthermore, when he looked for scapegoats beyond the White House and the monied interests of Bay Street, he pointed directly at Alvin Hamilton. In his words:

> One intervention that I did not expect was that of the Minister of Agriculture. On 8 June, Mr. Hamilton announced in Vancouver that the 92 1/2 ¢ exchange rate was a compromise between those in Cabinet who favoured a 90¢ rate and those who supported a 95¢ rate. He went on to indicate that he favoured the 90¢ rate as "defensible with Canada's negative trade balance". His statement did the government a great deal of harm.[37]

In this instance, accessibility to and open honesty with the press proved not to be the best policy.

Hamilton brought Diefenbaker a transcript of the interview and convinced the prime minister of the sincerity of his motives, but Diefenbaker never withdrew his condemnation.[38] Perhaps Hamilton should have learned his lesson, but he did not. Less than two weeks later, in the middle of the cabinet meetings held to find a way out of the exchange crisis, Hamilton appeared on a CBC television programme and declared that "there are no extraordinary fiscal problems in Canada." Again there can be no question of his motives. The economic indicators he regarded as most important showed that Canada's recovery was well underway and he believed that the government deserved credit for this. In the circumstances, however, especially when taken out of context, the statement was a monumental blunder and it might have cost Hamilton his cabinet position. Diefenbaker's reaction was as follows:

> In the midst of all this, Mr. Hamilton appeared on television 21 June to state that there was no crisis. Had the Minister involved been anyone other than Alvin Hamilton, who had retrieved the farm vote after the disastrous period of Douglas Harkness in the Agriculture portfolio, I would have fired him on the spot, as some of our colleagues demanded.[39]

Hamilton maintains that he never feared for his job, but his subordinates were not so confident. Faibish warned him that his reputation was at an "all-time low" because of these incidents,[40] and Mulroney asked M.R. Jack, executive assistant to George Hees, for any material that could "buttress Mr. Hamilton's position in the House" because:

> As a result of the Prime Minister's austerity program shortly after the election and in light of post-election statements by many of our financial experts, you will appreciate that my Minister is in pretty hot water.[41]

This episode is a sorry chapter in Alvin Hamilton's political career. It added to his reputation as a minister with "a tendency to put his foot in his mouth occasionally,"[42] and caused the government additional difficulty at a time when it had on its plate all that it could handle. Hamilton, as might be expected, tends to downplay the significance of both "slips of the tongue." He admits that neither did him nor the government any good at the time, but maintains that their political repercussions should not overshadow the benefits which occurred from his successful espousal in cabinet of the policies which put Canada on the road to economic recovery.[43] In the context of politics in the Conservative party it must also be remembered that the struggle in cabinet over the direction of economic policy was contained. Although lengthy and heated on occasion, it did not cause either resignations from the cabinet or demands for Diefenbaker's resignation. It is true that the government's management of the economy contributed to its decline in popularity, and to unease in certain Conservative circles over the prime minister's leadership. It was defence policy which led ultimately to the challenge to his position, however, and the fight for the crown which was to go on for the next four years.

In general, the government's record in matters of defence policy is one of commitments made, then refusal to accept the consequences of these undertakings. Specifically, the Diefenbaker cabinet failed to meet Canada's obligations to our allies in the North Atlantic Treaty Organization (NATO) and to the United States under the terms of the North American Air Defence agreement (NORAD). Canada had been one of the founding members of NATO in 1949 and had stationed troops in France and Germany since then as part of the forces safeguarding western Europe from the threat of Soviet invasion. By 1957 NATO military strategists had concluded that the defence of Europe would require the use of tactical nuclear weapons if the Warsaw Pact attacked and, in December of that year, the prime minister signed an agreement on Canada's behalf which committed this country to the acquisition of nuclear weapons for our army brigade and air division based in Europe. In May 1959, at NATO's request, the cabinet also accepted a "strike reconnaissance" rôle for the air division, a task which would require the RCAF to equip its aircraft with nuclear air-to-ground weapons. Diefenbaker, acting as his own minister of external affairs between the death of Sidney Smith and the appointment of Howard Green, pledged to have eight squadrons ready for such combat by 1 May 1963. However, the prime minister did not sign the agreement with the United States necessary to acquire the weaponry. Ten months later, cabinet decided to acquire the Honest John rocket for Canadian artillery units in Europe and despatched troops trained in its use in December 1961. Although a non-nuclear version of the rocket was available, the Defence Department did not order it. Therefore, to be of any use whatsoever the Honest John had to be armed with nuclear warheads. Nevertheless, the government once again would not obtain the necessary weaponry and thus Canada's contribution to NATO's fighting forces consisted of air squadrons unequipped for their rôle and artillery "armed" with bags of sand.

In the North American context, John Foster Dulles, the American secretary of state, visited Ottawa in late July 1957 and obtained the prime minister's approval of a plan to integrate both nations' air defences into a single central command. Both parties assumed that Canada's contribution to NORAD would be the CF-105 Arrow interceptor, then under construction. However, the Canadian government soon came to question the choice of the Arrow. They had no doubt that it was a superb military aircraft. However, it cost a great deal to build and neither the United States nor any other NATO ally would purchase it for their air forces and so reduce the drain on the Canadian taxpayer. The St. Laurent government had come close to scrapping the project prior to the 1957 election and, after much debate and nearly two years' delay, the Diefenbaker government arrived at the same conclusion. It was not an easy decision. It involved not only military but also financial, employment, nationalistic and political considerations, and one member of the cabinet believes that it was the turning point in Diefenbaker's career. According to William Hamilton, the prime minister became "unsure of himself and unable to act decisively after the Arrow fiasco."[44] Diefenbaker announced in the House of Commons on 20 February 1959 that the Arrow would be abandoned. Now the government had to produce a satisfactory alternative.[45] Major-General George Pearkes, the minister of national defence, and his chiefs of staff had recommended the Bomarc "B" ground-to-air missile as a possible replacement and now cabinet accepted the proposal. The prime minister further announced that Canada would build two Bomarc bases, one at North Bay, Ontario, the other at La Macaza, Québec, in place of the Arrow. These bases would not only fulfill our obligations under the NORAD agreement, but would also push the site of any future nuclear battle north from southern Ontario and Québec to the less populated regions of the country. The Bomarc, to be of any use at all, had to be armed with nuclear warheads, but the government would not agree to acquire them. The warheads could be obtained only from the United States, but American law insisted that such weapons be kept under American control and this most members of the cabinet could not accept. Thus, when the RCAF took over the completed Bomarc bases on 1 February 1962, the missiles, like the Honest John rockets in Europe, stood tipped with sand instead of the armament for which they had been designed.

Canada's refusal to arm the Bomarcs left a gap in America's defences and Washington understandably was concerned. The United States had agreed to the bases at North Bay and La Macaza at Ottawa's insistence and wanted these bases fully operational. However, the election campaign, the financial crisis, and the government's minority position all intervened to divert the cabinet's attention from defence policy, and negotiations with the Americans did not resume until the autumn. By this time, the government had decided to seek a compromise with Washington whereby "nuclear warheads would be held in bases in the United States to be moved to Canada to be available to the R.C.A.F. for use in Bomarc missiles and interceptor aircraft, on request by the Canadian Government when war appears imminent."[46] Ministers believed, apparently, that there would be sufficient forewarning to obtain the warheads from the United States in time of peril. The Cuban missile crisis should have convinced the government of the folly of its proposal, but it did not. Not only did cabinet not arm the Bomarcs or the Voodoos it had acquired earlier in the year when it realized that the day of the manned bomber was not yet over, it also refused permission for

American nuclear-armed fighters to fly over Canadian territory. Once again Washington was understandably upset. General Lauris Norstad, on his way home in early January of 1963 from a tour as NATO supreme commander, stopped off in Ottawa and, in response to a reporter's question, stated bluntly that Canada would be shirking her responsibilities if she did not accept nuclear weapons for her forces in Europe. Later in the month, the State Department issued a press release drafted in the White House which contradicted several statements Diefenbaker had made to the House of Commons on 25 January in which he cast doubt on the value of the nuclear deterrent and its rôle in North American and European defence. Pressure from the United States did not change the government's stand, however. If anything, it increased the anti-Americanism of the prime minister and some members of the cabinet. Until the end of its days, nearly three months later, the government continued to refuse nuclear arms for the Honest Johns and the CF-104s in Europe and the Bomarcs and Voodoos at home and thus, as Peter Newman summarized its defence policy, "Canada, under John Diefenbaker's management had spent $685 million for the most impressive collection of blank cartridges in the history of military science."[47]

Defence policy is often debated hotly and at length in Canada, but it seldom determines the fate of governments and their leaders. In the case of the defence policy of the Diefenbaker government, however, it not only had an adverse effect on our relations with our closest ally, it also split the cabinet, led to the government's defeat in the House of Commons, contributed to the Liberal party's victory at the 1963 election, and nearly brought John Diefenbaker's leadership of the Progressive Conservative party to an early end. The government's refusal to acquire nuclear weapons did not meet with the approval of everyone in the Conservative party, nor even the cabinet. As early as May 1961, Douglas Harkness, who had replaced Major-General Pearkes as minister of national defence in the cabinet shuffle of October 1960, began to urge his colleagues to accept the warheads which would make the weapons they had acquired or were about to acquire functional. To his way of thinking, Canada had made specific commitments to the United States and our NATO partners and had to acquire a nuclear capability in order to honour them.[48] In this he was opposed most strongly by Howard Green, the minister of external affairs. Green accepted Canada's membership in NATO and NORAD, but did not agree that we had to become a member of the nuclear club to meet our responsibilities under these agreements. In fact, Green believed that disarmament offered the only guarantee of a lasting peace, and he feared that if Canada acquired nuclear arms it would weaken his position at the United Nations, and undercut the work he had done for so long on behalf of the disarmament cause. The struggle between the two positions continued for months and gradually it became clear that Green's stand had the sympathy of a majority of ministers and the all important support of the prime minister. Nevertheless, Harkness remained in the cabinet in the hope that he might eventually win the day. He believed until the end that Diefenbaker would accept nuclear weapons for Canada in the right set of circumstances. The end for Harkness came when the prime minister refused to accept the unanimous agreement of a Cabinet Committee that Canada's obligations to NATO and NORAD might force her to acquire nuclear weapons and Diefenbaker threatened to call an election over the Americans' rebuttal of his 25 January statement on defence policy.[49] That was the final straw. After a final determined attempt to sway Diefenbaker and the cabinet, he submitted his resignation on 4 February. It read in part:

> For over two years you have been aware that I believed nuclear warheads should be supplied to the four weapons systems we have acquired which are adapted to their use. Throughout this period I believed that they would be authorized at the appropriate time. . .
>
> It has become quite obvious during the past few days that your views and mine as to the course we should pursue for the acquisition of nuclear weapons for our armed forces are not capable of reconciliation. Thus it is with a great deal of regret that I now find I must tender my resignation as Minister of National Defence.[50]

Harkness's decision to leave the cabinet came at a time when the government could ill afford it. It was in grave jeopardy in the House of Commons and had to prove that it could govern effectively despite its minority position. Furthermore, the prime minister had to show that he could provide decisive leadership and that he had the support of a united cabinet and party. Harkness's resignation, and the events which led to it, proved just the contrary.

Alvin Hamilton did not play as important a rôle in the evolution of the defence policy of the Diefenbaker government as he had in its economic policy. His interests and his positions as first minister of northern affairs and national resources and then minister of agriculture kept him at least one step removed from the process throughout most of the period. Nevertheless, as a member of cabinet he participated in the debates there, and as a member of Parliament he had to respond to the public's concerns. After the decision to abandon the Arrow he explained to his constituents that:

> This momentous decision was reached after the United States and Great Britain had declined to purchase the Arrow for their defences on the grounds that, in the light of recent advancement in ballistic missiles, the aircraft had become more or less obsolete. The same opinion was also shared by the Canadian Chiefs of Staff who worked in close consultation with the Government . . . it was the only decision the Government could make under the circumstances.[51]

As well, he began to receive mail on both sides of the nuclear arms question as early as 1960, and he too felt the pressure exerted by the Canadian Campaign for Nuclear Disarmament. Hamilton summarized his own position on the issue as follows in a letter to a constituent in October of 1961: "I personally feel that the extension of nuclear weapons to more countries adds to the danger of some international incident which would set off world conflict."[52] Despite, or perhaps because of, his experiences as a combat officer in the World War II, he found himself closer to Green than to Harkness on the question of acquiring nuclear arms for Canada although, unlike Green, his principal concern was for the domestic rather than the international political repercussions of the decision. Hamilton was troubled especially by the question of national sovereignty and the impact the storage of nuclear weapons on Canadian soil under American control would have on the government's prospects at the next election. In his words:

> the Conservative party [has] always had a reluctance to be under the American wing too much. We have an instinctive feeling about that. . .
>
> We did not believe that it [control over the warheads] should be under single American control which means you accept American sovereignty with the number of troops that they wanted to put in to look after that storage. We were opposed to that and we thought our alternatives should be examined by the Americans.[53]

When the boil came to a head at the end of January 1963, he advised Diefenbaker that:

> Generally speaking, I do not think that the nuclear issue is the main issue. The main issue in my opinion, is Canadian sovereignty . . . If the national sovereignty issue can be built up successfully, then it is an issue that might well affect from 25 to 40 per cent of the vote in Canada. If properly handled it will give us a fighting issue in Quebec . . . My conclusion, therefore, in spite of what some of our colleagues might think, is that the nuclear issue is not a political issue in the serious sense — beyond the question of indecision.[54]

His specific advice to the prime minister on the eve of Diefenbaker's speech on defence policy was to make it quite clear that whether Canada joined the nuclear club or not, the government would make its own decision "in the light of the facts and in the interests of Canada, and not on pressures from outside or from any group."[55] Political considerations were also those which brought Hamilton full-tilt into the fray at the time of Harkness's resignation. The fates of the government and the prime minister were at stake and he could not and would not remain on the periphery.

The first serious rumblings of discontent over Diefenbaker's leadership emerged after the near defeat in 1962. According to one Conservative, "the leadership question had been a festering sore ever since the June 1962 election, when our party dropped from the largest majority in parliamentary history to become a minority government."[56] The unhappiness grew as month after month went by without action on several important problems confronting the government, and led some cabinet ministers to begin consideration of the ways by which the prime minister might be forced from office. During this time, "the Cabinet was an unhappy family. Dief was nervous, indecisive and exploded at his colleagues. An average of four cabinet meetings a week were just talk, talk, talk. Ministers couldn't get a decision on important business for their departments."[57] Diefenbaker survived the party's annual meeting in mid-January without difficulty, despite rumours of a challenge to his leadership, but when Parliament reconvened on 21 January the discontent in cabinet soon spilled over into open revolt. Two quite different issues combined to bring the matter to a head: the government's need for House of Commons approval of essential interim supply, and the prime minister's response to Washington's rebuttal of his interpretation of the nuclear arms controversy which he related in his speech on 25 January. The opposition parties wanted a budget to debate and just before Parliament reopened George Nowlan, now minister of finance, and Gordon Churchill, government house leader, promised one by 1 March if the opposition would grant supply immediately. Diefenbaker, however, refused to place a supply motion on the order paper at that time, and scheduled the debate on external affairs and defence policy instead. This so angered Robert Thompson, the Social Credit leader, whose votes had kept the Conservatives in office since the election, that he threatened to withdraw his party's support from the government unless the prime minister were replaced. Diefenbaker gave his defence of his government's stand on nuclear arms as he wished and the State Department responded five days later. That press release so enraged the prime minister that he recalled Charles

Ritchie, Canada's ambassador to the United States, an action never before known in the history of Canada's relations with that country, and polled his colleagues for their views on an immediate dissolution of the House of Commons and an election which they would fight on the issue of American interference in Canadian affairs.

The prospect of an anti-American campaign at that time appalled some members of the cabinet, and ministers such as Hees, McCutcheon, Halpenny, Fulton, Balcer, and Sevigny met with increasing frequency over the next few days to plot Diefenbaker's removal. The prime minister did not ask the governor-general for a dissolution at that moment, but the thought lingered in his mind. He broached the subject again with cabinet on Saturday, 2 February, but could not obtain the support he wanted and, at Hees's request, agreed to a further meeting the next morning at his residence. Accounts differ as to what happened at that meeting, but the following sequence of events seems likely. Diefenbaker once again suggested an immediate election with Canadian-American relations as the centrepiece of the Conservative campaign strategy. Some ministers opposed this as before and Hees urged the prime minister to reverse his stand on the question of nuclear arms for Canada. Diefenbaker refused this appeal and Harkness then declared that the prime minister had lost the confidence of cabinet, the Conservative party, and the nation at large over this issue and should resign. Diefenbaker confronted his critics and demanded that those with him and those against him identify themselves at once. Approximately half those at the table remained seated when he asked his supporters to rise, although for different reasons. Some ministers apparently were unsure as to whether they would be voting on an election, nuclear arms, or the prime minister's leadership, and stayed where they sat. Diefenbaker then left the room with a threat to tender his resignation to the governor-general. After some minutes' confusion, the meeting resumed with Green in the chair and Harkness again attacked the prime minister. This brought Alvin Hamilton to Diefenbaker's defence and the debate became somewhat less than parliamentary in tone and language. Patrick Nicholson quotes Hamilton as saying, "You treacherous bastards! No Prime Minister has ever had to deal with so many sons of bitches."[58] Peter Stursberg cites Hamilton's recollection as follows: "That was enough for me. I just asked him where his integrity was. I said that I knew a son of a bitch when I saw one and there was only one place for sons of bitches to go and that was out. Either I was walking out or he was getting out."[59] Almost twenty years after the event Hamilton admits that "I lost my temper and when I lose my temper I don't hold back. I pointed out in the language of an army sergeant exactly what he had said and exactly what it meant, that he had violated his oath as a member of cabinet, and that he wasn't fit to sit in our cabinet."[60] According to Hamilton, most ministers agreed with him and Harkness had no choice but to resign. It is likely that Harkness had decided to do so already for he undertook to resign without delay and left the meeting. No one else went with him. Cabinet then drafted a memorandum urging the prime minister neither to resign nor to call an election and Diefenbaker returned to the meeting. No further decisions of any consequence were made however, and finally the gathering broke up. Some ministers left to pick up the pieces of an extraordinary Sunday and others to consider other ways of forcing the prime minister out of his position. Hees and Fulton returned later in the evening with an offer to appoint Diefenbaker chief justice of the Supreme Court if he would agree to go voluntarily, but he refused.[61] He would continue as prime minister and leader of the Progressive Conservative party until he lost the confidence of the House of Commons and the caucus of Conservative members and senators.[62]

Harkness made his resignation public the next morning, 4 February, and in the House of Commons Liberal Leader Pearson moved "that this government because of lack of leadership, the breakdown of unity in the Cabinet, and confusion and indecision in dealing with national and international problems, does not have the confidence of the Canadian people."[63] It was a motion the Socreds and New Democrats would find difficult to oppose and this added an even greater urgency to the conspirators' efforts. In the hope of keeping Thompson from voting with Pearson they chose George

Nowlan to replace Diefenbaker and Hees and McCutcheon delivered the news to the prime minister, again offering him the chief justiceship as a sop if he would go quickly and quietly. Again the Chief refused to resign and the fate of the government now rested with the minor parties, especially Social Credit. It appeared for a short time that the Socreds might forego their demand for the prime minister's resignation if he would agree to make a definitive statement of his government's defence policy immediately and to bring down a budget within a month. As Thompson explained later:

> Monday morning at caucus I reported that the government [probably Nowlan] had assured me of a budget by March 1, and fast action on the estimates. After that we issued a press release of the points we wanted fulfilled if we were to support the government. I sent a copy of it to Mr. Diefenbaker's office . . . so the Prime Minister would know our stand, and asking his assurance he'd comply. No communication came from him before I started to speak at 6 o'clock. So I stalled in my speech . . . I was waiting for the supper hour. I went out of my way to give him a chance to reassure us, but he wouldn't. So I went back to the House and moved my sub-amendment which sealed the government's fate.[64]

Thompson's sub-amendment read as follows:

> This government has failed up to this time to give a clear statement of policy respecting Canada's national defence, and has failed to organize the business of the House so that the 1963-64 estimates and budget could be introduced, and has failed to outline a positive program of follow-up action respecting many things for which this parliament and previous parliaments have already given authority, and does not have the confidence of the Canadian people.[65]

It would appear that the die had been cast, but the vote could not be taken until the following day and so the conspirators redoubled their efforts. First thing Tuesday morning Hees confronted Diefenbaker and demanded his resignation. Once again the Chief declined with vigour. As Gordon Churchill tells the story, "At 8:30 a.m. the Prime Minister phoned me at home to tell me that George Hees was in his study and had just asked him to resign. I said 'Tell him to go to hell and stand fast . . . I will take immediate action'."[66] Churchill at once contacted as many Diefenbaker loyalists in the cabinet as he could reach and told them to warn government backbenchers that they would soon have to make a choice between Hees and the Chief. Alvin Hamilton arrived at Churchill's parliamentary office at ten o'clock having just learned of the attempted coup on the radio. After Churchill brought him up to date, he too sought out Diefenbaker's friends in the caucus, particularly those from Alberta and Saskatchewan. He told them of the plot against the prime minister, warned that it was an attempt by the "eastern" old guard of the party to reimpose its control, which Diefenbaker had broken in 1956, and urged them to demonstrate their support for the Chief when he spoke in the House of Commons that afternoon. Hamilton also threatened to campaign against them in their constituencies at the next election if they failed to show their support. The threat proved unnecessary and Hamilton claims little credit for rallying the troops. In his words, "I simply put an idea loose in the minds of budding Paul Reveres and they were the ones who did it."[67] They most certainly did. Diefenbaker performed brilliantly that afternoon and his supporters cheered him to an echo. Even Hees pounded his desk enthusiastically after Lawrence Kindt, member for Macleod, Alberta, threatened to "pull your arm out by the roots and if I'm not big enough one of the Horners is."[68] Nevertheless, the display made no difference to the fate of the government. Neither the prime minister's performance nor the demonstration of support swayed the opposition members. All but two voted for Thompson's amendment to Pearson's motion and the government fell for want of confidence in it and its leader.

In anticipation of defeat, Diefenbaker had called a cabinet meeting for nine o'clock the following morning. Wednesday morning at eleven was also the usual time for meetings of the caucus and this fact gave the conspirators one final desperate hope for success. They planned to use their strength in cabinet to force the prime minister to resign, present caucus with a *fait accompli*, and ask caucus to ratify the deed for the sake of party unity in the face of the forthcoming election campaign. The scheme might have worked had Diefenbaker, on the advice of Alvin Hamilton, not switched the times of the meetings. Although not a party to the conspiracy, Hamilton sensed what was meant to come and urged the Chief to take his chances with caucus first. Again, accounts of that meeting differ in detail, but this much is certain. Hees tried with difficulty to read a speech in which he attacked Diefenbaker's stand on nuclear arms and argued against an election campaign based on anti-Americanism. The Chief offered to resign, but an overwhelming majority of caucus begged him to stay. Diefenbaker then demanded a pledge of loyalty, especially from those he knew had plotted against him, and all but Harkness fell into line. In Hamilton's words:

> God, that crowd was really out for blood. Those Maritimers! Those Westerners! It was a great caucus. And I didn't have to do anything. Diefenbaker motioned me away. I just sat to the side of the table in case he needed any help. He didn't. The only guy who stuck to his guns was Harkness. Even McCutcheon laughed and joined the hallelujah chorus. When they found two hundred men [*sic*] all behind the prime minister the other twenty who were lukewarm suddenly realized they didn't have any hope at all.[69]

Hees and others then met the press in a demonstration of party unity. The prime minister called upon the governor-general that afternoon to obtain a dissolution of Parliament and Canada plunged into its fourth election campaign in less than six years.

The election of 8 April 1963 should have been a disaster for the Progressive Conservative party. Most indicators pointed to a defeat of mammoth proportions at the beginning of the campaign. The prime minister stood accused of indecisive leadership and, indeed, the government had done very little in any area since its return in June 1962. The cabinet remained divided over the defence question and, in fact, two more ministers, Hees and Sevigny, resigned just two days after the campaign began because of Diefenbaker's stand on the issue and his attitude towards the United States. Unemployment, though dropping, remained high and the government's interventionist economic strategy adopted two years earlier had not yet produced all the desired effects in urban Canada. Little attention had been given to the party organization since the previous election and many party workers had become defeatist at worst and dispirited at best. In addition, the election of John F. Kennedy as president of the United States had created a mood for change among an important part of the Canadian electorate which the sixty-eight year old prime minister seemed ill-equipped to provide. Nevertheless, the result, while a defeat, was not a catastrophe. The campaign, and perhaps the near loss of his leadership, galvanized Diefenbaker. He went on the offensive from the very beginning. He accused the opposition parties of obstructionist tactics in the House of Commons which had prevented passage of his government's legislation. He attacked the Liberal party for changing its mind on nuclear weapons for Canada, and warned that if the Liberals formed a government the Bomarc bases would become nothing more than decoys to divert enemy missiles from American soil. He hinted darkly that Pearson had formed an unholy alliance with powerful interests in the United States to ensure his defeat. He railed at the unfairness of the press, ridiculed the Liberal "truth squad" which dogged his steps in the early days of the campaign, and did everything in his power to convince voters that he and he alone championed the cause of the ordinary Canadian. He came closer than any one thought possible to pulling it off. He forced the Liberal party onto the defensive and into unpopular errors of judgement. Late in the campaign he told one of his staff that "he needed two more Liberal mistakes. He had three already but he needed two more to pull it out."[70] All in all, it was a magnificent performance by the old Chieftain, but a losing one nonetheless. He kept Pearson from a majority, but had to turn over the reins of power just the same. In the circumstances, it is surprising perhaps that the 1963 election, at which Hamilton was returned with ease, strengthened John Diefenbaker's leadership of the Conservative party, albeit temporarily. Resignations and defeats provided him with a caucus more amenable to his leadership than at any time in the past year. In April 1963, his position was secure, but only for a short while. No party takes the loss of power lightly, and despite Diefenbaker's campaign the knives were soon unsheathed again, and next time, although the battle would be lengthy and hard-fought, neither he nor his friends would be able to save him.

Chapter 7
A Chance at the Ring

The fall of the government in 1963 marked the end of one era and the beginning of another for Alvin Hamilton, the Progressive Conservative party, and its leader John Diefenbaker. Not only did the party retreat from government into opposition but internal party politics replaced the partisan struggle as the most important issue of concern for many Conservatives. Diefenbaker became the protagonist in a tragicomedy staged by the party between 1963 and 1967. Electoral defeat strengthened the resolve of those in the party who wished to remove the Chief from the leadership and Hamilton soon found himself embroiled in the conflict, first as a Diefenbaker loyalist and later as a candidate for the leadership himself when he believed the man would step down. Although he pursued his various interests in several far-flung places over these four years, invariably Hamilton felt compelled to return to the civil war for the soul of his party.

If some Conservatives in Saskatchewan had had their way Alvin Hamilton would have been in no position to participate as fully as he did in the struggle for the federal leadership. They had leadership difficulties of their own and wanted Hamilton to return to Saskatchewan to take over the provincial party. Hamilton had kept in close touch with political affairs in Saskatchewan since his election to the House of

Commons in 1957. Diefenbaker made him the minister responsible for the province, Martin Pederson wrote often to inform him of developments in the province, and he believed that a strong provincial party would prove advantageous to the federal party's electoral fortunes. As he warned Diefenbaker in the autumn of 1959, "I think it would be a great mistake not to put every effort behind the provincial party in Saskatchewan . . . if there is a provincial disaster for us it will have serious repercussions on us all federally."[1] Thus, he did everything he could to help Pederson build on the federal party's success in the province. He served as honorary vice-president of the provincial association, contributed time and money to the provincial party, campaigned on behalf of Progressive Conservative candidates during the 1960 provincial election, and tried to ensure that actions taken by the federal government did not hurt the provincial party. For example, during the debate in cabinet over acreage payments, he advised the prime minister that:

> The matter of timing is the key to this whole problem. I believe it would be suicidal to Martin Pederson's efforts to announce an acreage payment before the election. As I see it, Martin has promised to pay $100 *and* make strong representation to the Federal Government to repeat the $200 payment of 1958.
>
> To help Martin we should accept the Farm Organizations' offer to meet with the Cabinet, but in the acceptance get across the idea that this meeting cannot be held until after the election in Saskatchewan.[2]

Despite these efforts and his own Pederson could not transfer the federal party's electoral success to the provincial arena. The party continued to be squeezed between the Liberals and the CCF and won no seats at all in 1960.

The magnitude of the defeat that year came as a great shock to those provincial Conservatives who had expected to duplicate the federal victory of 1958, and the sentiment grew that Pederson should be replaced as leader. For these people the opportunity to do so came with the defeat of the Diefenbaker government in 1963. They believed that since Alvin Hamilton was now out of power he might be enticed back to

Saskatchewan, and they had no doubts that his popularity as minister of agriculture would bring the provincial party instant success. Several people wrote Hamilton over the summer of 1963 to urge that he return to provincial politics. According to one of them:

> It is my positive conviction that if you were to come back and take the provincial leadership you could win power hands down and sweep the CCF from office . . . For the good of the party and the future of Saskatchewan I would ask you to ponder the pros and cons of this suggestion.[3]

This belief was shared by many of the party's prominents, including John Diefenbaker. As he wrote to his brother Elmer:

> I had Senator Pearson in today accompanied by Dr. Leishman and Jack Sangster. They are most anxious to get Alvin Hamilton to take over the leadership although they realize that his health being what it is he may not accept. They are strongly of the opinion that his acceptance of the leadership would ensure his being Premier whenever the election takes place. I agree with them . . . [4]

There is also some evidence that Diefenbaker was prepared to let Hamilton return to Saskatchewan. Faibish spoke with the Chief in August and related the following to his boss:

> He [Diefenbaker] said he told Martin Pederson last week that he did not have a hope in hell to win more than four seats, and that the only solution was for you to return to Saskatchewan as leader . . . He is completely convinced that you would win and he says you should stay a short time and return to Ottawa at the earliest opportunity.[5]

When Faibish suggested that the Chief might want to have Hamilton near because of the threat to his own leadership, Diefenbaker replied, "Alvin has been a close, dear friend and his loyalty has been exceeded by no one else. For this I will be eternally grateful and I admire him for it . . . But, I can look after myself."[6]

Hamilton refused to leave Ottawa for several reasons. He pointed to his health which had not yet recovered completely from his bout with Bell's palsy a year previously. He stated that he had confidence in Martin Pederson who deserved the same chance to prove himself that he had had when leader.[7] He would not be a party to any attempt to remove Pederson if his protégé did not want to leave, and he would not embroil the provincial party in the destructive infighting that had begun in the federal party over the question of leadership. Furthermore, he remembered his years of frustration as leader and did not wish to repeat them.[8] Pederson's complaints during the remainder of his leadership must have evoked sour memories of his own difficulties a decade earlier. After the 1964 election, Pederson wrote to the party's national director that:

> I must state emphatically that the reason why we do not have more Members is two-fold. First of all is the age old problem that seems to be peculiar to the Conservative party, namely top-ranking Conservatives wanting to support almost any political party except the Conservative party . . . The second major problem that prevented the election of more candidates was the incredible lack of funds.[9]

At the same time, one of the workers sent by the federal party to assist in the campaign reported that:

> Prior to the election campaign, Martin Pederson was offered a certified cheque in the amount of $75,000, made out to him personally, together with a guarantee of $150,000 to run the campaign if he would saw-off with the Liberal Party to the tune of 15 candidates . . . When asked who made the offer, Mr. Pederson told me it was "Conservative doctor and Liberal Party money" . . . He did not accept . . . The fact that we did not saw-off with the Liberal Party almost split the Conservative Party.[10]

Matters had not improved much by the time of the next election. In Pederson's words:

> In the 1967 campaign, as usual, we were strapped for funds. Alvin Hamilton arranged with the late Bobby Brown of Calgary, president of Home Oil, for a substantial donation to our party. I instructed our Finance Chairman to go to Calgary to pick up the money. He reported to me, a week later, that he had indeed picked

> up the $26,000, had taken $1,000 to pay off a note at the bank owed by the Party, and, he claimed, given the other $25,000 to Ross Thatcher on the instructions of Bobby Brown, because we didn't have a chance to do anything. These were the kind of internal, behind the scene ways that the Regina group used to bring me to heel for my lack of cooperation in 1964. [11]

No one would give up a successful career to return to that situation. Most important of all, though, Hamilton's heart lay with federal politics. The provincial leadership had never been more to him than a stage on the journey to the House of Commons and he was determined to remain in Ottawa despite the flattering offers of support.

Nevertheless, he continued to take an active interest in the fortunes of the provincial party. He undertook a speaking tour of Saskatchewan at Pederson's behest in the autumn of 1963. He contributed financially to the party's campaign in 1964 which, incidentally, Diefenbaker did not. He also campaigned actively on behalf of Conservative candidates in that election which saw Pederson win, without Liberal support, the first unadulterated Conservative seat in the province since 1929 and Pederson was grateful:

> I wanted to place on the record how much I appreciated the tremendous help you gave me, both before the election was called and during the election campaign. The impact of you taking part in the campaign had considerable bearing and I'm quite sure had marked effect on the outcome in the Arm River seat.[12]

He helped out at the by-election in 1965 in Moosomin, a provincial constituency within his federal riding, and during the general election of 1967 he advised his constituents that:

> In the provincial election in Saskatchewan, I support the Conservative candidates. With the third party slipping in Western Canada, it is very important that the Conservative party move into the position of being the alternative to the present administration . . . If Conservatives get elected in the Provincial Ridings which constitute Qu'Appelle Federal Constituency, I guarantee to you that

> the Liberal Minister in charge of the Canadian Wheat Board will learn that Western Canadians are dissatisfied with his actions. [13]

Important as these activities may have been, however, they remained peripheral to his life as a federal politician. By this time his career was fixed firmly on federal politics, on issues of national concern and, of course, on the internal politics of the federal Progressive Conservative party.

One of the issues of the utmost importance to Alvin Hamilton throughout this period was China. The grain sales in the early 1960s began a relationship between Hamilton and the People's Republic which continued over the years. Beijing did not forget the pledge he made in April 1961 to help China sell her products abroad, nor the efforts he made while in office to keep that promise. While in Hong Kong in 1961 he had invited the Chinese to send a trade mission to Canada as soon as possible and, on his return to Ottawa, helped arrange the tour which took place in October. During that visit he advised his guests to send more specialized missions the following year, and again, he did everything he could to ensure their success. In addition, he contacted companies across Canada and urged them to take advantage of the opportunities created by the grain sales. Then, when the business community failed to respond, he turned to Canada's friends in Asia and Latin America and asked them to welcome Chinese trade stores as a favour to this country. They did, and China's exports increased dramatically, although not to the extent desired in Beijing.

Thus, in early 1964 when the Chinese wanted advice on their international trading operations they turned to Alvin Hamilton, despite the fact that he no longer held a cabinet post. Hamilton arrived in China in March and spent several weeks in various parts of the country. He visited Beijing early in the trip to fulfill the main purpose of the invitation. While there he discussed several aspects of international trade with Chinese officials, including communications channels, credit arrangements, and the difficulties of a state-trading nation doing business with private enterprise economies. Later, he and his wife Beulah toured the country:

> We walked on their streets; we shopped in their department stores; we visited their kindergartens, elementary schools and universities; we examined their tremendous plant for all types of sports; we toured factories and farms; we climbed the Great Wall and marvelled at the palaces and tombs of their Emperors; we rested at their recreational centres; and I even tried their acupuncture treatments at Peking [Beijing] and Shanghai hospitals. [14]

The visit also included several banquets the Chinese laid on for their guests, and at each of them the host thanked Hamilton and Canada profusely for selling grain to China. This gave Hamilton more than a moment's pause because he regarded the sales, however important, as a business transaction unworthy of such fervent expressions of gratitude and, when he asked for an explanation, was told the following:

> Our pride was rudely shattered by the weather difficulties of 1959 to 1961. We had to slow down our "Big Leap" forward in industrialization. We had to move our labour battalions from the cities to the country to build dams and drainage ditches to guarantee the basic need of our country, namely its food and fibre. Just at the moment when we were in the midst of this tremendous national effort thinking we had no friends, you came selling wheat. [15]

This not only explained Beijing's thankfulness, it also suggested that perhaps China was beginning to regret her isolation from the rest of the world.[16]

Hamilton's suspicions were confirmed during a lengthy conversation with Zhou Enlai before he left Beijing. The Chinese prime minister invited Hamilton to meet with him and they spent an hour and a half together. They touched briefly on Hamilton's discussions with the trade officials and then Zhou turned to his principal theme — his country's current economic and political difficulties. The prime minister admitted that China could not reach her economic objectives without foreign trade, and he agreed that she would have to restore links with her former trading partners, regardless of the differences in their economic and political philosophies. Further, he declared that China's security required her to return to the world political stage. He made it clear that Beijing feared the Soviet presence on her northern border more than any threat posed by the Americans, that she regarded Taiwan as her only major difference with the United States and that she was prepared to wait fifty years if necessary to settle the question. In Hamilton's words, "After ninety minutes I realized that he was trying desperately to tell me that the one thing he wanted to do before he finished his political life was to bring the United States and China back into some form of harmony."[17] China wanted to end her isolation. She wanted a rapprochement with the United States and Zhou would welcome discussions with American politicians and businessmen to that end. That was the understanding Alvin Hamilton took with him at the end of his first visit to the People's Republic.

At first he attempted to deliver the message to America's politicians. In the summer and autumn of 1964 he approached several senators, congressmen and members of the campaign committees of both President Johnson and Barry Goldwater, but they would not talk to him until after the election later that year. Then, in January 1965, Senator Fulbright, chairman of the Senate Foreign Relations Committee, arranged for him to meet unofficially with some members of both the Senate and House Committees and a representative from Vice-President Humphrey's staff. Hamilton informed them of Zhou's wishes and urged them to accept the invitation to visit China. The Americans split on the question — some wanted to go, others did not because, in accordance with prevailing sentiment at the time, "they thought that dealing with a Communist was like dealing with the devil."[18] Nothing of immediate significance came of that meeting and so Hamilton carried the message further to the American people. He talked to several boards of trade in cities on the west coast in an attempt to convince America's businessmen of the advantages of restoring trade with China. This led to an invitation from church groups in the American Midwest to participate in a series of debates on the issue of Sino-American relations culminating in a conference sponsored by the Kansas Institute of International Relations in March 1965. During the final debate Hamilton put forward the argument that would become his lodestar for the next twenty years. This was Peace Through Trade — the belief that "the quickest way to achieve peace with your enemies is to start trading with them."[19]

> I personally wish that the Americans had more confidence in their real strength. I am not referring to their great military strength. I am not referring to the American concepts of self-determination or American style democracy. I am referring to the economic system that has developed in North America . . .
>
> My appeal to you is to let this great force loose all over the world, not just in the hegemony of the friends of the United States. . .
>
> I am not talking about give-aways. I am talking on behalf of the tremendous desire for all the people in the world to have a better standard of living. Their pride will not allow them to accept charity, but they know that trade among nations builds wealth faster than by trying to live within the boundaries of one country. The Chinese know this. They are willing to trade. They are willing to talk. In time our political differences can be resolved if basic interests are accepted, but first let us get on with the task of raising the standards of living by bringing the newly developed nations into the orbit of World trade. If we have faith in the ability of our economic institutions to prevail, then there should be no doubt that we can arrive at political solutions.[20]

This argument had some appeal. Even former Governor Alf Landon, "Mr. Republican" in conservative Kansas and one-time candidate for the presidency, concluded that "we should trade with the bastards."[21]

Unfortunately, the demands of Hamilton's own political career and events in China intervened to interrupt his efforts in the United States although he did not abandon them altogether. As he wrote to an American acquaintance five years later:

> In 1966 the Cultural Revolution began and I have been unable to get even Canadian businessmen beyond Canton. Last year, however, the Cultural Revolution seemed to have quieted down and on behalf of a number

> of your Representatives and Senators I wrote a personal letter to the Prime Minister suggesting that whenever the time was "propitious" he should consider re-extending the invitation of 1964. [22]

The letter to Zhou informed the Chinese prime minister that:

> Several high-ranking Senators and Members of Congress have indicated to me that they would like to visit China and discuss relations between China and the United States.
>
> Last month the Honourable J.W. Fulbright . . . wrote me. In his letter he pointed out that the United States Government has relaxed restrictions on travel to China and asked if I thought that your government would give him and one or two other members of his Committee visas to visit China.
>
> I submit this inquiry to you personally in the light of our conversation in 1964.[23]

Ultimately, of course, "ping-pong" diplomacy superseded Hamilton's efforts and led eventually to Richard Nixon's visit to Beijing. Nevertheless, Hamilton is satisfied with his early attempts to encourage a dialogue between China and the United States. He carried Zhou's invitation to the United States as requested, he planted the idea of rapprochement in the minds of several powerful American politicians, and he helped soften the extreme anti-Chinese attitudes of some of the American public. It would have been difficult for a man in his position to do more for he also had a great deal on his plate in Canada, including work to help overcome China's trade problems.

Hamilton understood that China's difficulty in increasing her exports could not be solved by any one approach alone and so he tackled them on several different though related fronts. First, he continued his efforts throughout the 1960s to convince Canadian businessmen of the profits to be made from trade with the People's Republic, and he returned to China in 1966 in an attempt to smooth the way for Canadian firms, albeit with little success because of the suspicion of anything foreign which characterized the Cultural Revolution.

Second, he kept a close watch on Canada's continued grain sales to China and urged the Pearson government to do more to help Beijing balance her large trade deficit with this country. In May 1965, for example, he rose in the House of Commons to declare that:

> I think we can gather from the announcement made today [of further sales] that this is no longer a temporary type of market. I think we have to assume now that this is not a windfall type of arrangement but will be here permanently.
>
> Therefore, in view of its importance I am going to ask the . . . Government to take effective action with regard to the desire of mainland China to set up in this country . . . an unofficial trade office where their representatives can meet with Canadian businesmen, so we can show some effort on our part to get their goods into this country, which are not coming in any amount at all at the present time. [24]

His reasons were straightforward and to the point:

> Trade with China is not going to be a one way street. We are selling them approximately $150 million worth of wheat a year and we are buying back a handful of millions — $4 million or $5 million — of dollars worth of materials. Canadian policy should be to help the Chinese in every way to establish legitimate trade relations with us.[25]

Furthermore, "Canadian Government policy should be to persuade the Americans to change their regulations . . . to allow American businessmen to trade with China."[26]

Hamilton's third approach was global in scope. He advised the government not to forget the less developed nations of the world when formulating its trade policy and not to join other industrialized countries in erecting barriers against trade with the emerging economies of Asia, Africa and Latin America. He feared that the GATT negotiations underway in the mid-1960s would perpetuate the poverty of the Third World, and he made several proposals he thought should form the basis of Canada's policy on foreign trade. His most comprehensive set of recommendations came in a speech to the House of Commons in the autumn of 1964. At that time he urged the government to:

1. Accept international commodity agreements which would raise the living standards of underdeveloped nations even if these increased costs to Canadian consumers
2. Create an agency to facilitate contact between Canadian businessmen and countries such as China which do not have the resources to develop their own selling organizations
3. Form purchasing boards in Canada with the authority to sign agreements with countries such as China which have a single selling agency
4. Encourage Canadian companies to combine their efforts at expanding exports
5. Press for the establishment of a world trading bank to facilitate credit sales and to take care of the paper work involved in such arrangement
6. Reduce tariffs on certain goods on a bilateral basis with as many countries as possible as proposed in the negotiations with the United States over the Auto Pact.[27]

Three years later, he added an expanded "export credits program" to his recommendations because:

> If we are to send our small companies around the world to enter into world-wide competition and ask them to get out and sell in world markets . . . we should establish a system of credit that will allow the salesmen of Canadian companies to get credit quickly so they may complete the sale at the earliest possible moment and beat out their competitors.[28]

Hamilton emphasized that in helping the underdeveloped nations of the world Canada would also be helping herself, and he returned to this theme time and time again. In the June 1967 speech he warned that:

> We in the industrial nations are now faced with two major choices. One is that we should use our great and growing wealth in a combined operation of giving handouts to the newly developing nations to try to keep them

> afloat and the other choice is to push self-help proposals. One of these self-help proposals is epitomized in the phrase 'trade, not aid'.[29]

Hamilton left no doubt as to which choice he would make:

> I think we should deliberately send our representatives to UNCTAD this autumn with instructions to state that it is Canadian government policy, supported by all parties, that we as a nation will enter into commodity agreements with the newly developing nations so they will receive an enhanced price for their primary products and so that their producers will be given a much better chance to attain a better living standard. We on our part will voluntarily accept any greater costs which come to us in this regard.[30]

The Third World deserved better than it was receiving at that time from industrialized nations, and Hamilton used an example from Canada's trade relations with China to prove his point:

> We buy $10 million worth of rice each year. China is selling rice on the world market and is buying our wheat on world markets; yet we in Canada do not buy one single dollar's worth of rice from China . . .
>
> I say it is in Canada's interest to help the countries that are buying from us by selling their products in this country.[31]

This was the same philosophy which had guided his thinking on ARDA and the World Food Bank. People everywhere preferred to help themselves rather than accept charity. If countries such as Canada helped nations such as China to prosper then Canada would benefit in return.

The prosperity of Canadians in general, and the farm population in particular, was also an issue of great concern to Alvin Hamilton throughout this period. Diefenbaker chose him to be the opposition critic for agriculture, made him chairman of the caucus committee on agriculture and appointed him to the committee on northern affairs and national resources. In addition, Diefenbaker named him chairman of the Caucus Policy-Making Committee — a tribute to his reputation as the principal "ideas man" of the previous administration. Hamilton regretted losing office in 1963 as much if not more than most Conservatives. He needed more time to see his plans for Canadian agriculture through to fruition and believes that the farm population would be better off today had he been able to do so.[32] Nevertheless, he adapted quickly and easily to life in opposition, despite having been a member of the governing party since his first election to Parliament in 1957, and he had acquired a vast background of knowledge and experience on which to base his criticisms of the new government. Hamilton also accepted his new rôle graciously, at least to begin with. He briefed his successors, Harry Hays in agriculture and Mitchell Sharp in charge of the Wheat Board, as to the problems they would face and pointed out to Maurice Sauvé the opportunities which lay ahead for the minister with responsibility for the ARDA programme. Furthermore, he convinced his fellow Conservatives on the Commons' Agriculture Committee to support any initiative which would assist farmers regardless of whether it was government sponsored or not.

Hamilton's contributions to the work of the House of Commons during the years of the first Pearson government reflect his major concerns and responsibilities at the time. Most of his questions and speeches dealt with agriculture and resources policy and no aspect of either escaped his notice. He urged the government to introduce a programme for eastern farmers, and to permit China to establish trade offices in Canada. He attacked the government over its grain transportation policy, for its stand on freight rates, and its refusal to take action to reduce the cost of farm machinery. He demanded information on grain sales, rail line abandonment, and the impact of the labour code on the operation of country elevators. He did his homework, read widely to prepare himself, and became a formidable force on the opposition front bench, so much so that Diefenbaker gave him the go-ahead to pursue other issues which attracted his attention. Thus, over these two years he also spoke on federal-provincial shared cost programmes, problems of international trade, the transportation of natural gas, off-shore mineral rights, forestry, aid to Tanzania to establish an air force, and during the debate on the new Canadian flag in which, contrary to his leader's position, he proposed his own design and urged that a national plebiscite be held to settle the matter.[33]

Hamilton attacked the government mercilessly when he believed circumstances required it and his zest for battle sometimes brought down upon him the wrath of both Liberal members and the Speaker. On one occasion, for example, he charged the prime minister with deliberately misleading Parliament, a claim that Pearson could not ignore and one that led the Speaker to ban Hamilton from the House of Commons, the first Canadian Privy Councillor to be so barred to that time. In response to a question from Gordon Fairweather, member for Royal constituency in New Brunswick, the prime minister assured the Commons that the sound cameras which had been taping a day in his life for a television programme had not been present during a cabinet meeting. This answer did not satisfy Hamilton. He had talked to some of those who had been present that day, at least one cabinet minister and a few of the journalists, and their accounts convinced him that Pearson had not told the whole truth. Hamilton raised the matter again and once more the prime minister denied that he had permitted any violation of cabinet secrecy. Hamilton then stated that "on the basis of the evidence we have, I say that is not the complete truth," and he charged that Pearson had "deliberately misled the House."[34] The prime minister objected to this, of course, and the Speaker asked Hamilton to withdraw his remarks. When he would not, the Speaker "named" him for disregarding the authority of the chair and he had to leave the House of Commons for a day.

After the election of 1965 and the death of George Nowlan in May of that year, Diefenbaker moved Hamilton from agriculture to be the Conservative party's finance critic. This gave Hamilton a chance to spread his wings even further and, in light of his growing knowledge of that complex subject, he did so happily. This did not mean that he ignored those areas in which he had been interested in the past. On the contrary, in his speeches and questions he continued to harass the government over grain sales, trade with China, a national power grid, development of the mineral resources of the north, forestry, grain transportation, oil and gas distribution, and rural development. He also had something to say about the plans for the Centennial, which had begun under his stewardship, the pollution of boundary waters, development of a Canadian film industry, federal support for universities (which he thought essential), unification of the armed forces (which he opposed), redistribution of federal constituencies in Saskatchewan, and morality in government, specifically the improper conduct of some members of the Pearson cabinet. In fact, it is fair to say that Alvin Hamilton became one of the star performers of the Progressive Conservative front bench during this period, and on one occasion he single-handedly forced the government to reverse a position it had announced publicly, an occurrence increasingly rare in the days of over-sensitive governments and disciplined party supporters.

Hamilton calls the event the Great Lakes Affair and regards it as the highlight of his first term in opposition. In 1965 it became clear that Ontario would require a substantial increase in imports of natural gas from western Canada and a year later the National Energy Board approved construction of a new pipeline south of Lake Superior through the United States to the refineries at Sarnia. Immediately there were cries of outrage from northern Ontario and, faced with two important by-elections in the area, the cabinet overturned the board's decision and ordered the pipeline to be built north of the lake. To Hamilton:

> This meant higher construction costs, no opportunity for summer storage along the route and hence a reduced load factor and higher unit costs per mcf. The resulting price in southern Ontario would be higher than competitive American gas and the big markets of southern Ontario would be lost to Canadian gas.[35]

As always, Hamilton did his homework on this issue. He consulted his friends in the industry and spoke to officials at TransCanada PipeLines Ltd. The speech in the House of Commons which resulted from this research was a tour de force. Hamilton took each argument presented by government spokesmen for their decision, demolished it, and presented counterarguments as to why the initial energy board decision should have been accepted. He also knew that TransCanada PipeLines would agree to increase the carrying capacity of its all-Canada route if permitted to proceed with its American plans, and when he recommended that the government meet again with TransCanada PipeLines officials the Liberals jumped at the chance, and eventually reversed their initial insistence on the Canadian route. According to Hamilton, "It was a sweet victory. I knew that there weren't too many cases where a one-man stand by an Opposition M.P. changed a Government's decision 180 degrees. I remember Diefenbaker doing it in 1951 on the Foot and Mouth disease outbreak . . . Now I had my own victory."[36]

Given his new responsibility as finance critic, Hamilton came to concentrate more and more on the government's monetary and fiscal policies and their economic and social effects as the period drew to a close and as John Diefenbaker ran out his string as leader of the Progressive Conservative party. His speeches during the budget debate in 1966, and on the estimates for the Department of Energy, Mines and Resources in 1967, provide excellent examples of his thinking on economic affairs. In them he outlined in some detail the philosophy of development he believed any Canadian government should pursue. His critique of Mitchell Sharp's budget in 1966 set the stage as follows:

> The tragedy of this budget, Mr. Speaker, is that the minister has not faced up to the fundamental decision which confronts Canada, and that is how to utilize the human and material resources of Canada so that the economy can operate closer to its essential capacity. The minister's policy would leave these human and material resources for ever and ever untapped at a time when consumer demand is there . . . The government last year introduced a general expansionist budget that had no regard for region or industry. The heating up of the economy in 1965 in certain areas has become alarming. The rise in prices to those who have low or marginal incomes is a disaster.

> During the last year the Bank of Canada reacted to the inflationary situation by imposing tighter money restrictions. The government at that time put some slight restrictions on some construction. This budget, however, adds several dampers to the economy. In some sections of the country and in some segments of the economy this is helpful. In other areas where we should be encouraging expansion to fully mobilize the nation's resources, it will not be helpful.[37]

His solutions to the problems facing Canada at the time were these:

> First, I ask why does the government not use the restrictive items of the budget on a selective basis, industry by industry, and region by region . . . ?
>
> Second, I should like to propose temporary manpower policies . . . Long-range policies involving education, immigration, retraining of workers, and so on, must go forward. In the meantime let us utilize the reserves of manpower available. . .
>
> Another point I wish to make . . . has to do with a policy on saving. I have figures to show that Canada is the most saving nation in the world. Yet we are short of capital . . . Is it not about time we gave incentives to people to own property and equity shares in the industries of this country . . . ? Think what relief from inflationary pressure the additional investment would bring and what a help it would be to people to have a type of savings which would grow with the country and help offset rising costs.[38]

At the same time he urged the government to raise old age pensions to one hundred dollars per month and to make better use of the treasure house of experience possessed by the nation's aged. In his words:

> The idea that people are handicapped or useless when they are over 65 years of age is altogether wrong. Their potential usefulness is tremendous. If we could employ these people in trouble spots to help us meet the shortage of skilled labour there would be no need to employ the restrictive devices which are used in the present budget.[39]

Just over a year later he returned to the attack:

> Our economists use the great ideas of Lord Keynes. Lord Keynes developed a system of economics designed to suit a homogenous, integrated country such as the United Kingdom, a country which was an exporter of manufactured goods and an importer of raw materials. He developed this economic system as a means of avoiding the ups and downs of the economic cycle. We in Canada have transferred this doctrine to our own country without taking account of the fact that Canada is not a homogenous or even an integrated country. We are a country of regions. We are not a sophisticated, mature industrialized country yet. Nevertheless our policies at the national level assume we are all in the same boat. We are not. So if we find two provinces threatened with inflation and eight provinces stagnating, we seek to cure the inflation in two provinces by imposing the same restrictions on the whole country, whether all parts need it or not.
>
> The whole concept of fiscal, monetary and trade policies fails because governments have failed to accept our need for a resource philosophy.[40]

Canada needed a comprehensive resources policy because:

> Canada undoubtedly is a resource nation and will continue to be one for many years to come. But though we have been a resource nation from the very beginning, there has never been developed in this country a resource philosophy which dominates the thinking of ministers of finance, which dominates the thinking of governments. If our future depends on the use made of these resources, then the whole organization of tax laws should be oriented to this end.[41]

Such a comprehensive resources policy could be found in the Second Stage of the National Development Program prepared by Hamilton and his advisers in 1961 but never legislated. If adapted to new circumstances it could provide direction and purpose for the nation's economic, trade, and manpower policies in the future.[42] It could also and would also provide the basis of Alvin Hamilton's run for the leadership of the Progressive Conservative party at the appropriate time.

The House of Commons was an important forum for Alvin Hamilton between 1963 and 1967, but his contributions there were only a part of his efforts on behalf of his party during those years. In fact, his reputation in party circles, his obvious concern for party policy, and his intense desire to strengthen the party in every region of Canada led him far beyond the confines of Parliament Hill. He received numerous invitations to attend various party functions at the provincial and constituency levels and fitted as many as possible into his crowded schedule, speaking on topics as diverse as national development, cooperative federalism, and the need for an urban renewal policy. Hamilton also took a special interest in provincial election campaigns and never refused a plea for assistance. In addition to his assistance to Pederson in Saskatchewan, in 1966, during the campaign in British Columbia, he asked voters to remember that:

> There are several parts of the federal P.C. program of Pacific development which require provincial action and cooperation before they can be proceeded with effectively. Land zoning, transportation and city planning are examples of provincial jurisdiction that would be helped if the P.C. point of view was available in the Legislature.
>
> I would like to see Vancouver become the champion of the North West. It would be mutually advantageous to the people of the interior and the people of the Lower Mainland. This wish would be expedited if the P.C. voice could be heard at Victoria.[43]

Hamilton had fought Social Credit attempts to take over the Conservative party in Saskatchewan for too long to accept Premier Bennett's claim that his party represented the only free enterprise alternative to the NDP, and what was true for British Columbia was also true for Alberta. A year later he wrote Peter Lougheed, the new leader of the Alberta party, to express his concern about:

> the proposals that are now appearing about a union between the Social Credit party and the Conservative party federally. These statesmen that make such comments aren't aware that such a proposal would destroy for a generation the efforts of many of us to build

> Provincial Conservative parties in Western Canada. Even considering the matter from the point of view of adding up votes, all that a Social Credit alliance would mean in Western Canada would be four extra seats federally. We have their votes now. It is obvious to me there is no need to sell any more of your homestead if it means achieving very little and destroying what can be very worthwhile in Western Canada.[44]

Perhaps Hamilton foresaw what lay ahead for Peter Lougheed in his struggle to overthrow the Social Credit dynasty. Hamilton had kept in close contact with Alberta politics over the years, especially when he was minister of agriculture. Then, in the summer of 1963, he toured the province at the behest of the then leader of the party, Milton Harradence, to assist with the campaign. Four years later, at Lougheed's request, he helped draft the party's agricultural programme for the election of 1967, and immediately after the results showed that the party had won enough seats to become the official opposition he wired Lougheed the following advice:

> I know you will be exhausted but try to take full advantage of present momentum. Call meetings of all candidates and campaign managers almost immediately in Calgary and Edmonton to get maximum local publicity. Try to get organization meetings called in each city riding immediately. In rural areas get organization meetings called after seeding. Try to get as many good candidates publicly committed as possible. Call for organization meetings in all seats where no candidates nominated for this summer. After all that advice Congratulations on stirring up so much interest in our party in Alberta. In two weeks take a holiday.[45]

This advice carried some weight. In reply, Lougheed thanked Hamilton for his assistance and added that "I have followed up your suggestions with respect to maintaining our present momentum."[46] This momentum would carry Lougheed and the Alberta Progressive Conservative party to a stunning victory four years later.

Hamilton also played an important rôle in the federal party's campaign during the 1965 federal election. Prime

Minister Pearson called a snap election for 8 November on the advice of Walter Gordon and others who hoped to catch the Conservative party unprepared because of its leadership difficulties, and he very nearly succeeded in winning a Liberal majority. The national organization of the Progressive Conservative party was in some disarray due to the appointment of a new director, James Johnston, in the summer of that year, and the mounting tensions in the organization between the pro- and anti-Diefenbaker factions. Nevertheless, the party soon had a comprehensive platform to take to the electorate, thanks largely to Alvin Hamilton. According to Johnston, "Fortunately, Alvin Hamilton was also a member of the Conservative Party, and a few days later I was able to go to work with him, putting together the party's platform."[47] Even Diefenbaker admitted that "our platform was drafted and appeared in ample time, and I must give credit to the Honourable Alvin Hamilton for excellent work in overseeing the preparation of our policy papers."[48] The platform reflected Hamilton's ideas on a host of diverse issues. In the words of the *Monetary Times*, "Most of the Conservative policies which Diefenbaker has been pouring out since the opening day of the campaign originated in Alvin's fertile mind."[49] The platform contained proposals for urban redevelopment, education, national resource policy, new trade techniques and, of course, agriculture. Hamilton drafted both a western and an eastern farm policy for this election and the seven proposals for eastern agriculture — an eastern grain board, increased production of feed grain, a pasture programme, forage banks, an eastern PFRA, a dairy programme, and increased use of ARDA in eastern Canada — wrought what Diefenbaker's staff called the "Miracle of Ste. Perpetue" when the Chief announced it to a large group of Québec farmers at a campaign meeting there. Much to their surprise, since Diefenbaker was by no stretch of the imagination the most popular politician in Québec, the policy was welcomed enthusiastically and boisterously and provided a great boost to his campaign. Hamilton also campaigned vigorously across much of the country. He spent over half of October in Ontario, Québec, and the western provinces, and the last two weeks of the campaign in Qu'Appelle and other Saskatchewan constituencies. Once again the Liberals failed to win a majority despite the advantages they held coming into the campaign. Although they came very close — within four seats — Diefenbaker proved to be a formidable opponent once more, especially when fed the proper ammunition by Alvin Hamilton, and despite the fact that he led a party that was becoming increasingly tired of his leadership.

The results of the 1965 campaign convinced Hamilton that the Progressive Conservative party had two major problems to overcome before it could expect to return to power — the intra-party fight over the leadership and a lack of policies that appealed to a sufficiently wide spectrum of the population. In addition, he believed that if the party concentrated its efforts on the latter problem the former would diminish in importance.[50] He had participated at the National Conference on Canadian Goals in Fredericton in 1964, a conference sponsored by the Progressive Conservative Association of Canada and organized by its new president, Dalton Camp, and he recognized the utility of a focus on party policy. As he wrote to Brian Mulroney, a former member of his staff, in the winter of 1965:

> You have probably gathered by now that a great majority of the Caucus and the Executive want an end to all this bickering . . . I am going to get a group in caucus to join me in presenting to the Party, policy suggestions which I think will prove acceptable. These we will be prepared to take to the Annual Meeting of the Party whenever it is called. In the meantime we will be asking various groups in the Party to discuss these . . . suggestions publicly as well as privately. Because the ideas are fairly imaginative and constructive it may get the Party back on the rails again.[51]

After the election of that year, Hamilton tried to organize extra-Parliamentary committees across the country, especially in urban areas where the party was the weakest, to contribute ideas on policy to caucus.[52] The following year, after the meeting which voted to hold a leadership convention, in his capacity as chairman of the Caucus Policy-Making Committee he attempted to reunite the caucus by holding a series of meetings on party policy for the future. Members of the caucus met in December 1966 and January 1967, and produced Practical Policies for People — "not a complete statement of Party policy, but rather a direction of the Caucus discussion of policy."[53] The document made recommendations in the fields of agriculture, defence and external affairs, family life and divorce, federal-provincial relations, finance and trade, health and welfare, housing, labour, resources, trade and commerce, and urban affairs and several bore the distinct imprint of Alvin Hamilton. In agriculture, for example, caucus proposed to "Revitalize the ARDA program and utilize the federal initiative to a far greater extent to solve rural problems and resource development for the benefit of all Canadians," to "Increase Livestock capacity in both Eastern and Western Canada by . . . A program specifically directed to the increased production of feed grains," and to "Modernize grain handling, storing and marketing procedures for Canada by . . . New sales technqiues such as long term contracts and reciprocal trade arrangements."[54] With respect to resources, the government should proceed on the principles "that first and cheapest access to energy should be provided for Canadians by east-west connections for gas, oil and electricity, including a national power grid, as common carrier," and "that regional development policies be continued and expanded . . . with special attention to our long term objective of bringing the economy of the Atlantic Provinces into balance with the rest of Canada," all the while remembering that "the consistent principle must be the philosophy of developing and conserving Canada's resources to meet Canada's need first."[55] In the area of trade and commerce Canada should develop her export markets by:

1. Expanded use of export credit and export insurance to enable Canadian producers to sell their products in the export market as easily as they do in the home market
2. A greatly intensified drive by our trade commissioners abroad to find new markets for Canadian products,

with particular stress on agricultural and fisheries products

3. Expanded use of foreign trade fairs to better inform Canadian producers of the opportunities to sell their products in the export markets
4. Bringing foreign buyers to Canada to see first-hand what Canadians have to offer, both in large trade exhibitions in our principal cities, and in production plants.[56]

Unfortunately for Hamilton, and perhaps the Conservative party, the fight for the leadership intervened to kill this promising initiative. Concern for policy alone could not keep either caucus or party united as both headed for the leadership convention. Hamilton put in a brief appearance at the Montmorency Conference in August, a gathering staged by Camp and the extra-Parliamentary party to avoid the chaos of policy formation at the leadership convention,[57] but was not an active participant. By this time, Hamilton was a candidate for the leadership himself and had already set out his stands on what party policy should be. He had little to gain, therefore, from participation at a conference put on by those who accepted neither his policies nor the prospect of his leadership. The same was true for Diefenbaker, and he did not attend at all. The Montmorency Conference, however, did have important repercussions for both men. It was at Montmorency that the "deux nations" idea first gained credence in the Conservative party, a rather innocuous statement on the Canadian founding in itself, but one whose implications were anathema to Diefenbaker and one which he decided to oppose at all costs. He took the fight to the floor of the convention as one of the candidates for the leadership and in so doing dashed whatever chance Alvin Hamilton had to lead the party he had served so faithfully for so many years.

Hamilton's involvement in the struggle for the leadership which went on in the Progressive Conservative party between the election of 1963 and the leadership convention in September of 1967, is the story of his attempt to reconcile two deeply held loyalties — one to John Diefenbaker and the other to the

Progressive Conservative party itself. The results of the 1963 campaign convinced Hamilton that the party would never win the support in urban Canada which it needed to return to power as long as Diefenbaker remained leader and the verdict in 1965 confirmed this belief. Thus, he was open to the argument that the Chief must go for the good of the party. Nevertheless, he was not prepared to force Diefenbaker out of the leadership and would not countenance any attempt to embarrass the Chief or to push him out against his will. He wanted to orchestrate an orderly succession, one which would allow Diefenbaker to leave with dignity and, at the same time, unite the party behind a new leader who stood a good chance of becoming prime minister after the next election. This is the reason he agreed to support Dalton Camp's candidacy for the presidency of the Progressive Conservative Association in February 1964. Camp promised to keep the anti-Diefenbaker faction in the extra-Parliamentary party in check while Hamilton arranged the succession.[58]

The arrangement worked well for a time as each man kept his part of the bargain. Hamilton convinced a majority of caucus not to oppose Camp's candidacy, Camp won the presidency and banked the fires of revolt within the extra-Parliamentary party, and Hamilton had his chance to find a replacement for the Chief on terms that Diefenbaker might accept.[59] Hamilton did not consider himself a possible successor. In fact, he did not believe that anyone in the Conservative caucus at that time was of leadership calibre. He wanted a person new to federal politics who accepted the development philosophy of the previous government, someone who would retain the rural support Diefenbaker had acquired, and who would also lure back the urban voters who had turned against the Chief. He planned to invite potential candidates to run for Parliament, prove their mettle in the House of Commons, and enter the leadership contest with Diefenbaker's blessing and the support of caucus. He approached the Chief with the idea in the summer of 1964 and Diefenbaker told him to proceed.

Over the summer Hamilton contacted the five people on his list of whom Diefenbaker approved — Robert Stanfield, premier of Nova Scotia; Lucien Saulnier, chairman of

Montréal's Executive Committee; John Robarts, premier of Ontario; Robert Macaulay, former minister of economics and development in Ontario; and Duff Roblin, premier of Manitoba.[60] The only one to show definite signs of interest was Duff Roblin. Hamilton then sought and obtained assurances from a majority of Conservative MPs that they would give Roblin every chance to show himself worthy of the leadership and Gordon Churchill agreed to resign his seat and create a by-election at the earliest possible moment if Roblin decided to enter the House of Commons.[61] It seemed at the time that Hamilton's plan would succeed. He and Churchill had found a successor apparently acceptable to Diefenbaker and a majority of caucus and the candidate seemed willing to spend some time proving himself in the Commons prior to the Chief's resignation.

The plan began to fall apart almost at once. Diefenbaker's opposition to the proposed new flag in the autumn of 1964 antagonized the Québec wing of the party and caused a split in caucus. Roblin decided to wait for a more propitious time to enter Parliament. A few months later, in February 1965, Léon Balcer, appointed Québec lieutenant a year earlier, demanded that the National Executive of the party call a leadership convention. His motion was defeated, though only by a small majority of two, and Balcer left the party soon afterward. Then, just as these wounds began to heal, Pearson called the election of November 1965, which forced the issue as far as Roblin was concerned. Hamilton moved immediately to persuade Roblin to run in this election. He arranged for seventy-three of the ninety-six Conservative MPs to contact Roblin in one way or another to urge him to enter federal politics.[62] When Roblin hesitated, he had Diefenbaker and Stanfield add their weight to the appeal but, in the end, Roblin would not take the plunge. He decided, or perhaps allowed himself to be convinced, that the risks were too great to give up his position as premier of Manitoba with no ironclad guarantee that Diefenbaker would step down soon in his favour, or that caucus would select him as the best person to assume the mantle. Roblin's refusal to accept the draft in 1965 ended Hamilton's efforts on his behalf and may have cost him the leadership when he sought it two years later. Hamilton had done for Roblin all that one could be expected to do, but without result. He had mortgaged his reputation with his colleagues for Roblin and Roblin's rebuff cost him personally. In his words, "We could have won the election in '65 with Duff. My popularity and usefulness in caucus were literally ended [because of Roblin's decision]."[63] The election also ended the understanding with Dalton Camp which had given Hamilton his chance to arrange an orderly and peaceful change in the leadership. Hamilton campaigned for Camp in his attempt to win a seat in 1965 and paid tribute to the president's efforts to maintain party unity. Camp, for his part, fought valiantly for the party and its leader during that election, but ended the campaign convinced that something had to be done quickly to replace Diefenbaker, and he broke his agreement with Hamilton and began to use his office to do just that. The struggle for the leadership thus entered a new phase and put the two men on opposite sides in the battle to come. Although Hamilton believed that the party would do better electorally with a new leader, his sense of loyalty would compel him to fight to keep Diefenbaker in the leadership until the Chief indicated that he was ready to go.

The battle began in earnest in the summer of 1966 when Camp called for a review of the leadership and began to seek support within the party for a leadership convention and to win a second term as party president. The struggle proved to be easier than he could have imagined because Diefenbaker refused to fight him on his ground. Although the Chief was well aware of Camp's activities, and supporters such as Hamilton urged him to build a counter-organization, Diefenbaker refused to do so, apparently in the mistaken belief that he had little to fear from the people he so contemptuously dismissed as the "termites." Even Hamilton treated the threat lightly at first. In a speech to a party gathering in Moose Jaw he referred to Camp and the calls for a leadership review in this vein:

> It reminds me of a prairie slough at dusk; you can hear a million bullfrogs croaking there on the lily pads.
>
> You sneak up through the bullrushes and quickly grab one of them, and 50 percent of the noise is gone.[64]

The consequence for Diefenbaker was that he lost this initial battle almost by default. By the time the party met in Ottawa in November a majority of delegates supported Camp and his position on the leadership. Furthermore, and to compound his problems, the government scheduled a debate on a proposed change to the rules by which the House of Commons granted supply to coincide with the opening of the convention. This meant that staunch Diefenbaker loyalists, such as Churchill and Starr, could not devote much time to campaign on his behalf. It was left to Alvin Hamilton, who saw the writing on the wall, to round up a few members in a desperate last minute attempt to convince delegates not to desert their old Chieftain. In his words:

> Never in the field of human endeavour have so few made so many people so mad. We just brutalized those poor delegates. I told fellows who I'd helped out in various constituencies . . . if you go and gun down this guy Diefenbaker, I'll be in there speaking against you. I don't care if you're running for dogcatcher. I'll tell them what a lowdown dirty skunk you are.[65]

The pressure did change some votes, but not enough. Nor did Diefenbaker's speech to the convention. He underestimated the strength of feeling against him. He was booed, heckled, and embarrassed on national television, the butt of "the most humiliating political scene in Canada's history."[66] When the votes were counted, Camp defeated Arthur Maloney, Diefenbaker's choice for president, by 564 votes to 502. Then, with the pro-Diefenbaker forces disheartened and in disarray, the convention adopted the following resolution:

> That this party expresses its support of the Right Honourable John G. Diefenbaker, its national leader, and acknowledges its wholehearted appreciation of his universally recognized services to the party, and in view of the current situation in the party, directs the National Executive, after consultation with the national leader, to call a leadership convention at a suitable time before January 1, 1968.[67]

First the rose, then the crown of thorns. The motion passed by 563 votes to 186.

This vote was a crushing blow to Alvin Hamilton, for it wrought the very occurrence he had worked for so long to avoid — the public humiliation of John Diefenbaker by his own party. In his words, "It was a dreadful experience to see one human being hounded by other human beings."[68] In retrospect, he wished he had never accepted Diefenbaker's refusal to organize his support prior to the convention, and he blamed himself for allowing Camp's people to take over delegate nomination meetings almost without a fight.[69] Furthermore, the strong-arm tactics he had used on delegates at the convention made him wonder if he had any friends left in the party.[70] The entire affair left him sick at heart and disgusted with his fellow Conservatives and, for a few days, he seriously considered leaving politics altogether.[71] In the end, he could not do so. Bitter though he may have been, and despite his loyalty to Diefenbaker, who held the leadership proved to be of secondary importance to him. As he explained to his wife Beulah:

> That's my party. No matter how sick it is, I'm going to stay there and fight for all I'm worth for what I believe in because my main pitch hasn't really been for Diefenbaker or for Bennett or for Bracken or for Drew. My main pitch is the ideas that I represent and [although] the party is the most stupid party I . . . could ever be in, at least . . . if they only know what the right thing is they tend to do it.[72]

This is the reason he refused to have anything to do with the proposal floated at the time by some Diefenbaker supporters in caucus that they leave the Progressive Conservative party and form their own independent group in the House of Commons. He realized that this would place him outside the mainstream of Canadian politics, that his ideas would never see the light of day as legislation, and Diefenbaker simply was not worth that sacrifice. Nevertheless, his allegiance to John Diefenbaker remained sufficiently strong that he would fight to keep the Chief as leader for as long as he was certain that Diefenbaker wanted the post. He signed the petition circulated by Gordon Churchill just after the annual meeting which urged the Chief to "continue as Leader of our Party" and which repudiated "the action of the party's annual conference in calling for a review of leadership and a national convention in 1967 at which the leadership would be at stake."[73] In addition, he began a counterattack which he hoped would weaken Camp's position and reunite the caucus behind its leader. He could not turn back the clock perhaps, but he could try to give John Diefenbaker a better chance of winning the leadership at the forthcoming convention, if he chose to run, or of dictating the conditions of his departure, if he decided to go. Hamilton wanted to build the organization of pro-Diefenbaker supporters he felt he should have put together when Camp's tactics first became apparent. Near the end of November he advised Maloney that:

> It is clear that we were 'taken' at the Annual Meeting by a well organized group. . .
>
> Therefore, on my own responsibility, I am quietly moving to straighten out this matter in the three provinces in the West. I think some thought should be given to Ontario.[74]

At the same time he began to contact individual party members he knew to be Diefenbaker loyalists to urge them to take on the challenge to the Chief's leadership. For example, in a letter to Mrs. J.G. McDougall of Blyth, Ontario, he wrote that:

> You have probably heard by now that 71 members of Caucus are standing firmly behind Mr. Diefenbaker and we will be asking constituency Associations to name pro-Diefenbaker candidates in the next election. In other words we may have lost a battle but there are others to come.[75]

Further, he used his chairmanship of the Caucus Policy-Making Committee to call those meetings which led to Practical Policies for People and which he thought might bring back the anti-Diefenbaker MPs into the fold, or at least divert them from their attacks on the Chief.[76] All of these plans withered on the vine, however, when Diefenbaker called for an early convention to settle the issue of his leadership. Events began to move too swiftly for anyone to control and Hamilton began to weigh his own chances at the ring.

If the party's decision to hold a leadership convention "belled the cat," then the National Executive's announcement, on 29 January 1967, that the convention would be held in Toronto at Maple Leaf Gardens from 5–9 September "put the cat amongst the pigeons." Although Diefenbaker, in his call for an early convention, had not made his intentions clear, the general feeling was that he would not enter the race to succeed himself and this left the way open to anyone in the party, Diefenbaker loyalist or opponent, with leadership aspirations. At first, Alvin Hamilton did not see himself as a likely successor to the Chief. He recognized his own shortcomings and doubted that he would be regarded as a credible candidate.[77] Further, he realized that his rôle in the events of the past few months, and his public identification with John Diefenbaker, would undoubtedly hurt his chances of success.[78] In these early days, as before, he preferred to throw his weight behind someone who shared his philosophy and who could turn the Progressive Conservative party into a viable electoral force. If any candidate met these criteria, then Hamilton would not seek the leadership and he urged his friends in caucus to join him in a waiting game. In fact, he pleaded with those who had signed the pledge of loyalty to the Chief:

> not to make a decision to support anyone, to try to stay absolutely free until we saw which way the cookie was going to crumble and we could recover the loss of Diefenbaker by putting in the man that we wanted as opposed to the man that Camp and his crowd wanted and who I assumed would be either Stanfield (his first choice) or Roblin (his second).[79]

It was not until this effort failed, and the pro-Diefenbaker group in caucus began to split amongst various candidates, that Hamilton began to listen seriously to those who urged him to run himself.

There proved to be no dearth of people who wanted Alvin Hamilton to enter the race. He received letters and telegrams of support from all parts of the country and slowly but surely he succumbed to their pressure. By the end of March he would write one supporter, "It looks very much if Diefenbaker does not stay that I will have to take a go at it [the leadership]."[80] In mid-April he informed another that:

> It was very good of you to write suggesting that I offer my services for the Leadership. Many others have done the same thing. Organizations have sprung up in Vancouver, Alberta, Manitoba and Ontario to support my nomination. I have said publicly that if enough groups show an interest that I will let my name stand.[81]

Finally, on 26 May he threw his hat in the ring. He did not do so capriciously. In fact, he had many misgivings about his candidacy including the knowledge that he would need a miracle to win.[82] There were many reasons for his decision. Certainly the promises of support he received from all over the country convinced him that he could put together a creditable organization and that he would not be embarrassed by a paucity of votes at the convention. Secondly, none of the provincial premiers touted as potential successors — Robarts, Roblin or Stanfield — had entered the race and Hamilton believed himself to be better for the party than any of the candidates who had declared — Fulton and Hees — or any who might declare — Fleming and McCutcheon. Thirdly, Diefenbaker encouraged him to run. The Chief told him simply that "if you want to preserve what you've fought for all these years you must run."[83] Diefenbaker also urged others such as Starr and Fleming to put themselves forward, but Hamilton regarded this as an advantage. It convinced him that the Chief would not enter the race, it overcame his nagging suspicion that Diefenbaker wanted to use him as a "stalking horse" for his own candidacy, and it added to the impression he wanted to create that he was more than a mere shadow of John Diefenbaker.[84] Finally, he ran for the leadership because he wanted the Progressive Conservative party to continue on the course it had followed since 1956. As one of his opponents in the race, Davie Fulton, put it, "He ran to preserve a place in the party for prairie conservatism."[85] In Hamilton's own words, "I went into it for one purpose only and that was because I knew that I would be the best guardian of the policies I wanted the party to adopt and I said that all across the country. The only reason I ran was to push these policies."[86] Hamilton saw himself as the conscience of the party, the custodian of the advances of its recent past and the fount of its policies for the future. He had fought for his ideas for too long to let them go by default.

The press release Hamilton issued to announce his candidacy set the tone for his campaign. He would emphasize policy and party unity, both of which he deemed essential to restore the electoral fortunes of the Progressive Conservative party.[87] First of all, he reminded delegates of the party's recent history:

> You will recall that for many years the people of Canada regarded the Conservative Party as the spokesman for Big Business. John Diefenbaker changed that image to one in which our Party spoke for all groups; the farmers, the workers and the businessmen. He made Canadians aware of the Prairies, the Maritimes and the North and that they had not fairly shared in the general prosperity of the nation. As a result many people, who ordinarily did not trust the P.C. Party, started to vote for us. These newcomers to our Party will leave us just as quickly if that bond of trust and those things which John Diefenbaker stood for are questioned.[88]

His promotional literature evoked memories of the many successes of the Diefenbaker government — the grain sales to China, the Pine Point Railway, the Saskatchewan River Dam, the Atlantic Provinces Power Development, the Red River Diversion, the Columbia River Dam, the World Food Bank, the Law of the Sea Conference which secured Canada's control over the resources of the Arctic, and the northern mining and oil regulations that preserved the resources for Canadians — "all accomplishments in which Alvin Hamilton is recognized as playing a major role."[89] Then he urged delegates to look to the future. In general:

> any new leader must be able to hold the confidence presently held in John Diefenbaker and move into rural Quebec and the urban areas with policies to meet their needs. If that new leader can build an alliance among these various groups and regions, then the P.C. Party will

> predominate in the last third of this century as it did in the last third of the 19th century.[90]

Specifically, in a briefing paper prepared for the convention, the following points were made:

> In 1963 [*sic*] he caught every one's attention by his "Growth Theory" paper at the Fredericton Thinkers' Conference. In 1964 his speech in the House of Commons on new types of trade institutions to bridge the gulf between industrial nations and the newly developing nations was a landmark in new policy concepts for a trading nation like Canada. In 1965 he produced the nine point Urban Policy that was based on the needs of people living in built-up areas. More important he has been questioning the wisdom of the application of Keynsian doctrines "holus bolus" to Canada which is not a homogenous mature industrial country, but a regional country with various levels of development . . . His theories on flexibility by region and by industry have not been contradicted by economists. His "peaking" policies for labour and "capital accumulation" are unique and a practical means to attack any nation's basic problems of keeping full employment without serious rises in the cost of living . . . Alvin Hamilton is the only public figure putting forward a positive approach. He has been proposing . . . that Canada choose an expansionist, dynamic, type of nationalism that is world motivated . . . In 1967 in his Confederation Centennial Speech . . . he set an economic target of an average 6% growth rate for Canada over the next 25 years. With his coherent policies on finance, trade, urban matters, resources, development and administration of government he is confident that target can be reached. If it is reached, Canada's per capita income will exceed all other nations.[91]

In addition:

> No statement about Alvin Hamilton would be complete without mention of his concept of a package policy for social security. Sooner or later in a universal system the weight of abuses increases to a point which endangers the whole system. Some have proposed a means test. Alvin has put forward an individual incentive approach

> whereby the individual increases his final pension by using the other forms of service at a minimum. Special arrangements are made for the chronic cases. This idea will probably save more hundreds of millions than any other proposal advanced to date.[92]

Furthermore, "There is the question of loyalty to one's organization. That is not a test which Alvin Hamilton would fail. Loyalty to John Bracken — Loyalty to George Drew — Loyalty to John Diefenbaker."[93] Finally:

> The chief reason that the Progressive Conservative Party should choose Alvin Hamilton as their [*sic*] leader is that he is the only candidate, and one of the few men in any of the parties who is abreast or even in advance of current economic thinking at our Universities. He combines this quality with the skills acquired in 25 years of public life . . . He is a man who would bring Canadians national purpose, and would inspire by his dynamic brand of Canadianism a new sense of national unity and accomplishment.[94]

This was the message Hamilton and his supporters took to the delegates throughout the summer of 1967. It was a clever appeal designed to attract those who wanted the party to retain the best of its recent past and those who wanted it to strike out in new directions. In brief, it told delegates that given his past performance, and his plans for the future, Canadians everywhere could expect a better life with Alvin Hamilton as leader of the Progressive Conservative party and the next prime minister of Canada.

Hamilton looked to several long-time friends to assist in his campaign — among the most important Donald Johnston, still with TransCanada PipeLines and a man who had held a "watching brief" on Hamilton's leadership prospects from as early as 1960;[95] Roy Faibish, his one-time executive assistant, now in business; Kenneth Binks of Ottawa, a former national secretary of the party; David Sinclair, an accountant in Vancouver with experience in the oil industry; and William Whiteacre, a Toronto lawyer and president of the Progressive Conservative Businessmen's Club. These men formed the circle of his closest advisers and ran his organization. In addition, Hamilton sought help wherever he could find it — in caucus, in provincial organizations, amongst Progressive Conservative youth, and in the academic community. Although he did not have much open support in caucus, Robert Coates from Nova Scotia and Warner Jorgenson, his former parliamentary assistant from Manitoba, offered to campaign for him in their respective provinces. Martin Pederson, leader of the party in Saskatchewan, kept in touch with Binks throughout the summer and promised to persuade as many of his province's delegation as possible "to stand together . . . in support of Alvin."[96] Daniel Johnson, premier of Québec, provided an organizer to help in that province, in repayment of debts owed, despite his personal preference for the bilingual Duff Roblin. Whiteacre in Toronto and in Montreal André Leroux, a consulting engineer, and J.T. Copp, a professor at Loyola, organized Committees for Alvin Hamilton. Several university student Progressive Conservative Associations jumped on his bandwagon, and eventually Ed Mayernick, president of the Ontario YPC, and Les Horswill, president of the BCPC Student Federation, created a Youth for Hamilton Committee because "he, more than any other candidate, is expressing our generation's concern and also presenting well considered solutions to meet the real problems in Canadian political affairs."[97] University faculty also entered the lists on his behalf even though they were not members of the party. Two of them, Donald Smiley and Paul Tennant, both at the University of British Columbia, gave their reasons for their decision in the following statement midway through the campaign:

> We believe that Mr. Hamilton will be able to maintain unity within the Progressive Conservative Party and to increase support for the Party among those not now giving out their allegiance. He would be able to preserve and improve the better elements of Diefenbaker Conservatism — especially its sensitivity for the aspirations of ordinary citizens. We are especially impressed by the fact that, more than almost any other politician we know, Mr. Hamilton is informed of what the Academic community is saying and thinking about Canadian Affairs.[98]

Budget for the entire campaign was set at seventeen thousand dollars, a modest figure even at that time.

There is no doubt that Alvin Hamilton made the major decisions with respect to his campaign strategy.[99] He chose where, when and how to approach delegates and, in the beginning, he took several steps which left the impression that he did not think much of his chances of victory and that he had entered the race simply to make a point. He refused large contributions offered by friends in the oil industry on the grounds that they should back a winner — a mistake he would later regret when his people overspent the budget by ten thousand dollars in an attempt to match other candidates' handouts and hospitality at the convention, and he had to pay most of this out of his own pocket.[100] He told both Coates and Jorgenson that he would accept their support only on condition that they shift it to Stanfield or Roblin should either or both of these "favourite sons" run because "you've got to back the local champion or the local machine falls apart."[101] He ignored Saskatchewan and Alberta almost entirely, apparently for several reasons. In the first place, he did not believe that he had to campaign there to win votes. In his words, "if they didn't know what to do, there was nothing I could do to persuade them."[102] Secondly, he wanted to dispel the image that he was merely a regional candidate with appeal to westerners alone. Finally, as the convention drew near, he began to suspect that Diefenbaker might yet seek to turn back the clock, and he did not want to engage in a public fight for delegates in areas where both could expect to do well, or to place his friends in a position of having to choose between himself and their old Chieftain.[103] Thus, it can be seen that Hamilton's campaign was not based on a determination to win the leadership at all costs. He wanted the crown, but was not prepared to hurt the party to obtain it.

In these circumstances, Hamilton took his crusade into British Columbia, Ontario and Québec and spent little time on the prairies or in the Atlantic provinces. In fact, in the last month of the campaign he visited Saskatchewan only once for two short days and divided the remainder of his time between Ontario and Québec, devoting the last ten days exclusively to "la belle province." For a while it appeared that the tactic would be successful. He picked up support everywhere he went, except Québec, and entered the convention certain that he would do well on the first ballot. He had especially high hopes for Ontario. At the end of July he had approached the province's MPPs with the following proposal "of mutual interest":

> You will be facing a Provincial election soon. You have to face considerable resentment among the Progressive Conservatives in Ontario over the events of last November at the Annual Federal Meeting concerning the treatment of our Federal leader . . . This is where the mutual interest enters. Is it possible that your support for me federally would ease the strain with your pro-Diefenbaker supporters without alienating your young people or your anti-Diefenbaker P.C.'s?[104]

The response from at least one section of the Ontario élite seemed promising. According to Hamilton:

> Because of the effectiveness of the campaign that I had waged among the delegates in southwestern Ontario, John White had come up here to Ottawa to see me, as a spokesman for what we called the London 'mafia'. He indicated to me that in talking among themselves — and I assume that would be Frost and Robarts and so on who controlled that bloc of votes — they had decided that they would swing those two hundred votes either to Duff Roblin or myself, depending on the circumstances at the time of the convention . . . This chat with John White was very encouraging to me, and I visualized that, even with Stanfield and Roblin in, if I got the two hundred delegates I might be in the five hundred class on the first ballot.[105]

The rest of the five hundred would be made up by his "almost complete support in Saskatchewan and Alberta," "a proven group in B.C.," "a few from the Yukon," and "a bloc from northern Ontario."[106] Some of this support may have been "soft" and some of it conditional, but such is the stuff of which dreams of leadership are made. As long as Diefenbaker remained on the sidelines, and no other candidate performed better than expected, Alvin Hamilton had good reason for optimism as he entered the convention.

Hamilton came to Toronto on Sunday, 3 September, two days prior to the official opening of the convention, to meet delegates who arrived early and to plan convention tactics with his campaign team.[107] He took a suite at the Royal York for his personal use, booked the Alexander Room at the Westbury for his campaign headquarters, and set up hospitality suites in both hotels. He was in good spirits at the time. He had waged a creditable campaign by his own standards and reports from his staff gave him reason for hope, if not overconfidence. Six days later, on the day of the vote, his campaign was a shambles due to his own mistakes and to circumstances over which he had no control.

The first blow fell on Tuesday evening, 5 September, at the policy session at which all candidates had the opportunity to meet the party's Policy Committee and to outline the direction the party would take under their leadership. Hamilton, by his own admission, underestimated the importance of this meeting. He reminded the delegates there that policy was his forte and gave them as much of his plan for Canada as time would allow, but his remarks were "off the cuff" and "not a finished or polished performance."[108] Stanfield, by comparison, delivered a brief but "highly polished, prepared speech."[109] This mistake cost Hamilton dearly. Policy was his great strength and his entire campaign was based on the assumption that his vision of the Canada of the future would have a greater appeal to delegates than that of any other candidate. That did not happen on Tuesday evening. According to one observer, "The poor showing of his competitors plus the reverberating effect of the news media's choice of Stanfield as the best performer made that Tuesday evening speech the convention's turning point."[110] Momentum began to swing toward Stanfield from that moment, and it did not take long for the bad news to reach Hamilton. In his words:

> The next morning when the . . . papers came out that this was the man for all seasons, I knew what the score was. I finally got confirmation of that because John White was courteous enough to have breakfast with me and tell me

Alvin Hamilton with John Diefenbaker during the election campaign of 1957.

Alvin Hamilton, M.P. and his colleagues in the Diefenbaker cabinet, 1957.

NAC PA 129237

Minister of Northern Affairs
and National Resources, c. 1958.

NAC PA 129236

Chairman of the Cabinet Committee on the Columbia River, c. 1959.

J.G. Diefenbaker Centre JGD 383

Alvin and Beulah separated by other head-table guests appreciating John Diefenbaker's after dinner humour, c. 1959.

SAB R-A 11,470(7)

Alvin Hamilton looks on as Queen Elizabeth inspects a 4-H Club display at the Wells's farm, Tuxford, Saskatchewan, 1959.

SAB S-B 2590

Minister of Agriculture, c. 1960.

SAB S-B 2649

Minister responsible for the
Prairie Farm Rehabilitation Act, c. 1961.

"The Importance of ARDA," Chamberlain,
Halifax Chronicle-Herald, *27 March 1961.*

"On Top of the World," Chamberlain,
Halifax Chronicle-Herald, *31 March 1962.*

"More Political Hay," Sebestyen,
Saskatoon Star-Phoenix, *3 May 1961.*

"The Road to Hell," Jones,
Edmonton Journal, *14 November 1962.*

"Lower Dollar — Higher Exports — Greater Prosperity,"
Innes, Calgary Herald, *13 June 1962.*

"Protecting Canadian Sovereignty?," Reidford,
Globe and Mail, *8 March 1963.*

Alvin and Beulah met by Chinese officials Lee and Yao Wei as they arrived at Tientsen station, March 1964.

SAB S-B 2526

Candidate for the leadership of the national Progressive Conservative party, 1967.

SAB S-D10

Leading the procession of pall bearers at John Diefenbaker's funeral, 22 August 1979.

Being sworn in by Dr. B. Koester, Clerk of the House of Commons, after his election victory in 1984.

Brian Mulroney with his "friend and mentor," c. 1985.

With the Prime Minister on the occasion of Alvin's seventy-fifth birthday celebration, 30 March 1987.

"Advising the Prime Minister," Spring 1988.

"Still in Harness," Alvin Hamilton being greeted by John Fraser at the Speaker's Garden Party, June 1989.

> that the Ontario votes would now be going to Stanfield.[111]

The events of Tuesday evening also cost Hamilton the man he had asked to nominate him — William Davis, then minister of education for Ontario and later premier of the province. After White's visit, Hamilton telephoned Davis to assure him that he would understand if Davis wished to withdraw his support in the circumstances, and Davis did so "with much relief."[112]

The second blow came on Wednesday when the Policy Committee adopted the "two nations" theory of Confederation which had emerged from the Montmorency conference. This resolution coincided with Diefenbaker's arrival at the convention and it brought the Chief into the fray immediately. He despised the concept and would fight with every weapon at his disposal to ensure that it never became party policy. The resolution would have to be approved by the entire convention on Saturday to become official and Diefenbaker would use every opportunity to oppose it. His first chance came Thursday evening when he delivered the leader's address to the convention. Camp and the convention organizers hoped that this would be the night that John Diefenbaker accepted his fate and bowed out gracefully with the good wishes of a grateful party. Instead, the Chief used the occasion to deliver a ringing denunciation of the "two nations" resolution:

> The adoption of the two nations concept would segregate French Canada. I am not going to agree, whether it's popular or not, to erect a Berlin Wall around the province of Quebec . . . Laurier said, "This is one nation." Cartier said, "This is one nation." Langevin, Bourassa, St. Laurent said the same, all through the years. We are asked today to go back to the period between 1841 and 1867 to two Canadas. . . Furthermore, let us be Canadians. Let us not deny equality to those whose surnames are not of the parent races.[113]

Privately, he informed Hamilton that if the convention did not "get rid of that resolution on two nations . . . he might have to run for the leadership."[114]

Diefenbaker did in fact submit his nomination papers the following morning, fifteen minutes before the deadline, and ever since there has been speculation as to his reasons for the decision. Diefenbaker maintained that he did so in order to give himself another chance to speak to the convention to persuade delegates to oppose the "two nations" resolution:

> the absolute reverse of everything I had stood for in life, and the very reverse of everything the Conservative Party had stood for, from Macdonald to me . . . I realized that I would be clobbered in the voting, as I told my friends and supporters, but as no other candidate was prepared to pit himself against this monstrous course, it was up to me.[115]

Others, such as James Johnston, believe that Diefenbaker decided to run because he felt that since he had been elected leader by one convention only another convention could relieve him of the position and, further, that he wanted to show the party that its leader was not the tool of its president.[116] Newman suggests that Diefenbaker wanted to run all along and simply used the "two nations" resolution as an excuse to do so.[117] Hamilton tends to accept Newman's view. Years after the event he is convinced that Diefenbaker probably never intended to give up the leadership without a fight and that he saw the "two nations" resolution as a means to a last minute reprieve.[118] Whatever his reasons, Diefenbaker was now a candidate and this dealt the final blow to Hamilton's chances for the leadership. In his words:

> I knew the meaning of that to me and to Mike Starr. He said that he was not going to let the party adopt such a resolution, that it was against Conservative principles and against his views, very much so. I understood that and I've never done anything else but admire him for his stand, but it destroyed Mike and me as serious candidates.[119]

In an attempt to repair the damage, Hamilton announced that he agreed with Diefenbaker's stand on the issue but that he did not believe it should be allowed to dominate the convention. When this tactic failed he then "ordered" Pederson to instruct the Saskatchewan delegation to vote for Diefenbaker on the first ballot and passed the word to his other supporters that he would "understand" if they did the same.[120] This time his loyalty to the Chief and his concern for party unity did him in. Without these votes he would be too far behind after the first count to threaten the front runners and delegates would not look to him as *the* compromise candidate on future ballots.

There is no evidence that Hamilton ever thought of withdrawing from the race as he might have been expected to in the circumstances. Although his chances of victory had been hurt he had not decided to run for reasons of ego alone. He had a set of policies he wanted the party to adopt and this mattered more to him than the person who would put them into effect. In addition, he had attracted a group of dedicated followers who shared his purpose. They would not go to Diefenbaker automatically and he could not disappoint them. Furthermore, he had one last opportunity to present his case to the delegates and perhaps recoup the losses of the past couple of days. All the candidates would address the convention on Friday evening and Alvin Hamilton would not pass it by. After the obligatory "spontaneous" demonstration by his supporters and his nomination by Margaret Campbell, controller of Metropolitan Toronto, and Jean-Jacques Martell, MP for Chapleau between 1957 and 1962, Hamilton took the podium. Once again, he did not deliver a highly-polished performance. Only hours before he lay exhausted on his hotel bed tossing out ideas that Donald Johnston, his chief writer, attempted to put into speech form.[121] Nevertheless, according to the press, he gave one of the best speeches of the night.[122] He spoke openly of his high regard for John Diefenbaker and asked delegates not to penalize him for his loyalty to the Chief. He reminded the convention of his rôle in the successes of the Diefenbaker government. He warned of the threat to Canada's survival as an independent nation from the Liberal party's desire for commercial union with the United States, and urged delegates to adopt his policy of "expansionist nationalism" which would strengthen the Canadian economy by increased exports to countries all over the world, including Communist China to which he would extend official recognition. He outlined his plan for national economic development in which business, labour and government would each play an important rôle. This, he promised, would ensure a place for labour in the Progressive Conservative party. He also drew attention to the other source of the party's electoral misfortunes — its lack of support in the cities — detailed his proposals for urban Canada and called for a "new relationship between the modern city and the central government." Finally, he asked delegates to remember that the Conservative party should always be known for its humanity and never forget its responsibility to the nation's underprivileged — a keystone of his philosophy from his earliest days.[123] It was a powerful speech in which Hamilton gave full vent to his years of concern for party policy, one which accomplished his goal of providing the party a direction for the future if it wished to follow, and one which caused Peter Newman to write at the time that "whatever happens to the Conservative party, there will always be a touch of Alvin in the night."[124] Just the same, Newman also commented that "he was talking in his private shorthand, his visions too high-flown for his listeners"[125] — and the results next day would show that while the speech probably bound his followers more closely than ever to him, it did not attract many new converts. In this instance, those delegates who liked Hamilton's ideas but preferred someone else as leader could have their cake and eat it too, for the ideas would always be there for the taking without fear or favour.

Hamilton and his team played out the string to the bitter end. The next morning, Saturday, voting day, delegates awoke to find the following document available for their perusal and consideration. Titled ALVIN HAMILTON FOR THE FUTURE this handout reminded delegates that:

> Today YOU vote. So please ask yourself the four [*sic*] questions of paramount importance to all of Canada.
>
> — Which candidate has a record of unwavering loyalty to the Party leaders . . . Bennett . . . Bracken . . . Drew . . . Diefenbaker?
>
> ALVIN HAMILTON HAS!
>
> — Which candidate is identified with devotion to the all-important development of the nation's great Northland?

ALVIN HAMILTON IS!

— Which candidate has created a co-ordinated program for the development, re-development and enrichment of Canada's cities?

ALVIN HAMILTON HAS!

— Which candidate is internationally esteemed for his balanced approach to foreign affairs?

ALVIN HAMILTON IS!

— Which candidate is thoroughly acceptable to all members of our party in ALL parts of Canada?

ALVIN HAMILTON IS!

ALVIN HAMILTON CAN UNITE THE PARTY

ALVIN HAMILTON CAN UNITE CANADA

EVERYONE, EVERYWHERE TRUSTS ALVIN HAMILTON![126]

Late that morning, events at the convention brought a glimmer of hope to the Hamilton camp. Two of Diefenbaker's closest friends, Gordon Churchill and Joel Aldred, suggested to the convention chairman that the recommendations of the Policy Committee be tabled instead of voted on. Eddie Goodman, conference chairman, and William Davis, chairman of the Policy Committee, agreed to the compromise and Diefenbaker no longer had his self-professed reason for remaining in the leadership race. With Diefenbaker out, Hamilton's chances would improve dramatically. However, for reasons as yet unknown, Diefenbaker did not withdraw.

The results of the first ballot put Diefenbaker in fifth and Hamilton in seventh place on the eleven-candidate ballot. Together their votes would have totalled 407, enough to put Hamilton into a solid second place.[127] Of course, he would not have received all the votes that went to Diefenbaker, but it is likely that he would have obtained enough of them to remain a viable contender. According to Donald Johnston:

> I think if Diefenbaker had stayed out we might have gone through that magic three hundred barrier. Joe Clark is living proof of how important that first ballot position is and if we had come out ahead of Hees and closer to Fulton there is no telling where Alvin might have gone because even when he was obviously a loser his vote did not decline — it increased.[128]

Even at this late stage Hamilton hoped Diefenbaker would withdraw. In his words, "he had made his pitch and when he wasn't in front he shouldn't have stayed in. But he seemed to lose his judgement. Diefenbaker used to become very unstable at moments of emotional decision and once there had to be another ballot he couldn't seem to get out."[129] Once again, his hopes were dashed. Diefenbaker hung in and the count saw him remain in fifth place while Hamilton moved to sixth. Their total vote dropped to just below 300, Diefenbaker's substantially, Hamilton's marginally, but still enough to tie Hees for fourth place and close enough to Stanfield to have a chance. Finally, Diefenbaker decided to withdraw and the word spread throughout the convention. Finally, Hamilton thought, he would have the opportunity to show his true support which even then he believed to be in the range of 300.[130] However, it was not to be. Diefenbaker did not make up his mind in time to be removed from the ballot and his hard core supporters gave him a vote of 114 while Hamilton languished 8 votes behind. Even when added together the vote would have left him in fifth place, far behind Hees. In Hamilton's opinion, "When Diefenbaker's supporters realized he wasn't going to make it they began to piddle off, but instead of coming back to me where they should have they gave their votes to the other candidates."[131]

Hamilton stayed on for the fourth ballot and saw his vote increase by over 50 percent to 167. However, by this time it was too late to stage a comeback. He finished in last place and had to be dropped from the ballot. Hamilton had stayed in the race despite pleas from Roblin to withdraw in his favour. Ralph Hedlin, one of Roblin's staff, offered him his choice of position in a Roblin cabinet, but Hamilton would not play that game. He did not think his supporters would follow him to Roblin and, in any case, he believed to the end that he was the best person to implement his plans for the nation.[132] Furthermore, he felt that his open support of Roblin might leave the impression that the Diefenbaker loyalists had polarized behind one candidate and he would do nothing that might further disunite the party.[133] Stanfield and others maintain that Hamilton's decision to remain for the fourth ballot helped

Stanfield to victory because it kept Roblin in second place after that important count.[134] Hamilton, for his part, does not accept this view, again because he does not think he could have delivered his supporters en masse. Furthermore, Fulton chose Stanfield over Roblin on the final ballot and, even if both men had brought with them each and every one of their votes, a Stanfield victory would have ensued. In the end, Stanfield defeated Roblin by 1,150 votes to 969.

This result ended John Diefenbaker's leadership of the Progressive Conservative party and Alvin Hamilton's chance at the ring. He would never seek the leadership again. He had given it his best shot and had come away a loser. He could take some comfort in the fact that he had waged the campaign he wanted to on the issues he believed to be important and that his poorer than expected showing was due to Diefenbaker's intervention — a factor he could not control. Nonetheless, the convention was a bitter pill to swallow. He left it in debt, his party divided, his influence on it in decline and, to make matters worse, within a year he would no longer have a seat in the House of Commons.

Chapter 8
The Stanfield Years

Hamilton did not dwell long on his convention defeat. It was not in his nature to do so and circumstances did not permit. He remained a loyal servant of the party and Stanfield needed his experience on the opposition front bench. The two men met several times after the convention to discuss party policy and tactics and quickly established an "easy relationship" based on their common philosophy of activist government and their shared desire to defeat the Liberals.[1] Hamilton would help his new leader in any way he could to return the Conservatives to power at the earliest opportunity, and Stanfield would put Hamilton's parliamentary expertise and his links with the Diefenbaker rump in the party to good use.

Hamilton interpreted his brief broadly, especially in the weeks before Stanfield entered the House of Commons.[2] In early October, he led the Conservative attack on Mitchell Sharp's budget, reiterating his long-held belief that Keynesian economics could not be applied holus-bolus to a country such as Canada without unnecessary hardship for some regions.[3] Later in the month he used one of his party's "Opposition days" to castigate the government for its lack of action in an area dear to his heart — national resources. His motion began:

> That this house is of the opinion that the government should state immediately its policy on national resources and clearly set out its intentions and objectives generally; and particularly with respect to:
> (a) A national energy policy, including natural gas, oil, electrical transmission grid and uranium.
> (b) A national water policy.
> (c) Forestry, agriculture and fisheries policy.
> (d) Human resources.[4]

Further, and in response to the wave of environmental concern beginning to sweep over North America, he asked the government to set forth its policy to deal with the pollution which is "endangering any or all of these resources."[5] Over the next four months he made major speeches on rural development, northern affairs and energy,[6] and pressed the government for information on offshore mineral rights, grain sales to China, oil exploration in the Arctic, and pipeline construction — all matters of long-standing importance to him. At the end of March 1968, in recognition of these efforts and his concerns, Stanfield appointed Hamilton chairman of a caucus "super-committee" on regional and resource development to coordinate the work of existing committees concerned with agriculture, energy, mines and resources, Indian and northern affairs, forestry and rural development. The job proved to be temporary, for Hamilton lost his seat at the general election fought three months later.

For Hamilton, the genesis of his defeat on 25 June 1968 began in early April, just after the change in the Liberal leadership, when he was asked by Mitchell Sharp and Paul Martin to represent Canada at the meetings of the Inter-Parliamentary Council to be held in Dakar, Senegal, later that month. He feared an early election and knew he should not go. However, the conference would give him an opportunity to put forward his ideas on the importance of primary industries to developing countries and on methods of assisting developing countries improve their foreign trade, and "both Sharp and Martin assured me that their new leader would take several months to get the feel of things and that there wouldn't be an early election."[7] The announcement of the election caught

Hamilton in Dakar. Had Hamilton been contesting his old riding of Qu'Appelle, his absence in the early weeks of the campaign would not have made so much difference. In this election, however, he was running in Regina East.

Redistribution had combined the two Conservative seats of Qu'Appelle and Moose Mountain in southeastern Saskatchewan into one and, of course, only one of the sitting members — Alvin Hamilton or Richard Southam — could represent the new constituency. At first, Hamilton decided to seek the nomination in Qu'Appelle-Moose Mountain and even offered to compensate Southam financially if Southam would step aside in his favour. However, Southam refused the offer, pleading financial hardship, and proposed instead that Hamilton run in Regina East, a new riding without a sitting Conservative. He also convinced Stanfield and Martin Pederson, among others, to intercede on his behalf and they did so with some effect. They knew, as did Hamilton, that the party faced a strong challenge from both the Liberals and New Democrats in Regina and they argued that only a candidate of Hamilton's reputation could save the party one of its urban seats. Ever the loyal party man, Hamilton finally succumbed to the pressure when the executive in Regina East offered him the nomination uncontested, and promised a campaign fund of ten thousand dollars minimum, a complete campaign organization, and a public relations staff. At the time it seemed to be the proper course to follow. In the end it proved to be a political mistake of the first magnitude, for the prominent Conservatives of Regina did as little for Alvin Hamilton in 1968 as they had done during his years as provincial leader.

> The tragedy was that the man who was supposed to collect the money went off to England for a holiday all during the period the money was supposed to be collected and never collected it. There was no work done on organization and, typical of Regina, Conservatives became demoralized and simply dropped out of sight when there was a fight on.[8]

This was the situation which confronted Hamilton on his return from Africa five weeks before election day. He had neither money nor organization in place for the campaign and had to obtain the one and build the other almost from scratch. Nevertheless, he nearly pulled it off.

He won the nomination on 15 May and began his campaign in earnest. He built an organization which consisted primarily of students from the Regina campus of the University of Saskatchewan. He rented a bus to carry his message to as many voters on as many streets in the riding as possible. This prompted one journalist to compare his tactics to those of the osculatory prime minister, Pierre Elliot Trudeau,[9] in this headline, "Hamilton favours Bus over Buss."[10] He attacked the Liberal government over its trade and agriculture policies blaming it for the drop in both grain sales and price received. He produced his own Policy for a Greater Canada in which he outlined his ideas on national and regional development. The "Canada-Wide" proposals included: a national power grid, eastern reforestation, a national transportation policy, a national energy policy, a national resource policy, a national water policy, a continental resource pool based on an exchange of growth rates with the United States, Continental Shelf exploration, the creation of new industrial complexes in all regions of the country, new trading techniques to expand exports, and national conferences on human and non-renewable resources. His specific proposals for the prairies promised a new farm policy, a second Trans-Canada highway, new marketing companies for prairie fish, potash and newsprint, a technical survey of Hudson's Bay and the diversion of waters from the rivers of the north to the drought-threatened regions of the south.

Hamilton's literature borrowed heavily from his campaign for the leadership the previous year. It reminded voters of his record of achievement as a member of the Diefenbaker governments and drew attention to his vision of the future, a vision which included the cities as well as the rural areas of the country. In addition, it tried hard to convince the electorate that he stood the test of comparison with Trudeau and the "new" Liberals and that he should not be dismissed as "yesterday's" man. For example, one pamphlet advised the voters of Regina East that:

> It is not the past alone that makes Alvin Hamilton attractive. His record on Resources and Agriculture is well established. It is the range of ideas for the present and future of Canada as a nation that he has evolved and made known in the last four years that makes him a necessity for Regina and for Canada. In particular, he has a broad knowledge and a deep interest in the affairs and problems of our cities; this became very evident in 1965 when he produced the nine point "Urban Policy" dealing with the needs of City people.[11]

Furthermore, after a lengthy exposition of Hamilton's development proposals, the literature pointed out that:

> Time after time Hamilton has "laid it on the line" and has been proved right. But the important thing is that he has been prepared to think and speak out. As Douglas Fisher said, "The exhilaration we have had from Alvin Hamilton, politician, rests on something untypical of most Canadians in politics. He has no sense of class or 'pecking-order', no over-respect for conventional wisdom or the order of the past. He not only believes experts are to be used by politicians, he approaches them with the confidence that if they have anything to contribute he can use it and popularize it for the common elector."[12]

Over the course of the campaign Hamilton also found time in his busy schedule to speak on behalf of Conservative candidates in Ontario, British Columbia, Alberta, Manitoba, and other Saskatchewan constituencies. Perhaps it was a mistake to leave Regina East but few would have predicted as close a result — John Burton (NDP) — 13,641; Alvin Hamilton (PC) — 13,449; Ken MacLeod (Liberal) — 11,986; W.C. Beeching (Communist) — 230 — a loss by 192 votes.[13] Hamilton won a majority of the rural polls in the riding but lost most of the more numerous urban polls in Regina itself. Nevertheless, just one more vote in each of the 227 polls would have brought him victory.

Hamilton's defeat came as the "biggest surprise" of the election for much of the Saskatchewan media and it seems that they fell prey, as did many Conservatives, to the erroneous assumption that Hamilton's reputation alone could overcome all the forces arrayed against him. They ignored his late entry into the campaign, his lack of money and organization, the time he spent away from the constituency, and the high quality of his opponents. They forgot that Alvin Hamilton's prestige in Saskatchewan was based primarily on his work in agriculture and would not necessarily impress the predominantly urban voters of Regina East, despite the importance of agriculture to the entire provincial economy. They downplayed, although Hamilton did not, the impact of Trudeaumania on the "sophisticates" of Regina East which drew off some of those who would have voted for any party likely to defeat the NDP. Finally, they underestimated the strength of the New Democrats, now rejuvenated after the pummelling during the Medicare crisis in 1962, and their defeats at the hands of Ross Thatcher and the Liberals in the provincial elections of 1964 and 1967. In fact, Hamilton at first laid the blame for his defeat "at the feet of Liberal and New Democrat versions of the P.C. stand on Medicare."[14] Later, he attributed the result as well to the ill will which pervaded the Conservative party after the leadership convention and the party's treatment of one of Saskatchewan's favourite sons — John Diefenbaker. As he explained to Peter Stursberg:

> It wasn't only Diefenbaker who lost. I lost the election in '68 and Mike Starr lost that election too. The old people said your party wouldn't keep Diefenbaker, and even though Starr and I had been strong Diefenbaker supporters we both lost on that issue because these old people just deserted us. So they gunned us down not because we were against Diefenbaker but because we belonged to a party that had gunned Diefenbaker down.[15]

Whatever the explanations for the result, and all the above played a rôle, nothing could detract from the fact that Alvin Hamilton lost in Regina East. Although he masked his disappointment well to the many who offered their condolences, and promised that the setback would be temporary, it was indeed a personal as well as a political tragedy. In his words:

> It was a heartbreaker . . . After all those years of frustration I'd had in the party, to be sent back to oblivion again was a hard, hard blow. And worst of all, of course, was

> the loss of my place in the pecking order amongst the other politicians. Once you've been defeated, regardless of the circumstances, you still get the name of a "loser." So there I was with no great money at hand and an election lost and what do I do for a living?[16]

He might also have added that the defeat cost him the forum he needed to put forward those ideas he believed essential to the future prosperity of his country. He gave some thought to an early return to the House of Commons via a by-election and Stanfield attempted to convince Southam to resign in his favour, but neither Southam nor anyone else would step aside, so he had to reconcile himself to the fact that the next Parliament would convene without Alvin Hamilton on the public payroll.

The loss in 1968 left Hamilton without a regular income for the first time in thirty years and his first concern had to be to secure his financial future. Although the Hamiltons were nowhere near the poorhouse, a life in politics had not made Alvin a wealthy man and at age fifty-six he could not afford to retire on his Parliamentary pension and the small amount of capital he had accumulated. He first thought he might return to teach at Nutana and later considered offers of academic/administrative positions at universities in Ontario and Québec, but neither of these options appealed greatly to him. He wanted to stay close to federal politics, as well as earn a living, and he concluded that both objectives could be accomplished only by remaining in Ottawa. Thus, he turned to writing, lecturing, and in accordance with his philosophy of "self-help" — the world of private enterprise. Within a month of the election he informed Tom Symons, then president of Trent University, that "I intend to remain in Ottawa and have set up my shingle as a consultant."[17] He would continue to do what he had done for years — give people advice — only now they would have to pay for his expertise. He wrote for the *Toronto Star* and several magazines, he lectured to Canadian and American audiences, and he initiated or became involved in several business ventures both national and international.

Some of these endeavours paid dividends immediately. Within a year, he had an income of close to five thousand dollars from writing and lecturing alone. As well, he helped the staff at CJOH-TV in Ottawa develop a new format for the station's news telecasts and shortly thereafter he became a director of the company. Other ventures took longer to bring to fruition. For example, Hamilton spent two years without success trying to raise the capital to establish a company that would sell Chinese goods in the international marketplace. He knew that China needed to sell her products abroad in order to finance her industrialization and feed her population, and he believed that he could help in this respect. However, his efforts went unrewarded until 1971 when the Chinese once again asked him to come to Beijing to advise them on methods of increasing their exports and reducing their trade deficit. That visit marked the beginning of a long and mutually beneficial business relationship. According to Hamilton, "I recommended that they beef up their tourist industry and I put forward a lot of other ideas, but the one thing they were really interested in was my proposal to develop their oil and gas resources."[18] The recovery rate of oil and gas from Chinese fields was low in comparison to other countries but could be increased substantially with the proper equipment. The Chinese asked if he would acquire the machinery for them and he agreed to try, although he told his hosts that this time he would not help them for nothing. He explained that he had assisted free of charge in the past because he had been a politician with a steady income, but now as a private citizen he owed it to his family to earn something for his services. Nevertheless, he did not send Beijing a bill. Instead, on his return he approached one of the largest oil equipment companies in the United States, Baker Oil Tools, to see if they would provide the equipment the Chinese needed. Baker agreed to do so, but American law at that time prohibited trade with the People's Republic of China and so Baker created a new company, Baker Trade, incorporated in Hong Kong, to complete this transaction and others to follow. Hamilton received 12.5 percent of the shares in the new subsidiary. Baker Trade acquired the machinery from its parent and other American firms, established a school to teach Chinese technicians how to use the equipment, and the resulting increase in productivity enabled Beijing to sell Japan several billion dollars worth of oil within a decade. Baker Trade orchestrated several other deals between China and the capitalist world as well, and within five years its sales reached $50 million per year. The arrangement satisfied all parties concerned. The companies sold their products, China obtained the machinery she needed, and Baker Trade, including Alvin Hamilton, received facilitator's fees from the companies involved. Canada also benefitted because every dollar China earned elsewhere in the world enabled her to purchase Canadian grain without insisting that Canada buy an equal amount from China in return.

Baker Trade and another company Hamilton founded in the late 1960s to expedite trade between non-Communist countries — Resources and Industries Associates — eventually proved very profitable, but they did not solve Hamilton's immediate financial problems and he looked instead to investment opportunities in Canada. One appeared very shortly in a field of some familiarity to him — mining. In the mid-1960s he had been approached by Merril Menzies for funds to enable Menzies's twin brother Morris to test a method he had developed to extract low grade ore from promising deposits at a profit. Menzies tried the technique on an ore body in British Columbia discovered earlier but abandoned by the mining companies as too costly to develop, and it proved feasible. Now the original partners had to find the funds to put the mine into production and they offered shares on the stock market at $1.05. Hamilton received thirty thousand of these shares as one of the original partners and later bought an extra five thousand at $9.00 each. After an initial period of a couple of years, when the value of the stock fell in response to changes in the tax law concerning mines and capital gains, it rose eventually to $42.00. Of course, this did not happen overnight and, in fact, Hamilton skated on very thin financial ice for much of the time he was out of Parliament,[19] but the money he received from CJOH and his writing and lecturing carried him through and, in the end, his investments in Brenda Mines and later the Cypress Anvil mine in the Yukon, together with the income from Baker Trade, laid the basis of what later became a sizeable and stable portfolio of stocks.

Although financial security was one of Hamilton's major concerns between 1968 and 1972, he soon found that he had neither the time nor the inclination to devote himself exclusively to its pursuit. In fact, within a few months he became involved in a myriad of activities which kept him as busy as he had been when in the House of Commons. People by the hundreds continued to write him for assistance as if he were still a sitting member and he answered each and every request as best he could. He renewed his contacts in the civil service, the universities, and the business community, pushing his pet projects and trading ideas on matters of mutual interest. He participated at conferences on Sino-Canadian relations, such as the one held at the University of Guelph in the spring of 1969. He accepted a position on the advisory council of the United States based Fund for Peace whose aim was to promote better understanding between the United States and Communist China. He opposed the imposition of the War Measures Act in 1970 on the grounds that the situation in Québec did not warrant such draconian action and he participated in public protests against it. He served on a fund-raising committee to establish a memorial to Charles W. Lightbody — an old friend and much beloved member of the Departments of History at Brandon College and the University of Saskatchewan. He acted as midwife and founding member of the Biomass Energy Institute — a non-profit organization headquartered in Winnipeg — whose purpose was and is to advance environmental consciousness and the use of all available forms of renewable energy. He attended meetings — one of only two Canadians invited — of the Quadrangle, a group of top-level politicians, financiers, and industrialists from the United States, Japan, Britain and the European Community. Finally, he retained his interest in and concern for the future of the Progressive Conservative party in general and his own return to the House of Commons in particular.

Hamilton was not much involved with the internal politics of the party during these years. Not having a seat meant that he avoided most of the tension that pervaded the caucus as Stanfield sought to confirm his leadership victory, and as his supporters and those of John Diefenbaker fought for control of local organizations in constituencies all across the country. Once again Alvin Hamilton's major contribution to the party came in the form of proposals for new party policy. Stanfield did not give him specific assignments on a regular basis, but the two met occasionally to discuss issues of current concern. In addition, Hamilton served with Martial Asselin, member for Charlevoix, as co-chairman of the Resources Policy and Regional Development Committee at the Priorities for Canada Conference — a meeting of politicians and academics Stanfield brought together at Niagara Falls in the autumn of 1969 to develop new policies for the Conservative party. The report that Hamilton and Asselin submitted at the conclusion of the conference is too lengthy to quote in full, but its preamble provides ample proof of the importance with which the participants viewed their subject.

> Natural resources exploitation and conservation are the keys to future Canadian sovereignty. The Canadian nation will prosper or suffer permanent jeopardy, depending on the ability of Canadian Society both to develop our vast national heritage and to preserve natural resources for our own use.
>
> Not only the total output of our land and sea resources, but also the estimated reserves of those in the ground and in the ocean will create for Canada a substantial new position as an important world power in excess of the conventional posture we have maintained in foreign policy and defense policy. The national heritage consists of our natural and our human resources.
>
> Progressive Conservatives must build on what we have already done. A firm basis for what is needed was established by the Conservative government in 1957-1963. We must restore this momentum. We have the facilities. We have the political and historical frameworks. *A new Canadian destiny depends on the ability of Canadians*

> *to regulate the development of our resources and to share them with the world.*[20]

The committee's specific recommendations reveal the extent of Hamilton's influence. Among the many proposals one finds are a commitment to cooperative federalism — "National Resource Policy should be a cooperative enterprise of the federal government and the provincial governments and their departments. National policies should be implemented by regions"; a reiteration of the growth rate exchange technique "using water as one of the resources in a package for bargaining power with the United States or other countries"; an "aggressive marketing philosophy" in agriculture; "a fully-owned and controlled Canadian company to sell Canadian cereals abroad"; "taxation policies that recognize risk" for the oil and gas industry; "immediate ratification of the Law of the Sea Convention of 1958"; "federal aid in financing power development"; "development of a coordinated power grid"; and "a shift from traditional agriculture systems to beef and silviculture."[21] A year later, at Stanfield's request, Hamilton presented his leader with a seventeen-page updated version of the urban policy he had prepared for the 1965 campaign. Again, it is far too long to quote all of it, but its conclusion deserves mention, for it reveals the extent to which the problems of the urban environment had become a part of Hamilton's overall policy. As he tried to show during his run for the leadership, he did not deserve the reputation of a one-dimensional man with concern for the rural areas of Canada alone. After detailed recommendations dealing with everything from the need for a Canadian council on urban affairs to federal grants for public transportation and community recreation, he concluded that:

> It is time for the Federal Government to take the initiative in suggesting methods by which the three levels of government can cooperate . . . There must be a base for greater communication between the cities, provinces and federal government on water management, urban transit programs, airport location, etc. The federal interest is primarily economic. The provincial interest is quality [of

> life]. Both can achieve their objectives through developing a sense of community in our burgeoning cities. . .
>
> Finally, in the years ahead, one can visualize regional or urban governments having transferred to them some of the powers now possessed by the federal and provincial governments. *Not only will the city be the heartland of our industrial growth, it will be the cultural and political center for most of our people.*[22]

According to Hamilton, the recommendation that federal powers be transferred to the municipalities "terrified" Stanfield.[23] Despite the utility of the other proposals, the report never made it beyond the leader's office. Alvin also wrote the occasional speech for Diefenbaker, spoke to party gatherings when asked, and campaigned on behalf of Conservative candidates in the provincial elections in Alberta and Saskatchewan in 1971. Beyond this and other activities discussed already, the remainder of his involvement with the party during this period consisted of efforts to ensure his return to the House of Commons at the earliest opportunity.

Hamilton orchestrated his re-election with care and skill. In the first place, he sought and obtained Southam's assurances that he would retire before the next election, although they kept the agreement to themselves for some time to fuel press speculation as to where Hamilton would run. Secondly, he had Southam facilitate his candidacy among Southam's supporters in the old Moose Mountain part of the riding so that when the nomination meeting was held he ran unopposed. Thirdly, he put together an organization which integrated his and Southam's supporters, which covered every poll in the constituency, and which raised the money for his campaign. Finally, he used the media in Saskatchewan to ensure that he did not become a "forgotten man." In this he was so successful that almost no month went by from the time of his defeat to the announcement of the election without some reference in the provincial press to Alvin Hamilton and his activities — be it his attacks on the Government's LIFT (Lower Inventories For Tomorrow) programme which kept thousands of acres of fertile farm land out of production, his trip to China, or his proposals to increase grain sales and improve the efficiency of the grain transportation system.

Thus Hamilton was well prepared when Prime Minister Trudeau called the election for 30 October 1972. He had the nomination in hand, his campaign organization in place, and sufficient money in the bank. Nevertheless, he approached the election with some trepidation. In his words:

> I don't take things for granted and I didn't know those people in the southern part of the riding as well as I would have liked. I was terrified of Estevan because from the past record there was no clear winner there. I had to solve a lot of problems and I had to find the keys to certain situations and these didn't come in a blinding stroke of genius.[24]

Hamilton's campaign reflected his anxiety. This time he stayed close to home and spoke on behalf of only four of his colleagues in other Saskatchewan ridings. He campaigned in all areas of the constituency with a vigour that belied his sixty years, launching salvo after salvo at the Liberals' agricultural policy and their attitude towards the plight of the prairie farmer. He charged that Otto Lang, minister responsible for the Wheat Board, had cost farmers $50 million two years previously by selling barley at less than world prices.[25] He called it a "crime" that Canada should have to import foreign beef when Canadian farmers could double their production with proper government encouragement.[26] He accused the Liberals of playing havoc with prairie farm incomes by not ending the eight-month dockers' strike on the west coast.[27] He promised the farm population a much better deal from a Progressive Conservative government. He vowed to negotiate commodity agreements with various nations to halt the current price war amongst the world's wheat producers. He pointed to the agricultural policy western Conservatives had prepared for Stanfield which, when implemented, would provide livestock insurance, improved water storage, a feed-grain bank, easier farm credit, higher grain prices, and greater farm security. He offered the urban voters of the riding mortgages at 6.5 percent, residential land banks to lower the cost of building lots, and an end to the 11 percent federal tax on building materials.[28] His final advertisement, four days prior to election day, took aim at the recession which plagued all Canadians and offered the following Hamiltonian solutions:

> A 92 1/2 CENT DOLLAR
>
> The greatest economic growth in our history started in 1961 when we devalued the dollar to 92 1/2 cents. Now the dollar is at $1.02 and we have both stagnation and inflation.
>
> We Can Do It Again
>
> Buy equities in American Multinational Companies.
> This will bring our dollar value down and make practical use of our $5 billion U.S.A. reserves. This will do four things:
>
> 1. Help the U.S.A. in its balance of payments difficulties
> 2. Help Canadians own the companies that own us
> 3. Help our exporters of wheat and manufactured goods get better prices
> 4. Provide more Canadian jobs.[29]

In the circumstances, it is likely that Hamilton would have won the seat in 1972 without any outside help. Qu'Appelle-Moose Mountain had been a Conservative area in the past and the recent decline in farm income in a predominantly agrarian riding gave the Liberals little hope of increasing their vote. This left the New Democratic Party as the only remaining threat, but it was from this unlikely quarter that Hamilton's campaign received an unexpected boost. In the midst of the contest Lorne Nystrom, NDP member for Yorkton-Melville — the constituency which abutted on Qu'Appelle-Moose Mountain to the north — predicted that Hamilton and every other Conservative candidate except Diefenbaker would lose their deposits. Naturally, the local media sought Hamilton's response and, as he tells the story:

> When the press approached me I was old enough and smart enough to agree that I had never seen the NDP work harder, that I had never seen the Liberals work harder, and that the election was very uncertain here. This was all they needed. There were headlines and it was on the radio that I was in a fight for my life here.[30]

The publicity which attended the episode spurred Hamilton's supporters to even greater effort. On election day he received over 14,500 votes, a clear majority; almost 8,000 votes more than his nearest rival; and double the majority Southam received in 1968. According to Hamilton, "It was a sweet, sweet victory."[31] Despite his contention that the past four years had been among the most exhilarating of his life, since he had been able to pursue projects he never had time for previously, he was obviously delighted and relieved to be back in the House of Commons.[32]

Stanfield wasted little time in making use of Hamilton on his return. In a minority Parliament, with the prospect of power if he could force an early election, the leader of the opposition needed all the skills and talent he could muster. Initially, Stanfield considered making Hamilton the party's critic for agriculture and, in fact, Hamilton's first speech in the Commons after his return was an attack on the government's agricultural policies, especially the LIFT programme which he renamed the Lower Income For Tomorrow programme.[33] Nevertheless, when the two men discussed his rôle in the twenty-ninth Parliament, Hamilton suggested that he be made his party's spokesman for energy, not agriculture. He knew that the Conservative caucus contained several members competent to deal with agricultural matters and his contacts in Resources and Industries Associates and the Quadrangle forewarned him of the developments soon to take place in the international oil market. Furthermore, no one else in caucus had his knowledge of the oil and gas industry, which extended from his years as leader of the Progressive Conservative party in Saskatchewan, nor the experience he had gained as minister of northern affairs and national resources. Thus, he concluded that he could contribute more as opposition critic for energy, rather than agriculture, and Stanfield appointed him to the shadow cabinet with responsibility for that portfolio. This did not mean that he refrained from intervening in debates on agriculture when he believed he had something of value to say, and he did so on several occasions in the months prior to the 1974 election. However, he did not do so to any greater extent than one would expect of a former minister of agriculture and a member who represented an agrarian constituency. Nor did he have much to say with respect to his other great interest at the time — Sino-Canadian relations — for there was less need for him to do so. The Trudeau government had extended formal recognition to the People's Republic of China in October 1970, sales of prairie grain continued unimpeded, and Canada had begun to buy more from China to help offset the cost of the grain sales. Hamilton's brief was, of course, narrower than the one he had held when in opposition in Diefenbaker's day. Nonetheless, he was content. He had asked for energy, Stanfield had granted the request, and he devoted himself to the subject for as long as Stanfield remained leader of the party, and throughout one of the most difficult and disruptive periods in Canada's economic and constitutional history.

The decision of the Organization of Petroleum Exporting Countries (OPEC) cartel to double and then redouble its prices sent shock waves through the industrialized world and Canada did not escape unscathed. It left severe economic dislocation in its wake, and the Liberals' attempts to minimize its effects over the next decade caused fissures in the fabric of Confederation as great as the emergence of the Parti Québecois. All parties recognized the seriousness of the situation, and at first the mood in the House of Commons was one of cooperation to find solutions to the problem. The Standing Committee on Natural Resources, of which Hamilton was the most prominent Conservative member, met regularly throughout the only two sessions of the twenty-ninth Parliament to collect statistics on reserves of fossil fuels, consider contingency plans for eastern Canada in the event of a dearth of imports, and discuss alternative sources of renewable and nonrenewable energy. On behalf of his party Hamilton made several suggestions in both the committee and the House of Commons which he thought would help the country cope with the crisis. In the first place, he advised the government not to panic.

> Canada has nothing to fear within the short term or in the long term. We have plenty of resources of the traditional

> fossil forms and unbelievable resources . . . in the form of renewables.[34]

Secondly, he suggested that Canadians should regard the situation as not only a challenge but also an opportunity.

> Of all the industrialized nations, with the exception of Russia, Canada is the only one that can look with assurance to the future in the short term and in the long term . . . If we add up all our resources, according to conservative estimates our potential reserves of oil, gas and other energy resources will last us about 500 years at present consumption rates . . . Now, with the rising prices of energy offshore . . . all these things can be turned to advantage . . . I think the future we have talked about for a generation or more, or maybe longer, has a chance to be fulfilled in a very short time.[35]

Thirdly, he reminded the government that the problem was not one of supply, but rather of pricing, and he urged that Canada adjust to the new cost as soon as possible in order to take advantage of her privileged position with respect to resources.[36] Finally, he made several specific proposals to overcome the short-term problems caused by the price hike and to ensure an adequate energy supply for the future. He urged the government to alter its taxation policy to do away with the "front-end loading" which forced oil exploration companies to pay taxes at the very time their capital costs were the highest and before their new wells were fully in production.[37] He asked that the Ottawa Valley line, introduced by the Diefenbaker government as the basis of its National Oil Policy, be abolished and that pipelines to Québec and beyond be built to ensure security of supply for eastern Canada.[38] He advised caution in the export of Canadian oil and natural gas to the United States and alacrity in the implementation of plans for conservation of current supplies. He urged government support for further exploration in the Arctic and off the east coast and the development of alternate energy sources.[39] And, given his understanding of the nature of the Canadian federation, he advised the government to cooperate fully with the provinces in the shaping of its policies.

> To us, consultation means concrete plans with the provinces for the maximum and best use of resources. In the present situation, it means coordinating policies with producing provinces of oil and gas to lessen the impact of a world energy revolution on consumers. It means heavy emphasis on positive policies to enlarge our present industries and to add new industries based on the comparative advantage that our oil, gas, uranium, coal and hydro power potential gives us.[40]

In the spring of 1974, when the government introduced a bill to regulate the price of Canadian oil in domestic and foreign markets, the official opposition declared itself willing to cooperate — a most responsible tack to take in a minority Parliament. Given the severity of the crisis, and with an election just around the corner, the Conservatives might have been expected to use the situation more for their political advantage.

Between the elections of 1972 and 1974 Hamilton not only acted as his party's spokesman on energy in the House of Commons, but also chaired a caucus committee which attempted to develop a comprehensive Conservative response to the energy issue. The documents produced by Hamilton and the committee reflected their changing perceptions and concerns. The first, put out in May 1973, was titled A Natural Resource Policy for Canada and treated energy as but one of the several resources necessary for the future prosperity of the nation.[41] The second, in December, called An Energy and Resource Policy for Canada, focussed on the theme that in a time of growing world shortages Canada's resources of energy, water, land, forests and minerals represented an unparalleled opportunity for Canadians.[42] The third, in February 1974, called pointedly Energy Policy, made detailed recommendations to overcome the energy crisis in both the short and long term and provided the basis of a paper prepared for the general meeting of the Progressive Conservative party in mid-March. In general, the latter effort adhered to Hamilton's long-held belief that Canada required a comprehensive resources policy and it integrated energy policy into an overall National Development Strategy. In particular, Resources for Canadians proposed:

1. A new National Energy Council composed of representatives of both federal and provincial governments as well as of consumers, industry and labour to take over and expand the advisory role performed by the National Energy Board
2. A national pipeline system built wholly within Canada to bring existing supplies from the producing provinces to all Canada and to carry new supplies from the Arctic and the oil sands when brought on line
3. A national power grid to utilize all electrical energy sources, including development of the Fundy tides
4. Joint federal-provincial projects to develop all available energy sources, including nuclear power
5. Joint federal-provincial research into all forms of renewable energy, including biomass, solar and wind power
6. Federal-provincial cooperation in the preparation and publication of ways and means of conserving energy.[43]

These proposals became the "Energy and Resources" plank in the party's appeal to the electorate in 1974. Unfortunately for Hamilton, his committee and the party, energy and resource policy took a back seat to another section of the party's platform designed to dampen the inflation fuelled by the rising cost of energy — wage and price controls.

Hamilton had very little to do with the decision to make a ninety-day freeze on wages and prices the major thrust of the Conservative campaign in 1974. The issue had been debated in caucus but no agreement had been reached prior to the defeat of the government. Some of Stanfield's advisers — James Gillies, member for Don Valley, in particular — had given the matter considerable thought however and, with an election suddenly upon him, the leader decided to accept their advice. Hamilton did not like the idea. He believed that wage and price controls increased rather than decreased inflationary expectations, but he accepted the policy out of party loyalty and because of its projected short duration. Furthermore, he had no difficulty explaining its value to his constituents. One of his advertisements midway through the campaign stated bluntly:

INCOMES POLICY
THE FACTS
1972 — 6% Inflation
1974 — 10% Inflation
THE CHOICE
Do Nothing or Incomes Policy
PC INCOMES POLICY
90 Day Freeze
Consultation with Provinces, Labour, Management
Flexible Controls
As each industry puts into practice the agreed policies to lower prices, reward productivity etc., then controls are removed. Wages and profits can rise providing there is no increase in prices.
What is Your Choice?
VOTE ALVIN HAMILTON.[44]

Of course, Hamilton did not campaign on wage and price controls alone. Other advertisements attacked the Liberal's agricultural policies and promised a better life for farmers and, indeed, all Canadians should the Progressive Conservative party win the election. However, it was not to be. Although Hamilton and most of his western colleagues were returned easily, Stanfield's stumbling attempts to demonstrate the worth of his proposed freeze on incomes and prices could not compete with the prime minister's devastating riposte, "Zap. You're Frozen!" Conservative representation in the House dropped from 107 to 95, the Liberals won a majority, Robert Stanfield lost his last chance to become prime minister of Canada and, within a couple of years, older members of caucus, such as Alvin Hamilton, would be forced to give way to a younger generation of Conservative politicians.

When Parliament reconvened Hamilton continued his interest in energy matters, but now he was more critical of the government's actions and less willing to overlook its failings. Its greatest mistake in this area as far as he was concerned was the Petroleum Administration Act introduced in October of 1974 — a revised version of the legislation lost when the government was defeated. This act would give the federal government the power to set the price of all petroleum products in Canada except those which did not cross a provincial boundary, and to do so unilaterally if it could not obtain the agreement of the producing provinces. This time Hamilton did not quarrel with the intent of the legislation — to cushion Canadians against the shock of ever-increasing world prices:

> All parties in this House hope that, with God's grace, we will have energy available for many decades to come and that we will be advantageously placed in this competitive world to provide energy at lower prices for all Canadians. Not only must prices be lower for the benefit of consumers and industry, but they must be lower to attract investment to this country . . . All parties support that principle. This bill will make it possible; we do not dispute that.[45]

Nor did he dispute the government's jurisdiction in the area. "There is no question that the federal government has complete sovereign power in interprovincial and export trade."[46] However, he knew that the producing provinces, especially Alberta and Saskatchewan, would not like the price controls imposed upon them arbitrarily. In his words, "These people are as sensitive as cats at a certain season of the year, and you have to keep this fact in mind."[47] Furthermore, the third clause of the bill read that "This Act is binding on Her Majesty in right of Canada and in right of any province," and he argued to the end that this infringement on the prerogatives of the Crown in the provinces was both unconstitutional and destructive of internal harmony in a federal state.

> It may be difficult to determine when the federal government, by legislation, impinges upon the provincial legislative field; however, it is not so where the federal legislature impinges upon a provincial Crown prerogative. One need only look to see if there is a record showing that the provincial Crown has consented to this

> impingement upon the prerogative. If there is no consent, then the infringement is invalid . . . there is no doubt that the federal government, through parliament, cannot bind a provincial Crown prerogative without the consent of the provincial Crown.[48]

Hamilton wanted the government to agree not to act without the prior acquiescence of the producing provinces, and he proposed that Clause Three be amended to read that "where the legislative authority of the Parliament of Canada does not extend to bind Her Majesty in right of a province, then to the extent that Her Majesty in right of a province consents thereto."[49] He wanted to avoid a "war with the provinces," and, had the government accepted the amendment, the people of western Canada might have had less reason to believe that their interests had been sacrificed once again for the benefit of Ontario and Québec. It is not mere coincidence that the rise of modern western separatism dates from the passage of the Petroleum Administration Act and that it had its greatest appeal after the introduction of the National Energy Policy six years later.

The constitutional argument was the major thrust of Hamilton's opposition to the government's energy policy, but it was not his only concern. As he put it:

> This is not just a constitutional debate. It is a debate on a product which provides 50 per cent of the energy of Canada. This energy not only runs our factories, our trucks and our automobiles; it keeps us warm in winter. The actions of the government are driving the oil and gas companies out of this country, and hastening the day when we will have to go out and beg the world for supplies of oil to run our factories and keep us warm.[50]

Thus, in the sixteen months between the time the thirtieth Parliament began its sessions, and Stanfield left the leadership of the Progressive Conservative party, Hamilton made several suggestions designed to guide the government to a satisfactory response to the dislocation caused by the OPEC cartel. He again urged the minister of finance to alter the tax policy so as to encourage greater investment in exploration for conventional sources of energy; he asked for construction of a two-way pipeline from Montréal to Sarnia to secure supplies for both regions of the country; and he proposed that the government fund research into all likely forms of alternative energy including wind-power, heat pumps, solar heating, and biomass. He also attacked the government for its decision to establish the Petro-Canada Crown Corporation as doing nothing of substance to alleviate Canada's energy problems. On third reading of Bill C-8 he concluded that:

> We are just seeing part of a massive fraud on the part of the government to pretend it is doing something to meet the needs of the country . . . When we think of gathering the resources of this nation and expending $1 billion or $2 billion just to get started in this poker game, without any guarantee of an extra barrel of oil or one cent less per barrel in the cost structure, I think I am right in saying this bill is a pretence and a fraud.[51]

As always, his criticisms were not just negative. He proposed several alternatives — courses of action more in keeping with his belief that Canadians should own their own resources, but as individuals not as the state. His favoured scheme would have changed the tax law so that Canadians would have purchased shares in existing oil companies in such volume that we would control these companies, at least their subsidiaries in Canada, within a few short years. Once again, however, the government did not heed Hamilton's advice and today Petro-Canada's colours are planted firmly in all regions of the country — red flags to her opponents, banners of convenience to her customers.

The government's second egregious error in judgement during this period, in Hamilton's opinion, was its decision to introduce wage and price controls. The Anti-Inflation Act brought before the House of Commons on 13 October 1975 would give the federal government the power to limit increases in wages and prices in its areas of jurisdiction for three years. Hamilton opposed the legislation for two major reasons. In the first place, he did not think it could succeed in its objective. "The bill before us makes no effort to get after the fundamental causes of inflation . . . This bill in every one of its terms legislates inflation."[52] Given his conservative view of human nature, Hamilton was convinced that both management and labour alike would move heaven and earth to ensure that they obtained the maximum increases permitted by the legislation and thus prevent inflation from falling to lower levels. Secondly, he suspected that the bill was unconstitutional.

> The bill says that it is not binding upon Her Majesty in the right of the provinces or upon Her Majesty in right of the municipalities, yet the government is systematically sitting down with one province after another and conniving together to get around the constitution of the country. As some provinces are now indicating, the legislation will not work because of its unconstitutional nature.[53]

Hamilton's alternatives — ("I do not think it is right just to condemn this legislation for what it is, bad legislation, without putting forward some form of alternative that is credible and reasonable"[54]) — were to limit any increase in the government's income to 10 percent to ensure that it did not benefit from inflation; to lower interest rates to reasonable levels; to regulate the money supply so that sufficient funds would be available for "legitimate" growth; to control land costs to keep the price of housing affordable; and to provide greater security for working Canadians so that they would feel less need to press for higher wages. Hamilton's decision to oppose wage and price controls was courageous in light of the fact that Stanfield and a vast majority of the Conservative caucus supported the government initially. In fact, only Hamilton and two other Progressive Conservative members defied their party's whip and voted against the legislation on second reading. Hamilton, the "party man," did not do so lightly. He did not like the idea of wage and price controls at all. He had accepted Stanfield's proposals in 1974 because the freeze would have been in effect for ninety days only. The difference between three months and three years was too great for him to stomach. He believed the Anti-Inflation Act would do far more harm to Canada than good and, in his words, "You can't vote for party when it's absolutely wrong for your country."[55] Eventually, Hamilton's arguments won the day, at least within his own party. On third and final reading the entire Conservative caucus, except George Hees, voted against the bill, although the government's majority in the House of Commons guaranteed its passage.

Hamilton's third major criticism of the government during this period was over its failure to deal effectively with the manifold problems of western agriculture. As soon as the Commons convened he was on his feet to demand an end to the grain handlers' strike on the west coast which had paralyzed exports of prairie grain. Over the next few months he urged the Liberals to renew the International Wheat Agreement, which had protected Canada's share of the international market, and to amend the Farm Credit Act, so that young farmers would be given a chance to establish themselves before their debts ground them under. He fought the government's stated intention to repeal the Prairie Farm Assistance Act, and its evident determination to terminate the Crowsnest Pass Agreement, both of great importance to his constituents. His longest battle, however, began with the introduction of Bill C-41, the Western Grain Stabilization Act, early in 1975, and it continued for the rest of the year. As so often in the past, Hamilton paid tribute to the government's intentions but complained that the legislation did not go far enough to satisfy the prairie farmer. He liked the proposal to create a fund to cushion the producer in hard times, but he did not believe that the fund in itself would solve the crisis in western agriculture. He wanted more money and effort put into marketing, research, farm credit, and insurance programmes as well as a new international agreement to guarantee the grain grower a fair return for his labour.[56] In addition, he advised the government to seek the opinions of individual farmers and not only the farm organizations before making a decision on the vital question of voluntary or compulsory participation in the fund, and he warned Eugene Whelan [the minister of agriculture] and Otto Lang [the minister in charge of the Wheat Board] — the "two babes in blunderland"[57] as he called them — that the future of the Liberal party on the prairies would rest on their response to his request. When they turned him down, he predicted further that the farm population would not accept the compulsory aspect of the legislation without a fight.[58] In the end the farmers did accept the bill, albeit with reluctance, and some benefitted from its provisions, although the act did little if anything to restore Liberal fortunes in the west and Lang went down to defeat in his Saskatoon constituency in 1979.

This era in Alvin Hamilton's life ended abruptly when Robert Stanfield left the leadership of the Progressive Conservative party. In retrospect, Hamilton has more reason than not to look kindly on Stanfield. Although the two men had their differences during those nine years, Stanfield did restore Hamilton to his prominent position on the opposition front bench when he returned to the House of Commons in 1972. Furthermore, he encouraged Hamilton's interest in party policy and gave him his head to pursue it even though he did not always produce initiatives the leader could accept. Over the years, Stanfield showed an abiding respect for Hamilton's abilities, and he gave him a position of prestige and influence in the party. In turn, Hamilton accepted Stanfield's leadership on all but a very few issues and worked hard to justify the trust placed in him. All this would change considerably when the party chose Joe Clark as Stanfield's successor on 22 February 1976.

Chapter 9
The Clark Years

Alvin Hamilton did not contest the leadership in 1976. He knew that his candidacy would reopen wounds barely healed since 1967 and understood that in the eyes of most delegates his close association with John Diefenbaker would doom his chances from the start. Furthermore, he was scant weeks away from the age of sixty-four and he realized that in the International Year of the Child most people would consider him too old for the position. He did attend the convention in Ottawa, of course, but played no rôle in its proceedings, nor in the campaign of any candidate. In fact, he had a great deal of difficulty in deciding which to support. In his words, "There wasn't a person in that race that I could honestly back for the prime ministership of Canada."[1] In the end he chose James Gillies — another ideas man in caucus — and when Gillies withdrew after the first ballot he voted successively and with diminishing enthusiasm for Jack Horner — an outspoken Alberta member of Parliament who had fought at his side on many occasions since 1958 — Brian Mulroney — president of the Iron Ore Company of Canada and a member of his personal staff in the early 1960s — and Claude Wagner — another member of Parliament and a recent convert from Liberal ranks in Québec. Hamilton never did vote for the eventual winner. On the last ballot he chose Wagner over

Clark for reasons both personal and political. He had nothing against Clark. He simply did not believe the young member of Parliament had either the experience or the presence to be an effective leader. In his estimation, "Joe will always be the office boy to me, fussing around all over the place just like a photographer at a wedding."[2] He did not think much more of Wagner's prospects. "I knew that Wagner would never make it as prime minister. He'd express things beautifully, but he had no substance at all in policy matters."[3] Nevertheless, Hamilton saw in Wagner the chance to elect the party's first French Canadian leader and the attendant possibility of increased support for the party in Québec and this convinced him, as well as Diefenbaker and many other delegates from the prairies, to vote against their fellow westerner.

Clark's trackers at the convention undoubtedly informed him of Hamilton's move to Wagner on that final ballot, but there is no evidence that the new leader held it against him. He did remove Hamilton from the shadow cabinet but appears to have done so not out of spite but because he wanted his party to present a new and younger image to the electorate — an image which had no place for the old war-horses of the Diefenbaker era, such as Hamilton, Hees and Dinsdale. Furthermore, Hamilton informed his new leader that he would be content to work on policy without the responsibility of a single ministry to criticize. It is clear, however, that Clark did fear Hamilton's penchant for novel and not necessarily conservative ideas, for in caucus he forbade him to free-lance or fly trial balloons without his prior approval.[4] Both of these decisions had a considerable impact on Hamilton's position in the party and his effectiveness in the House of Commons. In the first place, Clark's supporters began to avoid him. Secondly, exclusion from the shadow cabinet meant that he lost not only his best opportunity to influence party policy but also the focus for his criticisms of government actions. Although he continued to fill *Hansard* columns at the same impressive rate as in the past, his major speeches ranged further afield than before and lacked the persistence that follows automatically when one is the opposition critic for a particular department. Furthermore, his interventions in debates no longer possessed *the* authority that ensues when one speaks for one's party.

Hamilton's contributions in the House of Commons between Clark's election as leader and the election of 1979 covered both old ground and new. Trade with China continued to be an abiding interest and he wanted to know:

> With all these opportunities, what is the government doing? For example, when is it going to get the cooperatives in Canada to go out and visit Chinese trade fairs twice a year and make sure all the goods they can sell in Canada are bought in China in order to help the farmers sell their wheat? . . . There are lots of opportunities, but somebody has to put the sock to these companies in order to make them move.[5]

He remained convinced of the utility of "selective" budgeting to encourage economic growth in all regions of the country, and used the newly touted theories of Professors Mundell and Laffer to back his claim that the old Keynesian doctrines which pervaded the ministry of finance were no longer appropriate to Canada in the 1970s.

> What would Mundell do in present day circumstances? Since our economic charts are slowly levelling off instead of rising, and since there is unused plant capacity and slack in the labour force, Mundell would advise a policy of fiscal ease. Some would call that a policy of budgetary expansion. But the expression should not be brought about by increasing the deficit, not brought about simply by cutting taxes across the board to encourage people to spend more and spend their way out of recession. That is not what he means. Neither is he thinking of handouts or transfer payments. He suggests that in times like these we should make full use of our labour force and plant capacity. We should achieve our purposes by instituting tax cuts which will affect regions and industries. In that way we could fulfil our social purposes.[6]

He continued to urge the government to bring forward a comprehensive development policy — one based on government intervention, Canadian nationalism, private enterprise, and growth rate exchange agreements with our partners.

> We need a national development policy . . . We know that development has to have the activist leadership of a government, not to run business, not to own plants, but to get things moving, especially in view of our geography, the nature of our markets and, above all, our transportation difficulties . . . I want Canadian mines and oil wells owned by Canadians as individuals . . . I would like to see Canadians, as individuals, own this country, as opposed to governments owning it or directing it. That should be included in an industrial strategy . . . Tariffs today are an obsolete technique between nations. Let us take advantage of our resources in the form of basic supplies of iron, water and energy, and deal with these blocs; the European Common Market, the United States, Japan and any other group or single nation, on our growth rate of exchange.[7]

He updated his ideas on energy conservation and asked the minister of finance [Jean Chrétien] to alter the Income Tax Act so that Canadians could write off their research and installation expenditures on heat pumps, solar energy converters, heat storage facilities, methane production, vertical axis windmills, solar absorption air conditioning, residential photovoltaics, water recycling, conversion of waste to energy and protein, energy plantation, and production of hydrogen.[8] In this same speech, he appealed to the minister to ignore the advice of his officials because "the advice civil servants have been giving their masters for 30 odd years has been consistently wrong" — a long-standing Hamilton complaint.[9] He returned to this theme time and again, charging those "nitwits" in finance "with responsibility for the country's current inflationary difficulties — for the high cost of government, the misuse of our money supply over the last twenty-five years, high interest rates, high urban land costs, and misuse of the floating dollar."[10] Finally, he suggested certain "corrective actions" through which the government could improve Canada's economic situation, several of which he had proposed in the past without success:

> 1. Bilateral defensive agreements with each of our trading partners roughly equivalent to our potential liability in trade between our two countries

2. Government should guarantee unilaterally to our exporters that our tax load on them will be no greater than the Japanese exporter has to bear, that they will at least compete equally, and thus we will destroy this temporary great imbalance in trade in our respective countries
3. We should keep our domestic costs down
4. There should be new types of trade institutions
5. Canada, above all nations, should be pushing hard for an international unit of exchange
6. I would like to put forward a constructive theory which I call growth rate exchange . . . I think that this is the technique which we should be employing in product after product so that there is real equality of bargaining power between the nations with certain resources they are trading off by growth rate exchanges
7. In conclusion . . . I would predict that if we prevent interest rates from rising for another six or eight months, the economy will stage a recovery, after five years of stagnation, and that by the end of this coming year our currency will achieve an international value of 90 cents. I believe that this is about the best level for our dollar for the best operation of our system at the present time. There would be more people working, more tax revenues coming into the coffers of the government, and it would alleviate our deficits abroad and at home.[11]

Hamilton also took a keen interest in several new issues which arose during this period. One of these was capital punishment and the government's decision to abolish it. Hamilton opposed the bill. As he informed his constituents, "I still believe it is a deterrent; consequently I shall be voting against the legislation."[12] Another was the government's determination to introduce the metric system in Canada. This time Hamilton accepted the idea in principle, but he argued against the government's plan to impose it on every sector of the country without first inviting their views. In his words:

> Serious-minded people in this House and in the country will, I think, accept the fact that we have to move to the worldwide metric system because there is only one

> world of trade. But let us go forward with some compassion for those who have to do the work in the fields.[13]
>
> What we are witnessing here today is metricification without representation.[14]

He also criticized the government's apparent willingness to allow an individual's Social Insurance Number (SIN) to be used for purposes other than the ones for which it was intended. This, he argued, was a serious encroachment on the civil liberties of Canadians.[15] In addition, he took up the cudgels in support of the mortgage deductability proposal Clark used with such effectiveness in the fifteen by-elections held in October 1978, although he pointed out that the idea had been in the Progressive Conservative party's platform since 1965.[16] Finally, he tackled the problem faced by the nation's orphans whose guardians were ineligible to collect family allowance payments under the existing legislation, and he applauded the minister of health [Monique Bégin] when she announced a few weeks later that the injustice would be remedied.[17] Strangely enough, Hamilton did not spend as much time on agricultural issues, old or new, in this session as in the past. However, he more than made up for it in his reports to his constituents, which he distributed four times a year, and which were crammed with his attacks on government policy and his advice on everything from farm income stabilization to rail line abandonment.

Hamilton loved the cut, thrust and parry of Parliamentary debate and used his quick mind and sharp tongue on more than one occasion to justify his reputation as one of Parliament's most colourful characters. He had become a master of devastating one-liners and used them tellingly to drive home his attacks on the government. Once, when Trudeau left the House of Commons just as Hamilton's indictment reached its climax, he remarked that, "Immaturity is a disease suffered by many people; it is too bad to see it among prime ministers."[18] Another time, during a debate on the rôle of the Historic Sites and Monuments Board, the old historian reminded the government that "a place without a history does not have a future."[19] Yet again, when the government introduced a bill to control its own expenditures, he complained pointedly, and perhaps with tongue in cheek, that:

> We talk about the necessity to cut down on everything. All members had their incomes frozen at $24,000. Aren't we good boys! Yet we have a minister [Otto Lang] running up and down the country at $750,000 a time to see his constituents rather than ride on Air Canada. I think maybe it is cruel and unnecessary punishment for ministers to have to ride on Air Canada, but at the same time this is what destroys our posture that we are trying to save money.[20]

Hamilton's sense of humour did not last the period however. In fact, as the months wore on he began to show signs of increasing frustration and exasperation, first with the government and then with his own leader, for their unwillingness to accept his advice. His desperation boiled over late in 1978 when the minister of finance came to the House of Commons for authorization to borrow additional funds for the fiscal years 1978-79 and 1979-80. He compared Canada under the Liberals to a speeding car with no steering wheel and no driver plunging headlong to its doom.

> These people are going along like this, and I plead with them: for Canada's sake, admit your failures; for Canada's sake, beg for help, you need it; for Canada's sake, no more of these interest rate increases; for Canada's sake, no more foreign borrowing to enter a gambling game; for Canada's sake, recall that this country is strong; we must get it turned around and we do not have to wait until after the election.
>
> Just because we are called Conservatives and are in the opposition most of the time, it does not mean that we are all bad. Some of these ideas [I have just mentioned] do have some merit . . . For God's sake, let us pull together for a few months, get some economic policy through this Parliament, and turn this country around so we do not have so many unemployed and so we have some hope for the future.[21]

In his closing peroration, Hamilton called the members of the Trudeau government "lame ducks." He might have used the analogy as well to describe his own influence on the Conservative leadership which had diminished considerably since 1976.

Early in that year, shortly after he won the leadership, Clark asked Hamilton to work on party policy generally and appointed him chairman of a Special Policy Committee composed of twenty politicians and academics named by the leader. The committee met regularly over the next two years and produced several policy proposals, the most important being a comprehensive set which they presented to Clark late in 1977. These papers made recommendations in six areas: social policy; national development; industrial and resource strategy; taxation policy; international trade; and constitutional affairs. The paper on social policy accepted the "social revolution" which had taken place in the last fifty years, but, in recognition that "our productivity has not kept pace" with the cost of the services, proposed that: the operational costs of government involvement in this area be streamlined and reduced; the social service safety net restore individual responsibility; the funded portions of the social security programmes participate in the capital earnings of the nation; a national portable accident insurance programme be introduced; and a Human Resources for Tomorrow conference be held. The paper on national development recommended: a national power grid; a national telecommunications network; the production of gas and oil on a renewable basis; new energy storage facilities; new techniques of financing capital intensive enterprises to promote Canadian ownership; and use of the latest technology in areas such as underwater exploration. The industrial and resource strategy included: the conscious development of four new industrial complexes in Canada; concentration on products for export where Canada already possessed a comparative advantage; use of an expanded transportation system to enhance these advantages; and the substitution of growth rate exchange between countries for obsolete tariff techniques. The tax structure would be reformed by: Canadian acceptance of an international unit of exchange; an adjustment in the domestic monetary system to a formula based on productivity and the flow of money; and a shift in the fiscal system to reward productivity and savings, to encourage regional economic growth, to reduce interest rates, and to end the "suicidal quarrel" between the provinces and the federal government over the resource industries. Proposals in the realm of international trade included: commodity agreements; international trading companies headquartered in Canada; an international clearing house for short and medium term credits; and joint enterprises with other countries. Finally, the paper on the constitution, called A Flexible Federal System, recommended: an exchange of powers between the federal government and the provinces and a delegation of powers by both levels to special agencies where there is unanimous agreement; the geographical enlargement of the resource base of the Atlantic provinces to equal size with the other provinces; the utilization of councils of ministers with respect to policy making in their respective fields; and the recognition of urban and regional governments as part of the federal system. All this was to be accomplished without replacing the British North America Act. The committee also produced papers on Poplar (tree) Farming and Geothermal Energy.[22]

In addition, and to a large extent on his own, Hamilton developed another set of proposals during these months which he called An Industrial Strategy for Canada. This document elaborated in detail on each of the general proposals made in the Special Policy Committee's Industrial and Resource Strategy, and provided a set of specific guidelines as to how those objectives could be reached. This too Hamilton gave to Clark, but with no obvious effect. In fact, there is no evidence that the leader paid any attention at all to the wealth of material he received from Hamilton and his committee. Clark released none of it himself and, to add insult to injury, told committee members not to publicize it.[23] In addition, he refused to bring the proposals to caucus and blocked Hamilton's attempts to do so, thus placing the work of the committee in limbo and effectively preventing Hamilton from having any influence whatsoever on party policy. In Hamilton's words, "It was a horrible thing to do to a person who had waited for so long and had done so much."[24] Hamilton had every right to feel frustrated and angry. He had worked long and hard at the task Clark had given him. He posed no threat to Clark's leadership and wanted only to contribute his ideas and his years of experience to the shaping of party policy. He had produced a comprehensive and detailed blueprint, which he believed would win the next election for the Conservative party and give direction to an inexperienced group of new ministers. He had contributed all of this and yet Clark ignored him for no apparent reason. It was a slight Hamilton would not forget and one Clark would pay for in 1983.

In the circumstances, and given his age, Hamilton might have been expected not to run in the election of 1979. However, he never seriously considered stepping aside. The prospect of defeating the Liberals and seeing his party return to power, even if he no longer had much influence on it, were temptations too great to resist. His campaign began with this damning indictment of the Trudeau record in office:

1. Five years of inflation higher than 7% — now nearly 10%
2. Four years of unemployment at around 8%
3. Five years of economic growth below our 5% growth potential
4. Four years of trade deficits greater than $4B
5. Six years in which the Federal Budget deficit has increased (now $13B)
6. From 1961-76 taxes for the average Canadian family increased by 239%, income rose 142%, expenditures for shelter rose by 128%, food by 66% and clothing by 64%
7. Farm income in Saskatchewan from 1974-78 rose 23%, but expenses rose over 50% in the same period. Therefore, realised net income will show a drop 40%-50% when final figures are published in June
8. The Petroleum Administration Act, 1974, the double taxation of resources industries in the Turner budgets of 1974, the setting up of Petrocan in 1974 [*sic*] were all attacks on the provincial ownership of resources leading to the constitutional clash between the Federal government and the provinces

9. The expensive Bilingualism program under the Trudeau Government changed the Pearson program of trying to get more Quebecers into the federal civil service into an attack on the provinces' rights to control language
10. The confrontation tactics with the provinces not only has led to inflation and unemployment but to stagflation in the economy that has lasted six years.[25]

Right through until election day the newspapers of Qu'Appelle-Moose Mountain carried advertisements reminding voters of the government's dismal failures, especially in the field of agriculture, but in all other areas of economic performance as well. Hamilton's literature also reflected the differences between his ideas to solve these problems and those of the official party platform. With his proposals shelved by the leader, at least for the time being, Hamilton could only "predict" that under a Progressive Conservative government:

1. Inflation will be met by a five-fold attack on the too rapid money supply, too high interest rates, too high city land costs, our costly labour-management relations, and our misunderstanding of how to use the external value of our dollar
2. Our domestic tax structure will change to a positive rewarding of those who produce and serve
3. Our social programs can be saved at a high level of delivery by building in an individual positive incentive to use the savings to provide a much larger Old Age Pension
4. Our P.C. National Development Program will be based on:
   a. producing energy from renewable sources
   b. inter-modal transportation
   c. new techniques of financing capital intensive projects
   d. new technology, especially under water
5. There will be the start of four new industrial complexes featuring the West, the Atlantic, Northern Ontario and Quebec
6. There will be a priority given to the value-added industries of steel, petrochemicals, agriculture, fishing and forestry

7. The obsolete tariff system will be replaced by Growth Rate Exchanges that gives leverage to our resource industries
8. Canada will be taking the lead in introducing a whole new type of Trade Institutions to harmonize with the New World Order
9. Canada will move to a more flexible Constitution that will bring decision-making closer to the people. All levels of Government will end up stronger.[26]

Hamilton's newspaper advertisements did not mention the leader of the party. It did not matter much on election day. He won 54 percent of the vote in the riding — the largest majority of any Progressive Conservative candidate in Saskatchewan. The party also did well, but not quite as well, taking just 36 percent of the vote nationwide but winning enough seats to form a minority government.

Clark did not invite Hamilton to join his cabinet and so he had no part in its few successes or the many miscalculations which led to its premature demise. He believes that he could have helped the government avoid some of its worst mistakes had he been asked for his advice, but he was never approached.[27] Nor did he play a very active rôle in the House of Commons, for government backbenchers, while not without influence, have far fewer opportunities to do so than their counterparts in opposition. He did speak once to oppose a proposal that Canada accept United Nations control over the sea bed beyond national territorial limits, on the grounds that this would simply turn the resources over to international mining companies and be of little help to the underdeveloped nations of the world. He served on the Standing Committee on Finance, Trade and Economic Affairs and argued throughout its sittings in opposition to John Crosbie — his party's minister of finance — that raising the bank rate, a practice followed for months by the Bank of Canada and condoned by both Liberal and Conservative governments, neither strengthened the dollar nor lowered prices.[28] He asked the Department of Agriculture to publish its figures on how much energy various forms of plant life can produce in his continuing quest for alternative energy sources, and he did what he could behind the scenes to coordinate the policies of the ministries of agriculture, energy, mines and resources, DREE and small business with a view towards energy self-sufficiency for Canada by 1990. A passable record for a government backbencher over a short period of time, but unusual for Alvin Hamilton and the reasons for this deviation from the norm lie not in the political but rather in the personal realm.

Death and illness stalked Hamilton during these months. The string began on 16 August with the sudden demise of John Diefenbaker. This brought Hamilton away from his summer retreat near Kenora to play his part in the Chief's elaborate and self-orchestrated funeral. He attended the memorial service in Ottawa and marched in the burial procession at the head of the honorary pallbearers in Saskatoon. Thus ended a rather strange relationship which had endured for almost half a century. The two men had known each other for more twenty-five years prior to Hamilton's election to Parliament, they shared a common background and similar philosophy, and this had brought about a meeting of minds on many policy areas. However, the relationship was never one between equals as far as Diefenbaker was concerned. He never trusted Hamilton's political judgement completely, he continued to refer to Hamilton as "Young Alvin" long after "Young Alvin" had become a grandfather, he savaged Hamilton's proposals often in cabinet and occasionally in public and, after encouraging Hamilton to run for the leadership in 1967, he refused to stay out of the race even though he knew that his entry would likely ruin Hamilton's chance of success. Nevertheless, and despite the above, Hamilton remained a loyal supporter of the Chief as long as Diefenbaker held the leadership, a good friend for the rest of Diefenbaker's life, and he will remain a faithful guardian of the Chief's legacy to the end of his days. Even today, Hamilton cannot speak of Diefenbaker for any length of time without some reference to his debt to the Chief. The reason for this gratitude is that Diefenbaker gave Hamilton an opportunity to serve after years in the political wilderness, a chance to put his ideas into legislation that he believed would benefit the nation. For that Alvin Hamilton will be forever grateful.

In order to attend Diefenbaker's funeral, Hamilton left his dying wife Beulah at their cabin on Dogtooth Lake — a further testimonial to his regard for the Chief and a tribute to his wife's courage and understanding. The Hamiltons returned to Ottawa on 4 September and Beulah died the following night. In his next report to his constituents, later that month, Hamilton summarized their long and happy relationship in this way:

> Our story is not exceptional. We met at school in Delisle, Saskatchewan. We married in the Depression while I was at University. She endured the loneliness of my long absences during five years of War. She endured my many political defeats before 1957. She worried over the constant exhaustion of my five [*sic*] years as a Cabinet Minister. She really enjoyed the last sixteen years when I was home more often. We had a good life together and we both knew it. We could ask for no more.[29]

Three months later, just as Crosbie brought down his ill-fated budget, Alvin Hamilton entered hospital himself. He came through the operation all right, but the Clark government did not survive the budget. Hamilton's absence from the House of Commons did not contribute in itself to the government's defeat — the Conservatives simply did not have the votes to withstand a determined opposition. However, he did miss the drama which attended the demise of the third Conservative government in his lifetime and, on his return to health, found himself facing an election called for 18 February 1980.

Once again Hamilton might have been expected to give up his seat. The double blow of his illness and his wife's death gave him ample reason to step down. However, he was not ready to go just yet. By mid-January the *Oxbow Herald* reported that "he had been cleared . . . by doctors at the Military Hospital in Ottawa as physically fit." Therefore, "Mr. Hamilton will campaign in his usual manner, but he will have to avoid getting chilled or excessive physical exertion during the healing period."[30] Hamilton did campaign during the last month of the contest, though of necessity his activities were curtailed somewhat. His advertisements defended the government and the Crosbie budget and reminded voters that:

The Budget that the NDP and Liberals defeated provided:
For Farmers and Small Business
— $500,000 — Interest at Half Rates
— $200,000 — Capital Gains Reduction
— Spouses Remuneration a Deduction
For Everyone
— 100% Write-Off for Renewable Energy Hardware
— Gasoline Tax Credit
— $100,000 Capital Gains Reduction at $10,000 a year for Canadian Common Stocks.[31]

Other literature made several specific proposals to assist grain farmers in general, and the electors of Qu'Appelle-Moose Mountain in particular. Among these were promises to work for: restoration of the International Wheat Agreement; a new rail line to the west coast; lower interest rates; a storage dam on the Souris River; heavy water, fertilizer, chemical and protein plants in southeastern Saskatchewan; and a rail link between Estevan and Hudson Bay to expedite exports of the region's coal, potash, lumber and grain to Europe.[32] Hamilton's Campaign Committee urged voters to support him "Regardless of Politics" and again made no mention of the party leader. Again, it made no difference. Qu'Appelle-Moose Mountain lived up to its reputation as the safest Conservative seat in the province. After the election the local press noted that:

> Monday, February 18, 1980, was federal election day across Canada . . . a day in which Canadians (perhaps we should say eastern Canadians) voted in a majority Liberal Government under the leadership of Pierre Trudeau.
>
> In the riding of Qu'Appelle-Moose Mountain, however, more than half of the Saskatchewan voters again chose P.C. candidate Alvin Hamilton.[33]

Actually, Hamilton won slightly less than a majority of the vote (49.6 percent). However, it was more than enough to return him to Parliament to pursue his interests and to reflect on the reasons why his party lost power. The leadership of Joe Clark would figure prominently in his calculations.

Whatever Hamilton's thoughts on Clark's rôle in the Conservative defeat, he kept them to himself for the time being.

Nevertheless, his own rôle in the party changed somewhat after the 1980 election, partly because of his own wishes, but moreso due to his deteriorating relationship with his leader. Hamilton might have been content then to play the part of elder stateman in the party, giving the young leader the benefit of his wisdom and experience, but Clark did not think of him in this light. He saw Hamilton as an irritating reminder of the Diefenbaker era, and a potential source of embarrassment, given his proven propensity for independent thought and deed. For his part, Hamilton had come to regard Clark as a leader who had isolated himself from his caucus and who did not understand his followers' need to be "recognized and consulted."[34] In these circumstances, and because of his recent illness, Hamilton asked to be relieved of all committee responsibilities in the House of Commons, which Clark granted readily, and Clark chose not to make use of Hamilton's talents to aid the party in any other way. Thus, in the period from 1980 to 1983 Hamilton was more on the periphery of party activities in Parliament than he had ever been before. He attended caucus meetings sporadically and his opinions were seldom sought in the shaping of party policy. Nevertheless, this did not prevent him from placing his ideas before those who might advance his causes and he had many, ranging from international trade to new sources of renewable energy.

During these years Hamilton lobbied anyone who would listen to him — cabinet ministers, civil servants, businessmen, academics, his colleagues and his constituents. He also spoke in the Commons, albeit less often than before, and one reads these speeches with a sense of déjà vu since many of the problems which had plagued the Trudeau government between 1972 and 1979 continued to trouble it into the 1980s and Hamilton's solutions to them remained much the same. For example, in the field of energy, "develop alternative sources," "give incentives in order to move forward in the very necessary social and economic purpose of reducing the cost of energy to our people and at the same time making more money for the tax collector."[35] With respect to interest rates, "people claim that if we do not keep interest rates high, our dollar will drop. The governor of the Bank of Canada or anyone else who looks at the evidence knows that there is no evidence of that; in fact, the evidence is to the contrary."[36] For international trade, "we in this House in all parties . . . will do everything we can to help the minister improve the performance of the Export Development Corporation, and the first step is getting a supply of capital at the lowest possible price so that we can compete with other nations doing the same thing."[37] In agriculture, "accelerate marketing," "stabilization of prices and income," "a modern system of farm credit," "international commodity agreements," and "announcement [of floor prices for grains] a month in advance of the planting season so that the farmer can consider his various choices."[38] For the economy, "I suggest that the dollar should be allowed to continue to float," "let us work out a money supply formula based on reality . . . Reality is the combination of money in circulation and the velocity with which it moves," "I would like to see the small business development bond restored immediately," "I would like to see action on that Conservative proposal of a few years ago — mortgage interest deductability and property tax deductability."[39]

The three issues of especial importance to Hamilton during this period were constitutional reform, the National Energy Program, and the revoking of the Crowsnest Pass Freight Rates. He opposed all of them in principle or in detail. In the case of the constitution, he did not object to patriation:

> Every party believes in it. We want the constitution back. We want that Canadian constitution to be continued as a Canadian constitution by this Parliament and the other legislatures so that we can get at the serious questions knowing full well we have not had to ask somebody else to do it for us.[40]

However, he did not think it wise to tie patriation to a Charter of Rights within a rigid time frame as Trudeau insisted. Given his experience during the discussions in cabinet on Diefenbaker's Bill of Rights he believed it would be virtually impossible to reach agreement on a list of rights and, further, that the attempt to do so would distract governments from the many economic problems of far greater importance to

Canadians. "No matter how honest or sincere a person is, it is very difficult to describe rights."[41]

> A time frame for this operation is a minimum of three years, but more likely five to six years. In the meantime, the political leaders could quit their posturing and confrontation and get back to making news by doing something on the economic issues.[42]

In his opinion, the Constitution Act should have been split into two parts. "We should repatriate the British North America Act, have an amending formula, get it back here and settle down to the job that we have to do over the next three to ten years."[43]

With respect to the National Energy Program, Hamilton not only objected to it in general but had a particular dislike of two of the pieces of legislation which put it in place — the Canada Oil and Gas Act, introduced on 9 December 1980, and the amendments to the Petroleum Administration Act of April 1982. He regarded both as attacks on the producing provinces of the west, destined to rend national unity, and he argued against both on the grounds that they would drive Canadian companies out of the business and leave the production of oil and gas in Canada to foreign multinationals. In his words:

> This bill has turned back the philosophy of oil regulations in the world some 50 years. We have gone back to the concept of grabbing as much as we can of the resource in the early stages. Because we are grabbing so much, we are putting the companies which are trying to develop the resource into a negative cash flow position in the early years of development. This means in practice that we put the whole oil and gas reserves of the future into the hands of the big international oil companies, because the smaller companies, which only have a few billion dollars worth of reserves, cannot cope with the tremendous money power of the big internationals.[44]

It would be far better for all concerned, in his opinion, if the government withdrew both bills and redrafted them in accordance with the following principles: conservation, "the maximum economic recovery of every field"; elimination of all front-end loading charges on new wells, "no profits should be taken out of the north, no royalties or taxes should be taken out of the north, until the debts are paid off"; elimination of the "back-in" provision which would give the federal government the right to 25 per cent of all future discoveries, "put in its place, in statutory form, a contractual agreement which gives the partners fair and equal treatment according to the type of oil and gas they discover"; and Canadian ownership, "a minimum of 50% of all shares of any private company. All shares of public companies should be available on the stock market . . . so that Canadians can freely own this country as individuals and not through some government corporation."[45] If new sources of oil and gas were to be brought online and if western Canada were to be satisfied with her place in Confederation, then those aspects of the National Energy Program which were causing all the trouble would have to be changed. It would take many months and the election of a new government before this advice, at least in part, would be heeded.

Hamilton reacted to the government's announced intention to remove the Crow rate as would any westerner taught as a school child that the rate for moving prairie grain to market would be "a cent a ton a mile — FOREVER."

> Rightly or wrongly, the Crow rate in the minds of westerners is part of our Magna Carta, protecting our rights for what we did in opening the west. No one is going to change that. It is just as sacred as a constitution that lasts a thousand years.[46]

At first, when just the Crow rate appeared to be at stake, he limited his arguments to the historical.

> The debate on the Crow is not just a matter of dollars and cents or a matter of giving in to the promotion and con job of railways over the last 50 years. It is not just a question of trying to negotiate in a democratic fashion . . . Rightly or wrongly, Crow rates are part of the agreement which built Canada . . . The Crow rate is a mighty important . . . part of our national Constitution.[47]

Later, when the government introduced the Western Grain Transportation Act in May 1983, and it became clear that the legislation encompassed the future of the entire rail system in the west, Hamilton expanded his horizons. Now he had other targets to aim at — in particular the decision to abandon two thousand miles of rail line on the prairies. He considered this a terrible mistake, for it ignored the fact that these lines could carry more than grain and that western Canada possessed many of the raw materials needed by the European Community which could be transported to the sea more cheaply by rail than by any other carrier.

> I am simply saying that . . . the great wealth of the future for this whole nation in the next 40-50 years will come primarily from the areas west of the Great Lakes. The tonnage of minerals, lumber, potash, coal and gravel will come from the west. The first thing the railways should do, if they want to make more money immediately, is to get their rates down . . . Then they would see how they would make more money.[48]

If the railways made a profit on these operations then they would have less cause to complain about occasional losses on the transport of grain in those years when the harvest was poor or sales were low. In addition, he believed the legislation would hurt not only the prairie farmer but also those engaged in manufacturing in central Canada.

> This Bill brings fear into the hearts of the unemployed workers of Ontario. They know what it means when we lose $1 billion in the West and cannot spend it in the East. They lose three times as much as we lose.[49]

He admitted that the west was not a monolith in its attitudes towards the Crow, but felt that the concerns of those who supported this legislation could be met without placing additional burdens on the grain producers already reeling from low prices and high costs. He appealed to the farm organizations representing the different types of producers helped and hurt by the Crow rate to quit squabbling among themselves and support the efforts of the new Conservative government in Saskatchewan, led by Grant Devine, to unite all parties in opposition to the bill. The opposition in the Commons proved so vociferous that eventually the government invoked closure to ensure its passage. In the final debate, Hamilton reviewed his arguments as follows:

> I personally wanted some settlement of this Crow issue on a fair and equitable basis . . . but all we have is this scam started by the CPR. They conned the cattlemen, the commodity groups, the mining and forest industries. They were told they would benefit if the farmers paid a few dollars more . . . If we allow a dying Government to impose closure on something which affects most directly an alienated part of Canada, the Prairies, at a time when we should bring them together with Quebec because of their common interest in protecting our resources, then this Parliament will not give justice.
>
> As the Speaker gave her ruling today, we heard the rolling of the guns for the Royal Salute. In my mind I spoke the old Latin expression which translates into English as "Though the heavens fall, let justice be done." Justice was not done today, Mr. Speaker, in this House.[50]

For many people in the West the Western Grain Transportation Act did not do them justice and provided them with another reason to vote anything but Liberal at the next election. Hamilton drove home the message in his very next *Report from Ottawa.*

> The political reality is that the Liberal Government has given up on the West. It does not know how to handle the railways or the grain companies. It has managed to make all groups mad and feeling double-crossed. It has pushed the C.W.B. [Canadian Wheat Board] out of action and Hazen Argue [Minister in charge of the Wheat Board] into silence. It just hopes the NDP will save seats in the West so they won't have any more Western PC's to face.[51]

Only a single Liberal won a seat on the prairies in the 1984 election, although western reaction to the removal of the Crow rate did not account for this result on its own. Other factors had their impact as well, not the least being a resurgent Progressive Conservative party with a new leader at its helm — Brian Mulroney.

Chapter 10

The Mulroney Years

The question of leadership returned to centre stage for many Conservatives after the defeat of the Clark government in 1980. Very quickly the party split into at least three groups — Clark supporters, Clark opponents, and those who wanted to see Clark go but who were not prepared to push him very hard in that direction. Alvin Hamilton fell into this last camp. He did not think much of Clark's "high-schoolish" leadership abilities. He resented the fact that Clark had rejected his ideas on party policy. He believed that Clark had hurt the party with his efforts to expunge all traces of the Diefenbaker/Hamilton philosophy, and he feared that Clark's public persona would make it very difficult for the party to return to power.[1] Nevertheless, he took no part whatsoever in the early attempts to replace the leader. He does not believe in biennial reviews of the leader's position and such scheming reminded him too much of what had been done to Diefenbaker. Whatever his opinion of Clark, he would not join any plot to remove him. Furthermore, he could think of no suitable successor to Clark at that time. In his words, "I looked down the front bench and prayed to God for a miracle."[2] He would give Clark one more chance to prove himself. He remained scrupulously neutral at the conventions of 1981 in Ottawa and 1983 in Winnipeg and advised the delegates from his riding to do likewise. He did not want any one associated with him linked to any attempt to replace Clark.[3]

Hamilton's position altered drastically after the Winnipeg meeting when Clark, on his own hook, resigned and called for a leadership convention at which he would be a candidate. Alvin Hamilton would not vote against Clark as leader, but he would try to prevent Clark becoming leader again. Aged seventy-one, he had no illusions about winning the leadership himself. He had to find a candidate who shared his views on policy who could beat Clark. At first, he encouraged several people to run — Michael Wilson, Don Mazankowski, Jake Epp (all members of Parliament), and Brian Mulroney (still in business). He sent these men and two other declared candidates — John Crosbie and David Crombie — updated versions of the policy papers Clark had rejected prior to the 1979 election and asked for their comments. The intent was clear. The candidate who shared his desire to unite the party on policy and whose views were closest to his own would have his support. The exercise found him his man very quickly. Although most of the candidates involved agreed to some of his ideas, only Mulroney accepted most of them and only Mulroney took the time to discuss them with him. He visited Hamilton shortly after he announced his decision to run and the two men compared notes on issues which ranged from economic development through national unity to trade as an instrument of international peace.[4] In the end Mulroney convinced Hamilton of his soundness on policy matters. He had matured considerably since he received Hamilton's reluctant support on the third ballot in 1976. This time he would have his former mentor in his corner from the beginning to the end of the fight.

Despite the first of his two operations in 1983 for cataracts, Hamilton made several trips to the west on Mulroney's behalf during the campaign. He wanted to prove to delegates that his candidate had as good a claim to their support as did Clark and he used an argument that still had some impact in the area. He described Mulroney as the only candidate who accepted the philosophy of John George Diefenbaker. What this would mean to westerners, he promised, was that a

Progressive Conservative government led by Brian Mulroney and advised by Alvin Hamilton would not only understand the problems of the region but would also take action to solve them in the same way as the Diefenbaker government had between 1957 and 1963. Furthermore, he predicted that the party would never return to power under Clark because Clark had shown Canadians everywhere that he was unable "to cut the mustard." Not too old, but definitely lacking in leadership capacity. A generalization as to the overall impact of Hamilton's intervention is impossible, but in Qu'Appelle-Moose Mountain he is certain that only five of twenty delegates remained with Clark on the last ballot.[5]

At the convention in Ottawa, 8–11 June, Hamilton sat with Mulroney in his box to show delegates that Mulroney had "people of substance" backing him.[6] He also warned Mulroney not to let his attractive wife Mila steal the show from him. Telecasts of voting day show Hamilton looking serene, almost bored, in anticipation of the first ballot results. He knew that his candidate could count on approximately nine hundred votes with sufficient potential to grow on succeeding ballots to put him over the top. The day went precisely as he wanted it to. His only fear was that Clark's first-ballot support would drain off to Crosbie in numbers great enough to threaten Mulroney's position as the candidate most likely to defeat Clark, so he spent his time between ballots in the Clark camp urging delegates to remain with their man. The final vote brought Mulroney the leadership and Hamilton the promise that once again he would have some influence on the policies of the Progressive Conservative party. Victory that day was sweet, and both men had waited a long time to taste it.

Hamilton began the Mulroney era with a renewed sense of mission. He knew that the new leader would not have much time to devote to party policy and he expected to fill the breach. He would try to do for Mulroney what he had done for Clark, albeit without result — that is, provide a comprehensive set of policies on which the party could fight the next election and to which a new Conservative government could look for guidance. He concluded that Mulroney would need a policy advisory body similar to the old Manotick Group and, in fact, asked its more prominent members to return to Ottawa after the June convention. However, these men had long since established other careers they would not leave.[7] They would advise from afar, but they would not come back to the day-to-day hurly-burly of the capital. Hamilton would have to find others to take their place or do it on his own. He tried the latter course, but did not get very far for reasons largely beyond his control.

In the first place, just after the summer vacation Mulroney asked Hamilton to co-chair (with Senator William Doody) a Task Force on Job Opportunities for Canada's Youth with instructions to report by the following March on "the number of youth that are presently affected by unemployment, or will be affected in the foreseeable future, to determine the causes of youth unemployment, and the possible remedies."[8] Unfortunately, Mulroney could not provide the funds to hire sufficient research staff and most of the work had to be done in the chairmen's offices. A report was submitted, although Hamilton takes little credit for its recommendations beyond his insistence that any new programmes be based as much as possible on the principle of "self-help" at the local level. As he explained to his constituents:

> The trick is to have everyone make more money and use existing administrative machinery so no new bureaucracy is required. So Municipal Secretary Treasurers, Town Clerks, etc. should be ready with things that should and could be done in their areas. I know from experience that imaginative and innovative help is available at the local level, but it needs the knowledge of professional and business people to get it organized and working. There is nothing so satisfying as to make money and to know that you have helped others at the same time. Self-help is the Code phrase.[9]

Another project which consumed Hamilton's time prior to the 1984 election was his effort to counter Trudeau's "peace initiative," the one hope the Liberals had of restoring their sagging popularity. He was determined that the government would not win another term by use of this stratagem and he developed a tactic he thought could prevent it. He had discussed the importance of international trade as a force for world peace with Mulroney prior to the convention and now Peace Through Trade became the keystone of most of Hamilton's speeches in the House of Commons. Hamilton could not resist the occasional pot shot at his long despised bêtes noires, "the morons in the Bank of Canada and the Department of Finance who believe you can stop inflation by raising interest rates,"[10] nor did he ignore the problems of western agriculture, but for the most part his major contributions came in the field of international trade, especially during debates on the government's plans for the Export Development Corporation. His message was simple: "If we want to keep peace in the world, the only proven technique to keep and maintain peace is to trade with people."[11] Meetings all over the world to discuss various forms of disarmament would not ensure peace. "Peace cannot be achieved by conferences. Peace is only obtained by people working and trading together."[12] In his opinion, the prime minister could assist the cause of peace more by practical efforts to expand international trade than by his peripatetic wanderings in search of it. Finally, Mulroney's election as leader coincided with an approach from Beijing which gave Hamilton another opportunity to honour the pledge he made to Zhou Enlai in 1964 and which diverted his attention even further from his original purpose.

Early in the 1980s the Chinese government came to the conclusion that its highly centralized management of the economy was neither increasing China's exports nor the standard of living of her people at an acceptable rate. Beijing decided therefore to grant her cities and provinces greater autonomy in planning the pace and direction of their economic development and in 1983 asked Hamilton for his advice and assistance in the experiment. He accepted the invitation without hesitation. He met with Bu Zhaomin, China's director of International Trade Relations, and Zhao Ziyang, China's prime minister, during their visits to Ottawa in June 1983 and January 1984. They informed him that China needed help in a number of areas and asked him to meet with officials in Beijing and the provinces to discuss how China could acquire the technology she required, and to suggest ways by which she could increase her exports to pay for the expertise. He spent two weeks in Beijing, Shanghai, Guangzhou and Fuzhou at the end of March and beginning of April and learned that the Chinese wanted assistance with their water supply, reforestation, petrochemical industry, communications, transportation and energy generation. Beijing also confirmed its intention to introduce more flexibility into its economic planning. This shift in policy delighted Hamilton because it overcame a problem he knew from personal experience to be a major obstacle in expanding trade with China — the necessity of having each and every agreement vetted and approved by Beijing's slow-moving and often inefficient central bureaucracy. China's provinces are now free, within certain limits such as the state of the country's external trade balance, to buy and sell on their own and this has encouraged initiatives unheard of in the 1960s and 1970s.

Already under the new "pragmatism" the Chinese provinces of Heilong-jiang, Jilin, Jiangsu and Sichuan have "twinned" with Alberta, Saskatchewan, Ontario, and the state of Washington, and other such arrangements are in the offing. At least three provincial premiers — Lougheed of Alberta, Devine of Saskatchewan, and Peterson of Ontario — have led trade missions to Harbin, Changchun and Nanjing, and Edmonton has hosted a trade fair to publicize the products for sale from Alberta's "twin" province. According to one reporter who attended the exhibition:

> The Chinese shipped 600 tonnes of merchandise in 16 huge containers. They are going home with three, having sold about $300,000 worth of merchandise to friendly Albertans and struck a handful of modest contracts for more. . .
>
> More than 225,000 people wandered through the exhibits and/or took in the accompanying circus. Many witnessed the unforgettable sight of upright Chinese gentlemen in baggy suits gleefully stacking wads of Canadian $50 bills.
>
> Somewhere in Edmonton about a dozen homes are showing off new $2,000 silk rugs. A local eatery even

> purchased the dumpling machine the visitors brought. On such things are sound friendships based.[13]

This article pleased Hamilton a great deal for not only did it draw public attention to the new opportunities for trade with China but its conclusion echoed his belief that trade can contribute to peace between nations.

The major purpose of the twinning arrangement is to facilitate contact between those regions of China which require modern technology for various projects and those businesses in Canada and the United States which can supply it. If successful, the expertise and machinery China purchases will enable her to produce goods which are both needed at home and marketable abroad, with enough exported to balance the trade account. For example, the knowledge Fujian buys from firms in British Columbia should increase the efficiency of her mines, railways and ports, and help her export coal to Japan on a competitive basis. Beijing's change of attitude and the twinning arrangements made Hamilton's task much easier than ever before. On his return to Canada he brought together Chinese and Canadian buyers and sellers and lobbied Canadian companies and government agencies with some success. Today, a Canadian company is producing tractors in China, several mining and petrochemical firms have representatives there, and Hamilton plans to have Canadian forestry, environmental and nuclear experts go as soon as possible.

The rapid success of these developments troubled Hamilton somewhat for they proceeded at such a fast pace that little if any thought was given to the long-term prospects of trade with China. Some Canadian and American businessmen were most persistent in their pursuit of sales to the Chinese provinces with little attempt to coordinate their efforts or much concern for China's ability to pay for all these products. Hamilton feared that if more attention was not paid to China's need to export, then Beijing would be forced to end the experiment and reimpose her rigid central control. Chinese delegates to a conference on international trade held at Lewis and Clark College in Idaho, in February 1984, insisted that China expected more cooperation in this area than she had received to date. Hamilton attended that conference as its keynote speaker and reiterated the Chinese complaint. He warned his audience that the future of trade with China would depend on Chinese perceptions of the fairness with which they were treated now and the benefits they derived from their contacts with Western businessmen. He urged that trade be conducted on a basis of mutual advantage and that the drive for profits not destroy the fragile new "pragmatism" in China by over-aggressive sales techniques.[14] The five American state governments which attended the conference agreed to inform each other and the Canadian provincial governments twinned with Chinese provinces of their activities, but whether American and Canadian businessmen heeded his warnings is today at best debatable.

Hamilton's participation at the Idaho conference and his trip to China two weeks later were not without some personal political risk. He had nothing to fear from the Canadian government nor the leader of his party, for he notified the ministers responsible for trade affairs [Gerald Regan and Edward Lumley] of the purpose and result of his tour, and he returned from Beijing with an invitation to Mulroney to visit China at his earliest convenience. Rather, Hamilton faced a challenge for the nomination in his riding of Qu'Appelle-Moose Mountain. Earl Silcox, a local farmer and vice-president of the constituency Progressive Conservative Association, decided to contest the nomination on the grounds that he would provide the riding with better representation in Ottawa, that he would not move to the federal capital region as Hamilton had done, and that he would commute "from Qu'Appelle-Moose Mountain to Ottawa — not from Ottawa to Qu'Appelle-Moose Mountain."[15] Hamilton loyalists warned that the threat from Silcox was worth taking seriously and advised him to cancel his travel plans in order to meet the challenge. Hamilton, however, could not accept the advice. Although the contest shook him and he did not take it lightly, he had promised the Chinese he would go and he did go.

As it happened, he was able to put the visit to good political use on his return. He reminded delegates that he had secured the Chinese market for their grain in the past, he told them of the prospects of new sales in the future, and asked if they wanted a member who would go out and work actively on their behalf, or one who would stay home and commiserate with them when other countries captured these new markets. In his speech to the convention on 14 April he informed the delegates that:

> Trade and development opportunities with China and the Pacific Rim are opening up rapidly. Since June things have moved so rapidly on trade and development that new markets are appearing for meat products in many Pacific countries and the world demand for grain is increasing. This is no accident. I have worked damned hard at these new techniques of trade and financing which are now coming into form as tangible agreements for markets that we could never before imagine.[16]

He concluded with a plea for the opportunity to continue his work and the convention granted his wish — narrowly. Hamilton won 618 votes; Silcox 514.

With the nomination in hand, Hamilton took the same arguments to the constituency at large at the general election fought shortly thereafter. His campaign literature highlighted Peace Through Trade, featured a picture of Hamilton shaking hands with China's Vice-Premier Li Peng taken during his recent visit and asked for the public's support in the work he had begun.

> During this election campaign, I trust that people of all parties will unite behind the revival of the Diefenbaker spirit in Canada. PEACE THROUGH TRADE.
>
> There is much that I have to do in the next few years and I will need all your support and help.[17]

His advertisements also asked voters, "How would you like . . . Interest Rates Reduced 50% for Farmers, Home Owners and Small Business? Elimination of Capital Gains Tax on Farms and Small Businesses? Farm Fuel Reduced 20 cents per Gallon? Farm Chemicals Reduced 50%?" — and gave the leader of the party a place of prominence for the first time since 1965.[18] On 4 September 1984 victory proved easier to achieve than the nomination. Hamilton won by more than six thousand votes over his nearest opponent [B. Sauter of the NDP] and nearly doubled the vote of all his challengers combined. The party did just as well nation-wide with a near majority of the popular vote and winning 211 seats — a result which replicated its massive sweep in 1958.

It is doubtful that anyone welcomed the Conservative victory more than Alvin Hamilton. He had waited over twenty years for the chance to implement his ideas and now the moment had arrived. In his words:

> It was indeed an historic day for the PC Party of Canada on September 4th and I am so pleased that I personally have been given the opportunity to serve in the 33rd Parliament of Canada. I am confident that under Brian's leadership we will be successful in getting this country moving in the right direction once again.[19]

The "right direction," of course, was where he had been pointing for a generation and more and he had high hopes that the new government would accept his guidance. He believed he had a special relationship with the new prime minister, who had referred to him publicly as a "friend and mentor," and he thought he could translate this association into influence and action. Unfortunately for Alvin Hamilton these expectations have been realized only in part.

Mulroney did not include his friend and mentor in his first ministry, although this did not bother Hamilton greatly since he had not expected a cabinet post. In fact, he had told Mulroney months before the election that he would be quite content in the rôle of ideas man for a new Progressive Conservative government. He would not intervene often in Commons debates in order to give the many new Conservative members more opportunities to establish their reputations before the next election.[20] Nor would he attend caucus meetings without important cause. Instead, he would make his contributions behind the scenes. He would work quietly with ministers and their staffs to develop the policies he believed would create a better Canada.

A year into the government's term he reported to his constituents with some satisfaction. On the economic side, he advised that "the record is quite good. With the national economy reviving faster than expected and the rains coming to the Prairies the future looks a little brighter."[21] On the political side, "the Government has done more than well. The end of twenty years of confrontation between Ottawa and the Provincial Governments hopefully has ended."[22] In particular, he was pleased to point out that the Mulroney government had fulfilled most of the promises he had made in the 1984 campaign in Qu'Appelle-Moose Mountain — the elimination of capital gains taxes on farms and small businesses, a twenty cent a gallon reduction in fuel taxes, and the elimination of front-end loading charges on the petroleum industry which should result in a dramatic decline in chemical costs. Most of all, he was delighted that the government had accepted Peace Through Trade as a major thrust of its foreign policy.

Hamilton began the Mulroney years determined to continue his efforts to increase trade between China and Canada, and indeed between Canada and any country on a bilateral or multilateral basis, so long as it benefitted all parties concerned. He had a host of ideas he hoped to see through to fruition, including the building of better storage facilities in China so that Canadian beef could be flown in and Chinese fabrics flown out with less wastage than before, the sale of small nuclear reactors to Chinese cities to supply energy for heat, electricity and the growing and preservation of vegetables, and the use of Canadian technology to provide clean water in rural China. He arranged the financing for some of his projects from the World Bank and led a trade and development mission to China in the spring of 1985 to follow up the discussions he had with Chinese officials the previous year. In November and December of the same year he travelled to South Korea and Japan at his own expense to pursue other trade prospects, and he plans further trips in the future in the expectation of improving Canada's trade with all of Southeast Asia. In May 1986, he returned to China just prior to the prime minister's visit to check on the structures being considered to facilitate the transfer of economic and scientific information between Ottawa and Beijing — one of the items in the agreement to be signed during Mulroney's visit — and was pleased to learn that the Chinese had already established a centre for such exchanges. Although he was not a part of the official Canadian delegation — once again he had paid his own way[23] — Hamilton was welcomed warmly by the Chinese. They hosted a formal dinner in his honour the evening before Mulroney and his entourage arrived, and they added Hamilton's name to the guest list for the state banquet they laid on for the Canadian prime minister the following day. At the banquet, the Chinese toasted Hamilton several times after Mulroney, in his speech, had paid tribute to Pierre Elliot Trudeau as the man who had ushered in the modern era in Sino-Canadian relations. This was a subtle yet pointed reminder to the official Canadian party that the relationship had in fact begun a decade earlier and that the man who had forged the first bonds should not be forgotten. This incident illustrates Hamilton's recent difficulties, for sometimes his efforts seem to be better received abroad than at home. He had hoped initially to create a special section in the Prime Minister's Office to assist him and obtained Mulroney's approval in principle to do so, although he had little luck in finding anyone in the Prime Minister's Office to follow through on the idea, and most of the work continued to be done in his Parliamentary office and occasionally in the departments responsible for international trade. Nevertheless, Hamilton's efforts did not go unrewarded. For example, an issue of the *China Daily* early in 1987 reported that, "more than half of China's 800 million rural population now have access to clean drinking water as a result of a nationwide campaign to improve rural supplies," and further that "80 percent of the country's total rural population will be able to drink clean and healthy water by the end of the century."[24] Alvin Hamilton did not single-handedly clean up rural China's water and would never make this claim. However, when Chinese officials brought the problem to his attention he helped them find a way to solve it. This is what he means by "helping people to help themselves" and this is the practical result of his belief in Peace Through Trade.[25]

Despite his approval of many of the Mulroney government's actions, Hamilton was by no means satisfied with its entire record. He stated publicly that the renewal of the Small Business Development Bond Program did not accomplish its purposes and that more had to be done to prevent farm foreclosures.[26] He wanted interest rates reduced further and was worried that Finance Minister Wilson's attempts to reduce the federal deficit might do the economy more harm than good.[27] He believed the government could do more to promote economic development and international trade, and he was concerned that its political difficulties throughout its term might deflect it from the goals he wanted it to achieve. He wanted the cabinet to publicize its philosophy and its principles with greater intensity and to act in accordance with them always. His advice to the prime minister: "When you are under attack about smelly fish bring out the hopes and dreams. Then pray you can find two or three Ministers to bail you out before the next election."[28] Hamilton knew this government had made mistakes. He referred to himself at times as a "teacher in a kindergarten."[29] Not all his ideas were acceptable to cabinet and he did not always receive the cooperation he needed to advance his projects as quickly as he would like. Nevertheless, he continues to believe that the country is far better off with a Progressive Conservative government in office than it would be under the Liberals or New Democrats, and he intends to remain as close as possible to the government in the hope that it will implement his vision of what is best for Canada and the world.

By and large, Hamilton kept his vow to speak less in the Commons than in the past. In fact, in the first two years of Brian Mulroney's prime ministership he rose only twice — once to support the erection of a statue to John Diefenbaker on Parliament Hill and once in a sad tribute to his old friend Tommy Douglas on his demise. Later, however, he spoke more often, perhaps because his "quiet diplomacy" with the prime minister and cabinet did not achieve all its hoped for results, but more likely because issues arose which had been a constant concern of his for decades: the plight of prairie farmers; the impact of interest rates on the economy; self-sufficiency in energy; government assistance to the poor at home and abroad; and Canadian control of our resources. His opinions on these problems had not changed much, nor had his solutions to them, and he continued to press them publicly as well as privately on the government. "Financing for prairie farmers is crucial at the moment."[30] "I will not be satisfied until interest rates are at their proper level. At best, the interest rate should be at 3 percent . . . (adjusted for inflation)."[31] "The future of this whole continent in terms of self-sufficiency in energy is based on the Canadian Arctic . . . The nation that has the resources wins wars, and the nation that has the resources wins when it comes to trade."[32] "One of the biggest problems for all western countries today is our attitude toward social services. We think we should pour money out. However, we must do it in such a way as to get all our money back and make more. It is so simple to do."[33] "I am in contact with 86 countries. They ask what they can do to make some money. I tell them what they can do. We do not give them money. They do not really want it. If you can show them ways in which to earn it themselves it is much better."[34] "Just say to Amoco that one of the terms and conditions we will consider is this. We would like to put your Amoco into a Canadian company registered in Canada and make every one of the shares of that company available to Canadians. That is the positive way to go . . . If one is truly thinking of the interests of Canada, one should not think in terms of building a wall around us . . . the correct term should be positive nationalism."[35] "About Freer Trade . . . Westerners have little choice. Our small numbers, our vast areas, our transportation costs, etc. have made it mandatory that we work together, regardless of party, for our survival and benefit. On Freer Trade we are one by necessity."[36] Such advice was based on decades of research and experience, and Alvin Hamilton continued to offer it because he believed his proposals could contribute to a better life for Canadians and others, no matter their nationality.

Nineteen eighty-seven marked two important occasions in Alvin Hamilton's life — the first, his seventy-fifth birthday on 30 March, and the second, the thirtieth anniversary of his initial election to Parliament on 10 June. He spent part of the former at a surprise party organized by his staff and attended by his family, the prime minister, the leader of the opposition and other political dignitaries, and dozens of friends acquired during his lengthy career in Ottawa. He spent part of the latter in the House of Commons receiving tributes paid to him and the other two members first elected in 1957 — Lloyd Crouse and Robert Coates — both Conservatives from Nova Scotia. The first to offer congratulations was Donald Mazankowski, the deputy prime minister, who, on behalf of the prime minister and the Progressive Conservative party, acknowledged the presence in the Commons of the Honourable Member for Qu'Appelle-Moose Mountain, Saskatchewan, his service in the Diefenbaker governments and "his imagination and creative approaches to dealing with our mutual problems [which] have certainly made a notable contribution to our country."[37] Then John Turner rose to add that in his view

> he [Hamilton] has never been given the credit he deserves for having authored the northern vision . . . He opened up our lands north of the 60th parallel to Canadian attention. The Roads to Resources program was his. The farmers of this country will always remember him as a spectacularly successful Minister of Agriculture. The only weakness in judgment he has ever shown is having hired Brian Mulroney . . . when he was the Minister of Agriculture.[38]

Finally, offering the best wishes of the New Democratic Party, House Leader Nelson Riis noted that "there are a handful of people in the House of Commons who command the attention of Members when they stand. When the Member for Qu'Appelle-Moose Mountain stands and makes a speech in this House, he has the undivided attention of all Members."[39] Then, as the only one of the class of 1957 in the chamber that afternoon, Alvin Hamilton took the floor to respond. It was a polished performance by an experienced parliamentarian. Speaking extemporaneously, he reminded members of the importance of the 1957 election in breaking the trend to one-party government entrenched in Canada since 1935. Then he paid tribute to the war veterans who had entered Parliament at that election and who had brought with them the view that future wars could be avoided only if people learned to work together both within and between countries. He drew members' attention to the presence in the gallery of Michael Starr and used the former minister of labour's Winter Works Programme as a practical example of the spirit of cooperation the

Diefenbaker governments had tried to foster during their years in office. He pointed out that succeeding Liberal administrations had continued to talk "cooperative" federalism but had made the grave error of confronting the provinces as a group, instead of treating each province individually, and letting each province have an arrangement which suited it best. He ended his brief remarks as follows:

> We had a group of people in the caucus who were very conscious of the fact that the only way to keep peace in the world was to cooperate not only with our own institutions in the country, but to cooperate on an economic basis with all other countries in the world. We are one world economically, we are one country nationally, and the only way we can make it work is through cooperation. *All that this Government has done is simply to put in a written form.*[40]

It did not take members long to realize that Hamilton's final sentence referred to the constitutional agreement worked out by the prime ministers and the premiers at Meech Lake, and Hamilton is convinced that the accord reached there will begin a new era of cooperative federalism in Canada as beneficial as that which transpired during his years in office.[41] The Speaker called Hamilton's remarks "vintage House of Commons"[42] while all members rose and applauded. In paying tribute to colleagues past and present, in reminding Canadians of the reasons for past successes and failures, in providing directions for future government activity at home and abroad and in supporting his leader in his attempts to build a better Canada it was also vintage Alvin Hamilton.

Epilogue

Alvin Hamilton did not contest the federal election of 1988. Redistribution erased his Qu'Appelle-Moose Mountain constituency from the electoral map and, at age seventy-six, he decided not to seek a nomination elsewhere. It is difficult to imagine a life without politics for Alvin Hamilton. Politics has been his profession for virtually all of his adult life, he has served his party, his constituents, and his country in almost every way possible, and Canadian political life will be the poorer because of his retirement for he possessed many of the qualities desirable in political leaders. He was a career politician, he had a desire to serve, and his ego extended no further than the belief that he could contribute something of value to the political process. He was not in politics for fame or fortune and his personal life was irreproachable — scandal of any type never touched him. He was loyal to his party and its leaders, but he followed neither blindly nor without reservation. He had faith in the democratic process and in the enormous potential of this country and its citizens. He had a healthy distrust of those who placed their interests above those of the nation, and a dislike of civil servants when they came to believe that they had a better conception of the national interest than the elected representatives of the people. He had definite views as to the short and long-term interests of the nation, but was prepared to adapt to circumstances as they arose. He had a fertile mind, was open to any idea which might further his ends, and was prepared to work unceasingly to achieve them. Finally, he was a politician interested more in the substance of policy than in the ephemera of image and in furthering the interests of his country rather than his own — traits looked for and hoped for, but not always found in our politicians. In sum, Alvin Hamilton, P.C., made a significant contribution to the governance of his country, and his personal qualities, his career, his successes and failures and the reasons for them, together provide a standard of public service against which to measure other politicians past, present, and future.

Notes

Preface

1. Rich Little, "My Fellow Canadians," RCA, 1963.
2. Canada, House of Commons, *Debates* (hereafter *Debates*), 22 July 1960, 6738.
3. Editorial, *Calgary Herald*, 23 July 1960.
4. Editorial, *Lethbridge Herald*, 25 July 1960.
5. Hamilton maintains that when he sat down after his response to Wooliams's question, his seat-mate, J. Angus MacLean, minister of fisheries, turned to him and said, "Alvin, you really are the kind of guy who leaves no stern untoned."

Chapter 1

1. Ralph, born 1910; Alvin, 1912; Ross, 1914; Fred, 1916; Hubert, 1918.
2. Alvin Hamilton, interview with author, 24 June 1981.
3. *Kenora Miner and News*, 6 July 1927.
4. Ibid.
5. Alvin Hamilton, interview with author, 24 June 1981.
6. The contest was sponsored by Saskatchewan politican J.F. Bryant, and named for him.
7. Alvin Hamilton, interview with author, 24 June 1981.
8. Alvin Hamilton, interview with Peter Stursberg, Hamilton Private Papers, Manotick, Ontario (hereafter HPP).
9. A lengthier description of the organization can be found in Escott Reid, "The Saskatchewan Liberal Machine Before 1929," in *Party Politics in Canada*, ed. Hugh Thorburn (Toronto: Prentice-Hall of Canada, 1963), 93-104.
10. According to Hamilton, Diefenbaker never trusted his judgement completely throughout their long association, and he believes that one reason for this lies in Diefenbaker's recollec-

tion of that speech as incongruous, if not foolish. Alvin Hamilton, interview with the author, 16 February 1981.

11. For a further account of the Ku Klux Klan and the 1929 election in Saskatchewan, see Patrick Kyba, "Ballots and Burning Crosses," in *Politics in Saskatchewan*, ed. Norman Ward and Duff Spafford, (Toronto: Longmans Canada, 1968), 105-23.
12. Alvin Hamilton, interview with Peter Stursberg, 30 April 1980, HPP. For a humorous account of life as a teacher in a one-room school during the Depression, see Max Braithwaite, *Why Shoot the Teacher* (Toronto: McClelland and Stewart Ltd., 1965).
13. Saskatchewan Archives Board (hereafter SAB), Department of Education Archives.
14. Ibid.
15. The school board also hired Fred Hamilton to replace Alvin Hamilton when he resigned to go to university.
16. For analyses of the rise of the CCF and Social Credit, see Seymour M. Lipset, *Agrarian Socialism: The Co-operative Commonwealth Federation in Saskatchewan* (Garden City: Doubleday & Co., 1968), and C.B. Macpherson, *Democracy in Alberta: Social Credit and the Party System* (Toronto: University of Toronto Press, 1962).
17. Alvin Hamilton, interview with author, 21 January 1981.
18. J.A. Archer, *Saskatchewan: A History* (Saskatoon: Western Producer Prairie Books, 1980), 215.
19. Diefenbaker Centre (hereafter DC), Diefenbaker Papers, MG26 MII (hereafter DP), vol. 7, N. Given to J.G. Diefenbaker, 13 and 26 November 1936.
20. Party platform, Saskatchewan Conservative Party, 1938.
21. DC, DP, vol. 4, Senator Aseltine to J.G. Diefenbaker, 18 December 1937.
22. DC, DP, vol. 4, Alvin Hamilton to J.G Diefenbaker, 23 April 1938.
23. The English course he took in his third year may also have been an attempt to vindicate himself. During his last year at Rhondda he enrolled in a correspondence course offered by Carlyle King. King gave him the lowest mark he ever received in a university course and "he tore me to shreds over my writing." King gave Hamilton 60 percent. He earned a grade of 76 percent in the second course. Alvin Hamilton, interview with author, 21 January 1981.
24. Alvin Hamilton, interview with Peter Stursberg, 30 April 1980, HPP.

25. Gordon Robertson won the Rhodes scholarship that year. Coincidentally, Robertson became Hamilton's deputy minister of northern affairs and national resources.
26. Alvin Hamilton, interview with Peter Stursberg, 30 April 1980, HPP.

Chapter 2

1. C.H. Higginbotham, *Off the Record: The C.C.F. in Saskatchewan* (Toronto: McClelland and Stewart, 1968), 55.
2. Party platform, Saskatchewan Conservative Party, 1938.
3. DC, DP, #003687, F.W. Turnbull to J.G. Diefenbaker, 2 April 1938.
4. DC, DP, #003781, F.W. Turnbull to H.E. Keown, 29 April 1938.
5. Ibid.
6. DC, DP, #003572, E.E. Perley to J.G. Diefenbaker, 28 January 1938.
7. T.C. Douglas to George Williams, 26 March 1938. Quoted in David E. Smith, *Prairie Liberalism: The Liberal Party in Saskatchewan, 1905-71* (Toronto: University of Toronto Press, 1975), 234.
8. George Williams to J.S. Woodsworth, 23 June 1938. Quoted in Smith, *Prairie Liberalism*, 235.
9. DC, DP, vol 3, J.G. Diefenbaker to D. Massey, 10 June 1938.
10. Alvin Hamilton, interview with author, 16 February 1981.
11. Alvin Hamilton, interviews with author, 16 February and 24 June 1981.
12. Former student, now employed at Nutana Collegiate, interview with author, 9 June 1981.
13. Nutana Collegiate Year Book, *Hermes*, 1940.
14. DC, DP, #003642, J.G. Diefenbaker to Alvin Hamilton, 20 July 1937.
15. Ibid.
16. Alvin Hamilton, interview with Peter Stursberg, 30 April 1980, HPP.
17. Nutana Collegiate Year Book, *Hermes*, 1942.
18. Alvin Hamilton, "Canada's Forgotten Flyboys," *Toronto Daily Star*, 19 October 1968.
19. See, for example, Winston Spencer Churchill, *The Second World War: Triumph and Tragedy* (Boston: Houghton Mifflin Co., 1953).
20. Alvin Hamilton, interview with Peter Stursberg, 30 April 1980, HPP.

21. Hamilton, "Canada's Forgotten Flyboys."
22. Entry in Hamilton's log book by W/C R. Gordon, O/C 436 Squadron, 4 May 1945, HPP.
23. National Archives of Canada (hereafter NAC), Hamilton Papers, MG32 B40 (hereafter HP), Box 268693, Alvin Hamilton to J.G. Diefenbaker, 24 June 1944.
24. Progressive Conservative party advertisement, *Rosetown Eagle*, 17 May 1945.
25. NAC, HP, Box 268691, script of radio address by Alvin Hamilton, 1945.
26. Both Bracken and Ramsay had taught in the College of Agriculture at the University of Saskatchewan. Ramsay was teaching there when he accepted the leadership in 1944. Bracken had left much earlier for Manitoba and had been premier of that province from 1922 until 1942, when he won the leadership of the national Conservativeparty, which changed its name at his insistence.
27. SAB, Progressive Conservative Party Papers, S-B5 (hereafter PCPP), Rupert Ramsay, "Report to P.C. Convention," Regina, 22 October 1946.
28. SAB, PCPP, Rupert Ramsay, "Report to the Progressive Conservative Advisory Board," 11 November 1947.
29. Walter Tucker, interview with author, 30 July 1981. Tucker returned from the House of Commons to take on the leadership of the Saskatchewan Liberal Party in 1946.
30. *P.C.P. News*, 15 October 1945.
31. Ibid., 1 November 1945.
32. NAC, HP, Box 268690, Alvin Hamilton, script of radio address, 6 March 1947.
33. Ibid., 11 February 1948.
34. Alvin Hamilton, interview with author, 16 February 1981.
35. It is rumoured that this slogan prompted more than one voter, who preferred anybody to the Liberals, to state that while he did not know much about this fellow "Tyranny," he would vote for him rather than Walter Tucker.
36. SAB, Pamphlet Collection, G-14, "9 Lessons for Voting for the Progressive Conservative Party Candidate."
37. SAB, Pamphlet Collection, G-14, "The P.C. Plan for Saskatchewan."
38. Smith, *Prairie Liberalism*, 259. This was confirmed by Walter Tucker in an interview with the author, 30 July 1981.

39. It should be pointed out that both the Liberals and Conservatives nominated but one candidate apiece in the two-member constituencies of Regina and Saskatoon where Ramsay ran. They hoped that both antisocialist candidates would win, but this arrangement still left them in opposition to each other as well as the CCF and Social Credit.
40. Alvin Hamilton, interview with author, 24 June 1981.
41. Alvin Hamilton, interview with author, 16 February 1981.
42. Ibid.
43. Alvin Hamilton, interview with author, 5 October 1982.
44. SAB, Pamphlet Collection, G-14, "Declaration of Progressive Conservative Policy."
45. Donald Johnston, interview with author, 6 October 1982.
46. SAB, PCPP, Rupert Ramsay, "Report on the 1948 Saskatchewan Provincial Election," undated, but before 28 June 1948.
47. SAB, PCPP, H.O. Wright to R.A. Bell, 28 June 1948.
48. R.A. Bell to Alvin Hamilton, 28 October 1948, HPP.
49. R.A. Bell, interview with author, 9 October 1981.
50. SAB, PCPP, Alvin Hamilton to T. Wedge, secretary-treasurer, Saskatoon Collegiate Board, 25 November 1948.
51. SAB, PCPP, Alvin Hamilton to Mrs. A.L. O'Farrell, 14 February 1949.
52. SAB, PCPP, Alvin Hamilton to R.A. Bell, 2 November 1948.
53. Alvin Hamilton, interview with author, 2 February 1981.
54. NAC, HP, Box 268690, Alvin Hamilton, script of radio address, 6 June 1949.
55. Ibid., 14 February 1949.
56. Ibid., 14 June 1949.
57. Ibid., 19 May 1949.
58. Election advertisement, *Rosetown Eagle*, 2 June 1949.
59. SAB, PCPP, M.J. Coldwell to Alvin Hamilton, 28 June 1949.
60. SAB, PCPP, Alvin Hamilton to R.A. Bell, 7 July 1949.
61. Ibid.
62. SAB, PCPP, Alvin Hamilton to Rupert Ramsay, 5 August 1949.

Chapter 3

1. Lieutenant Colonel Allan Embury did win one of the three seats reserved for members of the armed forces in the 1944 election but he could not win a "regular" seat in Regina in 1948.
2. A.H. (Hammy) McDonald in Moosomin.
3. SAB, PCPP, Executive Advisory Board, resolution, 15 November 1948. Ramsay had to leave the province because of his wife's ill

health, but the executive believed he might return when his wife recovered.

4. NAC, Progressive Conservative Party Papers, MG28 IV2 (hereafter PCPP), vol. 193, Alvin Hamilton, report, probably to R.A. Bell, August 1949.
5. Alvin Hamilton, interview with author, 25 June 1981.
6. NAC, PCPP, vol. 193, Alvin Hamilton, report, probably to R.A. Bell, August 1949.
7. SAB, PCPP, H.O. Wright to R.A. Bell, 15 August 1949.
8. SAB, PCPP, H.E. Keown to Alvin Hamilton, 5 October 1949.
9. McPherson had been attorney-general and provincial treasurer in the Anderson government and had run twice for the leadership of the national party in 1938 and 1942, coming in second each time.
10. Alvin Hamilton, interview with Peter Stursberg, 2 May 1980, HPP.
11. Alvin Hamilton, interview with author, 16 February 1981.
12. SAB, PCPP, Rupert Ramsay to Alvin Hamilton, 13 October 1949.
13. The Conservative candidate in the Battlefords was David Thiessen, a local school teacher who was fired shortly after the by-election. Hamilton believed the dismissal was politically motivated but he could not prove it. He found Thiessen another school in a different area of the province and seven years later brought him to Ottawa to serve as his executive assistant.
14. *P.C.P. News*, 13 February 1950.
15. Hamilton wrote most of the copy for the *P.C.P. News* himself.
16. Although he did not have a seat, both Douglas and Tucker agreed that he could sit on the floor of the legislature and attend committee meetings, but he had neither speaking nor voting privileges.
17. *P.C.P. News*, 26 December 1950.
18. See, for example, his radio broadcasts in the winter of 1951-52.
19. SAB, PCPP. Progressive Conservative advertisement, 1951.
20. NAC, HP, Box 268690, press release, 7 December 1950.
21. *P.C.P. News*, 22 January 1951.
22. NAC, HP, Box 268691, script of radio broadcast, week of 31 March – 6 April 1952.
23. SAB, PCPP, "A Personal Message from John Diefenbaker," script of a radio broadcast, June 1952.
24. *Moose Jaw Herald*, 6 June and 10 June 1952.
25. SAB, Pamphlet Collection, G-14, "Program to Develop Saskatchewan."

26. SAB, PCPP, script of radio broadcast, 7 June 1952.
27. G. Alexander Jupp in Regina.
28. SAB, PCPP, script of radio broadcast, 20 May 1952.
29. Editorial, *Saskatoon Star-Phoenix*, 16 May 1952.
30. Alvin Hamilton, interview with author, 16 February 1981.
31. *P.C.P. News*, 12 July 1952.
32. Walter Tucker, interview with author, 30 July 1981.
33. SAB, PCPP, Alvin Hamilton to R.A. Bell, 27 January 1949.
34. SAB, PCPP, Alvin Hamilton to W.H. Kidd, 16 November 1950.
35. SAB, PCPP, Alvin Hamilton to J.B. Lorimer, 28 September 1951.
36. SAB, PCPP, F. Robertson to Alvin Hamilton, 25 May 1950.
37. SAB, PCPP, Alvin Hamilton to W.H. Kidd, 9 November 1951.
38. Ibid., 10 October 1951.
39. SAB, PCPP, Alvin Hamilton to D.S. Taylor, 9 November 1951.
40. SAB, PCPP, Alvin Hamilton to W.H. Kidd, 7 May 1952.
41. SAB, PCPP, W.H. Kidd to Alvin Hamilton, 21 January 1952.
42. SAB, PCPP, C.F. Ironside to Alvin Hamilton, 14 December 1949.
43. SAB, PCPP, Alvin Hamilton to W.H. Kidd, 9 March 1951.
44. Ibid., 10 March 1952.
45. Ibid., 6 December 1950.
46. SAB, PCPP, Alvin Hamilton to J.G. Diefenbaker, 21 October 1949. T.C. Douglas admitted to the author during an interview, 17 February 1982, that he wanted to see Hamilton in the legislature in order to be able to respond more readily to his criticisms, and that he would have advised the Moosomin CCF constituency association not to run against Hamilton in a by-election, although he also cautioned that the final decision lay with the local association. C.M. Fines also maintained in an interview with the author, 11 May 1982, that "he felt we should make way for Hamilton if the constituency would agree."
47. It appears that Hamilton also had good reason to believe that McDonald would not resign his seat for any reason. Alvin Hamilton,interview with author, 7 October 1981.
48. Ibid., 25 June 1981.
49. McDonald replaced Tucker as leader in 1954.
50. SAB, PCPP, E.J. Medland to Alvin Hamilton, 17 May 1955.
51. NAC, HP, Box 268691, Report to Provincial Convention, 1954.
52. SAB, PCPP, W.Vaughan to Alvin Hamilton, 4 July 1953.
53. NAC, PCPP, vol. 269, Alvin Hamilton to W.L. Rowe (Kidd's successor as national director), 12 July 1955.
54. SAB, PCPP, Alvin Hamilton to G.C. Peters, 22 April 1955.
55. SAB, PCPP, Alvin Hamilton to W.L. Newman, 22 August 1956.

56. SAB, PCPP, W.H.Kidd to Alvin Hamilton, 24 September 1952.
57. SAB, PCPP, Alvin Hamilton to unnamed postmaster, 6 November 1955.
58. SAB, PCPP, Alvin Hamilton to G.C. Peters, 12 December 1955.
59. Kohaly had been elected at a by-election in Souris-Estevan in October 1953.
60. NAC, PCPP, vol. 247, Alvin Hamilton memorandum to W.L. Rowe, 9 December 1954.
61. SAB, PCPP, Report on Organization in Saskatchewan, 7 May 1955.
62. SAB, PCPP, I. Stothers to Alvin Hamilton, 15 May 1956.
63. SAB, PCPP, Alvin Hamilton to J.B. Lorimer, 4 January 1956.
64. SAB, PCPP, Alvin Hamilton to J. McBride, 25 April 1956.
65. NAC, HP, Box 268693, Alvin Hamilton to C. Mears, 12 December 1955.
66. NAC, Diefenbaker Papers, MG26 M (hereafter DP), vol. 79, H.L. Watson to J.G. Diefenbaker, 27 April 1956.
67. SAB, PCPP, undated, unsigned correspondence.
68. SAB, PCPP, W.Nelson to Alvin Hamilton, 1 October 1954.
69. NAC, HP, Box 268693, J.G. Diefenbaker to Alvin Hamilton, 30 April 1954.
70. NAC, HP, Box 268693, Alvin Hamilton to J. Scrymgeour, 4 January 1956.
71. SAB, PCPP, Alvin Hamilton to W.H. Kidd, 16 November 1953.
72. *Saskatoon Star-Phoenix*, 27 April 1955.
73. Ibid., 5 April 1955.
74. Speeches quoted in the Saskatchewan press, January 1954 to March 1956.
75. SAB, PCPP, speech to Regina Progressive Conservative Association, 4 April 1955.
76. *Saskatoon Star-Phoenix*, 19 January 1956.
77. NAC, HP, Box 268690, script of television broadcast, 23 May 1956.
78. SAB, Pamphlet Collection, G-14, "Canadians Robbed of Heritage: A Look at Natural Gas," 14 December 1955.
79. NAC, HP, Box 268690, news release, 20 October 1954.
80. *P.C.P. News*, 13 September 1954.
81. Ibid.
82. Ibid.
83. "Convention Resolutions," *P.C.P. News*, 13 September 1954.
84. SAB, PCPP, script of radio address, 12 January 1954.
85. Ibid.

86. SAB, PCPP, speech to Regina Progressive Conservative Association, 4 April 1955.
87. Ibid.
88. Saskatchewan Legislative Assembly, *Debates and Proceedings* (hereafter *Debates and Proceedings*), 18 February 1954.
89. See *Debates and Proceedings*, 3rd. sess., 12th Legislature, 1955.
90. Ibid., 4th sess. 12th. Legislature, 1956.
91. NAC, HP, Box 268690, Progressive Conservative Election Declaration, 1956.
92. NAC, HP, Box 268690, election advertisement, *Western Producer*, June 1956.
93. Ibid.
94. NAC, HP, Box 268690, script of television broadcast, 2 May 1956.
95. NAC, HP, Box 268690, news release, 15 June 1956.
96. SAB, Pamphlet Collection, G-14, election pamphlet, May-June 1956.
97. Quoted in the *Saskatoon Star-Phoenix*, 27 January 1956. Hamilton's running mate in Saskatoon was Lily Bowman, president of the Western Canadian Temperance Union, a formidable woman Hamilton still refers to as "Mrs. Rectitude."
98. *Saskatoon Star-Phoenix*, 9 June 1956.
99. Editorial, *Saskatoon Star-Phoenix*, 9 June 1956.
100. Editorial, *Saskatoon Star-Phoenix*, 18 June 1956.
101. Ibid.
102. SAB, PCPP, Alvin Hamilton to E.G. Harlton, 3 July 1956.
103. Ibid.
104. Alvin Hamilton, interviews with author, 26 June and 27 October 1981.
105. SAB, PCPP, Alvin Hamilton to S. Haggarty, 26 June 1956.
106. NAC, HP, Box 268690, "Report on the 1956 Election in Saskatchewan," undated.
107. NAC, HP, Box 268693, Alvin Hamilton to J.G. Diefenbaker, 4 July 1956.
108. SAB, PCPP, Alvin Hamilton to T. McConnell, 3 July 1956.
109. NAC, HP, Box 268692, Alvin Hamilton to G. Cloakey, 12 March 1956.
110. SAB, PCPP, Alvin Hamilton to R. Crowlie, 13 September 1956.
111. SAB, PCPP, W.O. Wright to R. A. Bell, 3 June 1949.
112. Editorial, *Saskatoon Star-Phoenix*, 9 August 1957.
113. Alvin Hamilton, letter to author, 16 March 1982.
114. Martin Pederson, interview with author, 17 June 1981.

115. Alvin Hamilton, letter to author, 16 March 1982.
116. Quoted in *Saskatoon Star-Phoenix*, 2 February 1953.
117. NAC, HP, Box 268690, press release, 13 October 1951.
118. NAC, HP, Box 268690, press release, 2 July 1952.
119. Quoted in *Saskatoon Star-Phoenix*, 31 July 1953.
120. Election advertisement, *Grenfell Sun*, 30 July 1953.
121. SAB, Pamphlet Collection, G-14, campaign literature, 1953 election.
122. SAB, Pamphlet Collection, G-14, "A 16 Point Pledge for Canada," General Election Manifesto of the Progressive Conservative Party of Canada, 1953.
123. NAC, DP, vol. 47, J.G. Diefenbaker to Alvin Hamilton, 31 August 1953.
124. George Hees, interview with author, 17 February 1983.
125. SAB, PCPP, minutes of meeting held in Edmonton, 13 March 1955.
126. SAB, PCPP, resolution passed at meeting of Western Progressive Conservative leaders, Edmonton, 24 January 1954.
127. NAC, HP, Box 268692, script of radio broadcast, 11 January 1955.
128. SAB, PCPP, Letter to the Editor, *Calgary Herald*, 15 April 1955.
129. NAC, R.A. Bell Papers, MG32 B1, vol. 41, resolutions submitted for the consideration of the Resolutions and Policy Committee of the National Convention, 1956.
130. Ibid.
131. D. Owen Carrigan, *Canadian Party Platforms, 1867-1968* (Toronto: Copp Clark Co., 1968), 110.
132. Ibid., 163.
133. G. Hogan, *The Conservative in Canada* (Toronto: McClelland and Stewart, 1963), 79.

Chapter 4

1. NAC, HP, Box 269107, Alvin Hamilton, unpublished "Declaration of Principles by the Progressive Conservative National Convention," February 1957.
2. Ibid.
3. Alvin Hamilton, interview with author, 22 January 1981.
4. NAC, HP, Box 268709, M. Menzies to G. Green, 1 December 1956.
5. Ibid.
6. Ibid.

7. J.G. Diefenbaker, *One Canada: The Years of Achievement* (Toronto: Macmillan of Canada, 1976), 11.
8. NAC, DP, "The Progressive Conservative National Development Policy," 21 May 1957.
9. Ibid.
10. NAC, HP, Box 268691, memorandum, Alvin Hamilton to J.G. Diefenbaker, undated but between the leadership convention and the calling of the 1957 election.
11. NAC, DP, vol. 20, J.G.Diefenbaker to Alvin Hamilton, 18 February 1957.
12. NAC, DP, speech files, memorandum, Alvin Hamilton to J.G. Diefenbaker, 1 March 1957.
13. Ibid.
14. Ibid.
15. Carrigan, *Canadian Party Platforms*, 227-28.
16. Ibid., 228-33.
17. NAC, DP, vol. 20, Alvin Hamilton to Allan Grosart, 11 April 1957. Grosart replaced Rowe shortly after Diefenbaker won the leadership.
18. SAB, PCPP, press release, 18 April 1957.
19. Election advertisment, *Kipling Citizen*, 23 May 1957.
20. Ibid., 30 May 1957.
21. *Indian Head News*, 13 June 1957.
22. Ibid., 20 June 1957.
23. Editorial, *Saskatoon Star-Phoenix*, 13 June 1957.
24. Alvin Hamilton, interview with author, 14 December 1982.
25. Ibid.
26. See, for example, *Saskatoon Star-Phoenix*, 7 August 1957.
27. J.G. Diefenbaker, quoted in *Saskatoon Star-Phoenix*, 20 August 1957.
28. Editorial, *Saskatoon Star-Phoenix*, 21 August 1957.
29. Editorial, *Grenfell Sun*, 28 August 1957.
30. Alvin Hamilton, interview with author, 14 December 1982.
31. For a fuller exposition of the multifarious strains of Canadian conservatism, see William Christian and Colin Campbell, *Political Parties and Ideologies in Canada* (Toronto: McGraw-Hill Ryerson, 1983).
32. Alvin Hamilton, interview with author, 13 December 1982.
33. Ibid., 21 January 1981.
34. Ibid., 20 November 1986.
35. Ibid., 22 January 1981.

36. NAC, HP, Box 225, Alvin Hamilton to J.G.Diefenbaker, 15 January 1963.
37. Alvin Hamilton, interview with author, 26 November 1986.
38. NAC, HP, Box 268709, Alvin Hamilton to J.G. Diefenbaker, 21 September 1961.
39. Robert Bothwell, Ian M. Drummond and John English, *Canada Since 1945: Power, Politics, and Provincialism* (Toronto: University of Toronto Press, 1981), 200.
40. Alvin Hamilton, interview with author, 6 October 1982.
41. Canada, Royal Commission on Energy, *First Report*, October 1958, Appendix A, 90-91.
42. NAC, HP, Box 269138, record of cabinet discussions, 31 October 1957.
43. Ibid., 21 December 1957.
44. Gordon Robertson, interview with author, 14 December 1982.
45. Alvin Hamilton, interview with Peter Stursberg, 2 May 1980, HPP.
46. *Debates*, 14 October 1957, 6.
47. NAC, HP, Box 228, "The First Steps of a National Development Program," unsigned and undated, but clearly in Menzies's style, and found with other materials pertaining to the 1958 campaign.
48. NAC, HP, Box 269136, election address, J.G. Diefenbaker, Winnipeg, 12 February 1958.
49. Ibid. Also quoted in *Debates*, 7 July 1958, 1980.
50. R.M. Campbell, "The Diefenbaker Years Revisited: The Demise of the Keynesian Strategy in Canada," *Journal of Canadian Studies* 18, no. 2 (Summer 1983): 111.
51. NAC, HP, Box 268707, R. Faibish to Alvin Hamilton, 16 February 1958. Faibish was a brilliant civil servant who had experience in the departments of natural and mineral resources in Saskatchewan. He joined Hamilton's staff within days of Hamilton's appointment to cabinet.
52. Ibid.
53. Canada, Privy Council Office (hereafter PCO), vol. 60, #1491, record of cabinet conclusions, 21 April 1958.
54. Alvin Hamilton, interview with author, 7 December 1983.
55. Alvin Hamilton, interview with author, 10 February 1988.
56. Alvin Hamilton, interviews with author and the York University Institute for Behavioural Research, 25 October 1982 and 26 October 1970.

57. PCO, file C-20-9 (1)-D, cabinet document DEV-1, Alvin Hamilton, "Action for a National Development Program," 1-10.
58. Ibid., 10.
59. NAC, DP, speech files, Alvin Hamilton, "A Statement on the Philosophy and Principles of the National Development Program," January 1960.
60. Ibid., 4.
61. NAC, DP, speech files, J.G.Diefenbaker, 20 August 1958.
62. Ibid.
63. NAC, HP, Box 269163, Alvin Hamilton to J.G. Diefenbaker, 16 April 1959.
64. NAC, HP, Box 269136, speech, Alvin Hamilton to Pacific Northwest Trade Association, 4 September 1959.
65. NAC, HP, Box 198, memorandum, Alvin Hamilton to J.G. Diefenbaker, 27 April 1960.
66. Ibid.
67. NAC, HP, Box 189, memorandum, Alvin Hamilton to J.G. Diefenbaker, 27 April 1960.
68. Alvin Hamilton, interview with author, 7 October 1982.
69. NAC, HP, Box 197, Alvin Hamilton to J.G. Diefenbaker, 16 April 1959.
70. NAC, HP, Box 269136, "Progress Report on Cabinet Committee on Oil and Gas Policy," 14 May 1959.
71. *Canada Gazette*, pt.2, vol. 94, Territorial Lands Act, Canada Oil and Gas Regulations 1960, 498.
72. Alvin Hamilton, interview with author, 5 October 1982.
73. PCO, file C-20-5, cabinet document #350/58.
74. Bothwell, Drummond and English, *Canada since 1945*, 201.
75. PCO, file C-20-5, cabinet document #109/58.
76. *Debates*, 10 July 1959, 5798.
77. NAC, Howard Green Papers, MG32 B13, vol. 4, "P.C. Policy Statement on the Columbia," October 1957.
78. For a fuller treatment of the subject, see J. McMenemy, "The Columbia River Treaty, 1961-1964," Ph.D. diss., University of Toronto, 1969.
79. Alvin Hamilton, interview with author, 17 November 1982.
80. NAC, HP, Box 208, minutes of a meeting of the Cabinet Committee on Columbia River Problems, 13 November 1957.
81. NAC, HP, Box 209, J.G. Diefenbaker, 17 January 1961.
82. NAC, HP, Box 210, E.Davie Fulton, minutes of meetings of the Canada-B.C. Policy Liaison Committee, 3-4 January 1961.

83. NAC, HP, Box 210, E. Davie Fulton to Ray Williston, 31 January 1961.
84. NAC, E.D. Fulton Papers, MG32 B11, vol. 46, memorandum, Alvin Hamilton to cabinet, 5 October 1961.
85. J.G. Diefenbaker, quoted by R. Duffy, *Globe and Mail*, 10 September 1959.
86. *Debates*, 10 July 1959, 5798.
87. Canada, Royal Commission on Energy, *First Report*, October 1958.
88. *Debates*, 18 May 1959, 3768.
89. Canada, Royal Commission on Energy, *Second Report*, July 1959, 143-44.
90. Ibid.
91. NAC, DP, speech files, Alvin Hamilton, "Statement on the Philosophy and Principles of the National Development Program," January 1960.
92. Ibid.
93. NAC, HP, Box 269136, memorandum, Alvin Hamilton to J.G. Diefenbaker, 7 February 1958.
94. NAC, HP, Box 269111, Resources for Tomorrow Conference Secretariat, "General Aims of Resources for Tomorrow Conference," 30 June 1960.
95. Walter Dinsdale replaced Hamilton in both positions.
96. Canada, *Proceedings of the Resources for Tomorrow Conference*, vol. 3 (Ottawa: Queen's Printer, 1962).
97. Ralph R. Krueger and Bruce Mitchell, eds., *Managing Canada's Renewable Resources* (Toronto: Methuen, 1977), 3-4.
98. Canadian Council of Resource Ministers, *Annual Report*, 31 March 1965, 2.
99. Alvin Hamilton, interview with author, 20 June 1984.
100. *Debates*, 25 January 1961, 1403.
101. NAC, HP, Box 268647, Alvin Hamilton to provincial ministers of agriculture, 31 January 1963.
102. Ibid.
103. *Debates*, 25 January 1961, 1406.
104. Canada, Department of Agriculture, press release, 1 May 1962.
105. Canada, Department of Agriculture, *Annual Report 1964*, (Ottawa: Queen's Printer), 56.
106. Canada, Department of Regional Economic Expansion, *Annual Report, 1970-71* (Ottawa: Queen's Printer), 32.
107. Alvin Hamilton, interview with author, 26 October 1982.

108. NAC, HP, Box 268598, Alvin Hamilton to J.R. Hill, 14 April 1961.
109. M. Timlin and A. Faucher, *The Social Sciences in Canada*, (Ottawa: Social Sciences Research Council, 1968).
110. J.N. McCrorie, *ARDA: An Experiment in Development Planning* (Ottawa: Queen's Printer, 1969).
111. NAC, HP, Box 198, memorandum, Alvin Hamilton to J.G. Diefenbaker, 15 July 1959.
112. Alvin Hamilton, "Dynamic Conservatism," *Concepts*, August 1961.
113. NAC, HP, Box 197, election strategy meetings with the Manotick Group, 9-10 September 1961.
114. Alvin Hamilton, interview with author, 13 December 1982.
115. Ibid.
116. NAC, HP, Box 268708, Alvin Hamilton to J.G. Diefenbaker, 22 February 1963.
117. For an excellent treatment of the evolution of the economic policy of the Diefenbaker government, see Robert M. Campbell, "The Diefenbaker Years Revisited."

Chapter 5

1. Alvin Hamilton, interview with author, 26 October 1982.
2. NAC, PCPP, vol. 412, Alvin Hamilton to his constituents, 26 October 1957.
3. PCO, vol. 58, #1451, record of cabinet conclusions, 9 December 1957.
4. *Debates*, 22 January 1959, 3624.
5. Alvin Hamilton, interview with author, 25 October 1982.
6. *Debates*, 30 August 1958, 4346-47.
7. NAC, HP, Box 268678, memorandum, Alvin Hamilton to cabinet, November 1958.
8. *Debates*, 30 August 1958, 4345.
9. NAC, HP, Box 268675, data distributed by the provincial wheat pools, 30 August 1958.
10. NAC, HP, Box 268674, M. Langeau to Alvin Hamilton, 2 August 1958.
11. NAC, HP, Box 268674, H.G. Stamm to Alvin Hamilton, 6 January 1960.
12. Carrigan, *Canadian Party Platforms*, 255.
13. *Debates*, 30 August 1958, 4346.
14. NAC, HP, Box 268674, H. Fathers to Alvin Hamilton, 3 July 1959.

15. Alvin Hamilton, interview with author, 26 October 1982.
16. Alvin Hamilton, remarks made during a radio broadcast on CKCK, Regina, 31 January 1959, quoted in the *St. Walburg Enterprise*, 13 February 1959.
17. *Winnipeg Free Press*, 9 March 1959.
18. *Western Producer*, 12 February 1959.
19. Editorial, *St. Walburg Enterprise*, 13 February 1959.
20. Quoted in *Western Producer*, 12 February 1959.
21. NAC, HP, Box 268675, H. Watson to Alvin Hamilton, 5 February 1959.
22. NAC, HP, Box 268676, H. Kreutzwieser to Alvin Hamilton, 9 April 1959.
23. NAC, HP, Box 268677, N. Roth to D.J. Thiessen, 16 July 1960.
24. Alvin Hamilton, interview with author, 25 October 1982.
25. PCO, vol. 76, #1781, record of cabinet conclusions, 23 February 1960.
26. Ibid., vol. 78, #1825, 10 June 1960.
27. Michael Barkway, article, *Toronto Star*, 27 August 1960.
28. Alvin Hamilton, interview with author, 25 October 1982.
29. Ibid.
30. Ibid., 26 October 1982.
31. NAC, HP, Box 268662, Alvin Hamilton to Dalton Camp, 14 October 1960.
32. NAC, HP, Box 269150, Alvin Hamilton to Mr. and Mrs. A.R. Stout, 14 October 1960.
33. Alvin Hamilton, interview with author, 26 October 1982.
34. Ibid.
35. Canada, Department of External Affairs (hereafter DEA), file #9030-40, vol. 6, memorandum, C.J. Small (Department of External Affairs representative with Canada's Trade Commission in Hong Kong) to Department of External Affairs (DEA), 7 November 1960.
36. Alvin Hamilton, interview with author, 26 October 1982.
37. See for example, NAC, HP, Box 269150, memorandum to cabinet from R.M. Esdale, Department of Trade and Commerce, 13 January 1961.
38. Ibid.
39. See, for example, DEA, file #9030-40, vol. 6, memorandum, N.A. Robertson to H. Green, 14 January 1961.
40. PCO, cabinet documents, file #A-1-7(a)-C2, record of cabinet decision, 16 January 1961.
41. Ibid.

42. PCO, vol. 84, #1940, record of cabinet conclusions, 9 March 1961.
43. Ibid.
44. Alvin Hamilton, interview with author, 26 October 1982.
45. PCO, vol. 84, #1940, record of cabinet conclusions, 9 March 1961.
46. PCO, file #A-1-7(a)-C2, cabinet document 151/61, Alvin Hamilton, memorandum to cabinet, 10 April 1961.
47. Alvin Hamilton, interview with author, 26 October 1982.
48. PCO, vol. 85, #1951, record of cabinet conclusions, 11 April 1961.
49. Cabinet approved the change on 16 June 1961.
50. PCO, vol. 86, #1960, record of cabinet conclusions, 2 May 1961.
51. DEA, file #9030-40, vol. 6, memorandum, N.A. Robertson to A. Green, 28 April 1961.
52. NAC, HP, Box 268694, memorandum, W. McNamara to Alvin Hamilton, 28 April 1961.
53. Alvin Hamilton, interview with author, 26 October 1982.
54. *Debates*, 2 May 1961, 4205.
55. NAC, HP, Box 269150, undated aide-memoire, "Wheat for China: Arguments for the Proposal."
56. PCO, vol. 84, #1940, record of cabinet conclusions, 9 March 1961.
57. Alvin Hamilton, interview with author, 26 October 1982. This is confirmed by a message from the Department of External Affairs (DEA, file #9030-40, vol. 6) to Canadian embassies on 2 May, which read in part, "At eleven o'clock this morning Mr. Hamilton spoke to Mr. Freeman . . . and informed him of the announcement he was about to make in the House."
58. PCO, vol. 84, #1940, record of cabinet conclusions, 9 March 1961.
59. Alvin Hamilton, interview with author, 26 October 1982.
60. PCO, vol. 84, #1944, record of cabinet conclusions, 16 March 1961.
61. DEA, file #9030-40, vol. 8, memorandum, O.G. Stoner (DEA economic division) to A.E. Ritchie, 11 May 1962. The memorandum read in part, "We have also received the file on President Kennedy's visit to Ottawa on May 17, 1961, and we find that while there was some discussion of the question of Chinese representation in the United Nations there was apparently no mention of Canadian grain sales to China."

62. NAC, HP, Box 199, memorandum, H. Green to J.G. Diefenbaker, 7 June 1961.
63. See, for example, DEA, file #9030-40, vol. 8.
64. NAC, HP, Box 199, J.H. Wilson to Alvin Hamilton, 13 June 1961.
65. NAC, HP, Box 119, H. Zondervan to Alvin Hamilton, 3 July 1961.
66. NAC, HP, Box 269150, submission of the National Farmers Union to the Government of Canada, 15 February 1961.
67. NAC, HP, Box 268712, A.P. Gleave to Alvin Hamilton, 4 May 1961.
68. NAC, HP, Box 268662, resolution, District #10, Saskatchewan Wheat Pool, 8 March 1962.
69. NAC, HP, Box 268656, F.L. Williams to Alvin Hamilton, 4 February 1961.
70. NAC, HP, Box 199, F.C. Quelenton to Alvin Hamilton, 16 June 1961.
71. NAC, HP, Box 199, M. Menzies to Alvin Hamilton, 1 June 1961.
72. NAC, HP, Box 269118, Alvin Hamilton to G. Mclean, 14 September 1961.
73. NAC, HP, Box 225, memorandum, Alvin Hamilton to J.G. Diefenbaker, 15 November 1961.
74. NAC, HP, Box 268644, D. Fleming to Alvin Hamilton, 11 July 1961. Fleming wrote to Hamilton as follows: "I am entertaining increasing concern over the credit which has been established to China through the Wheat Board to finance purchases of wheat. In particular, I am concerned over the enlargement from $50 million to $100 million in authorized credit at any one time. . . In view of the size and nature of our wheat contracts and 'intents' with China, I think we should instruct the Wheat Board to keep us fully and very promptly informed on payments or defaults. If she defaults in excess of 10 or 15 (or at the most 30 days) we should seriously consider suspending shipments until payments are up-to-date."
75. NAC, HP, Box 268265, submission, National Farmers Union, 19 November 1962.
76. NAC, HP, Box 269126, H.C.Kreutzwieser to Alvin Hamilton, 3 January 1963.
77. PCO, vol. 96, #2152, record of cabinet conclusions, 13 November 1962.
78. W.A. Wilson, "Hamilton's Humiliation," *Montreal Star*, 17 November 1962.

79. NAC, HP, Box 268695, memorandum, R. Faibish to Alvin Hamilton, 8 November 1962.
80. NAC, HP, Box 199, R.M. Bond to Alvin Hamilton, 23 October 1962.
81. NAC, HP, Box 268644, G. Hoseng to Alvin Hamilton, 10 December 1962.
82. PCO, file #A-1-7(a)-C2, cabinet documents, telegram, C. Ronning to DEA, 23 November 1962.
83. PCO, vol. 96, #2160, record of cabinet conclusions, 27 November 1962.
84. NAC, HP, Box 225, Alvin Hamilton to J.G. Diefenbaker, 19 December 1962.
85. PCO, vol. 95, #2145, record of cabinet conclusions, 23 October 1962.
86. Ibid., vol. 96, #2169, 20 December 1962.
87. NAC, HP, Box 268644, Alvin Hamilton, letter drafted in response to those received concerning the Sino-Indian dispute, 3 January 1963.
88. PCO, file #A-1-7(a)-C2, cabinet document 362/62, 5 November 1962.
89. DEA, file #9030-40, vol. 8, memorandum, R.K. Thomson to Department of Trade and Commerce, 12 July 1962.
90. DEA, file #9030-40, vol. 9, W. Riddell to Alvin Hamilton, 14 December 1962.
91. PCO, #A-1-7(a)-C2, cabinet documents, "Trade with Mainland China — Duty Valuation of Textile Imports," 5 November 1962. This memorandum to cabinet by Alvin Hamilton provides a more complete explanation of the Chinese position.
92. NAC, HP, Box 199, Alvin Hamilton to J.G. Diefenbaker, 23 October 1962.
93. See, for example, DEA, file #9030-40, vol. 9, memoranda from the far eastern division to the economic division of DEA, 10 January 1963, and N.A. Robertson to H. Green, 5 March 1963.
94. Alvin Hamilton, interview with author, 26 October 1982.
95. Alvin Hamilton, interview with author, 25 October 1982.
96. Ibid.
97. Ibid.
98. Agricultural Economics Research Council of Canada, pamphlet, January 1963.
99. Clive Baxter, "No Political Chains," *Financial Post*, 19 October 1963.

100. PCO, vol. 86, #1984, record of cabinet conclusions, 27 June 1961.
101. Ibid., vol. 91, #2085, 22 March 1962.
102. Ibid., vol. 92, #2093, 6 April 1982.
103. Ibid., vol. 92, #2182, 8 February 1963.
104. Ibid., vol. 98, #2186, 21 February 1963.
105. NAC, HP, Box 225, Alvin Hamilton to N. Crawford, 8 January 1962.
106. Rapp was member of Parliament for Melfort-Tisdale. Cabinet approved the recommendation on 15 June 1961.
107. NAC, HP, Box 268669, press release, Department of Agriculture, 22 October 1962.
108. NAC, HP, Box 268581, R. Faibish to J.S. McGiffen, 7 December 1961.
109. C.S. Barry, interview with author, 27 June 1983.
110. NAC, HP, Box 268707, memorandum, R. Faibish to Alvin Hamilton, 20 January 1982.
111. Alvin Hamilton, interview with author, 27 June 1983.
112. C.S. Barry, interview with author, 27 June 1983.
113. Gordon Robertson, interview with author, 14 December 1982.
114. NAC, HP, Box 199, press release, Department of Agriculture, 30 April 1962.
115. NAC, HP, Box 269102, memorandum, Alvin Hamilton to J.G. Diefenbaker, 18 April 1962.
116. NAC, HP, Box 268655, Alvin Hamilton to J.G. Diefenbaker, 15 November 1960.
117. PCO, vol. 89, #2052, record of cabinet conclusions, 28 December 1961.
118. NAC, HP, Box 268711, memorandum, Alvin Hamilton to C.S. Barry, 13 September 1962.
119. D. Johnston to Alvin Hamilton, 25 June 1962, HPP.
120. NAC, HP, Box 268630, R.V. Beamish to Alvin Hamilton, 15 May 1962.
121. NAC, HP, Box 269102, memorandum, J.G. Diefenbaker to Alvin Hamilton, 7 January 1962.
122. NAC, HP, Box 269147, Alvin Hamilton, speech delivered at Joliette, Quebec, 24 September 1962.
123. Ibid.
124. NAC, HP, Box 269102, memorandum, Alvin Hamilton to J.G. Diefenbaker, 4 January 1963.
125. NAC, HP, Box 220, Alvin Hamilton to J.G. Diefenbaker, 8 February 1963.

126. NAC, HP, Box 204, memorandum, Alvin Hamilton to J.G. Diefenbaker, 15 January 1963.
127. NAC, HP, Box 204, Alvin Hamilton to J.G. Diefenbaker, 8 February 1963.
128. NAC, HP, Box 202. Quotations taken from various speeches delivered by Alvin Hamilton during the 1963 election campaign.
129. NAC, HP, Box 268655, D.M. LeBourdais to Alvin Hamilton, 29 March 1961.
130. NAC, HP, Box 268662, F.H. Collins to Alvin Hamilton, 20 October 1960.
131. NAC, HP, Box 268661, B. Carr to A. Grosart, 24 January 1961.
132. Editorial, *Penticton Herald*, 21 January 1961.
133. George Hees, interview with author, 17 February 1983.
134. Alvin Hamilton, interview with author, 20 June 1984.
135. Gordon Churchill, correspondence with author, 24 July 1983.
136. NAC, HP, Box 268593, R. Hatfield to R. Faibish, 4 July 1962.
137. NAC, HP, Box 268596, Alvin Hamilton to George Drew, 4 September 1962.

Chapter 6

1. Based on interviews with several members of the Progressive Conservative party, principally from Saskatchewan, in the summer of 1981.
2. PCO, vol. 90, #2070, record of cabinet conclusions, 16 February 1962.
3. Ibid., vol. 80, #1876, 16 October 1960.
4. Ibid.
5. Alvin Hamilton, interview with author, 6 October 1982.
6. See also, G.C. Perlin, *The Tory Syndrome: Leadership Politics in the Progressive Conservative Party* (Montreal: McGill-Queen's University Press, 1980), 64.
7. PCO, vol. 70, #1666, record of cabinet conclusions. Agenda of cabinet meeting, 28 May 1959.
8. PCO, vol. 98, #2191, record of cabinet conclusions, 18 March 1963.
9. Alvin Hamilton, interview with author, 6 October 1982.
10. Ibid.
11. Ibid.
12. NAC, HP, Box 268580.
13. NAC, J.A. MacLean Papers, MG32 B17, vol. 5, memorandum, N. Crawford to executive assistants, 7 November 1961.

14. NAC, HP, Box 268642, memorandum, J.G. Diefenbaker to Alvin Hamilton, 29 August 1961.
15. Donald Johnston, interview with author, 6 November 1982.
16. E. Davie Fulton, interview with author, 7 June 1983.
17. Richard Needham, *London Free Press*, 30 March 1962.
18. George Hees, interview with author, 17 February 1983.
19. William Hamilton, interview with author, 8 June 1983.
20. Walter Dinsdale, interview with author, 26 October 1981.
21. Alvin Hamilton, interview with author, 6 October 1982.
22. Alvin Hamilton, interview with York Institute for Behavioural Research, 26 October 1970.
23. Editorial, *Winnipeg Free Press*, 30 March 1960.
24. Campbell, "Diefenbaker Years Revisited."
25. In fact, in retrospect Hamilton is convinced that Fleming's 1959 budget did halt recovery. See Peter Stursberg, *Leadership Gained, 1956-1962* (Toronto: University of Toronto Press, 1975), 210-11.
26. Alvin Hamilton, interview with York Institute for Behavioural Research, 26 October 1970.
27. Campbell, "Diefenbaker Years Revisited," 114.
28. See Chapter Four for details of these programmes.
29. PCO, file #2102, 2 May 1962. In March the bank spent $38 million of its reserves. On 1 May it spent $36 million.
30. Ibid.
31. PCO, file #F-1-25, note by R.B. Bryce, 21 June 1962.
32. Editorial, *Globe and Mail*, 9 June 1962.
33. PCO, file #F-1-5, cabinet documents, D.M. Fleming, press release, 10 June 1962.
34. PCO, file #2109A, cabinet documents, 24 June 1962.
35. PCO, file #2153, record of cabinet conclusions, 15 November 1962.
36. J.G. Diefenbaker, *One Canada: The Tumultuous Years 1966 to 1967* (Toronto: Macmillan of Canada, 1976), 121.
37. Ibid., 131.
38. Alvin Hamilton, interview with author, 13 December 1982.
39. Diefenbaker, *One Canada: The Tumultuous Years*, 131.
40. NAC, HP, Box 268694, memorandum, R. Faibish to Alvin Hamilton, 28 June 1962.
41. NAC, HP, Box 227, Brian Mulroney to M.R. Jack, 4 July 1962.
42. J. McArthur, article, *Toronto Star*, 16 November 1962. McArthur also stated in the same article, "I still think Alvin Hamilton is one

of the most honest, effective and competent cabinet ministers in a government which doesn't have many such members."

43. Alvin Hamilton, interview with author, 13 December 1982.
44. William Hamilton, interview with author, 8 June 1983.
45. PCO, file #1554, record of cabinet conclusions. Cabinet accepted the recommendation in principle on 21 September 1958.
46. PCO, file #2148, record of cabinet conclusions, 30 October 1962. The proposed agreement also covered nuclear arms for Canadian forces in Europe.
47. Peter C. Newman, *Renegade in Power: The Diefenbaker Years* (Toronto: McClelland and Stewart, 1963), 354.
48. See NAC, Howard Green Papers, MG32 B13, vol. 1.
49. The committee included Fleming, Churchill, Harkness and Green. For a fuller account of this issue see J. Granatstein, *Canada: 1957-1967* (Toronto: McClelland and Stewart, 1986), Chapter 5.
50. Quoted in Newman, *Renegade in Power*, 365.
51. NAC, HP, Box 268664, Alvin Hamilton, *Report from Parliament*, 4 March 1959.
52. NAC, HP, Box 268596, Alvin Hamilton to Mrs. J. Toth, 31 October 1961.
53. Alvin Hamilton, interview with York Institute for Behavioural Research, 26 October 1970.
54. NAC, HP, Box 226, Alvin Hamilton to J.G. Diefenbaker, 24 January 1963.
55. Ibid.
56. Unnamed source, quoted in Dillon O'Leary, "How They Tried to Get Rid of Diefenbaker," *The Commentator*, July-August 1963: 1.
57. Other unnamed sources quoted by O'Leary in the same article.
58. Patrick Nicholson, *Vision and Indecision* (Don Mills: Longmans Canada, 1968), 232.
59. Peter Stursberg, *Diefenbaker: Leadership Lost, 1962-1967* (Toronto: University of Toronto Press, 1976), 57.
60. Alvin Hamilton, interview with author, 13 December 1982. A similar account of the meeting can be found in J. Granatstein, *Canada: 1957-1967*, based on J. Waldo Monteith's diary.
61. Chief Justice Patrick Kerwin had died earlier that weekend. This account is confirmed by Gordon Churchill who has written, "I was present at Mr. Diefenbaker's residence on the evening when George Hees and Davie Fulton arrived . . . and I heard

Davie mention the intention of the rebel faction to offer the position of Chief Justice to Mr. D. provided he stepped down." Taken from a letter from Churchill to Dr. F. Vaughan, University of Guelph, 18 May 1983, and quoted with the kind permission of Dr. Vaughan.
62. This account of the events of 3 February 1963 has been based principally on interviews with Alvin Hamilton and Walter Dinsdale, the writings of Patrick Nicholson, Peter Stursberg, Dillon O'Leary, George Perlin, Peter C. Newman, and J. Granatstein, based in part on the diaries of J. Waldo Monteith.
63. *Debates*, 4 February 1963, 3377-3430.
64. Robert Thompson, quoted in O'Leary, "How They Tried to Get Rid of Diefenbaker," 4-5.
65. *Debates*, 4 February 1963, 3414.
66. Gordon Churchill to Dr. F. Vaughan, 18 May 1983.
67. Alvin Hamilton, interview with York Institute of Behavioural Research, 26 October 1970.
68. Alvin Hamilton, interview with author, 13 December 1982. Newman corroborates the story in *Renegade in Power*.
69. Alvin Hamilton, interview with author, 13 December 1982.
70. Donald Johnston, interview with author, 6 October 1982.

Chapter 7

1. NAC, HP, Box 225, Alvin Hamilton to J.G. Diefenbaker, 9 November 1959.
2. NAC, HP, Box 225, memorandum, Alvin Hamilton to J.G. Diefenbaker, 20 May 1960.
3. H.D. McPhail to Alvin Hamilton, 15 April 1963, HPP.
4. Quoted in Diefenbaker, *One Canada: The Tumultuous Years*, 198-99.
5. R. Faibish to Alvin Hamilton, 28 August 1963, HPP.
6. Ibid.
7. See, for example, his reply to McPhail, 28 June 1963, HPP.
8. Alvin Hamilton, interview with author, 26 June 1981.
9. NAC, PCPP, vol. 228, Martin Pederson to R. Thrasher, 29 April 1964.
10. NAC, PCPP, vol. 237. The report on the 1964 Saskatchewan general election was prepared by P. Champagne, Progressive Conservative National Headquarters, in May 1964. This report is confirmed by Pederson as follows: "His statement is correct in essence but not in detail. The sum offered was $83,000, and the number of candidates that I was asked to run was 10, the seats

to be selected by the Liberals. All other seats were to be by-passed by the PCs." Martin Pederson, letter to author, 14 September 1983.

11. Martin Pederson, letter to author, 14 September 1983.
12. Martin Pederson to Alvin Hamilton, 7 May 1964, HPP.
13. NAC, PCPP, vol. 237, Alvin Hamilton, letter to his constituents, 5 October 1967.
14. NAC, HP, Box 199, Alvin Hamilton, speech to the thirtieth annual Kansas Institute of International Relations, 29 March 1965.
15. Ibid.
16. Alvin Hamilton, interview with author, 17 November 1982.
17. Ibid.
18. Ibid.
19. Ibid.
20. Alvin Hamilton, speech to Kansas Institute of International Relations.
21. Alvin Hamilton, interview with author, 17 November 1982.
22. Alvin Hamilton to C.O. Porter, 7 September 1970, HPP.
23. Alvin Hamilton to Chou Enlai (Zhou Enlai), 10 December 1969, HPP.
24. *Debates*, 25 May 1965, 1604.
25. Ibid.
26. Ibid.
27. *Debates*, 8 October 1964, 8876-79.
28. *Debates*, 30 June 1967, 2159.
29. Ibid., 2155.
30. Ibid., 2156.
31. Ibid., 2158.
32. Alvin Hamilton, interview with author, 18 December 1982. In particular, he wanted to establish ARDA firmly and introduce a feed-grain assistance programme for eastern farmers.
33. Hamilton's proposal was to have two crosses, red and white, representing the two founding races, on a red or blue background. He was willing to add a maple leaf to the design if sufficient people thought it worthwhile.
34. *Debates*, 19 June 1964, 4521.
35. Alvin Hamilton, "The Great Lakes Affair," unpublished article, written in January 1978, and in the possession of the author.
36. Ibid. In the article, Hamilton pays tribute to his brother, Fred, and to George Cloakey for his early education into the economics of the industry , and to Bobby Brown of Home Oil, the

largest shareholder in Trans-Canada PipeLines, for providing the figures on which he based his case in 1966. See *Debates*, 2 November 1966, 9465-89.

37. *Debates*, 1 April 1966, 3751-53.
38. Ibid., 3754.
39. Ibid., 3755.
40. *Debates*, 14 June 1967, 1526.
41. Ibid., 1525.
42. See Chapter Four for details of the programme.
43. Statement on the British Columbia election, 7 September 1966, HPP.
44. Alvin Hamilton to Peter Lougheed, 20 June 1967, HPP.
45. Alvin Hamilton, telegram to Peter Lougheed, 24 May 1967, HPP.
46. Peter Lougheed to Alvin Hamilton, 14 June 1967, HPP.
47. James Johnston, *The Party's Over* (Don Mills: Longmans Canada, 1971), 32.
48. Diefenbaker, *One Canada: The Tumultuous Years*, 254-55.
49. Article, "If Alvin were. . . .," *Monetary Times*, 1 November 1965.
50. Alvin Hamilton to Arthur Maloney, 28 November 1966, HPP.
51. Alvin Hamilton to Brian Mulroney, 10 February 1965, HPP.
52. Johnston, *The Party's Over*, 96.
53. J.W. Monteith, G.W. Baldwin, Alvin Hamilton, "Practical Policies for People," January 1967, HPP.
54. Ibid., 1-2.
55. Ibid., 17-18.
56. Ibid., 20-21.
57. Dalton Camp, "Reflections on the Montmorency Conference," *Queen's Quarterly* 76 (Summer 1969).
58. Alvin Hamilton, interview with York Institute for Behavioural Research, 26 October 1970.
59. It should be pointed out, perhaps, that many in the party regarded Camp's election as a victory for the pro-Diefenbaker forces as Camp defeated Egan Chambers, member for Montreal-St. Lawrence-St. George, known to be opposed to Diefenbaker's continued leadership. The meeting in 1964 also defeated a motion moved by Diefenbaker's opponents to have the vote of confidence in the leader held by secret ballot. Instead, the meeting gave Diefenbaker an open and resounding vote of confidence.
60. Marcel Faribault was also on Hamilton's original list, but was removed at Diefenbaker's insistence.
61. Alvin Hamilton, interview with author, 13 December 1982.

62. Ibid. There is a discrepancy between Hamilton's figure and that given by George Perlin in *The Tory Syndrome*. Perlin gives the figure as sixty, still a draft of sizeable proportions.
63. Perlin, *The Tory Syndrome*, 103.
64. Johnston, *The Party's Over*, 187.
65. Alvin Hamilton, interview with the York Institute for Behavioural Research, 26 October 1970.
66. Robert Coates, *The Night of the Knives* (Fredericton: Brunswick Press, 1969), 52. Coates, a member of Parliament, attended the convention.
67. NAC, PCPP, vol. 259, resolution passed by the Progressive Conservative annual meeting, 16 November 1966.
68. Alvin Hamilton to Mrs. B. Happy, 28 November 1966, HPP.
69. Alvin Hamilton, interview with author, 14 December 1982.
70. Alvin Hamilton, interview with the York Institute for Behavioural Research, 26 October 1970.
71. Alvin Hamilton, interview with author, 14 December 1982.
72. Alvin Hamilton, interview with the York Institute for Behavioural Research, 26 October 1970.
73. Coates, *Night of the Knives*, 200. Seventy-one members of Parliament signed the pledge of loyalty.
74. Alvin Hamilton to Arthur Maloney, 28 November 1966, HPP.
75. Alvin Hamilton to Mrs. J.G. McDougall, 28 November 1966, HPP.
76. Alvin Hamilton, interview with author, 14 December 1982.
77. Alvin Hamilton, interview with the York Institute for Behavioural Research, 26 October 1970.
78. Alvin Hamilton, interview with author, 14 December 1982.
79. Ibid.
80. Alvin Hamilton to W.H. McEwen, 28 March 1967, HPP.
81. Alvin Hamilton to W. Crandall, 12 April 1967, HPP.
82. Alvin Hamilton, interview with author, 14 December 1982.
83. Ibid., 20 June 1984.
84. Geoffrey Stevens, in his book *Stanfield* (Toronto: McClelland and Stewart, 1973), 170, considers this to be Hamilton's principal reason for running. It was not, but it deserves to be mentioned.
85. E. Davie Fulton, interview with author, 7 June 1983.
86. Alvin Hamilton, interview with author, 14 December 1982.
87. Press release, 26 May 1967, HPP.
88. Alvin Hamilton, letter to delegates, 18 July 1967, HPP.

89. "Why the P.C. Party Should Choose Alvin Hamilton," undated briefing paper, HPP.
90. Alvin Hamilton, letter to delegates, 18 July 1967, HPP.
91. Ibid.
92. Ibid.
93. Ibid.
94. Ibid.
95. In 1960 Johnston wrote to advise Hamilton that, "You should start now to groom yourself as the Prairie Provinces' candidate when the question of succession arises . . . with the proper build up you could easily be in the right place in 1965-67 which is the most promising time." In 1965 he wrote that "An analysis of your delegate strength suggests to me that whatever you can pick up in Montreal, Toronto and rural Quebec is pure gravy. You can't start too soon to make your impression in these areas." Donald Johnston to Alvin Hamilton, 5 December 1960 and 5 May 1965, HPP. It should be pointed out, perhaps, that the above should not be regarded as a long-term Hamilton scheme to win the leadership.
96. Martin Pederson to K . Binks, 19 June 1967, HPP.
97. Press release, 22 August 1967, HPP.
98. Press release, 20 July 1967, HPP.
99. Donald Johnston, interview with author, 30 September 1983.
100. Alvin Hamilton, interview with author, 14 December 1982.
101. Alvin Hamilton, interview with the York Institute for Behavioural Research, 26 October 1970.
102. Ibid.
103. Alvin Hamilton, interview with author, 20 June 1984.
104. Alvin Hamilton to Ontario Progressive Conservative MPPs, 28 July 1967, HPP.
105. Stursberg, *Diefenbaker: Leadership Lost*, 191.
106. Alvin Hamilton, interview with author, 14 December 1982.
107. A list of "key"people prepared for use at the convention included Faibish, Johnston, Whiteacre and Sinclair, Bob Amaron, Lou Hodgins, Joyce Bowerman, Tom Strong, Doug Colborne, Bruce Brown, Muriel Hunt (his long-time secretary), and his son Bill.
108. Stursberg, *Diefenbaker: Leadership Lost*, 193.
109. Ibid.
110. Peter C. Newman, *Distemper of Our Times: Canadian Politics in Transition, 1963-1968* (Toronto: McClelland and Stewart, 1968), 171.

111. Stursberg, *Diefenbaker: Leadership Lost*, 193.
112. Alvin Hamilton, interview with author, 20 June 1984.
113. Diefenbaker, *One Canada: The Tumultuous Years*, 284-85.
114. Stursberg, *Diefenbaker: Leadership Lost*, 194. This was confirmed by Hamilton in an interview with the author, 20 June 1984.
115. Diefenbaker, *One Canada: The Tumultuous Years*, 281-82.
116. Johnston, *The Party's Over*, 230-31.
117. Newman, *Distemper of Our Times*, 174.
118. Alvin Hamilton, interview with author, 20 June 1984.
119. Stursberg, *Diefenbaker: Leadership Lost*, 194.
120. Alvin Hamilton, interview with author, 20 June 1984.
121. Donald Johnston, interview with author, 30 September 1983.
122. *Globe and Mail*, 9 September 1967.
123. This summary is based on press reports of the speech. No copy of the speech exists in Hamilton's papers, perhaps because so much of it was extemporaneous.
124. *Winnipeg Free Press*, 9 September 1967.
125. Newman, *Distemper of Our Times*, 178.
126. Leadership pamphlet, September 1967, HPP.
127. The figures presented in the table below were taken from Perlin, *The Tory Syndrome*.

Results of Ballots 1-5
Progressive Conservative Leadership Race, 1968

Candidate	1st Ballot	2nd Ballot	3rd Ballot	4th Ballot	5th Ballot
Stanfield	519	613	717	865	1150
Roblin	349	430	541	771	969
Fulton	343	346	361	357	—
Hees	295	299	277	—	—
Diefenbaker	271	172	114	—	—
McCutcheon	137	76	—	—	—
Hamilton	136	127	106	167	—
Fleming	126	115	76	—	—
Starr	45	34	—	—	—
Others	12	—	—	—	—

128. Donald Johnston, interview with author, 6 October 1982.
129. Alvin Hamilton, interviews with the author, 14 December 1982 and 20 June 1984.
130. Ibid., 14 December 1982.

131. Ibid.
132. Ibid., 20 June 1984.
133. Ibid. See also, Perlin, *The Tory Syndrome*, 103. Perlin also quotes Faibish as stating that Hamilton would not support Roblin on the last ballot because of Roblin's earlier refusal to serve in a Hamilton Cabinet should Hamilton win.
134. Robert Stanfield, interview with author, 14 December 1982. See also, Coates, *The Night of the Knives*, and Perlin, *The Tory Syndrome.*

Chapter 8

1. Robert Stanfield, interview with author, 14 December 1982.
2. Stanfield won a by-election in his native Nova Scotia and took his seat in the House of Commons on 15 November 1967.
3. *Debates*, 19 October 1967, 2927-31.
4. *Debates*, 23 October 1967, 3368.
5. Ibid.
6. *Debates*, 25 October 1967, 12 December 1967, 23 January 1968.
7. Alvin Hamilton, interview with author, 26 June 1981.
8. Ibid.
9. Trudeau replaced Pearson as prime minister 20 April 1968.
10. Mary Ann Fitzgerald, *Saskatoon Star-Phoenix*, 21 June 1968.
11. Campaign pamphlet, "Why Regina East Should Choose Alvin Hamilton," 1968, HPP.
12. Ibid.
13. Canada, *Report of the Chief Electoral Officer*, 1968.
14. Quoted in the *Saskatoon Star-Phoenix*, 26 June 1968.
15. Quoted in Stursberg, *Diefenbaker: Leadership Lost*, 177.
16. Alvin Hamilton, interview with author, 26 June 1981.
17. Alvin Hamilton to T. Symons, late July 1968, HPP.
18. Alvin Hamilton, interview with author, 26 June 1981.
19. Hamilton's financial difficulties at this time were compounded by the loss of his brother, Fred, while prospecting in the North West Territories. After the initial search failed to locate the crash site, Hamilton continued to search at his own expense until it was found. An investigation proved that mechanical failure, not pilot error, caused the crash, and the manufacturer of the faulty part paid Fred Hamilton's widow sufficient damages to enable her to live free from financial concern.
20. Alvin Hamilton and M. Asselin, report to the Priorities for Canada Conference, 12 October 1969, HPP. Author's emphasis.

21. Ibid.
22. Alvin Hamilton, "Suggested Statement on Urban Policy, 1970," HPP. Author's emphasis.
23. Alvin Hamilton, interview with author, 18 February 1986.
24. Alvin Hamilton, interview with author, 26 June 1981.
25. *Regina Leader Post*, 23 August 1972.
26. Ibid., 17 October 1972.
27. Ibid., 28 August 1972.
28. Advertisement authorized by the Alvin Hamilton Campaign Committee, *Oxbow Herald*, 11 October 1972.
29. Ibid., *Kipling Herald*, 26 October 1972.
30. Alvin Hamilton, interview with author, 26 June 1981.
31. Ibid.
32. Ibid, 20 June 1984.
33. *Debates*, 12 February 1973, 1198. Hamilton also advised farmers to ignore the programme and to grow all they could. He did so on the basis of international marketing information apparently unknown to or ignored by the government. In this case, as with so many of his proposals, his position was founded on a great deal of research.
34. Ibid., 28 May 1973, 4167.
35. Ibid., 4164-67.
36. Ibid., 4164.
37. Ibid., 17 May 1973, 3867.
38. Ibid., 28 May 1973, 4165.
39. Ibid.
40. Ibid., 1 November 1973, 7454.
41. Alvin Hamilton, "A Natural Resource Policy for Canada," May 1973, HPP.
42. Alvin Hamilton, "An Energy and Resource Policy for Canada," December 1973, HPP.
43. NAC, PCPP, "Resources for Canadians," paper prepared for the general meeting of the Progressive Conservative Party of Canada, 17-19 March 1974.
44. Alvin Hamilton, election advertisement, *Kipling Citizen*, 20 June 1974.
45. *Debates*, 31 October 1974, 919.
46. Ibid., 13 November 1974, 1293.
47. Ibid., 26 March 1975, 4519.
48. Ibid., 17 April 1975, 4951.
49. Ibid., 14 November 1974, 1320.
50. Ibid., 4 December 1974, 1955.

51. Ibid., 10 July 1975, 7450.
52. Ibid., 2 December 1975, 9653.
53. Ibid.
54. Ibid., 9654.
55. Alvin Hamilton, interview with author, 26 June 1981.
56. *Debates*, 6 May 1975, 5527-28.
57. Ibid., 5529.
58. Ibid., 11 December 1975, 9950.

Chapter 9

1. Alvin Hamilton, interview with author, 14 December 1982.
2. Ibid. Clark struck a lot of the older Conservative members that way. One is rumoured to have commented after Clark's first caucus meeting as leader that when Clark entered the room, he didn't know whether to stand up or send him out for coffee.
3. Ibid.
4. Ibid.,18 February 1986.
5. *Debates*, 1 March 1976, 11371.
6. Ibid., 8 June 1976, 14302. For further discussion of the ideas of Professors Mundell and Laffer, see R.A. Mundell, *Policy Formation in an Open Economy* (Waterloo: University of Waterloo Research Institute, 1972), and A.B. Laffer, *Private Short-Term Capital Flows* (New York: M. Dekker Ltd., 1975).
7. Ibid., 23 November 1977, 1181.
8. Ibid., 30 May 1978, 5880.
9. Ibid., 5881.
10. Ibid., 24 October 1978, 411.
11. Ibid., 21 November 1978, 1343-44.
12. Alvin Hamilton, *Report from Ottawa*, March 1976, HPP.
13. *Debates*, 26 January 1977, 2418.
14. Ibid., 28 March 1977, 4364.
15. Ibid., 17 November 1977, 1004.
16. Ibid., 24 October 1978, 412. Conservatives won twelve of these by-elections in a precursor of the 1979 general election result.
17. Ibid., 3 November 1978, 794, and 29 November 1978, 1632. Unfortunately, neither the Trudeau government nor any government since carried through with Begin's promise and Hamilton continues to push the issue.
18. Ibid., 23 November 1977, 1180.
19. Ibid., 26 December 1976, 2208.
20. Ibid., 16 November 1976, 1030.
21. Ibid., 24 October 1978, 414.

22. Reports of the Special Policy Committee of the Progressive Conservative Party, 1977. HPP.
23. Alvin Hamilton, interview with author, 18 February 1986. Clark did not agree to release this material until 1981.
24. Ibid.
25. Alvin Hamilton, *Report from Ottawa*, April 1979, HPP.
26. Ibid.
27. Alvin Hamilton, interview with author, 20 June 1984. It is interesting that every one of the cabinet ministers from the Diefenbaker era still in the House of Commons in the early 1980s believed the same — that they themselves or any of the others could have saved the government had they been consulted. George Hees, Marcel Lambert, Walter Dinsdale, interviews with author, 17 March 1983, and 26 October 1981.
28. See, for example, the proceedings of the Standing Committee on Finance, Trade and Economic Affairs, 29 October 1979. Hamilton also clashed with Crosbie on the issue in caucus, arguing that it would be suicidal for the government to continue to raise interest rates when it had just promised in the election campaign to lower them. Alvin Hamilton, interview with author, 27 June 1983.
29. Alvin Hamilton, *Report from Ottawa*, September 1979, HPP. I never had the good fortune to meet Beulah Hamilton. Nevertheless, I can say that of all the people in this book she is the only one to have drawn unqualified praise from everyone who mentioned her and her importance to her husband's career.
30. *Oxbow Herald*, 15 January 1980.
31. Hamilton campaign advertisement, *Oxbow Herald*, 29 January 1980.
32. Campaign pamphlet, Hamilton Campaign Committee, 1980, HPP.
33. *Indian Head News*, 20 February 1980.
34. Alvin Hamilton, interview with author, 28 June 1981.
35. *Debates*, 27 January 1981, 6625-26.
36. Ibid., 22 May 1981, 9842.
37. Ibid., 17 May 1982, 17516.
38. Ibid., 18 June 1982, 18628-29.
39. Ibid., 5 June 1982, 19013.
40. Ibid., 9 October 1980, 3560.
41. Ibid.
42. Alvin Hamilton, *Report from Ottawa*, September 1980, HPP.
43. *Debates*, 23 February 1981, 7563.

44. Ibid., 21 October 1981, 12050.
45. Ibid., 13 January 1981, 6172. See also his speech on 7 June 1982.
46. Ibid., 25 March 1982, 15841.
47. Ibid., 26 February 1982, 15444.
48. Ibid., 20 June 1983, 26542. Hamilton used the same argument in 1981 to gain a reprieve for a spur line in his constituency. He convinced a hearing of the Railway Transport Committee that while the line might not be profitable at the moment for the hauling of grain, it could be a profitable part of the rail link between the resources of southeastern Saskatchewan and the port of Churchill.
49. Ibid.
50. Ibid, 26542-43.
51. Alvin Hamilton, *Report from Ottawa*, August 1983, HPP.

Chapter 10

1. Alvin Hamilton, interviews with author, 29 March 1980 and 16 February 1981.
2. Ibid.
3. To Hamilton's knowledge, every delegate from Qu'Appelle-Moose Mountain at Winnipeg voted against a leadership convention.
4. Alvin Hamilton, interview with author, 28 June 1983.
5. Ibid.
6. Ibid.
7. For example, in the intervening two decades Faibish had become a vice-president of Rogers Cable Systems, and and Johnston corporate secretary of TransCanada PipeLines.
8. Brian Mulroney, press release, 6 September 1983.
9. Alvin Hamilton, *Report from Ottawa*, November 1983, HPP.
10. *Debates*, 3 May 1984, 3389.
11. Ibid., 23 September 1983, 27368.
12. Ibid., 12 December 1983, 106.
13. R. Sheppard, "Back door opens on friendship," *Globe and Mail*, 8 May 1984.
14. Alvin Hamilton, interview with author, 30 April 1984.
15. E. Silcox, campaign literature, March 1984, HPP.
16. Speech to the Qu'Appelle-Moose Mountain nominating convention, Whitewood, 14 April 1984, HPP.
17. Campaign pamphlet authorized by the Qu'Appelle-Moose Mountain Progressive Conservative Association, election 1984.
18. Alvin Hamilton, campaign advertisements, election 1984.

19. Alvin Hamilton, letter to author, 19 September 1984.
20. Alvin Hamilton, interview with author, 17 February 1986.
21. Alvin Hamilton, *Report from Ottawa*, Fall 1985, HPP.
22. Ibid.
23. Hamilton was later reimbursed when Mulroney heard of the "oversight."
24. *China Daily*, 27 January 1987.
25. The success of the rural water programme encouraged Hamilton to suggest a similar campaign in the cities of China. He returned to Beijing in March of 1988, again at his own expense, and three months later an agreement was signed between the Chinese government and Canadian companies.
26. Ibid. See also, his *Report from Ottawa*, December 1984.
27. Alvin Hamilton, interview with author, 17 February 1986.
28. Alvin Hamilton to Brian Mulroney, 18 October 1985, HPP.
29. Alvin Hamilton, interview with author, 10 December 1984.
30. *Debates*, 21 October 1986, 594.
31. Ibid., 20 February 1987, 3686.
32. Ibid., 27 April 1987, 5282.
33. Ibid., 21 October 1986, 598.
34. Ibid., 599.
35. Ibid., 27 April 1989, 5282-84.
36. Alvin Hamilton, *Report from Ottawa*, January 1988
37. *Debates*, 10 June 1987, 6956.
38. Ibid.
39. Ibid., 6957.
40. Ibid., 6958. Author's emphasis.
41. Alvin Hamilton, interview with author, 10 June 1987.
42. *Debates*, 10 June 1987, 6958.

Index